REMOTE
CONTROL

REMOTE CONTROL

Television and the Manipulation of American Life

•

FRANK MANKIEWICZ
and JOEL SWERDLOW

Times
BOOKS

Copyright © 1978 by Frank Mankiewicz and Joel Swerdlow.

All rights reserved, including the right to reproduce this book or portions thereof in any form. For information, address: Times Books, a division of Quadrangle/The New York Times Book Company, Inc., Three Park Avenue, New York, N.Y. 10016.

Manufactured in the United States of America. Published simultaneously in Canada by Fitzhenry & Whiteside, Ltd., Toronto.

Designed by Beth Tondreau

Library of Congress Cataloging in Publication Data

Mankiewicz, Frank, 1924–
  Remote control.

  Bibliography: p. 281
  Includes index.
    1. Television broadcasting—Social aspects—United States.   I. Swerdlow, Joel, joint author.   II. Title.
HE8700.8.M36   1977   301.24′3   76-9726
ISBN 0-8129-0649-7

For Benjamin, who will live his life in the Age of Television, and who loves enough to survive it whole.

F.M.

For my parents, Profs. Gertrude K. and Irving Swerdlow, with love.

J.S.

ACKNOWLEDGMENTS

This book includes facts compiled and conclusions drawn from a wide variety of sources. In the course of its preparation, we read and digested thousands of studies of the relationship between television and human behavior. In addition, hundreds of people across the country were kind enough to submit to extensive interviews. To those people—lawyers, doctors, nurses, policemen from chiefs through S.W.A.T. team leaders to homicide squad patrolmen, judges, students, teachers, school administrators—we are most grateful.

In addition, we acknowledge the assistance of those in the television industry who took the time to talk to us about their profession. Network presidents and other executives, actors, writers, directors and producers (of whom special mention should be made of Quinn Martin, Norman Lear and Grant Tinker)—all were most helpful and generous.

To Curt Suplee, now with the Washington *Post*, go special thanks and appreciation for his encouragement and his editorial skills. His judgment and sense of style were both deft and welcome.

We wish also to acknowledge the special help of Walter Staab, president of SFM Media Service, a veteran of the television business who has compiled and who kindly made available to us a storehouse of facts, figures, and helpful insights, and of Bernard Solomon of the Philadelphia school system, who took the time to acquaint us with the extraordinary success that system has had in using ordinary television programming in teaching children to read.

Many other people contributed in special ways, giving talent and time.

Eilene Rinsky, Matt Schneider, Willie Blacklow, Howard Schwartz, and Jackie Sands gave of themselves in such a way that it can safely be said that without their generosity this book would not have been possible.

• ACKNOWLEDGMENTS

Many other people contributed in special ways, giving talent and time in the best sense of friendship, and their contribution is very much appreciated. In alphabetical order, they are: Barbara Barse, Susan Blacklow, Sam Berkman, Lynne Bundesen, Gil and Judy Butler, Eileen Chiu, Marion Clark, Beth Cole, Amy Lynn Collis, Mary T. Dondero, Ed Egan, Selma and Sam Greenhouse, Hilly and Felice Gross, Kirby Jones, Frederick Hacker, Sandy Harrison, Chris Kobler, Beth Landau, Louise Lindsey, Jean Maurer, Jane O'Reilly, Robert Remes, Judith Rossner, Linda Ruffer, Marjorie Friedlander Schneider, Norman Sherman, Barbara Sweet, Paul H. Swerdlow, Jo Betty Swerdlow-Sommer, Harry Sommer, Carol Wanagel, Sharon Waterman, Paul Weeks, Cissie White, Bob and Pamela Zelnick.

Special thanks go to our editors at Times Books—Emanuel Geltman, who guided this project through some early shoals, and John Simon, whose wise counsel and encouragement in the later stages were very welcome.

As usual, Holly, Josh, and Ben Mankiewicz deserve special thanks for their advice and restraint, and for their willingness to forego whatever pleasure there might have been in spending more time with a husband or a father.

Finally, it must be emphasized that while all of these people made a contribution, the final product is our own, and we are responsible for it. If the picture is not clear, it is the fault of our transmitter; there is no need to adjust your set.

CONTENTS

I believe television is going to be the test of the modern world, and that in this new opportunity to see beyond the range of our vision we shall discover either a new and unbearable disturbance of the general peace or a saving radiance in the sky. We shall stand or fall by television—of that I am quite sure. . . .

Television will enormously enlarge the eye's range. . . . A door closing, heard over the air; a face contorted, seen in a panel of light—these will emerge as the real and the true; and when we bang the door of our own cell or look into another's face the impression will be of mere artifice.

E.B. White, in
The New Yorker
1938

I have just returned from a visit to the United States, where television . . . has become an habitual form of entertainment in many more households than here. Among persons of my own acquaintance, I found only anxiety and apprehension about the social effects of this pastime, and especially about its effect (mentally, morally and physically) upon small children.

Before we endeavour to popularize it still further in this country, might it not be as well if we investigated its consequences for American society and took counsel with informed American opinion about possible safeguards and limitations?

T.S. Eliot, letter to the editor
of *The Times of London*
1950

DEAR ABBY: This may sound crazy, but I need your advice. I am divorced and the mother of a sweet, 4-year-old boy named Ronnie.

We were at home recently when an armed intruder confronted us. The man was gentle, and he quickly put Ronnie at ease. He wanted only money and promised not to hurt us. We both explained to Ronnie that Mommy would have to be tied up for a while. He seemed to understand.

After I was bound and gagged, Ronnie was told to turn the TV on and when the program was over (about 20 minutes) he could help me or call for help. I was taken to another room and the robber left.

Abby, my son spent the next three hours watching TV, while I was bound and utterly helpless. I finally managed, through the gag, to tell him to go next door for help.

Could Ronnie possibly have some hostility toward me? Should I see a psychologist? Please answer.

> "Tied Up"
> Abigail Van Buren, Dear Abby syndicated column
> June 14, 1975

REMOTE
CONTROL

INTRODUCTION

—A northern California woman recently sued the National Broadcasting Company and its San Francisco affiliate for $11 million. She feels they are directly responsible for the gang rape with a pop bottle of her nine-year-old daughter and an eight-year-old friend.

Only three days before the rape, the television network had broadcast a program in which the leading character, a young girl, was raped with a broomstick while taking a shower at a state home for delinquent girls. The camera lingered over the scene, showing in graphic detail the pain of penetration. The real rape—whatever its motivation—was a re-enactment of the fictional crime, but the real crime occurred in a quiet, middle-class neighborhood and was committed by children with absolutely no prior criminal record.

—During the early 1970s, the United States government spent $225 million for the Apollo-Soyuz space link-up with the Soviet Union. Officials admitted that the program contributed to no scientific or technological advances. Its purpose, pure and simple, they said, was to provide a television spectacular for hometown audiences. Hard-pressed by some Senators to defend their actions, spokesmen for the National Aeronautics and Space Administration failed to note that the program was no different in purpose from such events, among others, as the Selma march led by Martin Luther King, Jr., and nearly every presidential trip overseas since 1952.

—In May, 1972, a national political pollster was testing voter opinion in California prior to the state's presidential primary election. In accordance with the newest, most sophisticated polling techniques, he first sought to identify the ideology, personal prejudices, hopes, and fears of his 1,800-respondent sample (a fairly large size by the standards of the business). Accordingly, interviewers went into the field and asked, among other questions, "What is your greatest fear?"

Later, when the responses were being coded and analyzed, the pollster observed that the voters seemed to fit more or less into the national model—with the exception of their fears. As expected, major fears included a devastating nuclear war, a major economic depression, and uncontrolled inflation. On a personal level, family illness or tragedy, drugs, and an increase in neighborhood crime led the list. But the answers yielded something else which seemed quite surprising. Slightly more than 2 per cent of those questioned indicated as their *greatest* fear, "having to live underground."

If extrapolated to the nation at large, this 2 per cent would mean that about 4 million people feared living underground.

This particular fear had never appeared before as even a single response anywhere else in the nation, and the pollster found the sudden 2 per cent surge sufficiently astonishing to warrant a check. He found the reason.

A few days before the pollsters took to the field, a local television station had broadcast a science fiction movie set in the future whose theme was that overwhelming air pollution had forced people to move underground. In the movie, life had been entirely re-organized without fresh air and without the sun, and its melodramatic plot worked itself out against this background.

—One day in January, 1976, according to United Press International, a burglar broke into a Chicago apartment occupied by a man and his three children, ages nine, eleven, and twelve. After a struggle, the burglar killed the father. Police entered the apartment nearly ten hours later, after neighbors had noticed that no one seemed to be entering or leaving. What they found shocked them. The three children were watching television, while the bloody body of their father lay a few feet away.

—The University of North Carolina consistently fields one of the nation's best basketball teams. It is always near the top of the perennially strong Atlantic Coast Conference. During the 1975-76 season, the North Carolina team defeated the Duke University basketball team 89-87. The game was televised regionally. A few days later, North Carolina fell victim to arch-rival North Carolina State. This game was also telecast, this time nationally.

North Carolina coach Dean Smith charged that arbitrary time-outs for television commercials had affected both games: "We had an eight-point run over at Duke Saturday and they got a TV time-out. Today we had a good stretch going and they got another TV time-out."

—At the end of the 1975 football season, college players met in Montgomery, Alabama, for one of the inter-regional all-star games traditionally played during the post-season weeks. An independent producer sold the game to television stations across the country. They contracted to take three hours of air time with the warning that anything more would require substantial overtime charges. It became clear in the first quarter that the game would be dominated by passing and not by rushing. The frequently incomplete passes stopped the official game clock, but real time, of course, was unaffected. So the producer began to fear that the game would run longer than three hours and ordered the referee to cut the first quarter short. He dutifully complied: the first quarter of the football game was reduced to only thirteen minutes of playing time, instead of the fifteen minutes called for by the rule book. The two rival coaches had, of course, not been consulted.

After halftime, a new fear struck the producer's heart. The teams had turned to the more time-consuming running plays. Now it seemed that the game might run short, perhaps filling only two and one-half or two and three-quarters hours—not enough time for airing the full three hours' worth of commercials, and time for commercials is what pays producers. Again, an order went out—and this time the officials started to delay the game through the third and fourth quarters. Two minutes of actual playing time were registered on the official clock as only about one minute.

The fourth "quarter" lasted about nineteen minutes. The "winning" team scored the crucial touchdown during the "last thirty seconds" of the game. But the television show of the game lasted three full hours, replete with commercials, and the producer, the advertisers, and the broadcasting stations presumably went home satisfied. The coaches, the players, and the fans, of course, were not satisfied—they had the impression that the game was played by different rules.

—The Educational Testing Service devises, administers, and scores the nation's leading standardized college entrance examination, the Scholastic Aptitude Tests. In 1975, it announced a disturbing pattern: every year since 1963 average scores had been dropping, and the drop from 1974 was more precipitous than ever before. Journalists, educators, and politicians promptly commenced to express gloomy predictions about the decline in literacy among America's young people. A blue-ribbon panel was appointed to examine, among other things, the validity of the testing procedures. A few commentators noted that 1963 was the first year that members of the post-World War Two generation—educated in a world with television—were old enough to take the exam.

All these events are a part of one of the most important changes in modern times: the advent of the Age of Television. None, it is safe to say, would have happened without it. And these examples barely begin to touch on the widespread and deep changes in our lives brought to us by television.

The Age of Television is now about twenty-five years old. Its beginnings may be said to date from the day in 1951 when the coaxial cable was laid from coast to coast, for the first time permitting everyone in the United States to see the same thing at the same time. No longer would movies, mail, radio, even the telephone, be the most important conveyor belts of information, impressions, and ideas. They were superseded just as surely as travel by foot or by horse had been superseded before them. No longer would people in Chicago, Denver, or San Francisco have to wait for news or entertainment to arrive from the East Coast. No longer would it be possible for a political figure to do or say something to please only a regional audience, and rest relatively sure that voters in regions where the speech or action might be considered hostile would never learn about it. Regional differences themselves have lessened, and will soon be blurred beyond recognition.

This force has entered with a power that was not anticipated and has not yet been fully recognized. Its impact may be compared to that of movable type in the fifteenth century or of the automobile in the early twentieth century. Like these previous inventions, television has revolutionized the society it was meant to serve. Indeed, historian Daniel Boorstin writes that the appearance of television was not a "revolution" but a "cataclysm."

With the Age of Television has come the Television Generation. It is a generation whose members have spent more time in front of a television screen than in a classroom. It has incorporated television images into its daily milieu years before it even learned from books. It has a heightened sense of sound, color, and image. "Television has produced a generation of children who have a declining grasp of the English language, but have a visual sophistication that was denied to their parents," Alistair Cooke noted in a recent interview. "They learn so much about the world that appeals immediately to their emotions, but I'm not sure it involves their intelligence, their judgment."

The Television Generation is the generation of the Vietnam-bound Marine who told a reporter, "I want to kill a lot of Vietnamese people and I want to get on TV." It is the generation of Harvard University seniors who ask guest lecturer Muhammed Ali if he still uses Brut—the men's cologne he advertised on television. It is the generation who urged that kiddie-show host Captain Kangaroo be given an honorary Doctorate of Human Letters, and that the actor who played television doctor Marcus Welby speak at medical school commencement exercises. It is the generation of Charles Whitman, the mass-killer, who carefully took a can of Right Guard deodorant along on his murderous errand, presumably so he wouldn't offend.

The Television Generation consists, roughly, of all people born since 1945. It grows constantly while pre-television generations die off. By 1980, by reasonable U.S. Census estimates, 58 per cent of the total population will be members of the Television Generation.

Statistics begin to give us an idea of what has happened. Ninety-seven per cent of all American households have at least one television set, more than are equipped with refrigerators or indoor toilets. Forty-one per cent of the households have two or more television sets. Nearly 100 million Americans are regular television viewers, and the average set is on for about six hours and fifteen minutes each day. A study subsidized by the National Institute of Mental Health estimates that "about one-third of all American adults watch an average of four or more hours of television per day."

The nightly television audience runs at around 60 million, and at midnight, industry figures show that over 2 million children under the age of eleven are still watching. The average preschool child in America today logs in over fifty-four hours each week; this will amount to nine full years in front of a television set by the time the child reaches sixty-five. Before he is fifteen, this same child will have witnessed somewhere between eleven thousand and thirteen thousand acts of violence. If one wishes to see fifty-four acts of violence one can watch all the plays of Shakespeare, or one can watch three evenings (sometimes only two) of prime-time television.

The figures are overwhelming from whatever angle they are approached. During prime-time hours, anywhere from 45 to 70 per cent of the sets in America are on. During one episode of *Gunsmoke,* the hero's sidekick forgot to limp, and about one million viewers wrote in. (Some said, "Thank God, Chester is cured.") About 20 million people watch daytime soap operas on a regular basis. In 1975, Americans spent over $17 million on new television sets and advertisers spent over $4.5 billion to reach them.

Television viewing is what Americans do more than anything else but sleep. (A 1975 survey conducted for the *National Enquirer* by the New York Psychiatric Institute reported that about one-fifth of all viewers say they sleep and watch at the same time. No explanation was offered.) The time spent with a newspaper by the average American has been dropping constantly, and has now reached only one-half hour per day. This decline holds true for all economic, educational, and age groupings. While the amount of television viewing is constantly increasing, the gap between amount of viewing by the well educated and the poorly educated is narrowing. Furthermore, there is no relationship between attitude toward television and amount of time spent watching. "When we examine our respondents' evening and week-end viewing, it turns out that the groups which like television least are watching it about as much as those who like it most," concludes *Television and the Public*, the definitive study to date on Americans' viewing habits.

Television stations are trusted by more Americans than any other institution. While trust in such institutions as local government, police, schoools, and the church is declining, trust in television stations is increasing. More than a majority of the American people believe that television is the most believable source of news; newspapers are in a distant second place with only about 20 per cent.

A best-selling book may reach several million people after coming out in paperback. A hit movie is seen by perhaps 6 million people and a super-hit play attracts a million. The nation's largest-circulation newspaper has 2 million readers. But a television program which enters less than 30 million homes is a failure.

The statistics that mark the Age of Television are not without their human side. In 1975, a college professor concluded a two-year study in which he asked children aged four to six, "Which do you like better, TV or Daddy?" Forty-four per cent, he announced, preferred television. That same year, a fifty-year-old British bricklayer literally laughed himself to death while watching his favorite television program. His widow told reporters she would write to the program's producers to thank them "for making Alex's last moments so happy." In Washington, D.C., in 1975, physicians announced that a mini baby boom had occurred nine months after the conclusion of the televised Watergate hearings.

What is seen on television? What images flicker from the screen into living rooms, bedrooms, kitchens, and recreation rooms? What enters the average American home for over six hours daily? What is given to the child for twenty thousand hours while he is passing through infancy, childhood, and adolescence?

It is a new world, full of facts and unfacts. By day, we are offered a little early-morning news and gossip; game shows, in which ordinary people combine with celebrities from other television programs to earn substantial sums of money by humiliating themselves; "true-to-life" dramas (called soap operas); motion pictures at least a decade past their box-office appeal; old cartoons; and reruns of television programs once broadcast during evening prime time.

As the day lengthens into evening, one or two talk/variety shows may provide the bridge to local news programs. After a smattering of fires, sex crimes, corrupt meter maids, sports scores, and weather, the national and international news comes on for one-half hour. Then come more reruns and game shows, interspersed with an occasional low-level documentary, usually about wildlife or the antics of a television-inspired celebrity.

The evening is now fully upon America, ushered in by the new "family hour" concept of programming. In the words of one top network executive, this is a *cordon sanitaire* designed to exclude, for one hour at least, programs which contain violence. This is achieved at the expense of making family hour an oasis for sex, light-hearted and otherwise. The end of the so-called family hour unleashes violence, usually as the modus operandi of police and other law-enforcement officials. Along with these policemen, we get doctors and lawyers—each taking a half hour or an hour to solve a serious problem in the lives of their colleagues, clients, patients, or fellow citizens. Almost without exception, the problem is solved through an act of physical or psychic violence. Late at night, there is another half hour of news, mostly local, and more talk shows. Again one celebrity talks—often amusingly—with other celebrities whom television has created.

On the weekends, we get a steady diet of televised sports, by now tailored to fit the screen and the increasingly violent appetites of the viewers. It is also on the weekends that the occasional "serious" program—usually an interview of a public figure by three often-worshipful newsmen—is made available.

What is the message that comes through? What is it we are really seeing? During prime time, the message of television is quite clear and consistent: there is no problem, however serious, whether it falls within the domain of a policeman, private detective, a doctor, a lawyer, or any of the other television heroes,* which cannot be fully resolved in an hour, to the satisfaction of the law, the participants, and the viewers. And the solution is almost always achieved by an act of violence.

The power of this lesson cannot be underestimated; almost every television program has the same pattern. The problem is stated, whether it is the stealing of cattle, the murder of a Mafia chieftain, a kidnapping, an outbreak of drug use, or the inability of a teenager to get his own car. The problem deepens, the plot complications appear, and in the final minutes the problem is resolved. The criminal is killed or wounded and, in any event, apprehended after a violent chase or fight (usually both a chase and a fight), the goods are restored, the addicts are cured, or the family agrees that the youth may have the car. The crucial event, almost without exception, is an act involving some kind of sudden or even sustained violence. Usually, this problem-solving technique involves the use of a gun or other lethal weapon.

* The occupation of the hero is cyclical: in the mid-sixties he was likely to be a cowboy or a Western marshal; by the seventies, reflecting demographic changes in the real population, he was more likely to be urban and concerned with law enforcement.

Much has been written on the subject of television violence and its relationship with violence in the homes and streets of America, both by those who see the connection and by those who wish they did not, but we believe this book to be the first survey of virtually *all* the scientific studies on the question. If there is a serious reported study of the relationship between television violence and human society which we have not read and noted, we will be surprised. The weight of the evidence is clearly on one side, and this book marshalls that evidence and, perhaps, will make decision-making and—ultimately—action easier for those charged with that responsibility.

This book also discusses the impact of television on our institutions. It examines the question whether the multiple but clear messages of television may have contributed in a major way to that decline of national confidence in our institutions—private and public—which is, by all accounts, the major domestic political development of our time.

The *politics* of television—the ways in which public opinion, legislators and legislation, the press, and the regulatory agencies have their impact upon television content—is also a part of this book. We have chosen the establishment and trials of the "Family Hour" idea to demonstrate this interplay, because it seems the best example of how this particular game is played—and by whom.

This book will discuss as well the role television has played in speeding up—and delaying—the two major "revolutions" of our age, those in the areas of race and of sex. Television's impact on civil rights, as well as on the "white backlash," and highly emotional issues, such as busing, is a significant story and one largely untold in its totality. In addition, the changing role of women on (and in) television has accompanied a change in public and private attitudes, and the question of the effect of television in raising—and lowering—national consciousness is an important one, which this book tries to answer.

This book also describes the whole learning and social adaptation process with which television overwhelms the children in its audience. Significant results can be gleaned from the many studies of how television has affected the learning process of children, both in and out of the classroom, and we have summarized that data and drawn certain inescapable conclusions.

News and politics—these are the areas in which television has affected national life most visibly, and this book includes considerable study of how television news has assumed the function of setting the national agenda, and of the enormous political consequences of that assumption of power. How television news functions, how much time is allotted to it in the day's schedule, how decisions are made to allocate that time—these are the factors which now determine the course of our politics.

Finally, we have included a survey and analysis of the *business* of television. This national medium is, at bottom, not a way to purvey news and public affairs to the viewers, not a way to entertain millions of Americans with comedy, drama, and music, not a way to educate and inform—but the most profitable method ever devised by man to deliver huge audiences to advertisers, who then deliver their commercial messages.

Whoever forgets this single high purpose of television will not understand it, and this book attempts to explain some of the factors which are immanent in that business and financial structure.

We have not presented, in these pages, "solutions" for the problems we raise. We have attempted, rather, only to show the nature of those problems. Television, in one generation, has become the dominant influence in our lives, and we have tried only to show the extent of that influence and the ways in which things have changed because of it. As a free people, Americans may decide to leave the scene unchanged, but this decision should not be made without a clear picture of where the society is and how, in ways barely understood, it is controlled.

Walker Percy's 1962 novel, *The Moviegoer*, introduces "certification," a notion that does more to explain the Age of Television than does any other single idea. The story's hero has taken a woman friend to the movies:

> Kate watches, lips parted and dry. She understands my moviegoing, but in her own antic fashion. There is a scene which shows the very neighborhood of the theater—Kate gives me a look—it is understood that we do not speak during the movie.
>
> Afterward, in the street, she looks around the neighborhood. "Yes, it is certified now."
>
> She refers to a phenomenon of moviegoing which I have called certification. Nowadays when a person lives somewhere, in a neighborhood, the place is not certified for him. More than likely he will live there sadly and the emptiness which is inside him will expand until it evacuates the entire neighborhood. But if he sees a movie which shows his very neighborhood, it becomes possible for him to live, for a time at least, as a person who is Somewhere and not Anywhere.

Television is the great certifying agent of our time. Most Americans do not believe in the reality of any event or emotion that they have not seen, at one time or another, on television. This is the first commandment in the Age of Television. The second commandment is that if people believe that an event has occurred, then they will decide that they have seen it on television. Thus, something over 70 per cent of Americans believe they saw John F. Kennedy's assassination live on their home screens. In truth, no one saw it live on television; and the general public did not even see it on film until the 1976 showing of closely edited portions of the Zapruder film. A third dictum is that if people see an event on television that so jars their expectations and beliefs that it is virtually unassimilable emotionally, then they will deny that they saw it on the screen. To them, the event really did not occur, so it was *not* on television and was never certified. This faith enabled a majority of the American people to believe, sincerely, that the violence at the 1968 Democratic convention occurred in ways precisely opposite from what they had seen.

There is a tendency on the part of many social commentators to blame television for all disturbing changes in our society, largely because it *is* so much involved with who we are and what we do, but also because it is an easy target. It is essential to remember that no one cause can ever explain complex phenomena. Television does deserve to be singled out, though, for two reasons. First, as already explained briefly, it is intimately connected with most of the things we think and do. And second—alone among the fundamental forces acting upon us—it has been exempt from public examination. It may be that television is too close to us, too pervasive, to permit detachment. "It is hard to hear a new voice," wrote D. H. Lawrence, "as hard as it is to listen to an unknown language. We don't want to listen."

It will be argued in this book that the people who are speaking in this new voice are not trying to inform, instruct, or entertain us. Nor is their goal to shock us or pander to our fascination with violence and sex. The purpose of nearly every television program, including a disturbing percentage of those presented on the so-called public broadcasting channels, is to deliver the maximum possible audience for advertisements. These advertisements accomplish more than just the sale of deodorants, cars, and floor waxes; they sell a set of values. "In one area the industrial system is uniquely powerful," writes John Kenneth Galbraith in *The New Industrial State,* "although less in the propagation of ideas than in general mental conditioning. This is radio and especially television broadcasting . . . [t]hese are essential for effective management of demand and thus for industrial planning. The process by which this management is accomplished, the iterated and reiterated emphasis on the real and assumed virtues of goods, is powerful propaganda for the values and goals of the system. It reaches to all cultural levels. In the United States there is no satisfactory non-commercial alternative. It would be good if there were."

The men and women who control the Age of Television are animated by little more than a simple search for profits. They are neither good nor bad people, but only good or bad businessmen.

1 TELEVISION VIOLENCE: BLOODY INSTRUCTIONS

> . . . we but teach
> Bloody instructions, which
> being taught, return
> to plague the inventor . . .
> MACBETH, *Act I, Scene 7*

If *Macbeth* is ever presented on television, it will be with a lot of "prestige" fanfare at a bad rating time, or on public broadcasting. The message has been lost, if it was ever learned. Consider the evidence:

By the early 1960s, the supply of motion pictures originally produced to play in movie theatres had begun to dry up, so great was the demand of television for old films. The television industry then began production of so-called "made-for television" movies. These became profitable, employing the same talented people who had once formed the backbone of the motion picture industry, even though, as one leading screen writer described the process, "it was like manufacturing used cars, or turning out, on new machines, the chewed-on bones of a chicken."

By the mid-sixties, made-for-television movies were a staple of prime-time entertainment, and on December 13, 1966, NBC aired for the first time a film called *Doomsday Flight*. The script was written by Rod Serling, a gifted writer who had previously created and narrated the science fiction series *Twilight Zone*, which had earned enormous popularity and critical praise. *Doomsday Flight* told the story of an extortionist who had placed a bomb aboard a commercial airliner in the United States. While the plane was in flight, he calmly notified authorities that a special pressure-sensitive device would explode when the plane flew below a certain altitude. Once the plot had thus established that the plane could not even descend to land without the payment of the extortionist's demand, an exciting story unfolded as the plane cir-

13   •

cled and the authorities searched for both the criminal and the bomb.

Before *Doomsday Flight* was aired, the Airline Pilots' Association saw advance publicity, and tried to convince NBC not to show the film because "the mentally unstable are highly responsive to, and easily provoked by, suggestions." Telegrams to NBC, to the producer of the film, and to Serling, brought no satisfactory response. A last-minute telephone call to the network failed. This kind of pressure rarely works: pilots, after all, do not license television stations.

But the airline pilots knew what they were talking about. While the movie was still on the air, a U.S. airline received a bomb threat clearly modeled on the unfolding fictional extortion. The next twenty-four hours brought four more calls, and eight similar threats were received within a week. According to the Federal Aviation Agency, this was several times the usual number of airline extortion threats in a comparable time period. In a highly unusual move, the FAA blamed *Doomsday Flight* and the network for endangering that portion of the public who flies every day. A similar pattern of threats followed the showing of the film on Australian television the following year, and once again in 1973, when a repeat performance of the film on NBC caused the emergency grounding of a commercial airliner flying from New York City to Madrid with over two hundred passengers aboard. Incredibly, the television industry at home and abroad still had not learned, two years after that (or had learned, but chose not to use the lesson): in 1975, yet another round of threats struck panic into French aviation when *Doomsday Flight* appeared on that country's television screens. Before his death, in 1975, Rod Serling told an interviewer, "Yes, I wrote the story [*Doomsday Flight*], but to my undying regret."

None of the real-life extortionists has been caught, and thus it has been impossible to determine what kind of person decided to commit the crime after seeing it acted out on television. Psychologist Victor B. Cline of the University of Utah points out that the failure to identify and apprehend a large number of those criminals who are motivated by television shows has impeded the efforts of physicians and social scientists to determine what it is about television that spurs them into action. We do not even know, says Cline in an ominous note, how many of them are truly "disturbed, unstable, or impulsive," or how far they are at any given moment from the kind of action that can be triggered by images on the television screen.

One person who may very well have learned a lesson from *Doomsday Flight* is Hollywood screenwriter Brian Garfield. A few years ago, when Garfield returned to where he had parked his convertible, he "found the top of it had been slashed by a knife. I had the universal gut reaction— 'my property has been invaded, I'll kill him.' Then it flashed through my mind, 'what if somebody actually *did* that?' "

So Garfield wrote *Death Wish,* a book about an urban vigilante who goes about his rounds killing suspected muggers. The book, and the subsequent movie version, glorified the vigilante. The movie was seen by sell-out crowds—which occasionally stood and applauded, and were enormously enthusiastic whenever Garfield's "hero" blasted away with his gun. *Death Wish* may have been the first urban Western—certainly the first successful one—since the movie called *M.*

CBS bought the television rights to *Death Wish,* and late in 1975 decided to air the film during the 1975-76 television season. When the movie was shown, Garfield would be entitled to a $50,000 royalty payment. Nevertheless, Garfield offered to turn the money down if CBS would forgo showing the movie; he feared the movie would inspire imitators if presented on television to tens of millions of people. CBS refused. (It should also be noted that some members of New York City street gangs, perhaps with the knowledge that they might very well have been among the targets of any who sought to imitate the avenger of *Death Wish,* also urged that the film not be shown; but they have even less clout than airline pilots.)

Imitations of television crimes, alas, are not rare. There is hardly a day in which the wire services and police blotters across the country do not carry stories like the following ones:

—In San Diego County, California, a nineteen-year-old boy chopped his parents and his sister to death and crippled his brother with an axe. Prosecutors and police officials familiar with the case say he acted after seeing a made-for-television movie about Lizzie Borden (who achieved notoriety in 1892 for the axe murder of her parents) and that the boy discussed the movie with his classmates in the days after it was shown. The boy was a high school honor student and athlete.

—Three weeks after the broadcast of a made-for-television murder movie in 1973, a seventeen-year-old boy, who said he had "memorized the film to the last detail," admitted to re-enacting the crime when he murdered a young woman. Police said she had been raped, her head had been bludgeoned, and her throat was cut—just as in the film.

—In New York City a taxi driver held up a bar and killed three people. Caught by police, he said his crime had been modeled after a recent television show.

—In Baltimore, an ex-GI in fatigues shot and killed five co-workers with an M-1 rifle; police later discovered that he had purchased some chocolate bars at the same time he bought the rifle. He made the purchases one week after a prime-time television program had portrayed a fatigue-clad veteran who munched chocolate bars while shooting at passers-by.

—A popular crime show depicted an urban killer who slashed the throats of Skid Row "winos." A few days later, in Los Angeles, a wino was discovered with his throat slit. It was the forerunner of the "Skid Row Slasher's" reign of terror, which claimed numerous victims, all killed in the same way.

—In Montreal, Canada, thieves used a 10 mm. anti-aircraft gun to rob a Brinks truck of $1.6 million. Their modus operandi showed a great deal of imagination and sophistication, closely paralleling events on a recent prime-time crime program.

—A seventy-one-year-old Seattle man tried to rob a bank and walked right into the hands of the police. "It looked easy on television," he said.

—In London, school principals asked parents of kindergarteners not to let their children watch *Kung Fu,* an American series combining pop Zen with pop martial arts, which had vast audiences in America, and was shown in London on Saturday evenings to an audience of 3 million. The reason: teachers' complaints that schoolgrounds at recess time were turning into battlegrounds as children punched, jabbed, and otherwise did bodily harm to one another, using the best Kung Fu techniques.

—In Lexington, South Carolina, a young couple picked up a hitchhiker, shot him, and staged a car crash in which his body was burned. The woman then tried to claim insurance on the victim's life. The Lexington County Sheriff believes the crime had "something to do" with an episode of a private-eye program, *Barnaby Jones,* with an identical murder-for-insurance plot—shown just before the killing.

—A Dallas police sergeant recites numerous examples of crimes he believes to be directly inspired by television, and focuses particularly on a gang of juveniles who succeeded in cracking the steering-column lock on new cars. When asked how they had acquired the technique, the boys told him they had seen it on episodes of a police program.

Defenders of the television industry insist that such crimes are committed by mentally unstable people who would have done something violent, illegal, or crazy whether or not television existed.

"It is a tiresome fact," Edith Efron writes in a stalwart defense of the industry in *TV Guide,* "that crime antedates network television. . . . Attila the Hun, the Inquisition and, in our own century, Stalin, Hitler and Mao cannot be surpassed. And, to my certain knowledge, none of these was inspired by television. The 'TV violence' controversy is merely one of the typically ugly quarrels raging in the social science community." It *is* a fact, and perhaps tiresome to some, but Ms. Efron has hardly an answer; not even social scientists hold television responsible for crime—just for the increase in violence.

Herminio Traviesas, NBC's director of program continuity—the chief censor who decides what does and does not get on the air—has another argument. When asked if he planned to show *Death Wish* despite Brian Garfield's protest, Traviesas replied, "Of course." He was asked about the example of *Doomsday Flight,* and whether it bothered him when it came to deciding whether or not to air *Death Wish.* "Once you start worrying like that," he said, "then you can't show any drama on television. . . . You can't judge things by the few nuts."

Actor Efrem Zimbalist, Jr., adds, "Violence has been intrinsic to drama since the days of Euripides."

But these answers—fairly typical among television's defenders—sidestep the point. First of all, no claim is made that perceived violence incites real violence in every instance; all that is claimed, on the basis of considerable data, is that some people are more prone to violence after seeing violence on the screen than when they had not seen it. That may or may not be a definition—in Traviesas' shorthand—of "nuts," but it still is a significant number of people.

Television violence, unlike books, motion pictures, or Euripides' plays, reaches millions of people every hour, every day. In 1945, the high-water mark for motion picture attendance, nearly 90 million Americans went to the movies every week. Considering the population at that time, and subtracting the number of infants, servicemen, and people in war-related tasks who could not regularly attend, this suggests that nearly everyone in the country who could go to the movies weekly, did so. That figure of 90 million has steadily declined over thirty years with the increase in alternate sources of entertainment, particularly television. It is now—despite a 60 per cent increase in population—a banner year for movies if one-half the 1945 number, or 45 million, go to the movies once a week. But if 45 million people go out to the movies once in a week, 85 million—nearly twice the number—watch television every single day. This audience, of course, includes children of all ages, and if anyone believes children—even those of tender age—watch only *Sesame Street, Electric Company,* cartoons and other "soft" programs, the statistics on children's television viewing habits will come as a rude shock. It probably comes as no great surprise that from 10:30 to 11 PM (after all, it's still prime time) there are 5.6 million children between the ages of two and eleven watching television every night. From 11 to 11:30, not what we would call a high-participation time for children of that age, there are still nearly 3 million two to eleven year olds watching. From 11:30 to midnight, 2.1 million are still there. From 12:30 to 1 AM, there are still 1.1 million two to eleven year olds in the television audience, just under 750,000 from 1 to 1:30 AM, and 435,000 from 1:30 to 2 AM. Put in other statistical terms, almost one million children are watching the average minute of television—each and every night—between midnight and 2 AM. If *Sesame Street* is a children's show watched by adults, and it is, then the late movie is a show for grown-ups watched by children.

Television not only reaches young children whose parents would

17   •

never take them—or permit them to go—to movies like *Death Wish,* it also enters into the viewers' homes and psyches in the intimacy and psychological support of the living room and bedroom, in contrast to the alien environment when one goes out to the movies.

To "go to the movies" involves a conscious decision to move from one place to another, usually some distance away, as well as a willingness to spend an increasingly significant amount of money. For adults, it may involve hiring a babysitter, and fairly elaborate scheduling arrangements. For both adults and children, it almost always requires some transportation, and on the way into the theater one is made aware constantly of the difference in environment between home and the trappings of a "show." The statistical dimensions of television viewing, on the other hand, are such that for most American families, the phrase "we're going to stay home and watch television" means little more today than did the same phrase twenty-five years ago—without the last three words. In contrast, watching a performance on television requires no movement or change of environment at all—in fact the absence of television constitutes a change in environment, since television functions as a continuous accompaniment to the sounds of the home, a sort of visual Muzak as a background for other activities. For most families, it is easier to watch television than not to watch television, once the evening has begun. You have to go to the set, after all, to turn it off.

Furthermore, performers as they appear on television screens are far smaller and hence more "life size" than the performers on the huge movie screens, where actors are truly "larger than life." While one is in awe of movie stars, television stars are one's friends: when Mary Tyler Moore or Telly Savalas appears on the living room screen, we smile with familiarity as though an old friend had come by for coffee.

There is no record that anyone ever poured poison into his brother's ear after seeing *Hamlet* performed on the stage, and it is quite possible that no one emulated the actions of the hero of *Death Wish* after seeing it in a movie house. Nor, for that matter, does television violence necessarily produce thousands—or even hundreds—of murders. Not everyone who watches *Kojak* or *Streets of San Francisco* or *Starsky and Hutch* goes out and shoots a policeman or deals in narcotics or slaps a prostitute around. But remembering the numbers involved in television viewing, it is easy to understand that even a slight inclination toward imitative violent behavior can significantly affect a substantial portion of the population.

We are a country of more than 215 million people, of whom each year about one-half million check into or are re-admitted into a mental institution. About 4 million of us receive out-patient mental health treatment annually.

A National Institute of Mental Health task force concluded in 1975 that at least 20 million Americans "suffer from some form of mental illness." In another study, a team of psychiatrists and sociologists tested people selected at random on the streets of mid-Manhattan. Only 18.5 per cent were found to be "well"; all others needed psychiatric care of one kind or another. By any standard, there are a substantial number of unstable people, although it is true that not many are likely to turn to violence. But if only one per cent of the people who seek mental health treatment—leaving aside, if we may, the large number who need the care but don't seek it—are moved to violence by television, that means 45,000 extra acts of violence. When one adds the number of victims, real and potential, a substantial number of people are now involved. What if an airplane were actually blown up because someone felt impelled to do so after viewing *Doomsday Flight?* What about those who are raped, shot, bludgeoned, knifed, axed—by television imitators? What is the calculus of entertainment? Could those deaths and pain and grief be written off as merely a part of the price we pay to maintain art?

There is another, even more disturbing way to look at the statistics. Each year, Americans watch 100 billion hours of television; they see rape, murder, mugging, assault, and other violent acts. If only one per cent of the nightly audience is then prompted into real-life action by what is seen, that means 850,000 violent crimes. Let us be conservative, and suggest the possibility that only one-tenth of one per cent of the television audience is prompted into real-life action by television crimes: this means 85,000 violent television-induced actions are added to the national totals every night.

The difference between violent actions and reported violent crimes should be noted. No one can measure to what degree Americans solve their problems via violent actions, although we do know there is an epidemic of child abuse and wife beating. Thus, the immediate effects of television violence may be incalculably greater than indicated by the reporting of specific crimes.

It is impossible to isolate and quantify entirely the incidence of television-inspired real-life violence, but the bulk of the evidence is alarming. During the summer of 1975, Senator William Brock of Tennessee surveyed the juvenile court judges in his home state about the impact of televised violence. He found that "a vast majority [of the judges] are convinced that violence on television has a real effect on juvenile crime in their areas." Many of the judges provided Senator Brock with specific examples of crimes committed in their jurisdictions that were modeled after television programs.

In Montgomery County, Maryland, the State Attorney's office points to a number of juvenile burglaries in which the "kids" said they got the idea from television.

New York State Assemblyman Alfred A. DelliBovi, chairman of a legislative subcommittee on the family court, conducted what is perhaps the most thorough examination of New York City street gangs to date. He reports that the New York City Police Department believes more than 50 per cent of the gangs are "adventure gangs," which are "formed because of media* coverage of other gangs in the city."

That is a remarkable statistic. Even assuming that the police exaggerated their estimate by a factor or two, it still means that fully one-quarter of the street gangs in New York City are the products of "media" coverage of other gangs.

DelliBovi's report also concludes that media coverage "has led to many advances in present gangs. They have taken the strongest elements of gang organization and tactics from the fifties and have wed them to what they have seen on television and in the movies. As a consequence, 1970s gangs are more sophisticated, highly organized, and engage in a broader pattern of crime."

But the report contains even more ominous conclusions. DelliBovi's subcommittee discovered that professional social workers working with the gangs feel that gang membership is spreading rapidly from poor to middle class neighborhoods once thought impervious to "adventure gangs." Neighborhoods in Queens and Brooklyn, the report says, now have gang problems where none previously existed. Juvenile arrest records bear out that conclusion—an increasing number of middle class youths have been arrested in the course of gang activities. Of course, there are many pressures and problems that might turn a suburban teenager to gang activity and to crime. But, DelliBovi points out, "some probation officers think that middle class youths might be moved to join a gang because *it is becoming a fad*" (emphasis added).

How does something become a fad in the suburban areas of Queens and Brooklyn in the 1970s? One answer, of course, is the same way in which something becomes a fad in Kansas City, Phoenix, or San Diego—and for the same reason—it is observed on television. "The effect of the mass media on present gangs," DelliBovi's report concludes, "cannot be overemphasized."

Free-lance writer William Gale spent a considerable amount of time with gang members in 1974, and in a 1975 *New York Times Magazine* article, he portrayed the close relationship between the violence in their lives and the violence they see on television. According to Gale, the gang members "had the television on nearly all the time." In an interview after the article appeared, he said that "it would be difficult to

---

* "Media" is a high class, "uptown" word meaning—television. Street gang members don't read newspapers often, or books—and they don't listen to news programs on the radio. The time they spend at the movies is inconsequential compared to the time spent watching television.

overestimate the role that it plays for them. It's always there; the set is always on."

Following are typical comments by gang members to Gale about the televised violence they see:

—"I like to watch rape on TV. It's exciting."

—"Bang, bang, you're dead. That's all. They show just the violence. No real pain. No funeral. No plot of earth. No sign of what happens to the wife and kids after that guy gets killed."

—"[I like *The Untouchables* because] it's got the action. A lot of shooting. Killing. Pushing people off roofs. Planting dope on guys and then the police bust in. I like violence."

—"I want to see who gets killed. Good guys or bad guys. I like to see the Indians kill the cowboys who come to take their land. And sometimes I like to see the cops get it."

Gale reports, somewhat surprisingly, that gang members worry about what televised violence does to the world around them. The young women attached to the gangs are concerned that television may encourage the boys they know to commit rape. Many of the gang members worry about what the effects of television violence may be on their younger brothers and sisters. They feel that the glorification of violence may teach the wrong lessons. One member offered advice to parents of children who watch television: "Tell the kid that's not the way life should be. That's not the right thing to do."

Even older children, said the gang members, shouldn't spend too much time in front of "the trick box" because of the violence. But they also say that time thus spent can be useful: it can provide specific ideas about what crimes to commit, including precise instructions on the best ways to commit them. Even among the gang members, it would seem, the professional ethic prevails over the one we like to call Judeo-Christian.

THE SCHOLARLY EVIDENCE

Some public and congressional concern over televised violence developed concurrently with the growth of television itself. House and Senate hearings, all replete with horror stories about deviant behavior and crimes imitating television programs, were conducted in 1954 and again in 1961, 1962, and 1964. But the results were never more than the issuance of some thick reports. The federal government and the general public seemed to lack either the will or the means to force the broadcast industry to change.

Meanwhile, television seemed unable to exist without violence. Psychologist Victor B. Cline studied television programming during the industry's first decade, from the early fifties to the early sixties. His conclusion:

> In 1954 . . . violence-saturated action and adventure programming accounted for only 17 per cent of prime-time network offerings; by 1961 the figure was 60 per cent. Transmitting such figures into concrete terms, during one week of television in 1960 there were 144 murders, 13 kidnappings, 7 scenes of torture, 4 lynchings, and a few more miscellaneous acts of violence, all occurring before 9 PM.

In other words, Federal Communications Commission Chairman Newton Minow may have been mistaken in 1961 when he called television "a vast wasteland"; he might more appropriately have described it as a combat zone.

Televised violence continued to increase through the 1960s, and first became the object of serious scientific measurement in 1967 when Dr. George Gerbner began his annual survey. The Gerbner "violence count" has since become well-known in the scientific literature. Gerbner found that in the late sixties violence prevailed in 80 per cent of the Saturday prime-time programs and half of the characters on these shows committed some act of violence. During a typical two-week period, 790 people died or were hurt; and "good guys" used violence as much as did "bad guys," with the ominous difference that the good guys used violence to better effect.

By 1968, the National Association for Better Broadcasting estimated that the average American child would see physical damage done to about thirteen thousand people before he or she reached the age of fifteen; other estimates ran as high as fifteen thousand. No one in the broadcast industry has ever challenged these totals.

Following the assassinations of Senator Robert F. Kennedy and Dr. Martin Luther King, Jr., *The Christian Science Monitor* assigned a reporter to tabulate television violence during the first week of July, 1968. The reporter found eighty-four killings in eighty-five and one-half hours of network programming. The pastoral hour and one half was unaccounted for; perhaps an environmental "special"—one can only guess.

In the late 1960s, political assassinations, urban riots, and dramatically increased crime rates, particularly among youth, produced new public concern. Between 1960 and 1973, arrests for violent crimes rose 245 per cent for juveniles and 109 per cent for adults, and far from all the increase was due to better crime reporting and statistical advances.

The National Commission on the Causes and Prevention of Violence, appointed by President Lyndon B. Johnson in 1968 after the King and Kennedy assassinations, concluded:

> . . . we are deeply troubled by television's constant portrayal of vio-
> lence, not in any genuine attempt to focus artistic expression on the
> human condition, but rather in *pandering to a public preoccupation*
> *with violence that television itself has helped to generate* . . . The
> preponderance of the available research evidence strongly suggests
> that violence in television programs can and does have adverse effects
> upon audiences—particularly child audiences.
>
> Television enters powerfully into the learning process of children and
> teaches them a set of moral and social values about violence which are
> inconsistent with the standards of a civilized society. [Emphasis
> added.]

This was very strong language, particularly from a commission whose
membership seemed stacked toward the conservative side. Dr. Milton S.
Eisenhower, rarely known to challenge the status quo, was the chair-
man. Members included Terrence Cardinal Cooke and Senator Roman
Hruska, and the resident radical seems to have been—of all people—
Eric Hoffer.

Under intense congressional pressure to "do something," the Nixon
Administration's newly appointed Secretary of Health, Education and
Welfare, Robert H. Finch, responded in early 1969 by asking the
Surgeon General to take action. The result was a twelve-member advisory committee charged with determining whether television violence
had an identifiable effect upon children. The whole enterprise began on
a highly conciliatory note, considering the possible conclusions. The
Surgeon General gave the three networks veto power over committee
members, and they promptly blackballed seven academicians, while at
the same time seeing to it that no less than five of the committee's
twelve members were either on the network payroll at the same time
that they sat on the committee, or had been on the network payroll earlier in their careers. According to a Russell Sage Foundation study, of
twenty-nine names put forth by professional and academic groups, only
one was chosen.

Given $1.5 million by the National Institute of Mental Health, the
Surgeon General's advisory committee sponsored twenty-three independent research projects, which were released in five volumes in January,
1972. Along with these five volumes, the committee unanimously endorsed a final report, impressively entitled *Television and Growing Up:*
The Impact of Televised Violence. This final report contained a conclusion in the opaque style customarily found in unanimous committee
decisions:

> The evidence does indicate that televised violence may lead to in-
> creased aggressive behavior in certain sub-groups of children, who
> might constitute a small portion or a substantial proportion of the total

population of young viewers. We cannot estimate the size of the fraction, however, since the available evidence does not come from a cross section sample of the entire American population.

However, coming from an extremely cautious summary of an extremely cautious group of reports by an extremely cautious committee originally stacked to be pro-industry, this is a very strong finding. It does no less than admit the possibility that a "substantial proportion" of the nation's children may indeed be adversely affected by television violence. Such backhanded statements seem to have a meaning, particularly to those who know the code. The Surgeon General's report also stated, for example:

> The accumulated evidence, however, does not warrant the conclusion that television has a uniformly adverse effect on a majority of children.

Almost like prisoners trying to get a message past the guards, the advisory committee used such statements to tell us much more than is indicated by a hurried first reading. It means nothing—of course—to say that televised violence does not have a "uniformly adverse effect." In the study of social phenomena, very few factors, if any, have uniform effects on anything. To say that televised violence does not necessarily have "a uniformly adverse effect on a majority of children" leaves open—indeed, strongly suggests—the conclusion that it does have an adverse effect, differing in intensity, on a substantial minority. How big a minority? Ten per cent? Forty-nine per cent? A detailed review in *Contemporary Psychology* of all five research volumes concludes that the summary contains many other examples of this sort of cautionary zeal.

The Surgeon General at the time of the report, Dr. Jesse Steinfeld, discarded even this much caution in public testimony. In presenting the report to the Senate Commerce Committee, chaired by Senator John Pastore, Steinfeld said:

> While the committee report is carefully phrased and qualified in language acceptable to social scientists, it is clear to me that the causal relationship between television violence and anti-social behavior is sufficient to warrant appropriate and immediate remedial action . . . There comes a time when the data are sufficient to justify action. That time is now.

Steinfeld was pulling at least one punch, and he doubtless knew it (for that matter, so did Senator Pastore). The report was not qualified in language acceptable to social scientists; it was qualified in language acceptable to the television networks.

Many of the social scientists who contributed to the five volumes of research, angered by what they saw as a watered-down summary, also stepped forward to state that it had been proved beyond a reasonable doubt that televised violence has an adverse effect upon some of those who view it. Dr. Robert M. Liebert, one of the principal researchers, notes that:

> In point of fact, the studies . . . involved children and adolescents from every type of background . . . No region, ethnic group, or type of economic circumstance is unrepresented in the data collected to date. One team described its results as revealing that "as for relatively average children from average home environments, continued exposure to violence positively relates to acceptance of aggression as a mode of behavior." Most of the other researchers could—and did—describe their findings in the same way.

Dr. Steven Chaffee, a major contributor to the correlational studies in the five research volumes, writes:

> The "predeposition to aggression" limitation is to some extent a mere universal or tautological proposition, in that most children almost surely have at least some latent aggressive tendencies and are thus "predisposed" to aggression if so stimulated.

Dr. Chaffee feels that the summary report selected the wrong group of children for special mention. "Perhaps a more defensible conclusion," he writes, "would be that there is a *small subculture of habitually passive and unaggressive children* who will *not* be stimulated to perform aggressively regardless of what they see on television." (Emphasis added.)

Dr. John P. Murray, research coordinator for the studies, says:

> I don't think there is any question that normal children watching large doses of television violence are liable to behave more aggressively than others who don't. But the committee report never states this clearly.

Even more telling than such statements is an extensive body of scholarly literature, to date encompassing several hundred independent studies involving well over ten thousand children. Many of these studies preceded the Surgeon General's research, and a great many are either follow-through or replicating studies, continuations of specific research projects undertaken by the Surgeon General's advisory committee, or initiated to answer questions posed by one or another of the findings contained in the five volumes of research.

The literature is now so extensive that the federal government and private agencies (such as the Rand Corporation) spend considerable amounts of money paying scholars to do nothing more than organize and summarize existing data. These summaries invariably reach the same conclusion: that televised violence has been proved to have an adverse effect upon some children.

The evidence is so overwhelming that even medical journals have been publishing articles warning of the dangers involved. The *Journal of the American Medical Association*, perhaps the least likely of any English-language publication to print any social science conclusion that is open to challenge—much less a call to action—recently presented an article by Dr. Michael Rothenberg, a Seattle child psychiatrist hitherto publicly uninvolved in the question of televised violence. Rothenberg reviewed the available data and then called for "a major, organized cry of protest from the medical profession." The AMA Board of Trustees voted to endorse Rothenberg's position, and a few months later an article in the prestigious *New England Journal of Medicine* stated that television violence "has contributed to an epidemic of youthful violence, an epidemic that seriously threatens the health of American youth . . ." The *Journal*'s editor-in-chief added a special note affirming his agreement that television violence endangers the health of every child who views it.

Among the research conclusions that have prompted these judgments are the following:

—A happy home life, complete with loving parents and sound non-violent adult role models, does not mediate the effects of televised violence.

—Television violence can shape lifelong attitudes and behavior patterns. Heavy television watching during early childhood often correlates positively with violent behavior after graduation from high school.

—Children are more likely to model themselves upon what they have seen on film than they are to follow verbal instructions from a real, physically present person.

—Children exposed to violence on film retain the lesson learned from these films, including the use of aggressive play, for months afterward, even if there has been no subsequent reinforcement.

—There is a relationship between the amount of television violence a child sees and the amount of violence in his behavior and attitude.

—Children model themselves after an aggressive film they have just seen, even if they are free at the same time to play with non-aggressive toys such as crayons or tea sets.

—Viewers of a violent film are more likely to administer an electric shock to "helpless" subjects than are viewers of a non-violent film.

—Exposure to *only one* violent cartoon can increase the aggressiveness of a child's play. This effect appears only minutes after viewing.

—Children who view a substantial quantity of television manifest signs of anxiety and irritability. Dentists report that these children frequently begin teeth grinding which requires professional attention.

—Televised violence can make certain children twice as aggressive as they were before viewing.

Most studies of the impact of television violence have used children as subjects. They watch the most television, and they are far more vulnerable and impressionable than are adults. However, there are also studies that show televised violence has an effect upon adults. A team of researchers at UCLA Medical School recently completed a fascinating experiment involving over two hundred married couples. The couples were divided into three groupings, with every possible relevant variable such as age and education held constant.

For a two-week period their homes were fed a steady diet of carefully regulated television programs. One group devoted each evening to viewing only violent shows, another spent an equal amount of time watching only non-violent shows, and a control group watched no television at all. The results: during the viewing period, adults who saw violent programs reported an increase in aggressive feelings in themselves and their spouses, while those who viewed non-violent programs reported a decline in such feelings.

"They [the violence viewers] also were observed to be acting more aggressively—grouchier with their families, less tolerant of the child leaving his bike in the driveway," the Associated Press reported.

Of course, all these studies are open to severe methodological questioning. Human behavior is rarely reproducible in the laboratory; what goes on in the home may have little to do with what social scientists see. Causality in human behavior is complicated and most studies measure only one slice of reality. Control groups cannot be maintained; many studies do not even have control groups because nearly everyone in the United States watches a lot of television at some time in his early life, and thus the non-watcher is by this definition "abnormal".

The very act of testing is a nice social science application of the familiar principle that the fact of observation may change the thing observed; children in almost all of these studies, for example, knew they were being watched by adults, although for what purpose was rarely clear to them. And, of course, in many studies, the children are observed only during a period immediately following the viewing of filmed violence; the actions studied and depicted in these studies do not demonstrate that a child or adult will actually cross the line, necessarily, from "acceptable" to "unacceptable" behavior. It is one thing, say critics of research of the effects of television—and they are quite right in this—to act aggressively toward a toy doll in a laboratory and quite another to commit rape or to telephone a bomb threat.

All of these strictures on research pointing to the causal effect of television violence on real violence are cherished by the networks themselves, and they have made an extensive effort to deny the validity of any scholarly study purported to "prove" that violence on television is harmful.

But when all the allowances have been made for methodological error, after the last qualifying phrase or word has been deftly inserted, after the facts have been placed in their soft bed of social science jargon—after all of this, there remains a hard residue of evidence which tells us what we all know anyway, that violence begets violence, that children learn from example, and from the example of entertaining violence best of all.

DESENSITIZATION

Unfortunately, television violence does much more to children than simply increase their aggressive tendencies. As some of the studies cited above indicate, children also become demonstrably less sensitive to violence. To a significant degree, this is because violence and death on television are so cheap.

Eighteen members of a New York City youth gang stabbed to death a young boy they believed to be a member of a rival gang, at odds with their gang over "rights" to a local public swimming pool. When asked why he did the stabbing, one participant replied in a matter of fact way, "I always wanted to know what it would be like to stick a knife through bones. After I stabbed that guy I told him 'thank you.' "

Two teenage girls strangled a seven-year-old boy. They took him to an attic, used their hands to kill him, covered the body with a blanket and hid it under the floor planks. They had planned the crime months in advance after seeing something similar done in a gangster movie. Their purpose: to see what death is really like.

These crimes bear a striking resemblance to the axe murders, shootings, and other violent deeds cited in the beginning of this book. On television, rape, maiming, and murder are not real. But the lessons they teach are real indeed.

Psychiatrist Frederick S. Wertham warns that "continuous exposure of children's minds to scenes of crime and brutality has a deeper effect on them than is generally realized . . . people develop a toleration of pain and an accompanying indifference to it. And most frightening of all, they don't recognize this is happening." They don't recognize that they are being de-sensitized because the violence they see on television rarely, if ever, shows its own realities and consequences.

Television violence produces little or no pain or discomfort,* and almost never produces any permanent disfigurement or other physical consequences. Violence on television often leads to quick (never slow) death, but injuries short of death are never taken seriously. Typically, the victim is beaten or stabbed or shot and then "left to die"; the next scene reveals him in a sparkling-white hospital bed in a private room, thankful to be alive, joking through gritted teeth, and apparently feeling few after-effects. The short and long-range consequences of serious injury are never shown. Thus, pain, fear, time lost from a job, the high cost of medical care, and the anguish of family members are not part of the program, nor is crippling, or drawn-out dying.

When death does result from a violent televised act, it is short and sweet. Blood does not flow, organs are not smashed, the bowels do not move in one last desperate reflex. The exit wounds of bullets, which in reality are often the size of a dinner plate, are not visible. Instead, viewers see only surgically clean and usually bloodless entry wounds, which miraculously never hit arteries. The true physical dynamics of death are ignored in favor of clean, sterile, motionless bodies. When a bullet from a rifle struck President Kennedy's head, its force scattered pieces of his brain a considerable distance away. If that killing in Dallas had been part of a private-eye or police drama on prime time, one would have seen only a slump of the President's body from a wide-angle camera shot, with perhaps a quick cut back to the assassin, methodically refolding his rifle and slipping downstairs.

The most frequent example of violence in prime-time television is probably the blow on the head with—as the old detective stories put it—"a blunt instrument." This is a favorite episode, and there is hardly a prime-time hour free of an example or two. A frightened citizen will pick up a chair and smash it over the head of a person seen creeping around a darkened office; a police officer or private detective, not wanting to shoot and kill, will fell an assailant with a karate chop to the neck; or the hero, snooping where he isn't welcome, will be cracked across the head by one of the bad guys. In each instance, the result is the same. The person hit on the head is knocked out—but only for a short time. He then wakes up. In almost every case, the time for total recovery is measured by the time required to show a few commercials.

In any event, the message which comes through is a clear one: a blow with all one's force on the head of another with a blunt object is a very

---

* The "pain or discomfort" in the commercials—for arthritis remedies, for example—seems more real, even if instantly alleviated by the advertised product.

efficient way to stop someone—without serious injury. The television episodes teach us daily that if one must perform this small act of violence in the service of a larger objective, nothing damaging will happen.

But this simply is not so. Physicians report that blows on the head with chairs and gun butts regularly cause serious injury. In addition to death and paralysis (there are very few people who can survive a straight blow on the head with a lead pipe), possible effects include the temporary or permanent loss of motor abilities, the inability to speak or to understand speech or symbols, convulsions, dizziness, or chronic headaches, as well as emotional problems such as anxiety, fear, irritability, and depression, and a disruption in the "capacity to conduct interpersonal relationships," including shyness, feelings of inferiority, and paranoia.

Even when death occurs, television sanitizes it. No unctuous morticians exploit the bereaved. There are few bereaved in any event, and if someone mourns a television death, the fact is conveyed to the viewer by, at most, a dramatic shot of a single tear.

For that matter, on both news and entertainment television programs, death is remote and highly circumscribed. On entertainment programs, fully developed characters or, as they are called in the trade, "regulars," never die in the ordinary course of the plot; when a real television personality in the news, a Kennedy or a Martin Luther King or a Jack Benny dies, the event is not placed in the perspective of death but is transformed into a spectacle of state. Television's coverage of Jack Benny's death in 1975, for example, provided no genuine portrayals of sorrow (of which there were many) but endless opportunities for his former colleagues to enlarge and sustain their own egos. "He was stingy until the end," smiled Bob Hope, "he didn't give us enough time." Who, one might ask, is the ultimate beneficiary of such an eulogy?

Film clips of Benny used in the coverage of his death—and the pattern is similar for the death of other personalities to which television will devote a "special"—showed a young man in his prime, as though his years of aging had never existed. Within a few weeks, Jack Benny television programs were brought out for a few months of syndication, as if to comfort viewers by convincing them that he had never really died. Bruce Herchensohn points out that when Carole Lombard died in the early 1940s many people did not go to see her final movie because they thought it would be in bad taste. In the Age of Television, such sentiment would be totally incomprehensible.

In fact, television commercials even play off the timelessness of film and the consequent immortality of those filmed. A particularly grisly example of this was the use some years ago of an anti-smoking message delivered by William Tallman, the district attorney on the Perry Mason Show. Tallman was ravaged with lung cancer when he made the commercial, and spoke of his condition, and the advertisement was used even after he had died of the disease. As late as 1976, bank commercials using the authoritative presence of Lee J. Cobb were being screened—some months after Cobb's death—perhaps in some subliminal way to suggest the survivor benefits of a joint account.

Michael J. Arlen of the *New Yorker* calls television death "a huge cool authority" that has rushed into the spiritual vacuum left by the decline in tribal and religious institutional authority. With the exception of the very famous, television tells us that people do not really die. And as we have seen, they especially do not die if they are regular performers on a series. A not uncommon conversation between young children and parents occurs while watching television when one of the good guys is, perhaps, felled by a gunshot (or arrow) wound. The parent, solicitous, says something like, "I hope he's not dead," to which the child will reply, "Don't worry, he's a regular."

This is particularly comforting because *all of us are regulars,* each in the supreme daily prime-time program that is our own life. Only a few television producers have permitted stars to die, and then only when the actor has died or moved to another job. An example of this reluctance occurred in the fall of 1975 when the actress portraying a leading character on the popular comedy series *Phyllis* was murdered, apparently a victim of random violence, in Los Angeles. The character had been established for about five weeks on the program, as a wise-cracking woman with whom the star of *Phyllis* had obtained a job. The "problem" caused by this untimely death was solved by substituting—with no explanation—a new actress, who bore a startling physical resemblance to the one who had died.

The producers' experience, from *Lassie* in the 1950s to *M*A*S*H* in the 1970s, has been that the television audience will not gladly—if at all—tolerate such deaths. In soap opera, where things move more slowly, dead characters have been brought back in response to audience complaints, such as Sir Arthur Conan Doyle was reluctantly forced to bring back Sherlock Holmes from his death at the Reichenbach Falls. Death, in any realistic sense, simply does not exist on entertainment programs. On news it is often an abstract number, and on programs designed specifically for children, even with their highly stylized violence, it is nonexistent.

In many ways, this is similar to a Jewish religious tradition. During the recital of the Yizkor, the memorial prayer for the dead, children in many congregations are excused from the temple. The elders reason that it is too upsetting, and that children will learn about death soon enough. Modern Jewish parents, however, are moving away from the practice. Some feel that the secrecy forces children's imaginations to manufacture an idea of death that is too mysterious and frightening;

others realize that in contemporary society such secrets cannot—or should not—be kept.

But television—the orthodox rabbi in the great American congregation—is still trying to keep the secret; it is sending all of us out of the temple. "We do not die, apparently," writes Arlen, "except in numbers in Rangoon, or with blank faces in a gunfight . . . Television—this great communicating force—has settled into a role of largely ignoring the reality of death." On television, violence is virtually the sole cause of death; it is only on soap operas, and then very rarely, that anyone dies of age or disease. But violence performs its death-dealing service quickly, and then the victim is whisked off camera. The connection of death to real people and real feelings is anonymous, clinical, and forgotten in the time it takes to spray on a new and longer-lasting deodorant.

Nik Cohn, a young writer born just six years before the laying of the coaxial cable, has written a novel that may give us a glimpse of what the Television Generation has been taught about death. Cohn's *King Death*, published in 1975, dramatizes the life of Eddie, a professional hit man.

A television producer discovers Eddie in the act of practicing his profession. He knows a potential winning television program when he sees one, seeks out Eddie in a bar, and tries to persuade him to move to Hollywood;

> I've never seen anything like it, not on TV, or even at the movies. The way you plowed right through him, all in a single movement, and he did not struggle in the slightest—if I hadn't seen it with my own eyes, I would not have believed it—I was thrilled. Perhaps I ought not to say that, perhaps it wasn't dignified. But my blood began to roar, my temples to pound and do you know, when you had departed and the stranger was still, I felt as limp as a dishcloth.

Eddie accepts the compliments graciously, with just an echo of Lieutenant William Calley:

> We are not butchers, you could not rightly call us criminals. In my own satisfaction, I'd like to think that we are performers.

What type of performer? "As God is my witness," Eddie explains, "I bear no hate for any man alive, and every act I commit, I render it with love." Eddie signs up, and his kills are telecast "live" coast-to-coast. Eddie is soon a national folk hero, the object of adoration and autograph seekers. The culmination of his career is a national lottery whose winner gets to be killed by the champ on live, prime time television.

Home viewers see the winner's last few moments, surrounded by long-legged young blondes. He says good-bye to his wife and daughter, receives a Cadillac, a Caribbean home and $50,000 in prizes, and then goes to meet Eddie:

> Like fudge exposed to the sun, he went all soft and sticky, he did not feel anything. He existed, no more than that, and he was at home.
>
> He opened his mouth, he closed his eyes: head back, throat upraised, he offered himself without shame or the least regret. Once again, a shadow passed across his face and, as it did so, he remembered that he still owed Brannigan five dollars for his entry fee, a debt which would not now be repaid. In the final close-up, this thought caused him to smile.

The description is pure Television Generation. In literature death has taken many forms. But rarely has it been so clean, cheap, and sweet. And, of course, none of our pre-television authors thought to describe an America so enamored of death that it finds entertainment in close-ups of a murder victim's face.

Cohn's book anticipated by less than a year a column by William F. Buckley in which he indirectly complimented prison authorities in Hong Kong for televising the firing squad executions of two convicted criminals. It was, Buckley intimated, something that our society could well comtemplate.

At about the same time, a film named *Snuff* began to appear in the nation's movie theaters. A normal, grade-D porno movie until the final ten minutes, *Snuff* claims to portray the real-life maiming and murder of a young actress who had not been told what her role really called for. The Washington *Star* described those ten minutes:

> The young man astride the woman suddenly reaches for a six-inch hunting knife . . . then begins cutting from the tip of her shoulder downward . . . the gushing of the blood intensifies . . . as the knife cuts deeper to apparently sever the arm from the shoulder . . . He exchanges his weapon for a small pair of wire-cutters he uses to snip off the ends of several of her fingers. He and his accomplices use an electric saw to sever a hand . . . For a finale, the man goes back to his knife, cuts open the woman's abdomen, reaches in with outstretched fingers to fondle and caress the innards, then suddenly pulls out a handful, holds them high in front of him and bursts into a fiendish yell and laugh.

Many television stations invested a considerable amount of time in local news programs in interviews with patrons who had just seen *Snuff*. As the camera searched their faces, finding delight on some, disgust on others, these people explained why they believed the film was or was not real, while television newsmen treated the discussion with the same evenhanded seriousness they would have applied—let us say—to the repeal of section 14(b) of the Taft-Hartley Act.

"We are what you have made us," a Charles Manson gang member once explained. "We were brought up on your TV. We were brought up watching *Gunsmoke, Have Gun, Will Travel, FBI, Combat. Combat was my favorite show. I never missed Combat.*"

In 1974, Evel Knievel was scheduled to jump the Snake River Canyon on a live television broadcast. To help create a big rating he spent the weeks preceding his jump saying things like, "Got to be a winner or loser [between Knievel and the canyon]. Can't be no draw." As it turned out, it was a draw; even though, as an NBC correspondent pointed out a few days before, the canyon had become the sentimental favorite.

In March, 1976, plans (later postponed) called for people to pay $25 a head to watch a live, closed-circuit television "death match" between "shark hunter" Wally Gibbons, and a man-eating great white shark. Publicity for the fight ran as follows:

> Gibbons will bring to the fight a spear gun and years of shark-fighting know-how. The shark will be helped by its great size, killer jaws, and knife-sharp teeth. The fight will go on until Gibbons kills the shark. Or until it kills him.

Such stories raise many questions, all perhaps best summarized by one review of Cohn's novel: "Are we as a people becoming so habituated to violence," asked Edward J. Reilly, "that it seems no longer real unless it directly touches us?" It is an old-fashioned question. The modern version would add, "Is it real even then?"

In the total spectrum of television violence, rape deserves particular mention. Journalism professor Caryl Rivers watched two hours of televised rape scenes for the *New York Times,* and came away shocked: "The rape on *Hawaii Five-O* was not horrifying, not ugly. 'Titillating' is the word for the way it was presented. Lovingly, the camera stalked the rapist's victims, it peeped at shapely legs in miniskirts, leered at a wiggly walk, watched a swaying bottom. It made rape seem like a subject for a *Playboy* centerfold, an incident without terror and pain . . .

"The camera ogled legs and bottoms, but we got only a glimpse of the victims' bodies. A gorgeous female hitchhiker in tight jeans and a blouse that bared her midriff climbed into the rapist's car. A few minutes later, her body rolled out of the car and down an embankment. For the audience, it was a brief glimpse of a cipher, not a human being."

Contrasting this sanitized portrayal with the brutality and lingering scars that accompany real rape, Ms. Rivers wants the networks to be more realistic. "Instead of showing us actresses with catchupy bruises or anonymous figures under blankets," she says, "why not use a real police photograph of a real rape-murder victim, exactly the way she was found . . . It might give the folks out there on the other side of the tube an idea of what the word 'rape' is *really* about."

Industry spokesmen argue with some justification that they cannot move in any other direction. What should we do, they ask, show violence in all of its horrible details and consequences?

That is a difficult question, but it is also the wrong question. It is true that people do not want to see all of the details, at least all the time. Whenever television covers a bloody news event, such as an airplane crash, viewers watch carefully, with a mixture of hope and fear to see if the film will show real mutilated bodies. When the bodies are shown, people call the television station to complain. Sometimes a medical show will reveal in some detail just how grisly and difficult and bloody an operation can be. When that happens, as it did with the recent *Medical Story* series, viewers tune out in sufficient numbers for the show to be canceled.

What is at work here, at least in the minds of television executives, is a recognition that most people do not wish to see the details of life's unpleasantnesses and cruelties on the living room set. For most viewers, television is an escape from life and a source of pleasure. It is reasonable for the networks to believe, as they apparently do, that if they began to show what violence and its consequences are really like, the number of viewers would drop so sharply as to put them out of business.

But the question of whether violence should be sanitized, as it presently is on television, or whether producers should show violence and its consequence in all of their gory reality, is one we need not answer. Both alternatives are equally antisocial. The question that must be asked is, why dwell on violence in the first place? There is no inherent demand for violence in the art of writing entertainment shows for television. The demand is placed there by producers, who feel it is placed there by advertisers, who feel it is placed there by viewers. Howard Rodman, a leading script writer for television, tells of a conference about a scene in one of his teleplays in which two characters engage in a crucial conversation while one is driving and the other is a passenger in the front seat of an automobile. Rodman was asked by the producer—who had clearly been approached by someone at the network—to "put some action into the scene." Rodman pointed out that the scene itself, containing a conversation crucial to the resolution of the plot, probably was "action" enough, but the producer persisted. Perhaps, he said, there could be some tension connected with the driving, perhaps some broken glass. Rodman, who knows his craft as well as anyone in the business, knows that menacing music and broken glass are classic evocations of violence to come. He saw the direction in which the conversation was headed, and capitulated. He rewrote the scene, with his tongue more or less in his cheek, so that at the height of the key conversation, the passenger made a homosexual pass at the driver, the car suddenly went out of control, swerved, and plunged over an embankment, bounced down a steep hillside, and burst into flames at the bottom.

But this rebellion by Rodman, a spiritual successor to Herman J. Mankiewicz (the father of one of this book's authors), who once showed his contempt for the Rin-Tin-Tin ritual film by writing a climactic scene in which the dog picked up a sleeping baby and carried him into a burning building, is not typical. Most writers go along with the menacing music and the broken glass—and ultimately the broken head—because that is the way the game is played. It is a high-rolling game, in which the money from a successful series can create a most pleasant life for the creative people, their families, and their tax advisers.

So the cycle continues. The programs contain lots of violence, they are viewed by lots of people, the advertisers pay lots of money to the networks for the air time in between violent acts, and lots of that money is retained for high salaries and profits. And when the do-gooders complain about violence, network spokesmen can point to this remunerative cycle and say that they are only "giving the public what it wants."

There is no evidence of any kind that this is what "the public wants"; no one has ever asked us. One is unavoidably reminded of the Mad Hatter's tea party. The March Hare has told Alice, "You should say what you mean."

> "I do," Alice hastily replied; "at least—at least I mean what I say—that's the same thing, you know."
>
> "Not the same thing a bit!" said the Hatter. "Why, you might just as well say that 'I see what I eat' is the same thing as 'I eat what I see'!"
>
> "You might just as well say," added the March Hare, "that 'I like what I get' is the same thing as 'I get what I like'!"

The size of the audience seems to confirm that we like what we get; but no evidence has been presented—nor is it likely to be—that we get what we like.

HABITUATION

Repeated exposure to television violence, said Dr. Bertram S. Brown, National Institute of Mental Health Director, in testimony before a Senate committee in 1974, can produce

insensitivity to cruelty and violence because it gradually extinguishes
the viewers' emotional responses and builds the feeling that violent behavior is normal and appropriate under some circumstances,

Extensive scholarly research supports this and similar conclusions. One
typical study measured the tolerance for real-life aggression among
third and fourth graders. Using a carefully selected control group, it
demonstrated that just one exposure to an eight-minute violent episode
from a Hopalong Cassidy cowboy movie induced children to tolerate,
"for significantly longer" periods of time, what they believed to be fighting among younger children they had been instructed to supervise.
Similar results emerged when a contemporary television detective program was used and when the subjects were fifth graders. "We have
provided evidence," the authors conclude, "that exposure to TV violence
can increase *normal children's* toleration of real-life aggression." Using
language rarely found in scholarly journals, they report that "the overall
conclusion is frightening."

Another study concluded that "some children who are heavy television watchers and therefore are exposed to more violence may become,
to some degree, habituated or 'desensitized' to violence generally." The
experiment consisted of showing children from five to twelve years of
age a short film which included both violent and nonviolent segments.
A physiograph, a photoelectric cell, and other equipment attached to
their bodies measured their response. Violent sequences in the film
came from a Kirk Douglas boxing movie titled *Champion* and consisted
of blows struck during a prize fight. Even this violence, it must be
noted, was much more tame and disciplined than what is normally seen
on television.

In a later interview, the study's principal author explained that "the
television kids tended to be turned off emotionally; the children not exposed to television still were able to respond emotionally, feel for and
empathize with the person who was suffering the violence, moderate
though it was." Confirmation of this conclusion is found in still another
study in which subjects repeatedly viewed a nonfiction documentary
film of an apparently painful genital mutilation ritual performed by an
aboriginal tribe. Responses of physical revulsion to what was being seen
began to decline—and continued to decline steadily—after the first
showing. Repeated showings proved sufficient to neutralize practically
all negative reactions, including involuntary physical responses.

This study's author concludes that his experiment ". . . suggests the
possibility that viewers can be 'cured' of this kind of anxiety toward horror and pain. If this sort of process is going on, viewers may be increasingly able to accept real-life acts of extreme violence without attempting

to interfere." And then, in a chilling foretaste of what further violence may hold for the future, he warns that viewers *"may themselves be less reluctant to engage in aggression when provoking circumstances arise."*

National Book Award winner Jerzy Kosinski recalls with some foreboding one of the experiences he had while teaching public school. Kosinski invited a group of seven-to-ten year olds to sit in a large classroom and hear him tell a story. The room was equipped with television cameras and monitors so the children could either watch him or see him on television. Suddenly, by pre-arrangement, another adult burst into the room and started to argue with Kosinski, pushing and hitting him. A third camera recorded the children's reactions. Not one child voiced a protest, and only a few watched it really happening. The rest kept their eyes glued to the television monitors.

In later conversations with the children, Kosinski asked why they had responded in this way. The answer seemed natural enough. By providing close-ups of the violence and the fear, the cameras permitted the children to see Kosinski's facial expressions as he was about to be hit; provided the children with the "real thing" completely cleansed of fears and responsibility. "You looked so scared and he was so mean," said one . . . "You could see *everything* on those screens. They are great. How much does it cost to buy one of those things?"*

Kosinski readily acknowledges that his experiment was far from scientific, that it was designed only to provide him with more insights into the Television Generation. "They (the children) sat transfixed as if the TV cameras neutralized the act of violence," Kosinski explained to an interviewer. "And perhaps they did. By filming a brutal physical struggle from a variety of viewpoints, the cameras transformed a human conflict into an aesthetic happening, distancing the audience and allowing them an alternative to moral judgment and involvement."

Psychologists have many words they use to describe this desensitization process; among the most frequently used are *habituation, adaptation, satiation,* and *accommodation.* But whatever word is used, the end result is the same: "normal" people begin to accept violence as an ordinary companion in their lives. We can only begin to speculate on the social cost this evokes. Is it possible, for example, that the Kitty Geno-

---

*Sports viewing offers another example of this phenomenon. Fans at the stadium now report a sense of incompleteness and dissatisfaction, traced to the absence of "instant replay," a television device permitting the home audience to see a particular play again and again. Now, many stadiums and arenas have actual "instant replay" screens in place above the scoreboard—presumably to make the real "more realistic." At the Capital Center, Washington's indoor arena, one may buy a season "box" high above the floor. There, you and your party will sit in comfortable chairs in a paneled room, complete with carpeting, waiter service, and food and drink, and watch the game. Unfortunately, the basketball floor is so far away that the game must be watched on large closed-circuit television screens.

vese murder or the My Lai massacre may somehow be related to this phenomenon?

Passive observation of exceptional violence—the nighttime habit of many Americans—was the role played by witnesses to the murder of Kitty Genovese. Thirty-eight apparently normal people did nothing while just below their windows, a man sexually disfigured and killed a young woman. No one called the police, or even called out in an attempt to scare the killer away. When one of the witnesses went to the window of her apartment, she could not get a clear view of the murder taking place on the sidewalk below. "Turn off the lights, dumbbell," her husband is reported to have suggested, "*then* you can see." She did, and they both pulled up chairs to the window to watch the show. Lest anyone think there is something unusually evil about these people, experts now advise that women about to be attacked or who are being attacked shout "fire" instead of "help" or "rape" because the latter two words have been shown in many cases to evoke only indifference. The fireman is more likely than the arsonist to be a television hero; as we have seen, the rapist is often a morally ambiguous figure.

At My Lai, American GIs—young men who had grown up as members of the Television Generation—methodically shot and killed, or stood by and watched others shoot and kill, several hundred women, children, and old men. Like the citizens watching Kitty Genovese, these soldiers were simply watching—and doing—the type of thing they had seen done painlessly and affectlessly so many times while growing up. Lieutenant William Calley, asked at his court martial if it was true that he had killed an elderly monk by smashing his face with his rifle butt, replied calmly, "It was no big deal, sir." The "sir" is a nice touch and demonstrates in a perverse way the effectiveness of Calley's training, but the "it was no big deal" reflects his—and how many others'?—view of what came to be called a "massacre."

Consider this exchange, which took place between CBS correspondent Mike Wallace and one of the My Lai participants, two years after the event:

QUESTION: "You're married?"
ANSWER: "Right."
QUESTION: "Children?"
ANSWER: "Two."
QUESTION: "How old?"
ANSWER: "The boy is two and a half and the little girl is a year and a half."
QUESTION: "Obviously the question comes to mind—the father of two little kids like that—how can he shoot babies?"
ANSWER: "I didn't have the little girl. Just had the little boy at the time."

QUESTION: ". . . huh . . . how do you shoot babies?"
ANSWER: "I don't know. It's just one of those things."

If those actions and comments seem bizarre and isolated, it is instructive to compare them with the recent reaction of Chicago elementary school children after viewing the film *Mandingo* at a local theater:

> FLOYD: "They wanted to have fun with the girl. They asked her if she was a virgin. She said yes, so he took the other one and led her over to the shed and took off her clothes and started beating her with a strap . . . I felt the movie was very entertaining."

> KIM: "I liked the movie because it was bloody and nasty. He took him in the boiling hot water and stabbed him with a rake. The white man drank booze and he told her to take her clothes off and the white man told the black woman to take her clothes off."

> DON: "I liked when he boiled the guy in hot water, especially when the guy was making it with his girl. Then the white guy made it with the black girl. They beat him with a big wooden stick till they bleed to death. My favorite part was when they whipped the man to death."

The point here is not to censor or suppress movies like *Mandingo,* but to take a hard look at the environment (television) in which the movie's audiences live. The relationship between twenty years of nightly (and, for the most part, rewarded) violence and the reception of the movie is one which must be explored. The relationship that exists can no longer be in any doubt. *Mandingo* is, in theory, a depiction of the "horrors" of slavery, but its enormous success is due, of course, to the audience's identification with the slaveholders. Similarly, a new group of exploitation movies, with titles like *Bertha, Bitch of the SS,* is having a bit of a vogue, and it's not hard to see identification there, either. A commercial "artistic" movie of 1975, *The Night Porter,* even achieved some critical acclaim, although it was little more than "Mandingo Meets the SS," tricked out with a little pop Freudianism to the effect that some women "need" the kind of kinky brutality that increasing numbers of Americans now accept without "reacting."

Perhaps the most frightening, strongest, and most widely publicized indication of this growing insensitivity comes from a series of experiments conducted by psychologist Stanley Milgram, and extensively analyzed by him in his 1974 book, *Obedience to Authority.*

Milgram placed volunteers in a laboratory situation that enabled them to comply with requests—and later, orders—to administer electrical shocks in varying degrees of severity to persons whom they believed to be subjects of a scientific experiment. The instructions and orders came from authority figures (dressed in white laboratory smocks and holding clipboards, just like real television doctors and scientists), who explained that the "subjects" had volunteered to participate in an experiment that measured their learning capacity. The true subjects of the experiment, seated with the "scientists" (who were in reality actors hired for the occasion) were told that they were participating in important scientific research. In reality, the apparent "subjects" were also actors, and as they received the "electric shocks"—which were of course never really delivered—they would convincingly plead for mercy, demand to be released from the experiment, show great pain, and at times pretend to suffer serious heart problems.

The authority figures ordered the true subjects of the experiment—the volunteers who had agreed to administer the shocks—to turn up the force of the electric shocks in increasing magnitude whenever the fake subjects failed to respond correctly to a question. All of this was well rehearsed, so the fake subjects gave incorrect answers sufficient to warrant extremely high levels of electric shock. The shock dial was labeled "Slight Shock," "Moderate Shock," "Strong Shock," "Intense Shock," "Extreme Intensity Shock," "Danger: Severe Shock," followed by two switches simply marked "XXX."

The results were, quite simply, chilling. Milgram writes that "psychiatrists predicted that only a pathological fringe of about one in a thousand would administer the highest shock." But most subjects, irrespective of personal background or educational level, obeyed every order to give shocks—including orders they believed to be causing severe pain and that they were told by the "scientists" might cause heart damage and death. Open-ended interviews conducted several months later established beyond any reasonable doubt that the participants truly believed they were hurting another person; many said they would do the same thing all over again, even after having had the chance to think it over, and even knowing that the results of the experiment had depicted them as people with—to say the least—some rather unattractive qualities.

Sociologist Gordon W. Allport calls Milgram's analysis "the Eichmann experiment," likening its findings to similar conclusions drawn from interviews with former members of the Nazi SS. Some similarities are, of course, inescapable. But an important distinction exists. The members of the SS were a carefully chosen group—selected on the basis of their unwillingness to question authority, and in some cases for the pathological pleasure they derived from dealing in terror, torture, and death. But Milgram's subjects underwent no such screening. They were Yale undergraduates and ordinary people who came in off the New Haven streets after reading a newspaper advertisement soliciting their participation in a presumably useful scientific experiment. The horrifying fact, of course, is precisely that they were just plain folks, regular Americans.

But they were also regular Americans in the Age of Television, and they had watched with growing indifference the thousands of beatings, maimings, and killings that make up the nightly diet for most of us.

Another measure of our acceptance of, even desire for, violence is the way in which it has come to dominate our professional sports. In a more innocent age, violence in professional sports—except for boxing—was limited to an occasional spikes-high slide into third base or a not-so-subtly-thrown beanball. It was rough, but it was individual and sporadic. Today, violence or the possibility of violence is systematic throughout most sports events. Violence, after all, makes good television, and in the Age of Television "professional sports" has become synonymous with "televised sports."

To be sure, gladiators fought to the death as far back as 264 BC, and some form of sports violence, whether it be bear-baiting or boxing, has been with us ever since. But the Age of Television has brought violence to sports that were once treasured marks of our civility and notions of fair play.

In major league baseball, physical roughness and fights are now epidemic in what is supposedly a non-contact sport; many baseball players sustain injuries that take them out of action for considerable periods of time. In professional hockey—perhaps the roughest of our professional games—players have attacked one another with such brutality that some players have been charged with criminal assault. In early 1976, David Forbes of the Boston Bruins went to trial on this charge, the first professional athlete in American history to go before a jury for his actions on the playing field. In professional basketball, fights, roughness, and technical fouls have become so common that it is now almost mandatory for a successful National Basketball Association coach periodically to rush dramatically onto the court or even to scuffle with the referee. Auto racing has become faster and much more unsafe than it need be. The violence in football, the nation's most popular sport (as measured by the size of the television audience), speaks for itself. Spectators themselves at sporting events have become more violent, and it is no longer uncommon for referees or players to be injured by fans, or to need close police protection to return to their locker rooms.

Television does more than simply report or reflect this violence: it idolizes it. "Children have had plenty of opportunities to view crunches from close-up angles," notes a *Time* magazine essay. "Replaying highlights of games that viewers have not seen, *ABC Monday Night Baseball* showed at length the on-field fracas of the Chicago Cubs - San Francisco Giants game nine days after it occurred. Football "cheap shots" and beanball brawls, hockey fistfights and basketball square-offs—exercises in passion that transgress the rules—are a minor part of any sports event. Yet they are given long and detailed attention, instant and incessant replay."

Violence has come to dominate sports as it has become bigger and bigger business—under the impact of larger and larger television contracts. When the price of one-half minute of football time approaches $100,000 for an advertiser, it is no wonder that the actual quality of the games has changed.

Football is a good example. The whole movement toward the specialist, the changes in rules every year—these are largely done to make the game more "visual," more easy to "cover," and thus more likely to deliver a large audience. There are Americans of voting age—football fans—who think the "two-minute warning" is traditional and not simply a device added some years ago to provide a convenient place for commercial interruption at a key point in the viewing.

Soccer is another case in point. The rules—unchanged for what seems like hundreds of years—called for continuous play. Thus a forty-five- minute half took forty-five minutes of real time, with no time-outs for any reason. A few years ago, the presence of Pelé playing for a team in the American professional league prompted CBS to televise some games. Alas, a commercial was on the air while Pelé, on the field, was banging in a goal with a spectacular header. The result: a change in the rules to provide for a (presumably traditional) time-out just before a penalty kick. Nothing better demonstrated the fact that the networks, at least, are betting on the increasing popularity of soccer to attract future generations.

The influence of television is sometimes subtle, and sometimes not so subtle. A hockey referee, preparing to resume play after a "break in the action," will not drop the puck for a face-off until a buzzer on his wrist has sounded—the signal from the television booth that the commercial is over.

(The sociology of sports is particularly interesting in hockey. Professional hockey, as played in the United States, is a game played almost entirely by Canadians. There are only a few "American" players, and those are likely to come from near the Canadian border. Naturally enough then, all of the players—with one exception—are white. The game expanded rapidly in the late 60s and 70s, from the six cities that made up the National Hockey League to more than three times that number, into cities where no one had ever (or would ever) grow up playing hockey, such as Atlanta, Los Angeles, or San Diego. In spite of the lack of any traditional identification with the sport, it became quite popular in all the cities where it was played. It is widely believed among sports owners and writers that the growing popularity of hockey had an unspoken, and unspeakable, basis: that it was the only sports event

Americans could attend without having to watch blacks play—or, as a matter of fact, without having to share the stadium with blacks; not unnaturally, a lily-white sport attracted a lily-white audience. If that is true, then the failure of NBC to renew professional hockey's contract for 1976 was a good sign. It meant that, while there may be enough bigots in each National Hockey League city to fill the stadiums, there were not enough in the country to provide a large enough audience for the networks to deliver, profitably, to their advertisers.)

"If they are not becoming actively delinquent—our 'good' middle class children, yours and mine—they are becoming passively jaded," writes psychologist Victor B. Cline:

> As a kind of protection, they develop thick skins to avoid being upset by the gougings, smashings and stompings they see on television. . . . [C]hild viewers cannot afford to get involved, for if they did their emotions would be shredded. So they keep "cool," distantly unaffected. Boredom sets in, and the whole cycle starts over again.

And Milgram has demonstrated that the "whole cycle" can consist not only of passive observation or brutality, but eventually, active participation in it.

PROBLEM SOLVING

Televised violence has another harmful dimension. It teaches that violence is an acceptable and normal method of solving problems: in fact, the message is that shooting, stabbing, and slugging are far more efficient and work better than more time-consuming techniques such as reason, logic, or understanding.

In almost all the programs with a violent content—particularly those involving police or friendly private detectives—peaceful options such as patience, understanding, compassion, or due process of law are not very important—and often impatiently dismissed—so long as the right side winds up winning. Good guys, in fact, use violence—the same kind of violence—more often than the bad guys, and the unquestioning, implicit approval that greets their actions teaches a powerful lesson. The staff of the National Commission on the Causes and Prevention of Violence concluded in 1968 that from television "the overall impression is that violence, employed as a means of conflict resolution or acquisition of personal goals, is a predominant characteristic of life." The more socially acceptable techniques such as "cooperation, compromise, and debate," the staff concluded, "are notable only for their lack of prominence." This is supported by an observation made later by Dr. George Gerbner of the Annenberg School of Communications, University of Pennsylvania. "To be able to hit hard and to strike terror in the hearts of opponents—that makes one count when the chips are down," he writes in describing the world of television. Who is the flawed man and which the flawed cause, he says, are determined by "the last man to hit the dust"; virtue is tested by "hurting," and to kill is to prove one's supreme manhood. "Loss of life, limb or mind," in this television world, according to Gerbner, are simply "the wages of weakness . . ."

One social scientist tells the story of a group of young children in 1963 discussing something they had seen recently on television—the killing of Lee Harvey Oswald by Jack Ruby. One child said it was wrong, because Oswald was helplessly handcuffed between two police officers when Ruby shot him at point-blank range. Another child did not even seem to believe that this question was worthy of note. How was the child, after all, to distinguish the moral and ethical dimensions of Oswald's "live" death from what he saw every night on film or his favorite entertainment programs? In a popular police program of that time, the heroes never flinched from hitting a suspect while two policemen held his arms. To a six year old, perhaps even to a sixteen year old, there may have been little operative difference between a hero-cop on television and Jack Ruby.

The networks argue that this is an unfair attack; that they cannot be blamed for every insensitivity and for every action of unbalanced individuals. They claim that violence on television has been substantially cleaned up since the 60s and that all programs clearly teach that crime is wrong.

There was much to clean up. One Western of the 50s showed a man lying on the ground with an arrow in his chest. Another man walked up and said, "Don't worry, it won't hurt much longer," and pushed the arrow in deeper. At least, the networks say, such overt sadism is now off the air. And leaving aside the question of how or why such material could have been broadcast in the first place, it must be said that some progress has been made. In an early episode of *Gunsmoke* (often regarded as a relatively nonviolent program in its time) Marshal Matt Dillon's sidekick, Festus, had just shot down an unarmed man accused of raping Festus' young cousin. Dillon: "Did you kill him?" Festus: "I hope so. I shot him six times." Dillon nods his head understandingly and suggests that they both walk down to Miss Kitty's for a drink.

These days, that would not happen. Festus would corner the rapist who, to keep the symbolism straight, would pull out a knife. Festus would duck, knock the rapist off a balcony and then pursue him after the double fall. They would scuffle on the ground; and just as the rapist was about to slit Festus' throat, Marshal Dillon would shoot him cleanly and painlessly in the shoulder. The moral of this imaginary episode, according to network executives who keep track of such things, would be that bad guys use violence and lose. But the moral that is being learned in some of America's living rooms is different: good guys and bad guys both use violence; just make sure that yours is the more effective use— make sure you use it last.

A 1969 cartoon in the *Saturday Review* captured the hollowness of the network shift away from overt sadistic violence. The television producer is talking to his writer: "As part of the new de-emphasis, play up the line that he's fighting evil because he hates evil, instead of fighting evil because he loves to fight."

The networks agree, of course, that to show criminals "getting away with it" would be the height of social irresponsibility. And true to their word, television religiously demonstrates that criminals are always caught, innocent people don't go to jail (except on the heroic-lawyer programs where innocent people are released unharmed after no more than fifty-two minutes in jail).

This simple version of social responsibility ("crime does not pay") comes through the screen as a two-edged value. For one thing, crime on television is almost always exciting, intense, and even fun-filled. The bank robberies have a fascinating appeal, and to lead the police in a high-speed automobile chase, particularly down slippery streets, always appears as nearly the ultimate in daredevil manliness.

Crime on television also seems to offer sexual opportunities that would be unavailable to more law-abiding people. Ordinary viewers rarely have beautiful, provocatively dressed, available women lounging nearby while they smoke cigars* and discuss their next adventure; the criminals on television are almost always surrounded by such women who seem, in addition, to be highly aroused by evil doings. There is a clear association, in the television world, of crime and sex.

The widely advertised showing, in four hours of prime time on CBS, of *Helter Skelter,* the dramatization of the Charles Manson family's killing spree, brought this connection to a fully conscious level. The program taught plainly that if one is undereducated, unattractive, and scorned by the "pigs" of society, it is possible nevertheless to be surrounded by fifteen or twenty enormously attractive, sexually eager young women simply by the frequent use of random, murderous violence.

Helter Skelter was well produced, and therefore even more dangerous. One of the girls, in a breathy whisper, describes to a cellmate the killing of Sharon Tate, complete with the stabbings, the blood, and the

---

* The women, the Surgeon General notwithstanding, smoke cigarettes.

possibility of ripping her nearly full-term baby from her body; the scene is overall as sexy—and as horrifying—as any ever on the screen, even though the violence count is zero and the criminal has been put behind bars.

Caryl Rivers writes that the most troublesome aspect of televised rape is not the insensitivity shown to female victims, or the callousness with which the victim's experiences are portrayed—rather, she maintains, it is that the rapists seem to enjoy themselves. The message broadcast in the last few minutes, that "crime does not pay," says Ms. Rivers, didn't measure up to the real message, the emotionally more effective and longer-lasting message: "Ah, but what fun it was!" In one episode she describes, the rapist was "slim, handsome and virile"; he swaggered, and he could easily be seen as an object worthy of emulation.

On television the consequences of crime—as well as the consequences of violence—are rarely visible. To be sure, the guilty are caught (usually after being superficially wounded first) and brought to justice, but always at the very end of the program, seconds before the final fadeout. The uncertainties and terrors of arrest, the physical discomfort, the horrors of long boring years locked in a cage—these never exist as a direct consequence of television crime. They are replaced by a few commercials, a time of relaxation for the viewer, and preparation for the next program. If there is a penalty to be paid, just what the penalty is rarely is apparent. "Crime does not pay" is thus a message dimly received, if at all, by television viewers.

Young children, of course, are a very different category of television viewers from adults, and when they watch television—children's television or adult fare—it is not clear just what messages are received.

Children under the age of three usually see life in isolated sequences. By age four, a child can follow a story but cannot tell reality from fantasy and does not understand causality. The child does not know, for example, that a character has been shot by the police, or, for that matter, that the child himself is yelled at by his mother because he did something wrong twenty minutes earlier.

There is a story of how a young child approached Fred Rogers (*Misterogers Neighborhood*) in a hotel lobby and asked how he got out of the television set. The child then listened to a lucid explanation—as only Rogers could explain it—about the difference between real people and television pictures. Then, in the best journalistic tradition, the child asked a follow-up question, "But Misterogers, how are you going to get back into the television set?"

Between the ages of five and seven, a child begins to distinguish between the real and the make-believe, and develops the capacity for abstract thought. He has not yet worked out a balance between reward and punishment in fantasies, remaining, for the most part, unable to associate an action with its motives or consequences. He is aware of things like frustration, pain, and violence, but has not yet learned to work them into his own life space. Morality is still a confusing notion. Logic, as a tool that is at the child's disposal, usually does not appear until age seven or beyond, and magical or fairy tale explanations for the world can dominate until this age (although they peak at around age four).

At the same time he is able to see, as child development specialist Dorothy H. Cohen puts it, "the unbridled primitive quality of his fantasy enacted as appropriate reality in the world of adults; his fantasies of anger or fear are discharged and glorified by grown-ups on the television screen and throughout the news reports, as though there were no alternatives."

The possibilities for what this barrage does to children are the more manifold as they are unknown. Too little is known about how the world looks to a young child and about how his informational input affects maturation. "The entire contents of our experimental psychological journals," writes Harvard psychologist Burton L. White, "have given us only modest amounts of information . . ." A child of six still has trouble comprehending that his father was a little boy once himself. A child of six or seven, Ms. Cohen explains, "can know by rote that Los Angeles is in California—but not before they are closer to ten do they understand the spatial, part-whole relationship, that is, that Los Angeles is part of the larger spatial area known as California . . . Adults take this kind of knowledge about time and space as something that has always existed and assume that it exists in children, too. But careful study reveals that it does not emerge before a certain amount of maturing has taken place."

Ms. Cohen goes on to argue that maturing "cannot be hastened." Television, then, is not changing the pace of maturation so much as it is hitting the still-maturing child with a frantic barrage of largely unassimilable ideas, images, and facts. A six year old who has learned which is his left hand, has yet to comprehend that a person facing him has his left on the other side. And yet, we expect this child to know that one television detective shoots a man because he raped his best friend's wife or that another shot the bank robbers because they killed a guard. When children describe programs they have just seen, for example, the stories sound strangely unfamiliar even to an adult who has seen the same program. Almost all of the nuance is gone, causality is confused, and action dominates. "They are offered perversion," writes Cohen, "before they have fully learned what is sound."

During the 1930s, citizen pressure forced the motion picture industry to flash the "crime does not pay" message on the screen before and after gangster movies. The idea was that even this modest effort would teach children the appropriate lesson. It achieved little, and the practice was soon dropped. The television industry believes it is now including a similar, unspoken message in its programming—but it works just as poorly now as it did then.

Furthermore, most children watch violent programs in the presence of their parents or other adults and this, in many ways, legitimizes what happens on the screen. Children receive a very important and very fundamental message from what gives pleasure to their parents or other adults. If the parents add a few choice "get 'em's" or "look at that, will you's" the program content is reinforced, just as their laughter helps to shape children's sense of what is humorous. Mahonney Kassima, a convicted burglar and rapist incarcerated at Lorton Penitentiary near Washington, D.C., told the Washington *Post*'s Sally Quinn, "a child sits in front of TV and sees violence with the approval of his parents. He has no idea in his mind what's real and and what isn't real."

Even the parents who take the time—during a commercial or after a program—to explain what just went on, perhaps even disapprovingly, are doing too little too late. After all, they have just been sitting there and enjoying exactly what they are now trying to explain away. That enjoyment speaks louder than a whole moral lecture; besides, time pressure—the next program is about to start—usually limits what can be explained or criticized.

Scholarly studies have shown that there are other problems with the "good motivation" arguments advanced by the networks. If children feel that a character is "good" (a view they have probably reached because of skillful attempts to make him believe that), and then they see him commit an act of violence, they will *not* think significantly less of him. Indeed, one study concluded that "there is a relationship between exposure to crime and violent media and endorsement of an ideology which makes the use of force in the interest of egocentric needs the essential content of human relationships."

The literature also suggests that even older children do not take advantage of the time between viewing filmed violence and the presentation of a real-life problem in which to develop non-violent solutions to the problem. Violence used by "admirable" television characters has been legitimized, and many children simply accept it as a given and admirable part of life.

A 1972 study of teenagers discovered that "those adolescents whose favorite programs are the more violent ones, more frequently approve of a teenage boy punching or knifing another teenage boy." Other studies, conducted with slightly younger subjects, have concluded that children who watch violent programs believe more in the legitimacy of violence as a problem-solver and, not surprisingly, are also more willing to use it when confronted with a difficult situation.

Of course, it must be said that these studies measure association, and not causation. It could be, for example, that violent children simply prefer to watch violence on television because it meets their already established tastes. Perhaps. But the authors of these studies—and others—generally agree that all the available evidence supports the conclusion that violence on television constitutes

> consistent independent contribution to the child's notion about violence. The greater the level of exposure to televised violence, the more the child is willing to use violence, to suggest it as a solution to conflict, and to perceive it as effective.

Indeed, the same might be said of adults. William Saroyan once observed that "every man is a good man in a bad world—as he himself knows." The television world of super-heroes, and super-violence as super-solutions to super-problems, is tempting and exhilarating. It appeals to some of our basic needs as well as our fantasies. Millions of Americans—at least for an hour or more a week—*are* Kojak, and an equal number roam in the *Streets of San Francisco* with a handsome, young partner, nabbing criminals.

The sanitized shootings and other violent acts seen every evening give 85 million viewers, almost none of whom have ever shot or been shot at, highly unrealistic notions. Lessons are learned, and they are lessons that are likely to have an impact on real life decisions. It is not too farfetched to note that every American adult, for example, is repeatedly asked to decide—by voting—whether or not to support domestic and foreign policies, or candidates who advocate those policies, which involve one human being shooting at another human being in order to solve problems ranging from "law and order" to war and peace. The image that goes through our minds may well be derived from *Kojak* or *Cannon*. Even if education and experience push some individuals toward discounting such notions, the early age of their acquisition and the intensity of their repetition will make television-induced impressions difficult if not impossible to erase later. For all of Saroyan's good men in this bad world, television has made easier the acceptance and use of violence. In the words of Alexander Pope:

> Vice is a monster of so frightful mien,
> As to be hated needs but to be seen;
> Yet seen too oft, familiar with her face,
> We first endure, then pity, then embrace.

"REAL LIFE"

Despite the apparently overwhelming evidence to the contrary, television industry spokesmen often argue that televised violence does minimal damage, if any, to children, because they know it to be fictional. After all, the argument runs, young viewers realize that the Road Runner, Tom and Jerry, and other cartoon characters are only make-believe. The same goes for the real life actors on *Six Million Dollar Man, Cannon,* and the *Bionic Woman,* Lieutenant Harrelson of *S.W.A.T.,* and the crew of the *Emergency* ambulance—the networks say children know that they are playing the pretend game.

Parents certainly don't take these shows at face value, it is said. If they worry that their children may, that's one of the new problems of bringing up children. Discretion must be used; perhaps a child should not be permitted to see certain shows if he gets involved in them too deeply. Ultimately, of course, there's always the on/off switch and the channel changer. Or so they say.

Unfortunately, it's not that simple. Not only children, but adults, too, are enticed into believing that what they see on television is what they'll get in real life. In fact, it can be said with some degree of certainty that all of television—daytime, nighttime, entertainment, and news—is based on an intense effort, more often than not successful, by the people who manufacture television programs to make the viewers believe that it is in fact a picture of real life.

Were this not the case, the bottom line of television—advertising—would not be nearly so costly, or so profitable. The fatal fallacy in the industry position—that people know they are watching make-believe and therefore will not be induced to act in the ways the characters act on the screen—is that it is totally inconsistent with the television business.

It hardly makes sense to claim that for ten minutes people will, while watching make-believe characters in a drama, resolutely put the thought of any emulation out of mind, and then that they will switch gears in a second, in order to emulate other characters recommending a toilet tissue, detergent, automobile, or beer—and then, after sixty or 120 seconds, once again switch back to make-believe. Indeed, it is precisely the validity of the claim that viewers *will emulate the characters they see in commercials* on which rests the entire financial empire of television. One cannot imagine a network telling an advertising agency that television is understood by viewers to be make-believe and can in no way influence real-life conduct. On the contrary: the reason the networks can sell, and the reason advertisers will buy, commercial time as often and for as much as they do is precisely because they know that a significant slice of the viewing audience will in fact believe in the "reality" of what they see, and be persuaded by the people they see to act accordingly. This is the *hard* message delivered to prospective sponsors by the sales office. It makes it difficult to believe the sincerity of the *soft* message about the non-effects of violence issued by the public relations office. One does not have to wonder what these vintners buy to know that it is nearly as precious as the stuff they sell.

Even though the efficacy of television commercials is by itself sufficient to show that television is believed, and at least some of its messages acted upon, other evidence can be cited. Soap opera stars report that they are frequently stopped on the street and treated as though they are actually the characters they portray. An actress who plays a beautiful young temptress may be told—in person, or, frequently, by mail—to leave her best friend's husband alone. The actor whose television role is that of a harried "workaholic," often indifferent to his wife's needs, will be told to shape up or lose her. The actors frequently find such confrontations annoying and disturbing; many say that they stay out of public places because of it. Some live in semi-seclusion because they have been physically attacked for the misdeeds of their on-screen persona. These physical and verbal assailants are not "nuts" or social deviants. They are "normal" people—they don't have a long string of arrests, or criminal records; they do have a confused sense of reality. This belief can be upsetting. A physician once wrote the producers of *Edge of Night* requesting an end to a string of deaths of major characters. The reason, he said, was that one of his elderly patients had become disturbed by the deaths of characters who had truly entered her life. And at CBS, programmers had to eliminate poor people from soap opera scripts because too many sympathetic viewers sent them packages of food and clothing.

"We have a student who lives with us who is not Jewish," a Jewish mother explained to child psychiatrist George E. Gardner. "She has a crucifix above her bed. When my four year old asked her about it, she gave him a very detailed explanation which ended with Christ's death and resurrection. . . . When he told me the story, I said, "Well, weren't you surprised that he came alive again?" He wasn't surprised at all. He explained that somebody gets run over by a steamroller on TV and just pops right back up again!"

The producers of *Sesame Street* say their research shows that "children are confused when a familiar TV character is presented in an unfamiliar context. Most children believe, for example, that the people they see on the program are real and that they really live on Sesame Street. They have little conception of actors. Many believe the cast knows them as well as they know the cast."

Newspapers frequently contain sad items about children who believe that the action-filled television life can be emulated. The fourteen year old who hanged himself after watching rock star Alice Cooper on television, the nine year old who strangled himself on his cape while performing Batman leaps, the kindergartener who pushed his hand through a window, and the eight year old who lacerated his liver on his bicycle handlebars after imitating Evel Knievel,* all had one thing in common: they followed through on their belief that what they see on television is real.

The same problems of the difference—or the perceived lack of difference—between television "reality" and the "real" reality of life may be found in public attitudes toward the possibility of becoming the victim of a violent street crime. The only extensive examination of this phenomenon has been conducted by Gerbner and his colleagues at the Annenberg School of Communications. They asked a national sample three questions, measuring the perception of (1) the likelihood of becoming a crime victim, (2) whether people can be trusted, and (3) what percentage of males working in America have jobs either in law enforcement or crime detection. They also asked how much television their respondents watched, and for other answers they could use to analyze responses.

The results were instructive: heavy television viewers are much more likely to overestimate the true dimension and dangers of crime. For light viewers (watching two hours or less a day) other variables such as education or newspaper reading may intervene to neutralize the apparent impact of television viewing. But for heavy viewers, television overrides even the impact of a college education. And viewers under the age of thirty—members of the Television Generation—showed a greater propensity to overestimate—that is to say, to believe television—at all levels of viewing. "Symbolic violence," writes Gerbner, "potentially trains victims as well as perpetrators."

Some polls taken in the 1972 presidential campaign are even more instructive. Cambridge Survey Research, sampling small rural towns in Wisconsin, New Hampshire, Oregon, and Nebraska, asked respondents what they thought was the major issue in their own communities. In the top two or three, and often in first place, was "crime in the streets." This was a truly astonishing finding, since many of the communities sampled barely had streets—"street crime" over the previous four or five

---

* So many children have hurt themselves playing Evel Knievel that some members of Congress have pressured the networks to stop televising his stunts, and a recent article in *Pediatrics* medical journal discusses the "Evel Knievel syndrome." Not content to leave well enough alone, ABC, whose "sports" programs have provided Knievel with most of his exposure, broadcast a family-hour special on his life story and had Fonzie, the nation's youth idol (a character on ABC's *Happy Days*), attempt a Knievel-style "world's record jump of fourteen garbage cans" on his motorcycle.

years had been limited to occasional exuberant teenagers shooting at streetlights with BB guns. But "crime in the streets" is very real in the living rooms of peaceful small towns all over America, and if the bank is robbed or the rapist races down the street pursued by a policeman emptying his service revolver, or if screeching car chases endanger everyone on the road for three hours every night, seven nights a week, is it strange that on leaving the living room those images have created a permanent fear in the viewer, wherever he may live? Or that he will then, in the political homework of voting and expressing opinion, speak and act on that fear?

The National Commission on the Causes and Prevention of Violence asked teenagers in 1967 whether they agreed or disagreed with the statements, "the programs I see on television tell about life the way it really is," and "the people I see on TV programs are just like the people I meet in real life."

A full 15 per cent of middle class white teenagers agreed with those statements. There are millions of middle class white teenagers in this country (12 million, in 1970, white teenagers in families with incomes above the poverty line); and most of them watch prime-time police shows on a regular basis. So if 15 per cent of them believe that what they are seeing is reality, that makes a disturbingly large army of believers, all from the very class that will provide the backbone of stability and leadership in America.

The figures are even more alarming for other racial and economic categories. Among impoverished black teenagers, 40 per cent reported that they believed in the reality of television portrayals, as did 30 per cent of poor whites.* Again, this means that hundreds of thousands of youngsters, many already under great non-television-related pressure to resort to crime and other antisocial activities, are being educated with unreal expectations about the role that violence will play in their lives. And, too, with unreal expectations about how to resolve problems—with violence.

THE NETWORKS RESPOND

The networks' attitude toward "outside research," i.e., research conducted by anyone they haven't hired, is reminiscent of the attitude of

* One out of every three black families has an income below the poverty line; there were about 700,000 poor black teenagers, then, in 1970. There were, at the time of that same census, approximately 1.3 million poor white teenagers.

cigarette manufacturers confronted with overwhelming evidence of causality between heavy smoking and serious disease. The cigarette manufacturers point to smokers who survive, and to failure of the data to "prove" causality when held to extraordinary laboratory standards.

But the networks have not been content with challenging the data of those whose research shows that televised violence is harmful. (So far, no one has seriously proposed that a message be put at the beginning and end of each violent program: "The Surgeon General has determined that watching television is harmful to your health.") In the midst of all the unfavorable research results surrounding the question of television violence, networks hired their own social scientists and did some "in-house" research. It has been reported that each network spent over $1 million on violence-related research. What they say they found comes as no surprise.

CBS had the most elaborate study, under the direction of Stanley Milgram. An entire special episode of *Medical Center* was produced for research purposes, with three separate endings. The basic plot concerned a technician at the hospital who had been laid off in an economy move, just at a time when his wife needed a major operation.

In the key scene, he was alone in a room with a large plastic container for cash contributions, in which the public had placed lots of money—visible money. As the disconsolate man looked at the container, the camera showed the audience that the container was broken, and that one could easily reach in and scoop out the money. In one ending to the show, the man took the money, and got away with it. In another, he took the money, and was caught. In the third, after a struggle of conscience, he walked away.

Three different selected audiences were asked to view the program, each with one of the different endings. In order to keep the experiment "scientific," they were told it was the commercials that were being tested. Each audience member was asked to watch the program, record his response to the commercials, and then come to a convenient midtown Manhattan address to receive a handsome transistor radio as the payment for participating.

When the audience members got to the place where the radios were to be given away, they discovered an almost empty office, with a table on which a sign informed them that the supply of radios had been depleted, and that a journey to a remote address in Brooklyn would be required to pick one up. Alongside the offending sign was a plastic contribution container just like the one in the television program—full of money, and broken so as to provide easy access to the cash within.

Hidden cameras then recorded the reactions, to see if those who had been exposed to the ending in which the criminal escaped undetected would be more likely to take the money. To no one's great surprise, there was no significant correlation between the actions of the subjects and the particular program ending they had seen. CBS's research claim: the behavior of television characters has no influence on the real-life behavior of its viewers. Q.E.D. Although the raw results of this elaborate experiment seemed to show that exposure to criminal behavior, even when the criminal gets away with it, had no marked effect on real-life behavior, the entire study, its methodology and its conclusions, came under severe and devastating attack from independent scholars, most notably George Comstock of the Rand Corporation. The CBS experiment did, however, illuminate some interesting facets of our society. The authors note that test subjects at one point, perhaps in anger, began "urinating on floors [and] threatening violence to our staff."

CBS's study concluded, among other things, that "exposure to aggressive television content did not lead to assaultive behavior," and "violent crime is the result of multiple causation and cannot be attributable to watching violent television programs." CBS research ignored the obvious implication that if the studies had come out the other way, the country's streets would be awash with blood. No one among the independent scholars, of course, had suggested even the possibility of such clear causality from a single program.

The social scientist heading NBC's research operation feels that those of his colleagues who conducted research for the Surgeon General are "a bunch of idiots," and argues that to find out if televised violence has any adverse effects, "it is best to rely on really wise people, the people who could take a detached view and have the experience to really know what's going on." NBC has been conducting a long-range study of television's effects, and the results realized to date are reassuring, he says, that there's really very little to worry about. A typical finding: "There is certainly no evidence in these data that TV plays an instigating role with respect to aggression. At most, it is possible . . . but not demonstrated . . . that exposure to violence on television either preserves existing aggression in boys, or helps re-establish a former aggressive behavior pattern." That is reminiscent of tobacco companies' statements—also in contradiction of an overwhelming body of evidence—that sufferers from lung cancer may possibly have been, at some time, smokers, but there's no demonstration of connection.

In addition to such studies, the networks have given the American people one other concrete response to the questions raised about television violence. This response is worthy of considerable note, not only because it affects the programs that reach nearly every American, but because it is—so far—the only product of decades of public concern and scholarly study. All of the congressional hearings, the millions of dollars and thousands of man-years spent studying television violence, did at last bring something new to television: Family Hour. It is the answer of the federal government and the television industry to all the evidence that television violence is harmful. By a happy coincidence, this answer does not cost the industry one dollar. Let us now praise ingenious men.

2 FAMILY HOUR: THE POLITICS OF TELEVISION

Between the news and the violence
When the night is beginning to lower,
Comes a pause in the day's occupations
That is known as the Family Hour
AFTER HENRY WADSWORTH LONGFELLOW

In 1975, we were given the Family Hour. For one prime-time hour each weeknight, and one hour preceding it, we have programs deemed suitable for viewing by all the members of the family. This came at a time of widespread concern over the amount of crime and violence in America, and the amount on American television—but it has not decreased the violence on our television sets, not even for the children in the audience. Indeed, Family Hour was not intended to affect the amount of violence we, or our children, see on television; it was created by the networks and the government, acting together, with the complacence of advertisers, and the intent was to dupe the public (and our elected representatives) into silence, into thinking that television violence had been reduced. In fact, total violence has increased. Eight out of every 10 programs (9 out of every 10 weekend children's-hour programs) still contain some violence. The overall rate of violent episodes, 5.6 per play, is, if anything, highest on record. Psychologist George Gerbner, having done a count of the violent episodes in the first Family Hour season, concluded that "network policy seems to have responded in narrow terms, when at all, to very specific pressure, and only while the heat was on . . ."

To understand the sham of Family Hour, it is necessary to look at how it came about—and to see something of the machinery of change in the television industry.

Family Hour arose, quite clearly, out of more than two decades of debate about how best to curtail televised violence—a debate that gained its greatest momentum in 1968 and 1969, when assassinations and urban riots propelled violence to the top of the nation's worries. In the early 70s, crime and violence still hovered at or near the number one issue concerning Americans.

Arthur Taylor, known as the father of the Family Hour, says the earliest stirrings of this idea occurred to him when he and Fred Silverman, in a San Diego hotel room in 1974, were watching a syndicated rerun of *The Untouchables* at 6:30 PM. Taylor was then President of CBS, and Silverman was CBS programming chief. Taylor says it suddenly struck both him and Silverman that this was hardly an appropriate program to present at the time of the highest viewing by children.

This awakening was not shared by other network executives, nor carried through in subsequent actions. In fact, it is clear from a review of the events leading up to the initiation of Family Hour that the entire concept was far more an exercise in political imagery than a sincere attempt to deal with the problem of television violence.

On June 21, 1974, the Appropriations Committee of the House of Representatives attached to the regular appropriation measure for the Federal Communications Commission, a stipulation that the FCC must "submit a report to the Committee by December 31, 1974, outlining specific positive actions taken or planned by the Commission to protect children from excessive programming of violence and obscenity . . ." Less than two months later, the Senate Appropriations Committee took a similar action, calling on the FCC "to determine what is in its power in the area of program violence and obscenity, particular [sic] as to their effect on children." Both bills obviously inplied the threat that FCC appropriations might suffer if nothing were done.* These mandates in the Senate and House put Chairman Richard Wiley of the Federal Communications Commission on the spot, while at the same time giving him important leverage with which to move the networks on the issue. Wiley had about two months to achieve—or to give the *appearance* of achieving—something that had never been done before; namely, federal action to curtail violence and sex on television.

There was no reason to believe it would be an easy task. First of all Congress, reflecting the lack of focus or concern shared by the public at large, had demonstrated over the years a significant lack of willingness actually to *do* anything about televised violence.

Evidence, to be sure, had been building for decades and the reports just compiled by the Surgeon General's Advisory Committee had made it quite clear that violence had a direct, measurable, and harmful effect.

---

* The burden placed on the FCC was a result of the Surgeon General's report, but nothing more was heard—in all the conferences, announcements, press releases, and meetings over the next months—of that seminal study.

And yet the demands on the broadcast industry had been largely un-focused. For one thing, the cries from the general public were divergent. From the political right came a denunciation of "sex" on television, which often translated into an objection to a looser moral standard reflected in the motion pictures shown on television. The political left was more concerned about violence, but its demands were diffuse and its efforts largely unorganized. No significant national mobilization, left, right, or center, had emerged on the question of violence or sex.

In 1974, when the Appropriations Committees stepped in, Wiley knew that two decades of debate by people far more knowledgeable than he on the question of televised violence had produced no specific proposals, let alone any solutions. After twenty years of intermittent discussions, and after the Surgeon General's report, Congress could do no more than muster up the strength to foist upon the FCC a deadline which was both dramatic and unrealistic.

The deadline was dramatic because it permitted members of Congress to turn out press releases informing the folks back home that they had finally forced the FCC into action—implying, of course, they were due for congratulations on this action, and it should be remembered when it came time to vote.

But the deadline was also unrealistic: the members of both appropriations committees knew very well that federal law already dictated that the FCC could not deal directly with program content in the prescribed time, if at all.

The Administrative Procedures Act specifies that any interested parties—in this case presumably networks, station owners, producers, sponsors, writers, and citizen groups—must be given adequate time to examine, debate, and appeal any proposed rules to be promulgated by the FCC. The notice and hearings mandated by law would obviously run beyond the deadline laid down by the committees. Thus, even if Wiley had been able to come up with an FCC rule that was constitutional, it was clearly impossible to meet the deadline.

Nevertheless, Wiley took some action. In early October, he called on the industry to respond to the congressional pressure voluntarily.

"KNUCKLE RAPPING"

In the last of October, Wiley "summoned" the presidents of the three networks to what was publicly billed as a "knuckle-rapping session." The billing was probably part of an elaborate minuet. The network presidents were wielders of extraordinary power and they were also Wiley's prime constituents, indeed his power base. Both Wiley and the network presidents knew that they and not he ran television, and that the relationship between the FCC and the networks over a wide range of issues—"pay" cable television, video discs, copyright laws—was such that they could make it impossible for him to function, at least so long as a business-oriented President was in the White House. Furthermore, it is very unlikely that Wiley, who had no history of concern about televised violence, suddenly decided to make this the issue over which to provoke a great moral confrontation. There was no attempt by Wiley to organize congressional, press, or public support on the issue prior to meeting with the network presidents. Congress had already made it plain that it did not wish to become directly involved—merely to *seem* to be involved—and one can search the records of Chairman Wiley's speeches, press conferences, and public attitudes in vain to find anything approaching a rallying cry on this issue.

It seems likely that the fix was in—that Wiley and the network executives had already arrived at a solution acceptable to all (and, they hoped, to Congress as well) and that by the time the "knuckle-rapping" session was called, tacit agreement at the congressional level and perhaps at the network presidential level had already been reached for at least the broad design of the Family Hour decision, if not for all its specifics. Such a broad agreement need not have been reached at a conspiratorial, late-night meeting in a Washington parking garage; it could have easily evolved through a series of almost routine lower-level staff meetings, upward-bound memoranda, and all the other informal arrangements through which American industry lets its government regulators know how it wishes to be regulated.

The network presidents were certainly aware that Wiley and the FCC would have to create the public impression that the Commission was forcing the networks to make some concessions on the issue, perhaps even extracting as well some public contrition for the past volume of violence on the air. Thus the concept of a "Family Hour"—a two-hour *cordon sanitaire* in which only news and entertainment programs suitable for family watching would be played—first emerged on the public record following Wiley's "knuckle-rapping" session in late October with the network presidents. Sander Vanocur, then the Washington *Post*'s television columnist and himself a veteran of network corporate infighting (in the same way that the pavement is a veteran of infighting between the cement mixer and the steam roller) would later write that the participants at the meeting of the network executives and Wiley seemed determined to make Family Hour appear as "an immaculate conception." (Vanocur was right, because the real explanation of the acquiescence of the networks and any evidence of advance agreement with the FCC, would have revealed the Family Hour concept as an example of industry "self regulation" with which Washington and some members of Congress were becoming only too familiar.)

Wiley opened the meeting with a list of specific proposals, including a request that the networks make "a new commitment to reduce the level and intensity of violent and sexually oriented material." Wiley further said, "Programs which are considered to be inappropriate for viewing by younger children should not be broadcast prior to 9 PM local time."

If, indeed, the network executives had not seen the script in advance, it is hard to imagine that they felt anything more than that Wiley was proving himself a colleague rather than an adversary. The creation of an hour of entertainment suitable to the family out of the three hours of prime time was not a great sacrifice, if it was a sacrifice at all, since some such programming was already spotted in prime time. A little adroit re-scheduling would permit them to live very comfortably—and with a great deal of favorable publicity.

After agreeing to official follow-up meetings between the networks and the FCC staff, the broadcasting executives returned to New York. Within government and broadcasting circles, it was known that the negotiations were proceeding well, and that the ultimate details of Family Hour, although closely guarded, would soon emerge to everyone's satisfaction.

The only serious attempt to crack this secrecy came in late November from former FCC member Nicholas Johnson. Johnson, an out-of-the-mainstream gadfly, a middle class member of the counterculture, with a good ear for absurd rhetoric, knew that the network chiefs were meeting with Wiley, and he asked to be invited along. He wrote to Wiley:

> If "negotiations" are to be conducted by the presidents of the networks and the chairman of the FCC, and those negotiations are designed to eliminate or self-censor programming from American television screens, then it is essential that representatives of the public be present.

Johnson was acting in his capacity as spokesman for the National Citizens Committee for Broadcasting. Aware that Johnson had no organized political base, Wiley had little difficulty dismissing the request with a polite, but firm, "No." Similarly dismissed was a later statement of interest and a request for participation from the United States Catholic Conference. In a statement attacking any policy "designed to regulate," the Conference declared that

> self-regulation is not a unilateral activity performed behind closed doors by a few powerful individuals at the top. Self-regulation, to deserve the name, is an *open, accountable and cooperative* process, involving both broadcasters and the public they serve . . . The very corporate struc-

ture of the networks, for example, is such a forbidding and complicated maze that it appears designed to guarantee that, insulated from public scrutiny, top management may without fear of challenge or other encumbrance, pursue the uniquely important broadcasting goal of maximizing profit.

The Catholic Conference's statement generated a few feature stories. But its only real power is to generate publicity, and here that publicity failed to materialize because the networks did not even bother to respond, either directly through an answer, or indirectly by referring to the demand on their news programs.

For that matter, television network news programs never once reported on the events surrounding the creation of Family Hour. This was, at the very least, questionable news judgment; the creation of Family Hour affected some 85 million Americans, far more than the forest fires, floods, and other disturbances that make up about half of the evening news on the networks. As will be clear from Chapter 3, this is not surprising. What happens *in* television is rarely carried by the news *on* television.

Had Wiley, or any of the network executives, felt openness would have enhanced their public image or increased public and congressional support for the decisions they were making, the meetings obviously would have been open. One can only conclude that had the meetings been open, the weak and ineffectual nature of the remedies suggested would have almost dictated a public and congressional response requiring sterner action.

Indeed, it was precisely the possibility of such openness that Wiley used to give the impression that the networks were being forced to make concessions. Wiley even went so far as threatening the networks with publicity (a curious tactic for someone whose negotiations were being conducted behind doors that he himself had closed). In a speech in early December, Wiley warned that if the networks did not act, "then we have to look at alternatives as far as government action is concerned." Inside the industry, the question immediately arose, what action? In an interview with the *New York Times'* Les Brown, the leading television writer in the nation, Wiley answered that question by revealing that public hearings on televised violence *and sex* could be "one of the Commission's initiatives."* Wiley said—with full knowledge that Brown's column is read first thing in the morning by network execu-

* Wiley's opening proposals in October had included, as stated above, a request that the networks make "a new commitment to reduce the level and intensity of violent and sexually oriented material." The sexual aspect got dropped along the way, until it was brought up again in this December threat—then no more was heard about regulation of sexual aspects. As we shall see (in Chapter 5), Family Hour in its final form could almost be said to replace violence with sex.

tives, and before that Brown would be likely to telephone the executives to get their reactions—"If we fail to get sufficient voluntary action from the networks, we are going to ventilate the subject a good deal more than it has been . . . [This is] quite a weapon and they know that."

Now the question must be asked: why should the Chairman of the FCC feel that a full "ventilation" of televised violence and sex would be "quite a weapon" against the networks? And if he did believe that such a "ventilation" would produce a strong remedy, then why was there no such "ventilation" in the first place? What did Wiley think would come out in such hearings that the public would not know if there were no such hearings? What mobilization of public opinion might occur? The obvious answer is that an informed and probably aroused public, determined to achieve real reform and an end to gratuitous violence and sex, might not have been content with a few reductions here and there in a mere re-arrangement of what had become a steady but unpalatable diet.

Les Brown called the networks and told them about Wiley's comments. None wanted to be quoted on the record, but one unidentified industry source told Brown that Wiley's threat was "an offer they can't refuse."

Family Hour was added to the National Association of Broadcasters (NAB) Television Code. The Family Hour addition, after all of the negotiation and pressure, read:

> Entertainment programming inappropriate for viewing by a general family audience, should not be broadcast during the first hour of network programming in prime time and in the immediately preceding hour.

The rule also required stations and networks to insert "warnings" whenever they scheduled a program that might not meet this standard.

"A DECEIT"

Norman Lear told the *New York Times,* "Basically the family viewing hour is a deceit. It is not a sincere effort to curb excesses of any kind. If the networks were to make a sincere effort, it seems to me they would have called a series of meetings with the creative community to talk about excesses. No such meetings were ever asked for."

Lear's point was telling. After all, it is the writers and producers who create the violence in the first instance, and any true effort to cut back on it would ultimately require their cooperation and support. As we have seen, if the producers (acting, so they say, at the behest of the networks who act, so they say, at the behest of advertisers who act, so they say, at the behest of viewers, who deny responsibility) had really wanted to cut back on violence they would have gone to Lear and his creative colleagues and, in a series of meetings, told them that the high level of violence would no longer be accepted. There is every reason to believe that the "creative community" of which Lear spoke would have been entirely cooperative. (Their financial interests would be protected, as well as networks' financial interests, one assumes, in such meetings.) Instead, the producers and networks opted for Family Hour—mostly a rearrangement of the schedule of existing programs.

Indeed, after the introduction of Family Hour, television violence increased, rather than decreased. Just a few weeks after Family Hour began, *Variety*—the house organ of show business—ran a page-one headline:

TV NETWORKS RAISE GORE CURTAIN
Open Season on Violence
Slime at Nine

The story in *Variety* explained that "behind the Gore Curtain dropped by the networks at 9 PM each night [at the end of the Family Hour] lurks as much violence as ever." Calling 9 PM EST "the starting gun," *Variety* lamented that "criminals may be a minority in society, but they own 9 to 11 every night." The statement in *Variety* and its placement were particularly significant because the paper has never been known either for its high social consciousness or for a willingness to attack the central institutional base of the entertainment industry.

Other industry comment was not far behind. Five days later, an editorial in the influential Madison Avenue organ *Advertising Age* pointed out:

> All but a few of this year's law and order vehicles are scheduled from 9 to 11 PM (EST), which means the so-called adult hours could be exhibiting more killing and mayhem on the average week nights this fall than last season, which had its full share of violence.

> Coming at a time when we've just watched another near-miss assassination attempt against President Ford, and when every day in many American cities new names are added to the murder statistics, it seems pertinent to ask: What TV violence cleanup?

A few months later, a study conducted for Action for Children's Television concluded, " . . . If the overall level of violence has been reduced in all of children's television, as is claimed by the new network productions, it is far from true for independent stations' programs."

Independent stations are the key to another indication of the hypocrisy of networks' public posture about Family Hour. To disarm any opposition from independent, non-network stations, the NAB authorized a
"grandfather clause." The clause waived for two full years application of
the Family Hour restrictions to the nation's independent stations. They
could continue to show violent programming during Family Hour while
network affiliates and network-owned stations were required to program
only material suitable for a general audience.

According to industry statistics, over 34 million American households
regularly tune in to these independent stations. If televised violence is
indeed sufficiently harmful to merit curtailment at all, and if Family
Hour is an answer to a severe problem, then clearly there would have
been no justification for exempting the independent stations. The independents can no more impose their will on the networks than Costa
Rica can impose its will on American foreign policy. The networks need
the independents, though, in order to present Congress and the nation
with a united broadcasters' front on matters such as pay television,
which are really important to network profits—and the grandfather
clause was of crucial economic concern to the independents, some of
whom might have suffered some economic hardship had they been
forced to honor contracts and pay for violent programs they could not
broadcast in prime time. But the grandfather clause was of little or no
economic consequence to the networks;* and since the purpose of the
exercise was not to limit television violence but to seem to be yielding to
public pressure, the concession was readily made.

It will be recalled that Wiley's original suggestion—reasonably widely
publicized—had been that family viewing time should not end until 9
PM *local time.* By the time the networks and the NAB got through with
it, however, Family Hour would end at 9 PM only in the Eastern and Pa-
cific time zones, and at 8 PM everywhere else. One may well ask why

---

* The trade press revealed why the networks did not consider this clause a major problem. "A few industry experts do concede," *Broadcasting* pointed out, "that with no violent-
action shows on the networks' schedules between 8 and 9 PM, male adults in big cities
may switch their dials on at least some nights to an independent station that's running off-
network re-runs of series such as *Ironside* and the *FBI*. But nobody at the networks
thinks those switchovers will be anything more than small potatoes in terms of statistical
significance."

Ordinary folks might read that statement in a way unintended by *Broadcasting;* the
"concede" is a nice touch, along with "male adults." The implication is clear that "simply
everyone" agreed that television viewing is determined by the male in the family and that
it is "male adults" who crave "violent action" shows even if they are re-runs of *Ironside*
and the *FBI* that they have already seen.

But the specialized trade audience who reads *Broadcasting* knew that "statistical significance" meant ratings, and that ratings and ratings alone determine how much sponsors
will pay for commercial time, and that since what was involved was "small potatoes," no
significant profit would have to be foregone to make the concession that eliminated the independents' opposition to Family Hour.

the broadcast industry deemed it a serious matter to deny rape and murder to a younger audience at 8 PM Eastern time, but entirely justifiable to offer violence at 8 PM Central time. Norman Lear put the question appropriately: "Why," he asked, "are the networks abandoning the little ones in the Bible Belt?"

The answer from NBC to Lear's question was, ". . . the thrust and purpose of the family viewing concept is to identify a time period when parents can be assured that the program material is suitable for young children, watching alone; and it recognizes that in other time periods parents have some responsibility to guide their children's viewing." In other words, the precise time frame of Family Hour is unimportant; all that matters is that it be there. But this answer is nonsense and does not begin to reach the concern which prompted the decision in the first place. The supposed purpose of Family Hour, and the need stated by the whole thrust of research and congressional testimony over the years, was to curtail programs that are harmful to children during the time periods children are most likely to watch them.

The networks' explanation to Wiley for the staggered hour change was that to make Family Hour 7 to 9 PM local time everywhere in the country "would require prohibitively expensive separate program transmissions to each time zone," a claim that is patently false. For years the networks have had the technical ability to put the entire nation on the same programming time schedule. In other words, a program on at 8 PM in New York City could also be seen at 8 PM *local time* in Chicago, Salt Lake City, and San Francisco. The ability and the equipment already exist to do this at no extra cost. The only additional cost would have to be borne by those affiliated network stations that still do not have video equipment capable of taping either of the network feeds. Almost all stations, however, already have such equipment, and the cost to the others would be far from prohibitive.

The most likely explanation for "abandoning the little ones in the Bible belt" does not involve the cost of technical changes, but cost from a loss of advertising revenues. During television's early years, when technology was not so sophisticated, the Midwest time zone had to "go live" along with the East Coast (hence the familiar phrase, "one hour earlier Central Time"). If *Playhouse 90*, let us say, were broadcast live in New York at 9:30 PM, it would be on at 8:30 PM in Chicago and a simultaneous transmission would be economical. Thus the networks forced an earlier prime time—by an hour—on the Midwest. That was as far as they could go then; even television-hungry Californians could not be persuaded to eat dinner with Walter Cronkite at 4 PM and go to bed with Johnny Carson at 8:30, and so, since the West Coast would have to film (at first the technique was kinescope, and later would be videotape) and replay in any event, it was decided to keep for California the Eastern version of prime time, 8 PM to 11 PM. Later, when taping capacity had been perfected, the networks continued the simultaneous broadcast—on the stated assumption that most Midwesterners are agricultural people whose life schedule follows the sun; that they are up earlier, finish work earlier, have their dinner earlier, want their evening entertainment earlier, and go to bed earlier.

This pastoral time cycle may have been true long before television, but it is certainly not true now, nor has it been true for at least several generations. The sturdy yeomen of the Midwest are city people, no less urban than New Yorkers or Californians. They rise by the alarm clock, not by the sun, and the early morning hours are as likely to be spent with an "artifical flavoring for imitation orange juice" while watching the *Today* show as they are in the effete East. The work day in Chicago is nine to five, and the schoolday coincides with those in other American cities.

But Midwesterners do have different expectations about television scheduling, now: they believe and expect that prime time will begin at 7 PM, that the network news will be on the air at 5:30 PM or 6 PM, that the late-night local news will begin at 10 PM, and that Johnny Carson will appear at 10:30 PM. After all, that is the way they and their parents have been living for more than a quarter century (with the exception that it was Jack Paar or Steve Allen their parents watched).

In a classic example, then, of nature imitating art, Midwesterners now do in fact eat dinner earlier, watch the news earlier and go to bed earlier—not because their work requires an earlier schedule but because their lives, as the lives of most Americans, are quietly regulated by television programming schedules.

So much for arguments that the change would be "prohibitively expensive." The prohibitive expense would come from ratings that dropped during the period of adjustment. After asking his industry contacts why the networks do not simply put the entire nation on uniform local clock time, Les Brown could conclude that "viewers in the Central Time Zone, having fixed their habits over twenty-five years, might protest." Lower ratings mean lower advertising revenues—and this is a risk networks were simply unwilling to take. The Central Time Zone, after all, includes approximately one-third of all television households, a revenue base with which certainly nothing as inconsequential as an excess of violence during children's viewing hours could be permitted to tamper.

Of course, even after 9 PM, millions of children are still watching television. Between 9 and 9:30 PM, 11 million children are watching, 5 to 6 million are still there when the 11 o'clock news comes on, and an astounding 2.1 million are glued to their sets at midnight. These figures don't even include twelve year olds or teenagers.

Obviously, everyone involved with Family Hour knew all along that even a 9 PM deadline for violence would have a severely limited impact. Publicly, though, the posture was that the industry consciousness was being raised: the *New York Times* reported that "throughout the industry there is a fairly general agreement that programs too sophisticated for children should be broadcast when most children are asleep." Noting the figures on children's viewing, though, *Broadcasting* reminded its readers (industry people) that "nothing in the declaration of a so-called Family Hour will turn those numbers off at 9 PM."

CBS was asked if the programming changes required by Family Hour might cut down on audience appeal in that early violence-free hour. Arnold Beck, CBS director of network research, told advertisers, "there are sociological conditions that cause adults to watch television at certain times . . . In other words, no one will switch off . . ."*

Beck's analysis is worth examining. The "sociological conditions" that prompt television viewing in the first place have rarely, if ever, been analyzed. It is doubtful, given the present state of the art, whether they ever will be properly analyzed. Clearly, viewing is related to a lack of excitement and entertainment in most people's lives; if Thoreau was right that "most men lead lives of quiet desperation," then television may have provided an anodyne in permitting them to watch other people lead lives of loud desperation. Those "sociological conditions" would include the urge in the American family to avoid conversation with spouses and children at the end of the work day, and the other factors that prompt people to defend their television-watching habits on the ground that they are seeking "escape." The unanswered question, of course, is "escape from what?"

Students of television viewing habits have also identified an interesting phenomenon, the theory of "L.O.P.," or Least Objectionable Program. This theory, with considerable evidence to support it, suggests that many, if not most, viewers are not watching individual programs,

---

* There was one slight indication at the beginning of the Family Hour season that some people might be "switching off." During the fall of 1975, the Nielsen organization picked up a slight decline in the total number of households using television. The drop was small, and barely reached the threshold of statistical significance; but it sent shock waves through the industry because until then, the number of households using television had always steadily increased. Some industry pessimists suggested that Americans had finally "caught on" to the tube and were simply turning it off (or worse, not turning it on) in increasing numbers. Others, closer to the situation, argued that methodological innovations—such as the inclusion for the first time in the Nielson sample of homes without telephones—accounted for the decrease. Others, including some network spokesmen, suggested that the more bland, less violent Family Hour had reduced viewership. This, they said, provided proof that the networks had foresaken profit for the public benefit.

But the decline, if there was one, had nothing to do with Family Hour since it actually began during the summer before initiation of Family Hour programming. In any event, all the discussion and the claims proved to be moot after a few months when the curve bottomed out and began to turn upward once again.

but are watching, simply, television. Once the decision has been made to watch television, the theory goes, it will be watched no matter what comes through the tube, and the option to turn it off is no longer real. At this point the L.O.P. process takes over, prompting the viewer or viewing family to scan the options—either literally by turning quickly from channel to channel, or figuratively by checking or remembering a guide to programs—and select the least objectionable or offensive of the available programs. Thus, whether or not there was a Family Hour, viewing will remain stable because families will continue to select the L.O.P., whatever it is.

So the Family Hour might not include the attractive violence and mayhem, but the hour is still a very high-rated one, indeed probably the highest rated hour of prime time. Charles Allen, ABC Vice-President for Sales Administration, made the point clearly in an industry magazine interview in which he reminded advertisers that only a bad business-man would withhold commercials from the time slot with the largest number of viewers. "No advertiser would be willing to lock himself out of a whole series of shows in such a cavalier way," Allen said. He was dead right; none did.

In a trade-press article, NBC's Robert Howard reminded the industry that the networks were doing very well financially, and had every prospect of continuing to do so. "NBC recently predicted that over the rest of the decade the television industry would have an overall annual growth rate [in gross sales] of 9 per cent, with local expenditures averaging as high as 13 per cent," he boasted. "By 1980, that would add up to industry billings [for commercials] of $7 billion, just about double the billings we had in 1971." And the profit figures for 1975 and projected profit figures for 1976 bore out Howard's bullish predictions.

In other words, Family Hour had no discernible impact on profit, practically no effect on viewer acceptance, and, as we have seen, precious little to do with reducing the amount of television violence seen by children.

3 TELEVISION NEWS: INVENTING PRIORITIES

"Busing is one issue that has not troubled either the candidates or the voters in this campaign year," says network anchorman Walter Harry Chancellor, "although in a number of cities federal courts have ordered that students be bused out of their neighborhoods in order to achieve racial integration."

Cut to Roger Mackin, standing, microphone in hand, at a street corner in a residential neighborhood. A group of junior-high children, all of them white, can be seen behind him, schoolbooks in hand.

"This is the heart of Locust Heights, a lower middle class neighborhood here in Metropolis," Mackin begins, in that earnest but informative style that has made his reports well known throughout the nation. "These children, who used to go to the neighborhood school two blocks away, are waiting for the school bus to take them to the Fillmore School, two miles away. The reason: a federal court ordered the local school board to adopt a busing plan which would, in the court's words, 'remedy the deliberate racial imbalance created by local authority.' And so these youngsters are now—some of them against their parents' wishes—going by bus to a school outside their neighborhood."

On the screen, we now cut from the street-corner view of the correspondent to the children, as a yellow bus comes into view. The children, with a little horseplay, file onto the bus, and the camera takes up a position in a vehicle behind the bus. The on-screen view continues to be that of the bus, as it moves uneventfully through traffic and eventually arrives at a school. The voice of the correspondent is continuing:

"So far this school year, there has been no trouble. The children seem to get along well, and the principal and the teachers report no incidents, either at the entrances or inside the classrooms. 'It's just an ordinary

71 •

group of seventh-graders,' one of them said to me yesterday. Thirteen schools in the county are under the court order, and they all report the same thing—the busing is proceeding without incident."

Now the camera shows the bus stopped, lingers a moment as the children get out and walk on into the school building, a few waiting to talk with friends. Among the children now in the picture are some black students. The camera cuts back to Mackin, standing now on the sidewalk in front, with the school building, and a view of the flag, in the background.

"The days are uneventful here in Metropolis," he says, "at least on the school-busing front. Folks have a lot to argue about here, including the election campaign, but busing is not one of the things that disturb them. This school, previously 90 per cent black, is now roughly 55 per cent white. And nobody seems to mind very much. Roger Mackin at the Fillmore School, Metropolis."

The whole thing has taken one minute and fifteen seconds—and you will never see it or anything like it. The reason is quite simple; there is no action. It is, except for the places and the names, a reasonably accurate account of what happens in cities across the nation where busing has been ordered by the courts to remedy the denial of constitutional rights to black schoolchildren. But unless there is violence or the threat of it, busing is rarely covered on television news.

It is a perfect example of the dilemma of news producers. They want to present the news, they want to keep it in perspective, but they are also a part of television, an entertainment medium depending at all times—including during news broadcasts—on attracting the largest possible audience to deliver to an advertiser. Since news is part of an entertainment medium, it must be entertaining.

And a peaceful bus ride is simply not entertaining. What *is* entertaining is a shrieking confrontation between blacks and whites, preferably with the shiny helmets of the National Guard for additional "color" and the threat of serious violence. That is why the only busing stories ever shown on network television are likely to be from Boston, and occasionally Louisville, the places of controversy and violence, and that is also why busing has become the "issue" it has in national politics, and it is finally why Congress and the federal courts—which surely do, in Mr. Dooley's famous locution, "follow the illiction returns"—are more and more abandoning a rather promising and successful tool for implementing the Constitutional guarantees of due process and equal protection of the laws.

Occasionally, newspapers will carry "round-up" accounts of busing, and when they do a close reading yields the information that, except for Boston—which has contributed its good "visual" television coverage every September as the school year begins—busing is accepted and "working" in every other city where it is going on.

Charlotte, Denver, Detroit, Indianapolis, Pontiac (the scene of some frightening confrontations in 1971, the last time the Pontiac schools made network television news), Prince George's County, Maryland— these are all communities where our fictitious newscast could have— but has not—taken place.

The emphasis has been on busing at the outset of this chapter because it demonstrates the power of television first to create "news," and then to shape it so that only one perception is possible. News executives will undoubtedly respond by saying "these things *did* occur; there *were* violent confrontations connected with busing," but that only makes the case against television even stronger. In the first place, no one is sure that these events would have taken place without the provocative presence of television. The purpose of a demonstration, after all, is to reach a wide audience, not just to make an impression at the immediate scene of the crisis. Otherwise, why are demonstrations so carefully orchestrated and why are "the media" notified in advance?

In the second (and more important) place, there are a lot of *other* things that happened in the course of the busing developments, and without them the turbulence and violence is not only an incomplete story, but a grossly inaccurate one. To take a significant example: the Department of Justice released an analysis on June 27, 1976, describing—with considerable supporting evidence—the belief that widespread violence occurs when schools are desegregated by court order as "one of the myths . . . widely propagated by the opponents of school desegregation."

The report flatly contradicted the implications in a statement a few days before by then-President Ford, who—locked in a battle with Ronald Reagan for the votes of a few uncommitted delegates at the Republican convention, had sent a message to Congress. In the message, the President called it a "tragic reality that, in some areas, busing under court order has brought fear to both black students and white students—and to their parents. No child can learn in an atmosphere of fear. Better remedies to right Constitutional wrongs must be found."

In making this statement, the President was not making up an atmosphere out of whole cloth. He was echoing the perceived reality of millions—indeed, a substantial majority—of Americans. After all, they had seen the violence that always accompanies busing on their home screens.

But the Justice Department report said there was less violence than most people believed, and that most incidents, where they had occurred, had been outside of school and had involved anti-busing protests. "There is no substance," the report said, to the notion that white students being bused into predominantly black neighborhoods confronted any greater danger. "If anything," it reported, "whites being transported within the inner city are safer than in other parts of the city, in part because of community patrols and other measures taken by the minority community."

Senators Edward Brooke of Massachusetts and Jacob Javits of New York, who had requested the Justice Department report, concluded in a separate statement that most communities go through desegregation "without experiencing as many injuries as can be expected on any high school football field on any Fall Friday night." Neither the Senators' conclusion nor the Justice Department report were ever mentioned, so far as we have been able to determine, on any network news program.

There has been for more than one hundred years, and in a heightened form for the past fifteen years, no more pressing issue on our national agenda than the question of how—if at all—the black population becomes integrated into the larger society. Since the decision of the Supreme Court in the *Brown* case in 1954, that question has centered in public education. Once busing began to be used by federal courts as a tool to carry out the mandate of *Brown,* most of the controversy has centered on the school bus.

And yet, the treatment of busing has been almost entirely a fragmentary one, full of action, violence, "color," and conflict, and except for an occasional documentary presentation, no serious discussion of the issue has taken place. No wonder that conservative columnist Patrick Buchanan can safely refer, in the pages of America's most popular mass magazine, *TV Guide,* to busing as "this most detested social policy since Prohibition." Some 74 per cent of Americans, says Buchanan, oppose busing, and there is little reason to doubt the figure. The wonder, considering the way it has been presented on television, is that 26 per cent either favor it or have no opinion.

We have selected the busing issue for this emphasis not because it stands alone as an example of how television sets the national news agenda, for it does not stand alone. But it does illuminate, perhaps better than any other issue, the state of television news, and its impact on the public—which relies, in increasing numbers, on the images and perceptions television provides.

According to polls taken in 1975 and 1976, roughly 75 per cent of all Americans get most of their news from television, and an astounding 50 per cent say they get *all* their news from the home screen. These figures are not surprising to the proprietors of newspapers, particularly afternoon newspapers, who have seen their product change drastically since the advent of the Age of Television.

For the most part, Americans no longer pick up a newspaper to find out the latest news; they have already heard it or seen it. The "Extra" has disappeared, and it is doubtful, for example, if more than a small percentage of readers followed the Watergate crimes or the impeachment of Richard Nixon, or the Vietnam war for that matter, in the daily press. When Neil Armstrong first walked on the moon, it was television, not newspapers, that brought us the news.

This has changed the character of newspapers, the best of which now provides services beyond the bare facts of the day's news. Newspapers today are more likely to give the background of the news, the direction in which it might lead, profiles of the people who make news or will make news, analyses of style, or so-called "soft" news away from the "harder" headlines. Of course, newspapers are also prepared to give readers what they can not get so easily from television—recipes, advice to the lovelorn, local advertising, a daily horoscope, motion picture and other entertainment listings. In what seems almost a suicidal tendency, newspapers also detail at some length what will be available on television.

With the providing of hard news thus increasingly a clear field for television, the industry has reacted in a seemingly curious way—one that has fixed rigidly the way in which the news is presented, and that has led inevitably to great and significant changes in American politics and society.

Beginning in 1969, Spiro Agnew, newly elected Vice-President, began and continued a spirited attack on the news media—specifically television—with the advice and active collaboration of President Nixon. (In retrospect, it is doubtful that Agnew had *any* original ideas; a politician these days who takes cash in plain envelopes at the office and has free groceries delivered at home can hardly be accused of innovative thinking.) The burden of Agnew's attack was that the news on network television came to us filtered by the biases of the owners of the networks, whom he referred to as "a small group of men living in New York" (for which, read "Jews," a meaning Agnew did not make explicit until later). Since all those "New Yorkers" were liberal, or worse, the news was bound to be distorted, he concluded.

Among his natural constituency, Agnew was wildly applauded, and his patron in the White House encouraged him to go on. His crusade had some of its desired effect: network news coverage of Vietnam and other "divisive" issues became markedly more subdued, the largest peace demonstration in all the years of the war went almost totally unreported, and CBS even stopped, for a time, its analyses following presidential and, to be sure, vice-presidential speeches and press conferences. There were not, in those days, very many profiles in courage.

Agnew's charges set off a debate that has lasted, in one form or another, to this day. Right-wing columnists, mainly gathered in *TV Guide* but also widely syndicated in newspapers, still like to write about the "liberal bias" of television news, and there is still a measurable percentage of Americans who believe the "left-wing media" drove Richard Nixon from office (a percentage, apparently, that includes Mr. Nixon). On the other side, one can hear liberals and radicals complain about the conservative, establishmentarian bias of television news, and there is a measurable percentage of Americans who believe Richard Nixon would have had trouble being re-elected if television news had not acquiesced in his refusal to be covered during the 1972 campaign.

But these arguments miss the point. Agnew, although not for the reasons he gave, had some truth on his side. There is a bias of those who own and control television through which the news is filtered, but it is not a political bias, liberal or conservative, radical or establishmentarian. It is a commercial bias. It dictates that out of at least twelve hours of daily programming, the networks will allow only one-half hour to be news—and at the same time require that the news make as strong an effort to get high ratings as the other entertainment programs. That is what distorts the news programs, not some mythical Jewish control.

Agnew missed the whole point. If he had correctly identified the reasons for the bias, almost every non-electronic journalist in the nation would have applauded him; instead, he turned the attack on television news into an ideological struggle, and so it remains. The result is that television news executives can count on a reasonably solid liberal phalanx of support when the crucial issues arise, and it is not always deserved.

TWENTY-TWO MINUTES' LAWS

Let us analyze that thirty minutes of daily news. In the first place, commercials and station announcements reduce it to twenty-two minutes, and in that time the producers must tell—and display on film if possible—everything of importance that happened during the day. This is true on days when there is much news as well as on days when there is relatively little. So the twenty-two minutes is alternately jammed and padded, but with no flexibility at all in the length of the broadcast.

In order to remind himself of the dimensions of his task, NBC news producer Reuven Frank used to keep a display on his wall. There was, first of all, a huge enlargement of a typical day's front page of the *New York Times*. Over that, he had laid a transparency, in the *Times*-size type, of a typical day's script for the NBC nightly news. Overlaid on the *New York Times*, the news script took scarcely two columns. The message was clear; what the *Times* could tell in forty-eight pages, he had to tell in two columns and some pictures. What's more, unlike the *Times*, he did not have a virtual monopoly; his twenty-two minutes had to be livelier and more visual than the competition's.

The producers of network news programs are able and sincere men, experienced in their craft. They are not expressly engaged in purveying entertainment as their prime-time colleagues are. The pressures, though, to deliver a larger share of the audience to the advertisers, are just as great.

The result is that some informal, unacknowledged laws of television news have developed: unattractive faces are almost never on camera in "good guy" roles; a fire at night will almost always be shown though an equally serious daytime fire won't; every news story must be complete within one minute and fifteen seconds, unless the program is doing an "in-depth" treatment, in which case one minute and forty-five seconds may be permitted. All this has led to an overriding law—The Trivial Will Always Drive Out the Serious. There are other limitations and strictures. A story with film, for example, will almost always take precedence over one that must be read from the anchor desk or reported in a "stand-up" on the spot. If there is film, the action film will almost always replace the film that includes only a conversation or a discussion—"talking heads" are to be avoided if there's any possible way.

This places a considerable burden on the producers. In that twenty-two minutes available to tell all the whole world's news, where is the news to come from? The answer is—wherever there are cameras, and almost surely from nowhere else. This places a premium on permanent assignments, well-staffed bureaus, and assignments made early in the day.

A number of factors, in turn, go into these judgments. Washington is always well-staffed, and will contribute its share of time for that reason if no other. Time zones are involved; if there is to be any news from the West Coast, it had better happen before noon or it will almost certainly not make the deadline.

By the middle of the morning, the producers in New York have made some preliminary judgments. The *New York Times,* the Washington *Post,* the Chicago *Tribune,* the *Los Angeles Times* and a few other newspapers have yielded some "possibles." Bureaus in Washington and Chicago (and other cities where networks own stations and have equipment available) and overseas have perhaps indicated some potential stories coming up. The "budget" of the Associated Press and the UPI "daybook" are valuable sources of news to come. There will always be a presidential story, whether the President is meeting with an important head of state, fighting with Congress over domestic priorities, or taking his daughter to her new tree house. If the President's press secretary has put on a "lid"—there will be no reportable presidential activities—then *that* becomes the story, delivered by the anchorman over a slide picture of the President, with a hint of a suspicion that he just might be either ill or planning a major foreign policy initiative.

As the day passes, the schedule becomes more firm. The Washington stories stick, a riot fizzles and becomes "no story," some film of a forest fire—at night—in Montana comes in and replaces some talking heads in an environment story. An angry estranged husband has seized a child in Chicago and is holding her hostage. Luckily, a camera crew is available. And so it goes, until 6 o'clock.

Through all of this, a sort of modern version of Bishop Berkeley's dictum prevails. If a tree fell in the forest, he wrote, and no one was there to hear it, it would make no sound. So it is with television news. Events may take place—important events by any standard—and if there is no camera and correspondent present to record it, it is not "news" and at least 50 per cent of our countrymen will never learn of it.*

The impact on American politics—in the larger sense, including social movements, national priorities, elections and legislation—has been incalculable. Television literally sets our national agenda; it determines what Americans will be talking about and the choices we will have about how we will live. Even more important, it determines what we will *not* be talking about, and the choices we will *not* have. Those are easily defined: they are the questions too complex to treat in one minute and fifteen seconds, or too controversial—that is to say, too far outside the boundaries of acceptable thought, outside of what is "normal," as defined by people in the industry. They are also the questions that arise, or the events that happen, where there is no network camera. It is one thing to please the audience too little; the possibility of offending is an unassumable risk.

---

* During the 1972 presidential campaign, a sort of corollary of the Berkeley theorem came into play. One of the candidates for President, Senator George McGovern, had selected a meeting of a local of the United Automobile Workers in Detroit to make a firm statement about busing. His campaign aides thought it a strong and newsworthy statement, and had outlined the key passages in the text, distributed the night before to the national correspondents traveling with the candidate.

The reason for this precaution was not only to save some time for the correspondents, but also to save them film. They could—and almost always did—instruct their cameramen to film only the marked passages. If the result was that the candidate got on the screen what he thought was most important, that was a small bonus. This particular morning, though, before he talked about busing, to the union members and their guests, Senator McGovern had something else to say. He had seen, on the *Today* show, some film of Spiro Agnew from a campaign appearance the night before. Agnew, true to type, had questioned McGovern's patriotism. So McGovern, impromptu, denounced Agnew to the union audience, shaking his finger with anger and speaking quite movingly about his own sense of the country. Then he turned to his prepared text.

Later, in the campaign airplane flying from Detroit to a noon rally in Rochester, New York, a network correspondent approached a McGovern aide with a rather sheepish look and a special request. The camera crew for that network, at the instructions of the correspondent, had saved its film for the marked passages in the prepared text, and so had missed the rather dramatic attack on Agnew. Since the other two networks had film of the

And so the agenda is fixed. People talk about busing, not segregation, and when they do, it is of violence and confrontation. There is talk of ways to meet an "energy crisis," not whether such a crisis really exists or of what it consists. "Cleaning up the environment" is treated as though it involved high school students gathering beer cans and not the possible loss of millions of dollars in industry profits. Americans argue over whether power in America is lodged in the White House or Capitol Hill, and rarely if ever whether it might be found elsewhere. Genuine intelligent discussion is "bad television"—talking heads again—so the most complex political issues are reduced to the trivial level, where they can be presented "visually."

This encouragement of trivia was demonstrated very well through the whole course of the 1976 presidential election. It was, largely through the events that led to the nomination of both candidates, the first genuinely all-television campaign. That is to say, it was the first campaign in which both candidates virtually ignored other ways to reach the voter, and concentrated almost all of their time, energies, staff resources, and money on the ways in which they would be seen—and heard—on television.

Both Carter and Ford had the same problem. Neither had any record in national politics nor any recognizable constituency. Through our recent political history, politicians have, because of their nationally publicized words or deeds, acquired a following, and some of them have a following which will support them almost no matter what they do or say. Thus, there are Reaganites, there are "Kennedy people," there are people who proudly declare themselves to be Wallace-ites. There are those who would follow "old Hubert" wherever he leads. There are even devoted followers of Richard Nixon.

But after the national conventions of 1976, there were no comparable

extemporaneous part, and would unquestionably use it on their evening news shows, the correspondent asked if the candidate could possibly repeat his denunciation of Agnew just before he delivered the prepared text in Rochester? If he would do that, said the correspondent, he would then hand-carry the film to New York and it would make the network's evening news.

Senator McGovern agreed to do the favor, and the candidate's advance men managed to get the correspondent and his crew placed directly in front of the speakers' stand in Rochester. True to his promise, McGovern preceded his prepared remarks with another denunciation of Agnew, which may have come as somewhat of a surprise to the other networks (some of the spontaneity was gone, but it was a good performance), but which greatly pleased the network correspondent who had missed it in the morning. He thanked the people who had helped him, and left for New York.

That night, all three networks carried the Agnew portion of McGovern's speeches, two from the Detroit appearance and the other from Rochester. Imagine the surprise in the McGovern press office, where aides were watching the evening newscast on the network they had befriended, when the correspondent himself appeared at the end of the program to discuss the McGovern campaign with the anchorman. "It's going badly," he said, "and they need everything good they can get. This morning, for example, he denounced Spiro Agnew, and it went over so well that he decided to repeat it again in Rochester."

groups identified with Ford or Carter. Each had to create his constituency anew each day, and hope it held together until the next day. Each had the ability, which other presidential candidates had lacked, to attract voters on one issue and repel them on another—sometimes on the same day.

As a consequence, each relied heavily on the television news and their paid commercial time to get across to the voters some personal, rather than political, impression. Both saw the election, correctly, as one that would be decided on the basis of the voters' judgment of the men, not their ideas. Their ideas, in any event, were too little known to begin to elucidate them with only three months to go to election, since television would afford no time to do so thoroughly.

Both had learned, as well, one major lesson from George McGovern's campaign four years before. The lesson was simple: never advance a new and reasonably complicated idea in the course of a campaign; no time is allowed to discuss it or even to explain it. McGovern had proposed a welfare reform which guaranteed an income of $1,000 per person, declining as earnings rose. President Carter proposed a quite similar reform, but has wisely allowed nearly three years for public debate.

Each candidate then played, in sports terminology, for the tie rather than to "win" anything each night on the news programs. It was a wise decision, considering the way television news covers a presidential campaign. Each candidate is allowed somewhere between one minute fifteen seconds and one minute forty-five seconds of that precious twenty-two minutes. Although no law or FCC rule requires it, candidates get "equal time" each day. The "equal time" requirement of the law applies only to commercials—paid time, not news—while the "fairness" doctrine is applied as a required balance only over a period of time. But television—aware that half its audience might be offended if one candidate or the other is "left out" of the coverage, and that the offended half might take out its anger either by switching to another channel or, worse, responding against the products sold in the news time—is most even-handed. On a day when a candidate is doing nothing, there are stories to be run about staff, or campaign anecdotes, or finances, or polls—*anything* to match the other man's news display.

That minute-plus that is used is precious. It is the only view of the election from the candidate's point of view that half the electorate will get that day. If the candidate is on the road, the coverage will be highly stylized. We will see a shot of the campaign airplane landing. (The press photographers and television cameramen are on a different plane than is the candidate, and it always lands first, just so they can get this shot. It is part of the "death watch" aspect of campaign coverage, which will be discussed later.)

There will follow a shot of the airport crowd—rounded up for the occasion by the advance men—and then of the candidate descending the steps of the airplane. In 1976 the coverage was so similar and the speeches so uninteresting, the only way to tell the difference between the two men was at this point in the newscast—was the candidate carrying a garment bag?

Then, still within the tight confines of the time allotted, a few seconds would be devoted to local dignitaries, if they were well-known (the Mayor of Chicago, the Governor of California, any primary opponent, any black mayor), and if possible a few seconds more to some "color"— pretty girls, a band, hostile signs. Once in California a man with a huge chicken head got more coverage at one campaign stop than President Ford; he was more "visual," and there is no stricture against *clucking* heads.

Finally, over the wind and the general hubbub, viewers both see and hear the candidate. He has now about thirty to forty-five seconds left of his allotted segment, and he knows it. He will, therefore, say as close to nothing while seeming as informed and sincere as he can. If he raises an important "issue," he will necessarily have to treat it in the most superficial way, and he will run the risk either of not being understood or of meeting strong criticism, which he must endure until he has the opportunity for another thirty seconds in which to answer. It is, in short, no wonder that the 1976 campaign was virtually devoid—as it became a cliché to say—of "issues." The way in which television news treated the campaign made it essential that there be no serious discussion of "issues," or for that matter of anything else. Thus, it became particularly ironic that the final two minutes of each of the network news programs would be devoted to "commentary" from some serious senior correspondent, usually Eric Sevareid for CBS, Howard K. Smith for ABC, and David Brinkley for NBC. Their styles were different—Sevareid cynical, Smith full of outrage, Brinkley ironic—but the message was almost always the same. The message was that the candidates were not talking about the issues.

Imagine what would have happened had either candidate walked into any network newsroom after the nightly newscast and announced that the commentary had convinced him. Why not, Carter or Ford might have asked, devote two hours a night to a thoughtful discussion of the softness of the pound and the lira, and whether the American devaluations might have been a contributing cause? Or perhaps an hour or two on proposals for a new international economic order, with special reference to new sources of funding to be made available to the less developed countries? Or a brisk seminar by the candidates' defense experts on the different positions with respect to new proposals for Mutual Balanced Force Reductions? The answer is obvious. A serious discussion of the issues would have meant pre-empting some violence-filled and profitable hour and replacing it with a "dull" non-visual hour of talking heads. Television knows no greater sin. Even a *daytime* fire is better than a discussion of issues.

It was precisely this refusal to yield time for serious matters that permitted Richard Nixon in 1972 to postpone any national awareness of the crimes of his administration and his campaign until after the election was safely behind him, and that made the discovery and reporting of those events entirely the province of newspapers. When people learned about Watergate from television news, it was almost always either in a formulation which began "the Washington *Post* said today . . ." or in live performances before Senator Ervin's committee. When George McGovern charged, quite truthfully as it turned out, that the Nixon administration was "the most corrupt in our history," Nixon spokesmen used their network-news minute to "refuse to dignify the charge with comment." And there it stood, save for some comment that McGovern was becoming "desperate" in his charges.

The required balance, neutrality, and inoffensiveness of television news stays away from real controversy. Once, in 1972, Cassie Mackin of NBC analyzed a Nixon speech characterizing some of his opponent's positions, and pointed out—on the air in a newscast—precisely how each claim was false. Within minutes, White House Communications Director Herb Klein was on the phone to NBC, and Ms. Mackin never did it again. Neither did anyone else.

In 1976, there was one possible forum on television in which issues could have been seriously discussed. In a transparent effort to use a loophole in the requirement that if any candidate is given time by a station, all candidates must be given equal time, the networks seized on a series of debates to be held by the League of Women Voters between the major candidates. The flimsy way around the equal-time requirement was that this was a "news event"; the League just happened to be holding these debates, and television cameras would just drop by and film them. And since only Ford and Carter had been invited by the League to "debate," no others need be heard.

But by the time the negotiations were completed among the candidates (who certainly didn't want serious debate) and the networks (who wanted it even less), the League (which did) was outgunned. When the debates finally took place, the programs became a sort of double "Meet the Press," in which the candidates had two and one-half minutes to answer rather than the usual half of that time. Fearful of opening up lines of argument they would be unable to close, the candidates still played for the draw and hoped for some blunder on the other side.

The only thing that emerged from the debates was that some of the reporters who asked the questions seemed better informed, more articulate, and more "presidential" than the candidates. They could afford to be; they had far less at risk.

The 1976 presidential campaign, of course, was a different type of campaign than Americans had experienced for some time—at least since 1960. There was no incumbent, in any ordinary sense of the word. President Ford had come to office from the Vice-Presidency, but unlike other Presidents who had done so, he had never run for Vice-President; he had never even been considered by his party for the nomination to either place on the ticket. He had been President for two years, but he came to office with almost no national record of any kind, and he was, in a very real sense, our first probationary President; he would not be the "real" President unless he was elected. And Jimmy Carter made *his* lack of any national impression a campaign asset; it permitted him to run against politics and, by implication, politicians.

Even the Kennedy-Nixon campaign of 1960 was not comparable. Nixon had been Vice-President for eight years, and an active one, and before that he had been a highly visible and controversial Representative and Senator. John Kennedy had been a Senator for eight years, and one not unaware of how to obtain a share of the nation's attention for his record, his personality, and his platform.

Thus, 1976 was truly the first all-television campaign, in the sense that television set the issues agenda. Since the issues thus defined were necessarily one-short-answer ones—i.e., busing, abortion—the campaign was a rather trivial one. Nothing better demonstrated the way in which this power of television to control the agenda contributed to the American people's being ill-served.

True, a contributing factor was the new set of campaign-funding rules. For the first time, not only were individual contributions of more than $1,000 outlawed in the pre-convention period but public funds were used exclusively for the post-convention campaign. One result was a national campaign, for each candidate, conducted on a much smaller budget than in previous elections. Except for staff salaries and travel expenses, the money was spent almost entirely on television commercials. Gone were the bumper strips, the pamphlets, the buttons, and other open paraphenalia of a campaign, and gone too were the intense organizing and vote-getting operations. Voters and even campaign volunteers felt far more distant from the campaigns, and the television commercials—and that minute-plus on the evening news—were all that were left.

Increasing the amount of public financing to be available for a presidential campaign will not change campaigning much. The candidates will simply increase their television budgets. The medium has turned politics into a spectator sport, and the only position in the game that matters is President, because he is the only player for whom everyone votes. Therefore, he is the only player in the game who will be covered every day by television—the only national product in the national market.

This practice comes into operation, so far as the network news programs are involved, immediately after the election. A careful watch from November 2, 1976, to January 20, 1977, yielded the finding that, at least on CBS, President-elect Carter was on the evening news for his allotted time every single day between election and inauguration. And the treatment was substantially the same, whether he was appointing a Secretary of the Treasury or carrying Amy's doll house to a truck.

One evening—Christmas Eve—the news story about Carter was that there *was* no news; he had given the press with him the day off. And it took some of the twenty-two minutes to tell us *that,* and reflect on its significance. An obsession with the activities of the President is on the increase, and extends as well to his family. On the first day after the Memorial Day weekend in 1977, one big story on the evening news was the President, doing nothing of national interest, but behaving in a very "visual" way, walking around his home town of Plains, Georgia, shaking hands with neighbors. Another big story was Rosalynn Carter, doing nothing in Jamaica on the first stop of her South American tour, but doing it also in a highly visual way—shaking hands with children, and entering and emerging from buildings with Jamaican officials.

Presidential travel is a serious matter. In the winter of 1974, after he had been in office several months, President Ford announced that he was going to pay a visit to China. He did so, and the trip was well covered. But is there any doubt that, if the networks had politely told presidential Press Secretary Ron Nessen that they didn't see any news in the trip, and that they would cover it through their "stringers" in Hong Kong, a reason would have been found at the White House to cancel the voyage? Almost without exception, Presidents travel in order to be seen traveling—on the evening news.

There is another aspect to this faithful recording of presidential traveling—and the travels of presidential candidates. That is the "death watch" element. Ever since Dallas in November, 1963, the one overriding fear of network correspondents is that it will happen again and they will not be there to record it. The result is that the cameras—if they can—go everywhere the President or the candidates go, and correspondents become almost frantic if they cannot.

One day in the 1976 campaign illustrates this "death watch" psychology quite well. Then-candidate Jimmy Carter was scheduled for an afternoon of making television commercials. He was to drive to a farm and sit quietly and talk about issues, in the style he had used successfully throughout the primary election campaign. His television adviser, Jerry Rafshoon, advised the network crews that the session would be closed to press and cameras. But one network asked Rafshoon for permission to come along and observe the filming of the commercials. "We won't film anything," was the plea, "we just want to be there in case somebody takes a shot at him. And if they did that, you wouldn't want to use that film for a commercial anyway." Stunned, but impressed with the logic of the argument, Rafshoon agreed.

Death watch or not, the camera crews are there. And if network camera crews and correspondents are with the President, shooting film, the network cost accountants can find several reasons why the film should be used on the evening news. Barring massive power failures, it is extremely doubtful if there will ever again be a nightly network newscast that does not include a story about the President—any President.*

NEWS THAT IS NATIONAL

Television—over the years since the installation of the coaxial cable in 1951—has given us national news for the first time, and with a completely new idea of what news is. Even radio did not unite us this way, in terms of public concerns. The only well known "national" newscaster was Walter Winchell, and his broadcasts were noted more for their excitement and inside scoops than for the regular presentation of news. And radio still required enormous efforts of imagination. What do these people look like? How are they dressed? How large is that crowd?

In fact, it was said at the time—and still is—that Franklin D. Roosevelt was probably the outstanding *radio* politician of all time; the proof of the truth of that assessment is that no one else is even mentioned as a contender. But could Roosevelt have survived television? Specifically, could he have been elected four times—or even once—if the voters had known, because they *saw* him, that he could not walk and spent most of his time in a wheelchair?

Whatever the answer, it is certainly true that if FDR got away with seeming robust and active and ambulatory (and, to judge from recent biographies, got away with much more as well), the *national* quality of news was missing before television. Even as late as 1956, candidate Adlai Stevenson could be praised by his admirers for "saying the same thing in all parts of the country." Translated, that meant that his mea-

---

* Reputable psychiatric opinion supports the view that attempts at assassination of presidents and presidential candidates are often stimulated by the presence of television cameras, and that if all publicity concerning the picture or identity of the assassin could be suppressed until the time of his or her trial, the number of assassination attempts would decline drastically.

sured advocacy of civil rights was no less clearly stated in the South than in the North.

Since television, that is taken for granted. No longer can a candidate make a special appeal in one part of the country and expect that it will go unnoticed anywhere else. What is said in San Diego is simultaneously heard and analyzed in Bangor. In fact, candidates have little desire to stress local issues, lest they seem parochial and obscure on the (national) evening news on television.

Historically, this is a fairly recent development, and coincides with the technological development of television. Andrew Johnson, to cite one well known historical example, could not "take his case to the people" without in fact leaving the White House for an arduous tour "around the circle," in order to answer his critics. And Woodrow Wilson—who would today simply have reserved a few hours with the networks for a fireside chat, to be followed by news conferences and addresses to Congress—was forced to defend his League of Nations policy by an exhausting cross-country speaking tour, the strain of which probably led to the stroke which effectively ended his presidency.

The result of this "nationalizing" effect of television is not confined to news. Television is in the process of "nationalizing" virtually the entire American culture. Linguists tell us that regional speech differences will disappear within a few generations. Children in Boston are dropping the broad "A" of their parents' and children in Hattiesburg their drawl in favor of the flat, faintly nasal "California" accent of television announcers.

As television became a national medium, it became a vehicle for national advertisers; one result has been a further homogenization of the culture. Very few cities still have a local brewery, and the number of local bakeries is declining. Regional food differences are disappearing under the relentless hammerblows of McDonalds and Colonel Sanders. Dress and architecture will soon follow. It is even now almost impossible, looking out the window of a train or an automobile, to tell what city one is in, or even what region. The suburban shopping center, the fast-food outlets, the drive-in movie house, the "rebuilt" downtown with steel-and-glass high-rise office buildings—all were built to market or to service the products advertised on national television. Hair and dress fashions, "alternate" lifestyles, and tastes in books, motion pictures and, to be sure, television drama—all are carried across the country at once and "certified" by television as appropriate.

For politicians, the nationalization of *news* has had enormous significance. And for office-holders where television is not accessible, the problems of Woodrow Wilson and Andrew Johnson remain. The state of New Jersey, for example, does not have a single VHF television station.

There is a channel licensed to Newark, but the FCC permitted—indeed encouraged—its sale to a corporation which puts it on the air as New York City's "public" television station. It is only in the state of New Jersey where the governor must leave the state in order to talk to the state's citizens.

The result of having no television is a serious one. A far lower percentage of New Jersey citizens than those of any other state knows even the names of their public officials. People in New Jersey are more familiar with Mayor Beame of New York and Mayor Rizzo of Philadelphia than they are with their own mayors. A result is that corruption is more likely to flourish. With no local news at all, it is easier to set up informal, non-governmental arrangements and avoid detection. Furthermore, the political remedies customarily available to the aggrieved are less available in New Jersey. Should a challenging or reformist political candidate seek to "go to the people" over the heads of elected officials, he will be thwarted; there is no way to do so.

Television had a different effect in Ohio, during the 1976 Democratic primary. The final primary elections in three of the largest states, California, New Jersey, and Ohio, were to be on the same Tuesday in June. The count takes a long time in New Jersey, and some California polling places don't close until midnight EST. In Ohio, on the other hand, voting is by machine, the polls close at an early hour, and counting is swift. All the signs, therefore, pointed to major coverage of Ohio, and only peripheral mention of New Jersey. California, in any event, would not begin to be a factor until well after most viewers had turned off their sets and gone to sleep, so it was not involved in a major way in the night's television coverage.

The result was a network focus on Ohio, and that decision, dictated not by political importance but by the technology of television news, guaranteed Jimmy Carter's nomination. Carter had a smashing victory in Ohio—that night's coverage was all Ohio. Virtually ignored was the fact that Brown, with a short campaign, had won as handsomely in New Jersey, the nation's seventh largest and most industrialized state, and would later win overwhelmingly in the largest state, California.

Late, late viewers could see Governor Brown in California, after midnight, exulting over his success that day. Brown spoke to an excited band of followers and proclaimed his victories in New Jersey and California, and announced he would leave the next day for states whose delegates had not as yet committed themselves. To those who had already seen the formal award of the nomination to Carter by the networks, it seemed almost churlish of Brown not to concede. It was all over; not only the networks but Mayor Daley had said so. But in truth, it was a near thing. If the results had been reversed, so that Brown had won in

Ohio and Carter had won in California, or even if New Jersey's election laws had permitted a vote for presidential candidates directly, instead of indirectly for delegates, the Carter drive to the nomination might well have been slowed, and perhaps stopped.

Certainly, George Wallace and Henry Jackson would not have thrown their delegates immediately to a candidate who had been seen by the nation to lose two big states, including the one Mayor Daley had described as the key to the nomination, and certainly not to a candidate proclaimed on the networks the night before as the "loser." And Governor Brown, with the "momentum" the network commentators would have bestowed upon him, would have emerged as a genuine contender.

Time controls events. Presidents now deliver "State of the Union" addresses to Congress at 9 PM EST, and neither the chief executive nor the members reflect on why this should be the hour rather than the traditional noon ceremony. It is in the evening, of course, because that is prime time, and it is precisely at 9 because that is 6 PM in California—and after 9 o'clock in the East audiences begin to drift away, and before 6 o'clock in California much of the audience is still looking for the homeward-bound off-ramp on the freeway.

It is all now a part of the way we do our political business. If it is an important hearing, or one that at least one network thinks is important, then the witnesses will be wearing colored shirts, the lights and cameras will be in place, and all the participants—witnesses and committee members—will have become, however subtle the change, actors for the occasion.

Television, now, can make "stars" of politicians almost overnight. At the time of the hearings on the impeachment of President Nixon, a first-term Representative from Texas, Barbara Jordan—whose political career prior to that time had been noticed only locally—became such a star. Black, female, and possessed of a powerful speaking voice, Representative Jordan was a national hit from the moment she began to speak at the impeachment hearings. To this day, her speech is remembered as eloquent and compelling, and it made her a national figure and earned her an assignment as one of the keynote speakers at the Democratic National Convention in 1976. Few can recall what it was she said on that occasion, however. It was a perfect example of a television news appearance constituting the news.

Some of this immediate quality of television news is understood, and to some extent deplored, by the people who have to deal with it, and indeed by some of those who deal best with it. Walter Cronkite, for example, calls network news "a front page medium," and has said that television can't really do much more than produce a front page, and perhaps give people some guide as to what is important. Cronkite thinks the general public dependence on television news is unfortunate, and thinks "ominous" the figures which show that half of all Americans now say they get all their news from television.

Along with this increasing reliance on the "front page" of television for all the news, has come an interesting development. Television news is increasingly not only absorbed but trusted. Even under the official attacks on the credibility of television news and newsmen by the Nixon administration, including—indeed, led by—the President and the Vice-President, the percentage of Americans who trusted and respected the accuracy and reliability of the news in their living rooms steadily climbed. From 1959 to 1974, including through those years in which television news came under attack, not only from Nixon and his people but also from a segment of the disaffected Left, who regarded it as a basic tool of the Establishment, the percentage of Americans considering television's performance to be "good" or "excellent" rose from 59 to 71 per cent. During this time, the people who held a high opinion of schools dropped from 64 to 50 per cent, of newspapers from 64 to 58 per cent, and of local government from 44 to 35 per cent. By 1974, television was in the lead as the "most believable medium" by a margin of 51 to 20 per cent over newspapers; * as the source of most news by a margin of 65 to 47 per cent; and record percentages opposed government control over television news (81 per cent) and television programs generally (41 per cent). The difference between the two statistics is revealing—people evidently feel that television news is more sacrosanct than the rest of the television entertainment schedule, although the law treats them equally. Both are subject to government regulation through the licensing process and requirements imposed by Congress and the FCC. The industry treats them equally, too—both are competing for audiences in order to sell time at a higher price to advertisers.

Other studies confirm the trend of these findings, not only in the United States but in Western Europe as well. News is more believable if seen than if read about. Just why this should be so is a question which has given rise to some debate. One study attempting to determine this reason elicited the finding that more than half the people who say they "rely more" on television for news do so because it is "more convenient" and because it requires less effort.

---

* The confirmation of the criminality of Nixon and his associates, as had been reported by television and denounced until proven true, gave television—"the bearer of the bad news"—a boost in popularity. There is irony in this finding, because the Watergate story was never a television news achievement, and thus it would appear that the work of investigative, linear, newspaper journalists was ultimately responsible for this increase in the credibility of—television.

THE FIRST AMENDMENT

There are significant differences between television and the written press. The most important is that television is a *licensed* industry, for the reason that the number of channels is limited, and allocated by the government to each geographic area. These channels are then licensed by the FCC for a period of three years to the applicant that, in the opinion of the Commission, will operate the channel in the public interest.

For the most part, unless a challenge of sufficient weight is made, the Commission will renew existing licenses, but that fact does not make the operator of a television station the "owner" of that channel any more than the issuance of a renewable driver's license makes one entitled to drive for the rest of one's life. In other words, the public owns the television channels, and the law is quite clear that those licensed to profit from their use must conform to certain standards in order to continue to be allowed to do so.

No such requirement is imposed—nor can it be—upon anyone who wishes to print, for example, a newspaper, a magazine, or a pamphlet. No one licenses the Washington *Post,* the Chicago *Tribune, Time,* or *Rolling Stone.* Government has no authority to interfere with them—to require certain stories, to require certain standards, to forbid certain sorts of writing or certain subjects.

But television licensees, network and affiliate and independent, who all know that the license guarantees enormous profit opportunities, accept such burdens and restraints. They may not, for example, open their air only to proponents of one political party or cause. They may not allow advertising time to one candidate for office without equal time for his opponents. They are forbidden to advertise certain products or to depict certain acts. They must give evidence of reasonable recognition of the groups in their community, through employment opportunity and the opportunity to be heard—and seen.

No such requirements are placed on newspapers or magazines. The First Amendment protects them. But television proprietors are not protected by the First Amendment. No court has yet held that the guarantees of freedom of speech, freedom of the press apply to television stations, nor is one likely to. If there is any "freedom of speech" to be protected in television, it is that of the viewers—the public—and not that of the broadcasters, who accept the restrictions when they apply for, and accept, a government license.

A combination of producers, writers, and actors sued for the restoration of their First Amendment rights, which they claimed were violated by the imposition of Family Hour restrictions. (In fact, the Family Hour threatened to restrict them financially, by preventing second-time-around sales of violent shows to non-network stations.)

Judge Warren Ferguson, the federal trial judge in Los Angeles who heard the case, did not say the law objects to government regulation of what's broadcast. There was, it seems, no First Amendment violation. (No one, judge, plaintiffs, or defendants, took note that censorship for profit has been traditional in television programming, and that the complaints were that a form of censorship for social values had been sought.) Judge Ferguson did say regulation must be done in proper fashion.*

"If government intervenes in the future to control entertainment programming," the judge said, "it shall do so not in closed-door negotiating sessions but in conformity with legislatively mandated administrative procedures. If the government has any power to regulate such programming, it must be exercised by formal regulations supported by an appropriate administrative record . . ."

Nothing more clearly describes the distinction between the First Amendment's application to speech and printed material and the exclusion of television from its protection. It is inconceivable that any such language could appear in a judicial opinion concerning government regulation of the content of newspapers.

---

* The court struck down the Family Hour rule on the ground that it was transparently not a voluntary decision by the owners of television stations, but an action of the government, done through the pressures applied by the FCC and the Congress—and proper government procedures were not followed. However, Family Hour is still with us, because the decision was quickly appealed.

4 RACE: MAKING AND UNMAKING A REVOLUTION

James Baldwin once wrote that the most frightening thing about the American white world was that it acts as though blacks do not exist. From its very beginning, Baldwin's statement has described television. Through the 1960s, the second decade of the Age of Television, on the medium of communication Americans used most, one-tenth of the population, 20 million blacks, were truly—in Ralph Ellison's words —invisible men.

Few, if any, black characters appeared in children's cartoons and Saturday morning programs; *Mickey Mouse Club* included no blacks nor did *Howdy Doody;* Dick Clark, whose *American Bandstand* originated from largely black South Philadelphia, was on the air for years before any local citizens joined his group of young Americans. On adult programs, black appearances were limited to supporting and stereotyped roles such as maids and waiters, and occasional guest appearances by black singers and dancers. On regular prime time dramatic or comedy programs, a black leading man or woman was unknown.

If an accurate history demanded that blacks be present, then that history was changed. *Riverboat,* a program based on Mark Twain's stories about the Mississippi River, operated on the rule that no blacks could be shown—although the black presence and culture dominated Mark Twain's descriptions. Historical truth was submerged totally on a series called *The Americans,* a program about two brothers on opposite sides in the Civil War—slavery was rarely mentioned.

In 1956, screenwriter Rod Serling tried to sell the *United States Steel Hour,* a program promoted for solid serious drama, a play about the real-life 1955 kidnap-murder of a fourteen-year-old Mississippi black youth, Emmett Till, accused of no more than whistling at a white woman. The woman's husband and another man shot Till, dumped the body in the river, and were, quite predictably, acquitted by an all-white jury. The program's producers wanted the story done without mentioning race. Serling returned with a script about a Jewish youth in Mississippi who met the same fate as Emmett Till. In the end, the story as played on the air took place in New England, no lynching occurred, and the central character remained Jewish. Otherwise, it was the story of Emmett Till.

Actor-producer Robert Montgomery has complained that in the 1950s, NBC told him that his anthology series, *Robert Montgomery Presents,* was using too many black actors. When he resisted cutting back—his immediate response, he says, was to change a script so as to call for two *additional* black actors—the network found cause not to renew the program.

To be sure, there were blacks regularly appearing on television. One was Beulah, the quintessential white family's black maid, another was Rochester, Jack Benny's valet and low comic relief. The most famous, of course, were Amos and Andy, reproducing their celebrated radio perpetuation of most white-held stereotypes. There was one difference: on television, these two forerunners of Sanford and Son had to be played by black actors—on radio, they had been played by whites.

A 1959 doctoral dissertation documented what seemed already to be the case to an ordinary viewer: blacks appeared on television as servants five times more than they did in all other occupations combined. The same study found one black doctor; that was all so far as a depiction of black professionals was concerned.

It should be noted that this dismal recital was not just of television in its infancy, in those dim, unenlightened immediate-postwar years. As late as 1968, fourteen years after *Brown v. Board of Education,* and thirteen years after Rosa Parks refused to go to the back of a Montgomery, Alabama, bus, Chrysler Corporation tried to censor a scene on a variety show in which black singer Harry Belafonte and white singer Petula Clark inadvertently brushed hands while appearing together on stage—and on camera. For Americans to see, however fleetingly, a black man having even the slightest physical contact with a white woman—under their auspices—was apparently putting too much at risk for one of the nation's most powerful industrial corporations. At about the same time, a dramatic program depicted the scene at the subway stop at 125th Street in Harlem, and only white faces were visible.

In 1972, Action for Children's Television commissioned an analysis of the racial content of children's programs. Among its conclusions: ". . . non-American and non-white cultures were referred to negatively almost every time they were mentioned, and black and other minority characters made up only a small percentage of characters—7 per cent blacks and only 2 per cent other minorities . . . [T]he subject of race was never discussed, and even in shows with black stars or characters, the blacks interacted only with white characters in the white community. Occasional black leaders had a white co-leader, while most shows have white leaders. All figures of authority or sources of information were white . . . Blacks and other minorities rarely appear in work situations." The study also found that all other minority groups, for instance dark-skinned foreigners, Orientals, and American Indians were depicted in "negative stereotypes." Similar conclusions have been reported in other content analyses of television programming during this period. A separate study by ACT of adult programming showed that in less than thirteen per cent of all episodes were there "significant or substantive" relationships between blacks and whites.

In 1975, Les Brown of the *New York Times* reported that motion picture producer Stanley Kramer, whose previous credits included such successes as *Guess Who's Coming to Dinner?* had completed a television pilot program for ABC. Included, according to the report, was "a bedroom scene in which a black man kisses a white woman on the mouth."

"Kramer did it as tastefully as you could ask for," Brown quotes an ABC executive as explaining, "but the physical contact was clearly going to cause hell out in the boondocks." When reminded that a very popular CBS comedy program had shown a white man passionately kiss a black woman to whom he was married, the executive responded, "[A] white man kissed a black woman and, terrible as it is to say, that's somehow not as objectionable in this society as when the sexes are reversed."

The episode they were discussing occurred on *The Jeffersons,* a Norman Lear situation comedy about an upwardly mobile black couple (formerly Archie Bunker's neighbors in Queens) who have moved into a largely white high rise apartment building in Manhattan. The Jeffersons see a lot of (he tolerates, she enjoys) a couple from upstairs who are racially mixed. It was this couple whom millions of viewers saw in the kissing scene. Tony Brown, the articulate producer-host of *Black Journal,* thinks it significant that Lear has the black-white couple a few floors *above* the black couple in the apartment building; it reinforces psychologically, he thinks, their status in society. Brown also noted, as did the ABC executive in the Kramer case, the preference for white male/black female and thought the reverse impossible to portray.

Lear himself discounts totally the question of the placement in the building of the two couples, but sees some merit in the argument about sex and interracial contact. Lear said he would introduce, also on *The Jeffersons,* an interracial couple in which the man was black and the woman white; such a couple appeared briefly in a 1977 episode, but there is no indication that their appearance will be a regular one.

Stanley Kramer's pilot never saw the light of day (actually, of night), and the strong implication of the *Times* article was that the interracial

love scene was the reason. Of course, there are other tangible and intan-
gible reasons for rejecting a pilot program, and it may be that the
Kramer program was turned down, as they say, on the merits. The assumption need not necessarily be made that every program with race
and sex is rejected on the basis solely of its content. But Stanley Kramer
has one of the best commercial histories in the movie business—a "good
track record"—and, as Les Brown pointed out in his case study, the
networks almost always buy programs presented by producers of his
calibre and reputation. All things being equal (that is to say, all characters being the same color), the risk is relatively low.

Furthermore, as we shall discuss further in Chapter 7, the networks
will carefully monitor, in selected movie theater audience reaction tests,
the response to such crucial racial questions as whether a black male
lead is "too strong"—i.e., threatening—or a black-white, male-female in-
nuendo too obvious. Programs or even scenes that "test" as beyond the
tolerable boundaries are modified or cut out entirely, often without
debate or publicity.

Programs in prime time with black leads and black-oriented plots
began to appear in the 60s, largely in response to the nation's increasing
awareness, to pressure brought by civil rights groups, and to the sponsors' growing and measurable perception of a black audience with
money to spend.

At the same time, a persistent pattern began to emerge: blacks on
television became more and more involved with law enforcement. It was
almost as though America was being told by television that blacks cannot survive save in an environment of violence and screaming police
sirens, while at the same time ignoring—for a variety of reasons, none
very noble—the single factor which continues to set the races politically
apart: most violent crime in big cities is committed by blacks—against
other blacks.

Thus, a remarkably high disproportion of blacks were shown in law
enforcement roles, while almost all of the very few blacks portrayed as
criminals either had British accents (less "black," but still a strong signal of degeneracy to a mass American audience, just as a broad "Amur-
rican" accent on a British dramatic television program is a sure portent
of crass vulgarity), came from unnamed African nations, or were described as "misguided geniuses." Ghetto "punks," or violent, desperate
heroin addicts, were never black, but always white when portrayed. The
few black criminal types ever offered to home viewers were portrayed on
the "Superfly" image—high-living, high-rolling con artists surrounded
by beautiful willing women and wearing what Tony Brown of *Black
Journal* calls "clothes a fool wouldn't buy."

In what seemed a transparent effort not to offend, not to appear racist
at a time when racism, publicly at least, was out of fashion, television

tried to tell its audiences that violent criminals were white. Those blacks who appeared on screen held positive, law-abiding values—but often posed against the values of other, nameless, invisible off-screen blacks, as in this statement by a black policeman to young recruits on *Dragnet:*

> I wanted to do something for my country, I wanted to do something for my own people . . . And I'll tell you something else, some of our own people talk about "white man's law." There's no such thing, not when black men like you and me wear this uniform . . . it's every-body's law.

But those "some of our people" were rarely, if ever, heard on television, even though a case could then (and can now, for that matter) be made that the law is a "white man's law" many times and in many places. The failure to make this argument, but only to deny its validity in an interracial situation, involves racist feelings, however softly or in-directly expressed.

But even with the introduction of black leading actors and actresses, blacks emerged to a significant degree in so-called "salt and pepper" combinations with inevitably dominant white co-stars. Furthermore, the scripts were written so that the blackness of the performers was irrele-vant. Except for the color of their skin, they were essentially white. The examples are numerous, but include certainly the black "team mem-bers" in such programs as *I Spy, Mission Impossible, Mod Squad, The Rookies, Ironside, Mannix,* and *Star Trek.* The role of the black science expert on the *Mission Impossible* team was particular appropri-ate to this analysis. The team was some sort of U.S. espionage group, presumably from the CIA, and they all often posed—successfully—as ordinary working folks in the country of their assignment, which, ex-cept for a few exotic African countries, was always a country in which there were no other black people at all. The "willing suspension of dis-belief" here involved the notion that a Balkan dictator, for example, would not notice anything amiss if his chef (or male nurse, or electronic expert or portrait painter) turned out to be a black man.

Some programs featured blacks playing "real" blacks, but these either died fairly quickly (e.g., *Shaft, Bill Cosby, Julia*) or survived, as in the case of the *Flip Wilson* show, because their comedy-musical format per-mitted frequent appearances by white stars. Indeed, the Wilson show was extremely successful principally because Flip Wilson himself could portray effectively the various black racial stereotypes that white audi-ences have always found terribly amusing, such as sassy, street-wise black mommas and con-artist revivalist preachers. Whites may be trou-bled by the portrayal of an Elmer Gantry or an Aimee Semple MacPher-son; Reverend Ike only makes them laugh—unquestionably, because at bottom his spiel is only separating *blacks* from their money.

"Black performers," concluded a 1970 study, "unless [they] are previously recognized stars, must conform to what is apparently the 'acceptable' black image." In all of this, it is important to remember that even a "black" television program, in order to succeed, must attract most of the white audience, or the total audience to be delivered to the advertiser will be too small to warrant the commercial dollars needed to keep the program on the air.

ALL IN THE FAMILY

Early in this decade, Norman Lear and Bud Yorkin revolutionized the treatment of race on television with the introduction of *All in the Family*. Lear and Yorkin, who had teamed up in production of motion pictures and television for many years (both successfully and unsuccessfully, mainly the latter), modeled a pilot film for a half-hour series after a mid-1960s British Broadcasting Corporation comedy entitled *'Til Death Do Us Part*. ABC, interested, paid for the production of two pilot programs but finally turned down the idea. CBS, then looking for a mid-season replacement (the television "season" is roughly coterminous with the public school year in the Northern hemisphere) for a series which had failed, first introduced the program to prime-time audiences on January 12, 1971.

Lear, in his words, wanted "to get the network wet completely," so the first episode opened with Archie's son-in-law cajoling his wife into having sexual intercourse one Sunday morning while her parents were in church. Although the show began slowly in the ratings, by May it was the most popular prime-time program, a position it has relinquished only occasionally in the years since then.

By the mid-1970s, more than half a dozen prime-time network programs on the air relied on black actors and actresses living presumably "black" lives, and almost all of them were highly rated—all in the wake of *All in the Family*. One (*The Jeffersons*) was a direct spin-off of *All in the Family,* one (*Good Times*) a spin-off of a spin-off (*Maude*) of *All in the Family,* and all, including a third (*Sanford and Son*), were produced by the Norman Lear organization, by now one of the largest production centers in Hollywood.

These programs—as well as *All in the Family* itself—have been the subject of substantial amounts of controversy, with sharply divided, and not always predictable, battle lines. It is not hard to understand why. Leaving aside (no easy task in itself) Archie's slurs aimed at Jews, Catholics, Orientals, women, Italians, Puerto Ricans, Poles, college students, and homosexuals, most of his many unkind and bigoted comments are aimed at blacks.

They are, in Bunker's words on the screen, "coons" and "spades" (although, as Laura Hobson noted in a sharp attack on the program, never the ultimate and most likely in Bunker's vocabulary—"niggers," just as, she pointed out, Jews are "Hebes" but never "kikes"). Christ and, for that matter, Santa Claus, *must* be white; blacks run faster because "they've got it in their blood inherited from the time their forefathers were in the jungle running barefoot through all them thorns and thickets with tigers on their butts"; and, of course, black men have a special stamina with women. Archie, naturally, refuses to drink from a glass that has been used by a black man.

Carroll O'Connor, the gifted actor who plays Archie, says, "I think that we're doing something that needs to be done and that is show a racist what *he* is doing. I mean show him *truthfully* what he is doing . . . I think the chips are going to fall on the right side."

Jack Gould, a television critic for the New York *Times,* writes: "Some of Archie's words may chill the spine, but to root out bigotry has defied man's best efforts for generations, and the weapon of laughter just might succeed."

All in the Family has received numerous "brotherhood" awards from the Los Angeles chapter of the National Association for the Advancement of Colored People and from many other black organizations. It also has won perhaps the most meaningful praise of all from the millions of blacks who watch it regularly (it should be noted that the Nielsen ratings consistently demonstrate that programs with black leading actors consistently attract the vast majority of black households; *All in the Family* is a significant exception); many write letters to their local newspapers, noting that for blacks it is always better to see and hear about blacks than to remain invisible.

If the laughter generated by the program is, in Jack Gould's phrase, a "weapon," it is a powerful one. On the average, 40 million Americans tune in each week. *All in the Family* has been the subject of countless analyses by experts in fields ranging from psychiatry to anthropology; the bibliography is so long that the program has clearly entered into that pantheon of intellectual phenomena which America's scholars consider worthy of in-depth study.

The conflict remains. Harvard psychiatrist Dr. Alvin Pouissant, himself black, says the program is harmful "not only in terms of how it might be influencing white attitudes, but also because it *does* have many blacks laughing at the kind of bigotry and racism Archie expresses." *Ebony* magazine accuses *All in the Family* of lulling American blacks into a false sense of security. The Committee on Racial Equality says Norman Lear is attempting to emasculate black men.

The Congressional black caucus officially complained to the FCC that such programs set back black progress. Criticism, to be sure, is not confined solely to the black political community. Spokesmen for other derided groups have joined in. A study commission of the Anti-Defamation League of B'nai B'rith blasted "the insensitivity of [*All in the Family's*] producers to the awesome power of television to imbed the stereotypes that have haunted most of America's minorities for many decades, and Jews for many centuries."

Some black spokesmen call the programs—including *All in the Family's* offspring—"coon shows," after the derisive name given oldtime minstrel performances, treating blacks in the same way as the movies did Stepin Fetchit, the character of Watermelon on the *Our Gang* comedies, the eye-rolling and mock fear of Mantan Moreland, and the black "assistants" to Charlie Chan.

Such criticism is supported by a number of studies that show many viewers "take it seriously," particularly those who agree with Archie in the first place. One study asserted that these people (pre-Bunker bigots) will begin to emulate him, that "they will start openly advertising their bigotry," now that television has certified it. Another study found that 60 per cent of the viewers "liked or admired Archie more than Mike (Archie's liberal, university-educated son-in-law)" And the same study reported that 35 per cent of the respondents found nothing wrong in the use of expressions like "coon" and "chink."

Carroll O'Connor reportedly complains to friends that many real-life bigots approach him in public and offer congratulations. And Richard Nixon, a foe of O'Connor's in real life (O'Connor made spot commercials for the candidacy of George McGovern), once complained that an episode deriding Archie for his hatred of homosexuals "[w]as awful. It made a fool of a good man." At the time, the praise from Nixon went largely unnoticed. But now that the White House tapes reveal that Nixon's language reflects his own previously hidden bigotry and use of "forbidden" words, the comment seems perfectly clear.

However bitter their disagreements, advocates on both sides agree on one thing: the stakes are very, very high. The controversy is not over a magazine article, even a cover story, or newspaper editorials. It is not over a popular motion picture, which might reach 20 million people, once. It is over television programs which reach tens of millions—of all ages—every week. In the case of *All in the Family,* its audience of 40 million is augmented by the re-runs of the program, which are shown in many cities every afternoon. Critics and sociologists alike argue that the program's popularity has demonstrated that it has reached into the nation's psyche.

While much of the controversy centers on the grandfather of "race" programs, *All in the Family,* the power of the others (many Lear-created) has not gone unrecognized. *Good Times* is supposed to portray life in Chicago's Cabrini-Green public housing project. It is, says *Ebony* magazine, "the tube's best effort to date at showing a real slice of ghetto black life." Writing of *Good Times,* a *New York Times* critic noted,

> whites are being given glimpses of black life that, however simplified, can't help but weaken artificial racial barriers. When more than 18 million American households tune into *Good Times* each week, when an ordinary black family becomes a mass-public favorite, at least one change is no longer in the wind. It's here, right in front of our eyes.

Good Times does confront a number of serious problems, such as youth gangs, gun control, busing, black militancy, culturally differentiated intelligence tests, and the recurrent theme of black male unemployment. But, say many of its critics, its answer to all this—even in public-housing Chicago—is the standard message of middle-class white suburbia: work hard (when you can find work), respect the law, love each other and, above all, keep faith in God, and everything will be fine.

Aware that thousands of young blacks, nevertheless, are emulating the cute, unemployed, uncommitted "J.J.", the son who rapidly became a star of the program, Jimmy Walker (the actor who plays J.J.) tells interviewers that "my advice is, do not follow me." But at the same time, he is the major beneficiary of sales of J.J. clothes, belt buckles, and dolls, many playing off his battle-cry: "Dy-no-mite!"

Such is the power of *Good Times* that it became a major cause of concern in many black organizations when the producers decided to "kill off" the father, rather than replace the actor who had left the show (to play the adult Kunta Kinte in *Roots,* as it turned out). Spokesmen for these groups complained that the image of the matriarchial black family would be unnecessarily reinforced for both black and white viewers. The program's executive producer's reply, "the fatherless family does exist in the ghetto," was not reassuring; the problem seems to have been met by the mother's keeping company with a solid bourgeois repair-shop proprietor whose object is clearly matrimony.

But in the end, when all the sociology has been set aside, it should be recognized that television, true to the delicate financial calibration that governs its every movement, presents American blacks and black ideas in precisely the formulation that the largest number of viewers with the proper demographic characteristics will accept. After all, it is not interracial democracy that is being sold, but deodorant; not integration, but bathroom tissue. To reverse Warren G. Harding, "not normalcy, but nostrums."

In doing so, television is often pulling Americans in opposite directions. It is pulling them forward into the recognition that America is shared by blacks and whites with great differences, but who also live and love and fear in many of the same ways. At the same time, it is pulling us back by presenting far too many blacks who most often fit into the old minstrel-show patterns.

There is much that can and should be said, both seriously and humorously, about black life in America; it is, by and large, not being said on television. But then, it is not being said there about white life, either. "For those [blacks] who may still be looking for a deep and satisfying social significance in black shows on television, the wait goes on," *Ebony* noted in early 1976. "But this is true," the comment continued, "in one form or another, for most white shows, and thus TV must be realized, if not accepted, for what it is."

And that is what seems to be happening in the black community, and some of this complacency dominates the entire American community, black and white. "As critical as I am," says Tony Brown of *Black Journal,* "I would prefer them ("black" programs) to nothing. As sick as they are, they're a step for us." And a *New York Times* critic, noting the trend of blacks toward comedy shows, came up with perhaps the best comment of all. In a column in 1975 titled "Good Times for the Black Image," he noted, "never underestimate the power of being silly on television."

But Brown, after conceding that being visible, even with the wrong message, is better than being invisible, has difficulty concealing his anger. When asked in an interview whether it was his opinion that racial busing was a media-created issue, Brown's answer showed that his concern over entertainment programming of and about blacks is never far from the surface. Here is his answer:

> I'm not going to agree with you that it [busing] is a media issue. I don't believe it's a media issue. I believe it's a psychological issue and I believe it's because television has induced in black people the need to be with white people and we have associated being with white people as progress. That is self-hatred. And as long as television keeps selling us *Good Times,* don't be with other blacks, and *The Jeffersons,* move on up with white people, we're going to continue to substitute or confuse integration with equality . . .

There is a question, of course, whether "visibility" is good—or even better than invisibility—for blacks in the ways television presents them to an audience that the producers are always aware is far more white than black. If *Amos and Andy* was bad because of the shuffling, Uncle Tom, shiftless image of blacks it portrayed, then why is *Sanford and Son* any better? And the upward-striving George Jefferson has a lot of the Kingfish in him, which he often seems to play to his mother's Madame Queen. Brown may be right about the lesson of *Good Times* and *The Jeffersons,* but the larger lesson seems to have been lost, as well.

Whatever the message that comes through, though, whether separatist, integrationist, or Uncle Tom, it may be that a great many blacks in the television audience accept these programs the way Americans accept so many other things about television—without any conscious affect. The programs are very popular in the black community.

A survey by the Corporation for Public Broadcasting (CPB) a few years ago measured the reaction to a sample of black-oriented programs as well as programs featuring blacks in regular roles. The programs were *Sanford and Son,* a situation comedy about a father and son who run a junkyard; *Flip Wilson,* a musical comedy-variety hour with a black performer-host; *Mod Squad,* a police show describing the adventures of three young and hip undercover agents, one of whom was black; the *Bill Cosby Show,* a situation comedy in which Cosby played a gentle schoolteacher; *Ironside,* a detective program whose hero had a black assistant; and *Soul* and *Black Journal,* public television programs about black art and life in America.

The survey revealed, first of all, an extraordinarily high audience for the programs among black urban respondents: 65 per cent said they watched *Sanford and Son* regularly; the figure for the *Flip Wilson Show* was 53 per cent, both substantially higher than in the general viewing population. Of the respondents, 90 per cent reported seeing the programs. Nielsen ratings confirm this high viewing level within black communities.

The CPB study also sought to determine what blacks thought various of the programs were doing to the image of blacks generally in America. The table below, reprinted from the CPB study, indicates that a negligible percentage of respondents found the programs offensive or harmful:

	Is helping create understanding of blacks	Is making fun of blacks	Is hurting blacks
Sanford and Son	27%	5%	2%
Flip Wilson	19%	5%	2%
Mod Squad	17%	1%	1%
Bill Cosby	22%	2%	1%
Ironside	12%	1%	1%
Soul	17%	0%	0%
Black Journal	16%	0%	0%

But what may be most interesting is a column that does not appear—those who had no opinion. It would show that from 66 to 86 per cent of those asked accepted the programs without apparently forming any opinion about their message or their impact. It may also be true that there is a sense of alienation so strong that many respondents simply did not choose to answer what was clearly a white man's questionnaire. Whatever the reason, the response of blacks to their portrayal on television is a function—and a direct function—of the events of the 60s and 70s that comprised what has been called "the black revolution."

MAKING AND UN-MAKING A REVOLUTION

The black revolution, or movement, first burst upon the scene in recognizable form in the early 1960s; and once again, it was television that determined the time and manner of its acceptance. Rosa Parks, for example, climbed aboard a Montgomery bus in 1956, and refused to take a seat in the rear, thus triggering the boycott and bringing a young minister, Martin Luther King, Jr., to national attention. The first sit-ins and Freedom Rides began soon afterwards.

For decades before that, black men and women had had their heads cracked and had been kicked and beaten—and black (and white) leaders had called for action. No one spoke of a black revolution, or even of a "movement." In fact, there was none discernible. But as the number of television sets in the country increased sharply, so did awareness of the struggle. In 1957, television set owners and their neighbors could watch as the National Guard protected black schoolchildren from the spit, kicks, and blows of angry parents in Little Rock, Arkansas.

By the early 1960s, the vast majority of all black homes had television sets (in fact, blacks became—and remain—the heaviest viewers in the national market), and what they saw was a largely new and fascinating world—new, at least, in the frequency with which it was displayed—paraded before them. It was a world of suburban comfort and endless, attractive consumer goods—a world denied to all but a small percentage of people, black or white, but one that appeared on television to be available to whites all the time. Black sociologist Kenneth Clark has written that growing up with television is the most painful of all experiences for black adolescents in urban ghettoes; the discrepancy between filmed images and real images was just too great.

That discrepancy of which Clark spoke has been felt not only in Harlem and other poor American communities, but wherever television is first made available to economically and politically deprived people. "Television brought [promises of change] with increasing impact into the lonely cottages and the shabby back-street homes of Northern Ireland," writes British journalist Robin Day. "It opened windows onto a broader view of the world; it helped stir a challenge to blinkered bigotry and traditional intolerance . . ." Surely it is more than coincidence that the first major mass black resistance leading to violence in South Africa occurred in 1976, roughly one year after its government finally permitted television to be introduced.

Newsweek sensed the force of television in the "revolution of rising expectations" when it noted in a July, 1963, major article about the black revolution that it was "in a sense, a television revolution . . . In a world of hungering men, even a soap commercial can throw off sparks of revolt if its setting is a modern suburban kitchen."

A more matter-of-fact analysis came from a Mississippi cotton planter, as reported by political journalist Theodore H. White: "You got to understand that every one of those Negroes on my land has a television set in his shack, and he sits there in the evening and watches."

Television in the 60s did more than just reach, finally, the mass of black Americans with its message of available opulence. By 1960, it had nurtured a cadre of young shock troops for the revolution—or, as it was called then, the civil rights movement. These were members of the Television Generation who believed in what they saw, and were prepared to demand that the promises of America be kept. It was television which gave them the notion that they, and their demands, were legitimate. And it also permitted these younger, more militant blacks to bypass established and more conservative institutions in the community—including the white press.

Television was—and remains—a perfect tool for organizing a revolution. There is no other way to reach *all* your members simultaneously with the identical message—even if they number in the millions. Television, with its network signal flashed everywhere simultaneously, had become by the early 60s an inanimate Committee of Correspondence. If you watched the message in the news—or in the commercials or "dramatic programs"—you knew, as you could never have known before, that millions of brothers were watching the same message and, presumably, drawing the same conclusions.

Network news executives discovered that black activism provided good television, and at the same time, black activists discovered that television provided an excellent propaganda forum. Soon, cameras began to follow the sit-ins and the Freedom Riders, and the confrontations they provided with local authorities provided the action and, where possible, the violence to serve up to Americans at dinnertime with the evening news. If there wasn't enough action, camera crews and reporters could—and sometimes did—cgg on either or both sides, thus making news as well as recording it.

Black leaders, at the same time, began to recognize the tremendous power inherent in television. It was one thing to take a lonely nighttime bus ride through the rural South, knowing that an ill-tempered crowd was waiting at the destination, being whipped up by local agitators to beat or maim you. It was quite another to know that in that crowd there would be network camera crews waiting to beam that beating into tens of millions of American homes. It was the classic example of how the act of observation changes the character of the thing observed. Demonstrators and local officials alike became, in some strained way, actors on the television stage, and acted in ways subtly different than they might have were they not observed. It is absurd to speculate how the civil rights revolution might have fared had it not been for television; it would not have occurred at all.

At first, the timing and tactics with which civil rights activist leaders sent bodies into the breach, to be attacked by police dogs and fire hoses, were extremely naive. The immense reservoir of courage of Freedom Riders and sit-in demonstrators was nearly wasted as the early targets were selected in small, local, largely black communities. The goal of raising national consciousness could not be accomplished by local skirmishes. Where the results were violent, the larger society ignored it because no cameras were there; where there was no violence, the point was lost anyway. A kind of pastoral socialism may have prompted the selection of these early targets, but a cooler, more pragmatic, and modern media-oriented leadership soon emerged.

Those new leaders learned the twentieth century electronic lesson quickly. They learned that television has a high emotional content, that it can force clear-cut moral judgments, that—unlike newspapers—it is truly a national medium, that it is immediate and, above all, that it is available. It was as though simultaneously in states with civil rights struggles, reporters were asking, "When is your next demonstration?" And civil rights activists were answering, "When would you like to come?"

NBC correspondent Bill Monroe has written that a reporter once asked a demonstrator lying on the floor at a political convention how long he planned to lie there. The correspondent had only two or three minutes until air time, but he need not have worried, according to Monroe. "How long do you want me here?" was the reply. More than one reporter can recall being told (and reflecting that there was much truth in it), "The demonstrators would go away if you would." And sensing the truth in this, police and local toughs in many cities attacked the camera crews before they attacked the black demonstrators.

There were reports circulated—and some of them were undoubtedly true—that television reporters were openly soliciting violence or lawlessness in order to film it, but far more important was what happened systematically and "naturally." The cameras, the sudden bright lights, the giant trailed cables, the sound equipment and the network logos boldly splashed across most available space—all promoted excitement and the expectant feeling that certification was about to occur. A newspaper reporter, after all, can conceal his notebook and his pencil; the television reporter, in both the old and new senses of the words, "makes the scene." Such was the power of television that the Ku Klux Klan began inviting crews to its meetings and rallies. After all, the Klansmen must have been saying, why can't we get some publicity, too?

By 1963, in the last months of the Kennedy Administration, television almost totally dominated the progress of the civil rights movement:

—The August 1963, March on Washington for Jobs and Freedom, in which 250,000 Americans rallied in the capital and heard Martin Luther King tell them his dream, was almost a pure media event—had there been no media coverage, the goals would have been sought in a different way. King became a national "star" from that day until his death five years later. Nearly every American saw and heard that speech, either live or later on a news program.

—When Governor George Wallace of Alabama literally "stood at the schoolhouse door" to dramatize his opposition to federally ordered integration of the state university, he had already agreed to abide by the Justice Department's instructions to admit the black students. But in return he had elicited from Attorney General Robert F. Kennedy permission to stand in the doorway and take his stand—once, and only for television.

—In mid-1963, pressure from Washington finally broke the absolute color barrier on one of the television stations in Jackson, Mississippi, and a black man, NAACP leader Medgar Evers, was given one-half hour of time to present his position and that of his organization. Evers chose to present a plea for compassion: "If you suffered these deprivations, would you not be discontent?" He was murdered less than one month later. In his 1976 book, *The Good Guys, the Bad Guys and the First Amendment,* former CBS news executive Fred W. Friendly reports that "In a bar on the edge of Jackson, a white man was reported to have muttered, 'maybe this will slow the niggers down' . . ." And Friendly quotes the news director of the station that gave the time to Evers: "The community was inflamed. I never understood the Civil War until then . . . If we had put more blacks on the air, the hotheads from Rankin County would have bombed the station." Those hotheads, just like Medgar Evers, had understood the power of television.

—Subsequent marches and voter registration efforts, whether led by Martin Luther King or others, had their major impact not upon the angry white mobs or brutal police who reacted violently to the marchers, but upon television audiences in other parts of the country. When Sheriff Jim Clark's men charged the marchers at the Selma bridge, it may not have turned around much public opinion in Selma, but it galvanized people in Syracuse and Sacramento. And that, of course, was the purpose of the march.

—When President Lyndon B. Johnson took network prime time to denounce the murder of a civil rights worker and to pledge an effort to find the killers, those five minutes of presidential television time were, according to Mississippi editor Hodding Carter, "secondary only to the Emancipation Proclamation and the surrender at Appomattox" in the history of the South. Exaggerated, to be sure, but not by much. The surrender and the Proclamation were not instantly national events—the nation did not learn of either all at once. The news reached each place at a different time and, one imagines, in a different form.

—The Democratic National Convention in 1964, a dull renomination celebration for President Johnson, was enlivened by a dispute over the all-white delegation from Mississippi, challenged by an interracial group. The stories told at public (that is to say, televised) hearings by those challengers who had been beaten and jailed for trying to register to vote were harrowing. But without the national pressure these appearances engendered, it is doubtful if the Convention would have yielded to the compromise that gave the interracial group two delegates and permanently changed the rules, foreshadowing the racially balanced delegations of 1972 and 1976.

—In Birmingham, Alabama, in 1962, hundreds of arrests followed voter registration demonstrations in which police dogs attacked peaceful demonstrators and powerful fire hoses were used to sweep men, women, and small children off their feet and literally roll them down the streets. Television cameras caught the brutality and the late Eugene "Bull" Connor, the Public Safety Commissioner and for years a power in southern and national politics, instantly became a symbol of evil to most Americans. At first, the demonstrations were small, involving only a few hundred marchers in the street. But then television coverage aroused the support of the local black population—particularly young people —and the crowds soon numbered in the thousands. "The jails are full," Dr. King noted at one point, "what are they going to do with us?" The answer, of course, was more dogs and more fire hoses, and better publicity for the black cause among the millions—black and white—who watched the network news broadcasts each night.

—The Voting Rights Act of 1965, unquestionably the most important civil rights legislation and arguably the single most influential law in the one hundred years since the Civil War, was the result of this outpouring of violence on our television screens. When President Johnson spoke to Congress—using the words "We Shall Overcome," which audiences had heard at countless marches and rallies—the news programs intercut his speech with scenes of the brutality that had met peaceful attempts to register to vote.

During the following decade, a peaceful revolution transformed the political face of the Confederacy, as black registration increased enormously. In fact, President Jimmy Carter can credit his election in 1976 to the passage of the Voting Rights Act eleven years before; Carter carried the "Solid South" (except Virginia), but he did so with only 45 per cent of the white vote. Without the 1965 legislation, Gerald Ford would have been comfortably re-elected.

Even after the voting rights law was on the books, television continued to play a major role as the means of informing unregistered citizens about their new rights, reminding them of the blood that had been shed to secure those rights, and of their "obligation" to register and vote. NBC's Bill Monroe told of a black woman asked by a local television correspondent why she was registering to vote: "Well," she said, "I saw President Johnson on TV, and he said everyone should go and register to vote, so here I am."

By 1967, a curious thing had begun to happen. The Civil Rights Act of 1964 was law, as was the Voting Rights Act. The "act" of civil rights leaders like Roy Wilkins, Whitney Young, and Dr. King had become stale and could no longer be counted on for a big rating. Dr. King himself had turned to the question of Vietnam, an ambiguous cause at best for the television networks, who as government licensees, and as advertising medium for companies with defense contracts, had so much to gain by remaining supportive of the war.

So television turned, almost consciously, to fringe leaders who promised far more color and far more action. Thus it was that minor, peripheral figures such as Stokely Carmichael and H. Rap Brown, whose strength was in their knowlege of the stimuli to which television cameramen and correspondents would respond, became the image of "black leader" on the American screen. Martin Luther King, Jr., had ordinary citizens as a constituency, even before his television exposure; Carmichael and Brown had a small constituency among the people— their major constituency was television employees. These people, the new, made-by-television leaders, were clearly outside the network-determined boundaries of political and social acceptability. "Look at these crazies" was the message that came from the screen, and the premise didn't need to be stated—it was that a cause led by crazies need not be taken seriously. The same technique would later be used with anti-war movement "celebrities." (Abbie Hoffman and Jerry Rubin were engaging talk-show guests, but who could take them seriously as political leaders?) When Carmichael, particularly if exotically dressed, raised his fist and cried, "Black Power," it was far more of a television spectacle than when Roy Wilkins soberly analyzed the failure of the Federal Housing Administration to provide federal housing, or Whitney Young argued cogently that urban renewal had become little more than a device to move out lower class black slums—and the tenants—in order to make way for luxury high-rise condominiums for upper class and upper middle class whites. A new news "fix" was needed, and Carmichael, Brown, and black nationalism came into vogue. Separatism, previously scorned as the narrow, sectarian view of the Black Muslims alone, now became the cause whose advocacy could grab that precious evening minute—and if the advocacy was outrageous enough, perhaps an extra thirty seconds.

Then came the urban riots—Watts, Cleveland, Newark, Detroit. With them, Martin Luther King's dream became a nightmare. Television coverage was intense and technically skilled, but it also played a role in the riots themselves. Studies indicate that many looters and potential looters watched television for status reports, and then used what they saw to plan their strategy.

During the riots in Washington, D.C., which followed the assassination of Dr. King, public officials put famed soul singer James Brown on radio and television. "Go home," he urged, "look at television. Listen to the radio. Listen to some James Brown records." The officials using Brown were using the power of the media to try to get blacks to go home or to stay home to resist the temptation to enter or return to the combat zone. Other prominent blacks—prominent because of television, often—made similar pleas in other cities and other riots.

After the riots, the industry was full of compliments for itself. *Broadcasting* magazine, for instance, commended its subscribers and clients for their performance during the riots following Dr. King's death: "Television and radio emerged with new esteem last week from what may have been the stormiest ten days of news coverage in their history." There may well have been "new esteem" for television's performance during the riots, but any deserved esteem was for technical performance—moving smoothly and swiftly from scene to scene as stations and networks vied with each other in putting teams on the street to bring the action to viewers, live and in color. Certainly it deserved little credit for "keeping things cool."

Except technically, television failed miserably during the riots. To treat those events, as television did, merely as sensational, violent, but isolated stories, missed the point entirely. Where, for example, were the reports of courage and integrity, of blacks saving blacks and whites alike, of false arrests and police brutality? Those were occurrences as widespread and important as fires and looting—but they were absent from the screen, and from, therefore, the audience's knowledge. Above all, where was—and, for that matter, where had been and where were to be—any treatment of what life was like in an American ghetto? Why was there no discussion of what had prompted riots in some cities when other cities had no riots?

Television treatment of the riots met with other criticisms as well. "The TV media," wrote Theodore H. White as early as 1965, "capped their [riot coverage with] interviews as inflammatory and provocative as any ever heard in so delicate a situation." Among the instances cited by White: reports that police intended to use bazookas in Harlem and another that police had deliberately shot a black woman. White anticipated what was to happen to riot coverage for the rest of the 60s. "There's a report that one or two policemen are surrounded, so we're going over that way for a look," reported an excited KTLA reporter covering Watts in 1965. The report, as it turned out, was false, as were to be other accounts of fires, Communist plots, and armed whites charging into black neighborhoods. But through the certification process which television handles so well, these rumors became "facts," and part of the lore of each succeeding riot, for millions of viewers.

White's criticism of television depictions of the riots and of black life in America came from the other side of the argument as well. By limiting the coverage to the "action"—the looting, the screaming sirens and the bellicose black and white spokesmen—television was ignoring the desperate reality of some of the black experience. But White had another part of the black experience in mind when he spoke of what television ignores, and there is wisdom in his argument as well.

Anticipating, in a way, the objections to be voiced ten years later by black leaders seeking to halt a public television documentary on the horrors of life in Harlem, White noted in 1965 that

> the national audience has never been shown the neat [black] homes, the children playing in pleasant happy schoolyards. Television, reaching for a distorted dramatic effect, has ignored the triumphant achievements [of black communities] . . . Harlem, to an overwhelming degree, is composed of decent people living in decency, [but] TV gave its implied absolution to the rioters, further embittering the best of Harlem's Negro leadership and terrifying the whites already simmering and ready for counter-explosions of their own.

And the Kerner Commission added three years later,

> it would be a contribution of inestimable importance to race relations in the United States simply to treat ordinary news about Negroes as news about other groups is now treated . . . [The] press repeatedly, if unconsciously, reflects the biases, the paternalism, the indifference of white America.

It may not be that bad; it may be only that in treating any news about blacks as news of violence and confrontation, television is merely reflecting "the biases, the paternalism, the indifference" of a ratings-conscious industry, where cost-per-thousand to the advertiser is more important than the fabric of the society.

An analysis of the 1967 riots in Detroit by psychologist Benjamin D. Singer suggests that television played an even more important role in the riots—it may have helped to spread the *idea of rioting* from one city to another. Singer interviewed 499 black males, about 10 per cent of the total arrested during and after the Detroit riots. He concluded that "the broadcast media were the most important primary source by which information [about developing violence] entered the black community."

"It seems likely," Singer wrote, "that this affective aspect [past riots in other cities shown on television], along with routine "instructions" on how a riot is conducted *when it arrives,* contributed substantially to the riot readiness of a large number of individuals . . . [T]he data suggest that the population was already primed as a result of personal experience in the ghetto and televised prior riots and other media presentations."

Singer maintained that the relevant Kerner Commission statistics— "actual mob action, or people looting, sniping, setting fires, or being injured or killed" occupied less than 5 per cent of television's riot coverage during the seventy-two hours before and after a riot—are deceptively low and in any event grossly minimize their actual impact. Neary half of the interviewers reported they saw "violent acts against persons" on television. This indicates, says Singer, that there exists a vast difference between what television shows and what people perceive. This, in turn, coincides with the broader judgment of the Kerner Commission that

> the portrayal of violence . . . failed to reflect accurately its scale and character. The overall effect was, we believe, an exaggeration of both mood and event. We are deeply concerned that millions of other Americans, who must rely on the mass media, likewise (as did the Commission) formed incorrect impressions and judgments about what went on in many American cities last summer.

It would be one order of problem—and one capable of solution—if television had engaged in these distortions on purpose, either through racism or ignorance. But the cause was much deeper, locked into the structure of television news itself. If it is true, as former FCC member Nicholas Johnson has said, that "all television is educational television; the question is, what is the lesson?" then it is also true that all television is entertainment, including television news; the question is, what is entertaining? If the news programs on all networks were not vying for the flashiest mode and content, America's perception of events, of priorities, of choices—of itself—could be radically different than it is. People do want to know the news, and would tune it in even if it were thoughtful news, not competing for entertainment value.

With only one-half hour each day to "provide the news" *and* be entertaining enough to deliver a substantial audience to the advertiser, what is entertaining is violence and conflict. Because it operates within these rules, television unquestionably hastened and abetted the black revolution in its first years, and then, equally clearly, delayed and distorted it and, indeed, provided the images that led to the "white backlash," an epoch from which we have yet to emerge.

For through the time of the urban riots the message that flashed across the screen to white Americans was clear: Blacks are dangerous. Be worried. You may be next.

Subtle biases can govern the nature of coverage, and only the occasional dedicated and sensitive correspondent can be expected to overcome them. For example, the urban disorders of the 60s were treated, for the most part, as though they were crime stories or, perhaps, war stories, with the blacks portrayed as the "invaders" or the "aggressors." For the most part, this was true because newsmen and camera crews, for understandable reasons, entered into riot areas accompanying the police and National Guard. This led to a reporting of the story primarily from their official perspective.

Any analogy to the coverage of Vietnam (also entered only with the cooperation of the official armed authorities) breaks down quickly. Although journalists in Vietnam began with only one perspective—and served that one point of view to their audience for far too many years—in time they came to use that perspective against itself, and to note the hypocrisy and, eventually, the brutality, of the official policy. No such skeptical examination of official policy, or of newscasters' assumptions and presentation, accompanied the urban riots—nor has any yet emerged. It takes, apparently, several years during which a news story has continuing dramatic value, or entertainment value—a war can meet this criterion neatly, though not all wars do—before television begins to treat the story as one in which there is continuity, in which there may be substance for a more than superficial analysis. Television news, for all of the millions of feet of film it has available, has a notoriously bad memory. There is almost nothing comparable to the newspaper "morgue" in television journalism—no well catalogued, cross-referenced files available for quick reference and/or thorough study. If there were, it would be for prestige or decorative purposes, not use—because television news is instant news, it's what the camera sees that will, in the showing, catch and hold the audience's eyes. Yesterday barely exists on television; last week is an extraordinarily long time ago, and if recalled at all, dismissed as "past history." To be sure, television showed clips of action scenes in past riots during coverage of current riots—but only to provide some sensation when there was a lull in the current action.

The Kerner Commission touched on this problem, but did not face it squarely. Its report said:

> The media have thus far failed to report accurately on the causes and consequences of civil disorders and the underlying problems of race relations . . . The communications media, ironically, have failed to communicate.

Then, in an echo of the criticism and analysis of the nation's needs made by Robert Kennedy, the Commission added:

> The media have never reported, or really even glimpsed, what it is like in a racial ghetto and the reasons for unrest there. This may be understandable, but it is not excusable in any institution that has the mission to inform and educate the whole of society.

The end of that sentence is, of course, the trouble. Network executives do not consider that television has that mission—although they claim it, and claim First Amendment rights for television when it looks as though the public and the public's representatives might be about to claim some share of the public's rights.* Television's mission is far different, and the nation is better served the more we understand it. That mission—alas, its only mission—is to entertain large numbers of people so that sufficiently high rates can be charged to advertisers so as to push ever-higher the rate of return to the shareholders. That is not an ignoble mission; it is one that has led to much of America's strength and standing in the world. But it will continue to seem ignoble if we persist in assigning to television a higher one, and if television continues to assign itself a higher one.

Ironically, an attempt within the past two years to put on television precisely what the Kerner Commission said should have been shown— "what it is like in a racial ghetto and the reasons for unrest there"—met with deadly resistance from many black leaders.

In the fall of 1975, public television sought to air a Swedish-made ninety-minute documentary, *Harlem: Voices, Faces,* a brutal examination of life there. But bitter attacks and extreme pressure from the black community across the nation forced a postponement. The National Black Media Coalition called the program "Eighty-eight minutes of winos and junkies . . . unadulterated racism . . . offensive to the dignity and self-worth of the majority of black citizens throughout the

---

* See page 90 for discussion of public and broadcasters' rights.

United States . . . Blaxploitation [in] our own living rooms." While acknowledging that the program was factual, but not a factual picture of the black experience, *Black Journal's* Tony Brown began to arouse negative pressure among the black intelligentsia: "So many black people who need positive images so desperately to overcome the despair the film so ominously reveals, will be even more psychologically destitute."

The film's producers seemed surprised. It is, they said, "a film against oppression. [I]t can't be a rosy picture if you are out to tell about the evils in a black, inner-city ghetto, created by poverty and racism." The program was eventually broadcast, although notice had gone like a shock wave through the broadcast industry that the producers of any such future programs could expect to be called racists, or worse.

As the black movement changed, becoming more frustrated, in some ways more resigned and in some ways more militant, so did its leadership. Even before Martin Luther King's murder, television had been turning to peripheral figures—but eloquent ones—like Stokely Carmichael, Huey Newton, Eldridge Cleaver, and even truly exotic figures like Los Angeles' Ron Karenga and occasional spokesmen for Elijah Muhammed of the Black Muslims.

This metamorphosis in leadership was not purely a result of television's endlessly seeking new and more exciting celebrities with which to "hype" the evening audiences. Obviously, Carmichael and Cleaver struck some spark within the black community—others were trotted out and failed. But it is difficult to exaggerate television's role, almost always a self-fulfilling one: when a spokesman, the more colorfully dressed the better, was called a leader, he almost automatically, through the exposure, became one. As early as 1959, Mike Wallace of CBS presented Elijah Muhammed to television viewers. According to students of the Muslim movement, his following doubled within a month after he had been "discovered" by the mass media, and it continued to climb sharply thereafter.

By the end of the 60s, with the fervor of the civil rights movement spent and with the frightening memories of the urban riots still fresh, television—in offering these new, militant, rather frightening figures as "leaders"—was essentially giving white America what it wanted and believed to be true. Also, by helping to create new leadership that was ambiguous at best and demagogic at worst, television was serving its own interests as well: for television news suddenly found itself unable to "cover" the civil rights movement once it moved north.

The bad guys were no longer so clearly separable from the good guys; the demonstrations and the demands not only no longer provided such good visual effects, they were no longer easily definable or supportable. It was one thing to seek the right to register to vote in Selma, Alabama;

it was quite another to demand good housing in Cicero, Illinois, a larger share of the education budget in Chicago, "control" of neighborhood schools in New York, or membership in lily-white construction unions in Philadelphia.

It also became clear that the power and interests that control television and most of the rest of commerce no longer were so willing to align themselves with the black cause. It became harder to find out what that cause *was;* one thing was certain, a large element of it expressed the notion that blacks wanted very little to do with whites. Partly, this was a natural development—the black backlash, the frustration that society failed to change much in response to black pleas, and the wide admission to black consciousness of the humiliating position of blacks. Partly, this was a television-made development, what with the newscasts' need for new faces and new, dramatic, easily stated messages. It served the interests of the industry to present young, emotional firebrands as "black leaders." They were not only easy to film and understand, but the policies they seemed to advocate—violence, disruption, offenses to community manners—all made for good thirty-second and sixty-second film pieces to present on nightly news programs with no need for tedious, complicated explanations and analyses of real issues.

In retrospect, it is easy to see why the coverage of news about race was easy for television in the years in which it was hastening the black revolution. The unique character of this movement matched almost perfectly the unique needs of television news: visual action, preferably violent; drama defined by the clash of directly opposed forces; themes— such as voting rights—that were sectional but had a national impact; and problems that seemed to have simple (black and white, as it were) solutions.

But once the action moved into northern and western cities, television could no longer find racial stories so morally or technically easy to handle. To tell the horrors of life in state prisons; to analyze the rationale behind "affirmative action" programs; to expose the cosy arrangements among real estate, insurance, and banking interests that guaranteed discrimination in housing; to document the corruption among law enforcement officials that supports the continued trade in hard drugs in the ghettoes; to identify the complex factors behind high recidivism rates among unemployed black youth—these all take far more time than the thirty or sixty seconds available. The result is they are rarely covered, and blacks have become largely invisible once again on the news.

Whites, particularly so-called "ethnics," who were in many ways excluded, ignored and patronized as were blacks, saw what television had done. It had given blacks high visibility, which had quickly been translated into federal dollars. It put black faces on television commercials and made some of them the stars of what went on between commercials. It certified them. Ironically, whites were reaching this judgment just as the presumed benefits to blacks were diminishing.

"On racial issues," wrote *New York Times* editorial board member Roger Wilkins, himself a veteran of the struggle, "the press seemed to adopt Vermont Senator George Aiken's prescription for getting out of Vietnam: declare victory and withdraw."

After the riots, it was all downhill. Even liberal politicians fled the ground, and when television news made a major issue out of busing (either "forced" or "court-ordered," depending on where you stood), it turned out George Wallace had the middle ground.

Blacks were even de-certified in news stories about crime. Before the 60s began, a typical news story, either printed or broadcast, might have reported, "a twenty-five-year-old Negro male was being sought by police today after fleeing a bank robbery at Thirtieth and Elm." As consciousness rose and the racial issues became clear-cut, the same story would ordinarily exclude any racial reference in the description; in the 70s, the word "white" *entered* the description when appropriate; otherwise, the description was free of race. So the people came to know: "Unless they tell us differently, it was one of *them.*" We are still two Americas.

Of all the media, television is by far the most used by blacks. Black women who watch daytime television, for example, watch approximately 40 per cent more of it than do white women, and black children watch eleven hours more weekly than do white children. Forty per cent of all blacks average six and one-half viewing hours each day, and the average black family watches 16 per cent more television daily than the average white family. Race, in sum, is the best single statistical indicator of viewing habits.

The accuracy of all statistics regarding television viewing, though, are open to some question, and these, it must be said, more than most. Blacks in America are less likely to have the physical surroundings—telephone, familiar neighborhood appearance, or steady job—that are usually needed if one is to be included in a survey. In addition, serious differences may exist between black and white word usage (one survey, for instance, found no black audience at all for Westerns—an unlikely finding), and black subjects frequently distrust white interviewers or authoritative-looking black interviewers.

Nevertheless, even discounting for a probable amount of error, the figures point to a number of factors that would increase black viewing. These would include low levels and poor quality of education, a sense of isolation, feelings of self-deprecation and the absence of parents or other authority figures. The Kerner Commission reported:

Television is a particularly potent force in families where parental influence and family group ties are weak or completely lacking, most notably in low-income areas. In these instances, television does not displace parental influence, it fills a vacuum.

All of this is not particularly surprising—but a related and unexpected statistic has received remarkably little attention: perhaps the only significant gap between blacks and whites in America that is narrowing, rather than widening, is in television usage. Before the advent of mass television, blacks were known as "low media users"—that is, they were assumed to read newspapers and listen to the radio less than did whites. But by 1964, data from the Survey Research Center at the University of Michigan demonstrates, racial distinctions in the use of media for political information had disappeared, and television clearly made the difference. This held true even when education and income were held constant: among blacks with less than a high school education, "low media use" went from 71 per cent in 1952 to 49 per cent in 1964; "low media use" among whites with similar educational levels rose by 5 percent. During the same time period, 1952-1964, 22 per cent fewer of all blacks were "low media users"; of all whites, "low media users" went up by 12 per cent. While there is no reliable data available since 1964, collateral findings at least suggest that the trends are continuing, although obviously at less accelerated rates.

The studies also show that black adults, more than whites, trust that television tells them the truth, and that blacks are more likely to view television as realistic. Other studies establish that black children are more likely than are white children to believe what they see, both in television programs and television commercials.

What are black children learning? The data here are particularly weak, and seem to lead, often, in opposite directions, and almost any answer to that question will arouse substantial controversy. But it is at least arguable that the following "lessons" should be included in any comprehensive answer:

—They are learning to buy the products that are advertised.

—They are learning to want the products advertised whether or not they have the money to buy them.

—They are learning about the white world, and what it expects. The lessons are mixed. One study found, for example, that black children with a strong sense of black identity associated themselves more closely with the law-breakers on the police program *Dragnet* than did black children with weaker racial identity.

—They are learning about family life, in this case white family life. One of the few studies of black children's perceptions concludes, "[T]hrough TV they acquire the behavior perceived as appropriate for family members in the predominantly white middle class world . . . In this way, the television acts as a 'third parent.' " To which one might add—if not always in a way the other parents would understand or approve.

—They may be learning a kind of self-hatred. Many black spokesmen argue that white-dominated television makes young blacks want to change their skin color.

—They are learning notions about a proper black "appearance." Along with a few magazines and some movies, television defines the right appearance for a proper "dude." At different times dashikis or flashy bopping Shaft clothes, straightened hair or Afro, cocaine spoons, wide-brimmed hats, soul handshakes, and other apparent accoutrements of blackness are presented as appropriate. Obviously, not all of these style guides come from the home screen, but many do. Black athletes reach millions of black (and, for that matter, white) youngsters when they slap hands at mid-court or mid-field, and black (and white) show-biz types reach a similarly large audience when they wear ornaments around their necks that are instruments used for the consumption of illegal drugs.

Finally, television has raised and defined the expectations of young black Americans. Psychiatrists and psychologists are in general agreement that television-influenced expectations, along with those engendered by motion pictures, enter the inner world of childhood and adolescent fantasy. Television has also played a role, albeit an ambiguous one, in raising a sense of black pride.

Although it is difficult to follow both lines of influence, the fact is that television carries enough bits of information to enough different kinds of black people—particularly young people—so that it can engender pride in some and self-hate in others. For the most part, the former comes from so-called "black" programming; the latter from the rest, or "white" programs.

The evidence to support the argument that television has played a role in the rise in black pride comes from the new militancy and political assertiveness of younger, more public blacks, and is supported by a variety of imaginative research. In one study several years ago, black children ages three to seven were asked to comment on otherwise identical brown-skinned and white-skinned dolls: 59 per cent said the brown doll "looks bad," and similar results were obtained from studies through the early 60s. But in the early years of this decade, similar tests produced a 79 per cent "looks bad" response for the white dolls.

Obviously, it is difficult to assess the role of television in change of this type, although the extraordinary high viewing among black children at least supports the notion that it has had some effect. Ratings and studies of considerable depth consistently reveal the finding that blacks, children as well as adults, vastly prefer programs with black characters, no matter what the program content. Even children of an age and temperament to prefer "action" programming to rather static family drama will prefer a black family program to a white police story. Black children are more likely to adopt as role models the blacks they see on television than they are the whites.

Black faces on television also have an impact on whites, and it is a changing one. Very interesting studies show that whites with little real-life contact with blacks depend heavily on television for notions of what blacks are "really like," compared to whites who are in touch more in real life with blacks. This is a significant finding for television programmers and political opinion watchers, in light of the continuing trend toward separatism in private life. Television even ranks high as a source of information about blacks among urban white youths, who might be expected to have a high personal contact rate. A 1970 study reports that over 20 per cent of urban white children in the fourth and fifth grades learned "about how blacks looked, talked and dressed" from television. For suburban children, the figure was over 30 per cent, and for those in rural areas, over 66 per cent.

These figures support some interesting—and even ominous—data gathered during the 1972 presidential campaign. Patrick Caddell, who was then polling for Senator George McGovern, surveyed extensively in small towns and rural areas in Wisconsin, Oregon, and Nebraska before the primary elections in those states, in an attempt to discover what local issues people saw as important. Surprisingly, high on the list everywhere was "crime in the streets" as a local concern, although in fact there was hardly any crime at all in those communities and, for that matter, not very many streets. But network television had brought the crime issue to rural America in a frightening way, and in a way that made it seem "black" crime to many rural citizens.

The study cited above concluded that "TV exposure to blacks for white children contributed to identification with blacks and black-featured shows, *while personal exposure did not.*" The finding suggests the not-entirely-facetious suggestion that integrated classrooms may not be so desirable as integrated television programs.

This significant 1970 study also presented one other noteworthy finding, a not surprising one to modern parents of young children: in sharp contrast to young blacks, who favor black performers, young whites seemed to be increasingly "color blind." They chose a large number of black performers as their favorites. This stands in sharp contrast to four other studies, conducted between 1947 and 1970, which found that white children did not select blacks at all as people to emulate.

Further confirmation for this hopeful conclusion—that at least white children of the Television Generation are becoming "color-blind" about race—comes from two studies conducted by the research department of CBS in 1975. Even though CBS properly points out that "the statistics here reported cannot be legitimately generalized to *all* viewers," since the sample was not designed to reflect accurately the universe not tested, the studies have some significance. In the first one, 687 white children viewed a popular Saturday morning program, *The Globetrotters,* which presented the famous black basketball team of that name. The children were then asked, "What kind of people are they?" Only 22 per cent thought the performers' race was sufficiently important to warrant mentioning. In the other CBS study, over 700 white children were asked to state how they did or did not differ from the characters on *Fat Albert,* a cartoon program featuring black children; 71 per cent of the respondents did not mention race.*

BLACKS AND ADVERTISING

The following assertions are from studies of potential consumers:

> Black children respond uniquely to advertising directed to them as opposed to advertising directed to children in general. Thus, a market segment (black children) emerges which is possessed with substantial potential . . .

> The advertised wine was selected [by whites] 14 per cent of the time in the black model condition and 11.6 per cent of the time in the white model condition. This difference is not statistically significant. Thus, it appears that white consumers' behavioral response (product choice) to models of different races, is the same whether the product is bath soap or "pop" wine.

> "Shades of Black" are also important when considered with a homogeneous or "salt and pepper" approach. At one end of the spectrum is the "milk chocolate" or mulatto black (suggesting white blood and/or achieved middle class status), and at the other end is the "bittersweet," or "dark chocolate" model . . . We have found the "dark chocolate" to be more acceptable nationally than the "milk chocolate."

These three quotations are fairly typical selections from racial market research conducted within the industry. It has a long and not entirely honorable tradition. In 1931, the first national study of black consumers was financed by three major corporations—Anheuser Busch, Montgomery Ward, and Lever Brothers—and one year later there was an ar-

---

* Another "color blind" study is described on page 135.

ticle on the subject in the *Bulletin* of the Harvard Business School Alumni Association.

By the 40s, white consultants on the subject of the Negro market appeared; in 1943, advice to advertisers in *Sales Management* included: "Among other things, avoid minstrels, the name 'George,' watermelon, chicken, crap shooting, pork chops, gin, pickaninnies, Negroes as servants and exaggerated facial attributes." The advice seemed to fall on deaf ears.

By 1960, the cash income of blacks had reached $20 billion and market researchers were busy identifying the needs. "The Negro is determined," concluded one optimistic survey, "to enjoy the symbols of status whenever he can, whatever the price." Ads aimed at blacks stressed conspicuous consumption and immediate gratification, more or less as did the ads aimed at whites. Television sets, it should be noted, were considered luxury items; conservative Congressmen hardly let a day go by without complaining of the forest of aerials visible in the "welfare" sections of big cities. The Cadillac division of General Motors let it be known it was troubled by the number of its cars sold to blacks.

But by the mid-60s, things had changed. Very few sales pitches were directed straight at blacks, the "black market" ceased to be a separate and discreet target, and blacks began to appear, in "salt-and-pepper" combinations, on television commercials. A research report published in 1970 by the Marketing Science Institute explained that the salt-and-pepper "formula was adopted as a matter of social policy to give employment to Negro actors and models, and to reflect a social acceptance of the Negro in the white world."

Were that so, it would be the first time any policy was adopted by the television industry for benevolent motives; but it was not so. The reasons were quite different—briefly put, they were pressure and profitability. Advertisers and broadcasters found themselves threatened with adverse publicity and boycotts by black organizations and, more important to the advertisers, white allies of black organizations. In the nature of American politics, these allies were likely to be wealthy, liberal, and suburban—by any demographic study the kind of people who will spend money and who ought not to be offended.

Furthermore, market research had begun to present the nation's corporate leadership with information even more important than protests and threats of protest. The researchers reported that whites would no longer consciously avoid products seen to be used by blacks in advertisements. While whites might not be stimulated to buy by the use of black models and actors, the evidence seemed to indicate they had at least reached a point of indifference.

"Perhaps the greatest challenge for marketing managers in reaching the Negro market in the 1970s," ran a typical marketing report, "is to continue to do a profitable business while simultaneously pursuing a constructive social policy." That, of course, is not just a challenge to those who wish to "reach the Negro market," it is the central dilemma of American capitalism. The statistics that reveal 90 per cent of all cancers are environmentally caused, suggest that the dilemma—to earn a profit while pursuing a constructive social policy—is as yet unresolved.

Much of this research was done in the South, on the theory, apparently, that racial prejudice was higher there, and that if Southerners will accept black faces and bodies in advertising, everyone will. If a white who is a small businessman from the Mississippi delta, will buy a deodorant he has seen used by blacks, the thinking seemed to be, then a white anywhere in the United States will buy it, too.

Market research also developed another trend—blacks will buy black. As recently as 1964, serious analysis demonstrated that black women preferred brassieres modeled by a white woman. But by 1970, a study concluded that while this preference for white models might "exist, the evidence to support it is not available." And two market research reports announced in 1975 that "there have been no reported studies of negative reactions by black consumers toward black models in commercials."

Once these truths were accepted, it was easier to see another and more relevant one—blacks have a lot of money to spend. By 1964, *Advertising Age* headlined an article:

> Negro Market Will be Controlling Factor in Profit
> Margins of Big U.S. Companies in Fifteen Years.

The article may have involved a slight overstatement, but blacks do now spend some $40 billion per year, a figure that may not be the difference between profit and loss for many companies, but can hardly be ignored by any national advertiser.

Finally, there slowly dawned the realization of a demographic fact of merchandising life, which ought to have struck the marketers many years before: ever since World War Two, blacks had moved in a steady migration from the rural South to northern urban centers, and had become a substantial portion of those media markets. Advertisers buying time in New York, Philadelphia, Detroit, or Chicago were reaching a significant percentage of black viewers whether they did anything about it or not. And that black audience, as the ratings began to demonstrate, not only watched television but watched it more than whites did. So blacks moved into commercials, playing essentially "white" roles but visible nevertheless.

By now, the number of commercials using blacks has increased to over 15 per cent, although the figures vary according to the regional market tested. And even these percentages are somewhat misleading and exaggerated because the percentage of blacks in "public service" commercials ("Buy Savings Bonds Where You Work") is higher than in those that seek to sell a product. But even so discounted, the emerging black commercial presence, according to *New York Times* television critic John O'Connor, is a "revolution [that] has been quiet but immensely significant."

The business of advertising could take a benign view even of the more militant separatist movements. Consider this summary of literature, published by the Marketing Science Institute:

> Many values of the Black Muslim movement are very close to those values ordinarily associated with the Protestant Ethic. Among these are the personal virtues of honesty, effort, and achievement. The purpose of the Black Power movement is to give Negroes a better chance to get the things they want, which in respect to goods and services are by and large the things that whites want.

And conservative Senator Daniel P. Moynihan, the author of some controversial works in the field, once said that "blacks in America want the same things as other Southern Baptists—a good job and a color television set." The period of the past ten years has been one of business' increasing adherence to this kind of thinking. At first astonished that black audiences could be measured—and that those measurements showed they were making selective judgments about programs originally projected for mass audiences—business quickly adjusted, and advertisers may now take advantage of special rating techniques. Thus, those manufacturers and advertising agencies with special interest—or special disinterest—in black audiences can tailor their commercial placements, and the population of the commercial drama itself. The bottom line, in this case, has led to progress. Unquestionably, there are substantial positive aspects. To the extent that commercials influence our behavior and attitudes—and billions of dollars are spent in reliance on the belief that they do just that—it is positive for the reason that it lets whites see that blacks exist, and in familiar surroundings. This is, as previously noted, especially effective in creating "color-blindness" in white children.

There are long-range problems to be watched, however, no matter how welcome the appearance of blacks in the commercial mainstream of television might seem. For example, blacks are far more likely than whites to appear as secondary figures in commercial "groups," and far less likely to appear alone. And advertisers have continued to exercise extreme care in presenting blacks in roles that are politically and socially "safe," particularly where sex is concerned.

Thus, Harry Belafonte and Petula Clark could probably touch hands—perhaps even hug—at the end of a variety program, but their counterparts could not appear on the Geritol—"she's my wife, and I love her because she takes care of herself"—commercial. One toothpaste advertisement shows a white male interviewer—almost all interviewers on commercials are white males—kiss a female consumer who, in an apparently "unrehearsed" sequence, says she uses the sponsor's product. The same, or a similar, sequence is used with different casts of characters: by a curious coincidence, the interviewer is black when—and only when—the woman is black, too.

On a commercial for a sturdy cigarette lighter—the Bic—a series was developed with highly sexual overtones, in which members of both sexes offered one of the opposite sex "a flick of my Bic." But the black stewardess offered a flick of *her* Bic only to a black passenger.

ROOTS

In January 1977, ABC pre-empted some of its prime time for eight consecutive evenings to play a special program, *Roots*. The drama was an adaptation of a book by Alex Haley, an American black. Haley had spent twelve years searching out his family history, which had included four generations of slaves. The book—and the television series—told that family history, with generous fictional additions which were, however, historically "accurate." That is to say, all the events portrayed in *Roots* could have happened to this family, and certainly happened to some families.

Roots came with substantial advance publicity, much of which stressed the first and second episodes: shocking portrayals of the horrors and brutality of the slave trade in the infamous Middle Passage. The other networks, fearing the worst, juggled their schedules so as to "counter-program" the ABC drama with weak opposition. Sometimes a network, sensing a strong entry at a particular time slot and anxious to preserve its own rating for that time as well as the "adjacencies"—the time periods before and after the hour in question—will counter-program with a strong selection; in the case of *Roots* both rival networks chose the opposite course, and left the field to ABC, probably assuming that after one episode, viewers would turn in droves to NBC and CBS rather than watch the rest of the *Roots* series.

The results were disastrous for NBC and CBS. On the first night, a Sunday, *Roots* was watched by nearly one-half of all the households in which a television set was in use. That only whetted the appetite for more, and of the seven remaining episodes, six emerged as the most-watched television programs in the quarter-century history of the medium. The other two episodes put all *Roots* episodes in the top eleven of all time.

It was a stunning ratings performance, in which more people watched each night than the night before. It was surely a new format for television—it immediately generated plans for "eight-parters" in the future, it started executives to wondering if the pattern of one program per series per week had been made obsolete, and it made a national figure of Alex Haley.

In addition, while the program was running, it seemed to stimulate some interracial violence—mostly in schoolyards—but not much. There were reports that it had vastly stimulated black pride, and it surely must have helped along some white guilt. What was it, exactly, that people had seen?

Roots told, in human terms, the story of slavery in America, a story surely known to almost every American, in its outlines at least, but never before seen in the living room. The picture was one-dimensional—there were no good whites at all until the final episode, when a poor white from Tennessee befriended the black family. But then, slavery was largely one-dimensional, at least on the plantations where *Roots* was laid.

It is surprising—perhaps it reflects the guilt many feel about slavery and the development of the races in this country—that there was no outcry at all about the savage violence present in almost every episode of *Roots*. Brutal, elaborately staged whippings took place in virtually every night's presentation, there were frequent rapes and references to rape, as well as other brutality. In one vivid early episode, the hero's foot was chopped off—the camera veered away to the victim's face just as the axe was descending—only, as the scene made clear, as an alternative to castration.

Roots, in this respect, was simply a better-made production of *Mandingo,* the first in a series of cheap movies that exploited the horrors of slavery, and the one which so "inspired" the youths in Chicago quoted earlier (page 40). The violence, of course, was all administered by whites against blacks—the reverse is unthinkable on television—and there seems little question that the repeated brutality was a major factor in building the ratings. *Roots* did make whites more aware, undoubtedly, of the historical burden blacks must live with; but its impact in this was overshadowed, it seems, by the titillation provided by its violence and its violent sex scenes. There also seems little question that, if *Roots* had been an ordinary historic melodrama and not concerned with our national shame of slavery, ABC would have been the recipient of an avalanche of protest from the PTA and every other group that monitors television violence. Until *Roots,* television always demurely kept its floggings and mutilations off-camera.

In the end, the presentation of *Roots* seems more important as an event in the history of television than in the history of the races in America. It will inspire other short-term series, it will undoubtedly spawn some imitators—*Roots II* is already on the drawing boards—for whatever else it demonstrated, it left the message that a lot of stars and a lot of violence in a well-made production will produce and hold an enormous audience. It is hard to believe that any other message will remain.

A WORD ABOUT RACE
AND CRIME PROGRAMS

One early evening in 1967, Robert Kennedy sat in his Senate office with a few aides and began to talk quietly about what he would do about the nation's racial crisis if he were President. The Detroit riots were hardly cool, and President Johnson had made it plain that the government and the Congress would not support anything more than the appointment of a high-level commission (it turned out to be the Kerner Commission), and that signaled to Kennedy that nothing serious would be done.

RFK said he would call in, in small groups, the real leaders of every major urban community. He talked about mayors and district attorneys, chairmen of chambers of commerce, but he also talked about neighborhood leaders, popular policemen, students, unofficial black spokesmen, business, church, labor—the whole fabric of trust in terms of local community responsiveness, the kinds of people originally sought to be reached by the community action segment of the War on Poverty.

He would say to them, he said, "It's your problem." As President he would discuss the resources that were available and not available, but he would impress upon the local people, he said, the need for local solutions and proposals—which could then be assisted by presidential leadership and congressional action.

Kennedy began to talk, then, softly, about what it meant to be black in the American city. He talked of the education programs on which billions of dollars have been spent in "enrichment," and how inner-city schools were worse than when the programs began. He talked of students *losing* points on their IQs between the fifth and eighth grades. He talked about the principal at a New York high school who had told him that he would continue to give diplomas to functionally illiterate students, as long as the telephone company and Sears insisted upon a high school diploma for a starting job. He talked about what it was like to raise small children in rat-infested apartments, he talked about the deterioration of housing in the inner city after years of federally sponsored housing programs. He talked about unemployment, which was then— as now—approaching and holding at 40 per cent among precisely that group of young men and women to whom a job was crucial to the beginning of a family and the acquisition of some stake in society. He talked about the job programs and the training programs that prepared people for jobs that no longer existed. He talked about "minority hiring programs" that resulted in "minority firings programs" when the slightest seismic tremor hit the local economy.

Above all, he talked about the loss of hope and of a life of permanent despair, disaffection, alienation, and hostility. He talked about the preachments of "Stay in school" and "Make something of yourself." And he talked about the view of life that a young teenage black must have whose older brother had heeded those admonitions, stayed in school and out of trouble, and now was unemployed with not much hope of ever being employed at anything that could realistically be called a job.

A second approach, he continued, would be to call in the chief executives of each of the television networks, either alone or together, and perhaps accompanied by the major film-making talent at their disposal. He would urge them—a smile crossed his face as he thought of the "ruthlessness" of the proposal—to show on national television, in prime time, with all the enormous skill at their disposal, just what ghetto life was like. It couldn't be done in a few hours, he thought, but it might be done in a year, or perhaps less, of constant, skilled, prime-time exposure. "We're never going to do anything," he said, "unless people in the country understand what that life is like." It was clear, at least in his mind, that the way people would "learn about that life" was to see it night after night after night on television.

Robert Kennedy never lived to put any of those proposals into practice, and there is no way to know what might have happened if he had. But that was (and remains) surely one way to demonstrate the black urban experience to America—through television. It is hard to believe that it had not occurred to many people in high positions of authority in the television industry. But the industry collectively chose instead to "stay out of trouble"; it created a system of crime to be displayed in prime time every night—not for one year, but for several—from which urban blacks had been almost totally removed. It was as though the ancient slogan had been reversed and had become: "If you won't join 'em, beat 'em."

Crime on television is directed almost entirely at white, middle class, white-collar victims. Their securities are stolen, their jewelry is heisted, sometimes they are killed in obscure plots having to do with inheritance or control of the business, or they kill in order to better their personal social life. The criminals are also almost always white.

But that is not crime in America. Street crime, which is the crime people fear, and on which fear public policy is often based, is a vastly different matter.

The victims of crime are far more likely to be black than white, and the most played upon age group is the young. But even a black physician, for example, living and practicing in the newer suburbs, is more likely to have his car stolen than is his white colleague or neighbor. And in real life, more than half of the people arrested in America for murder and robbery are black as well, as are 45 per cent of those arrested for rape, and 30 per cent of those charged with burglary and larceny. This presents an enormous problem, and can be dealt with in two ways. First, television crime could reflect real crime, in which case roughly half of the nightly television criminals would be seen as members of some sort of black urban underworld, preying on, largely, black victims, without further comment. This could be defended, however improperly, and one can imagine it being defended, on the grounds that "it reflects reality." Second, the networks could use the incidence of black crime to begin to get to the consciousness of America in the way in which Robert Kennedy suggested—by some treatment, *any treatment,* of the reality of black experience in urban America. Even today, when it has become part of a pervasive conservative social chic to blame crime solely on the criminal, and to ignore with a light, scoffing tone fifty years of criminology (sometimes, to be sure, soft-headed and inaccurate) that tells us surely and clearly that the environment of the criminal is a strong and determining element in his behavior. Such a treatment, for example, would talk about the unemployment rate among black teenagers in our cities—which goes up when the economy is bad, and *continues* to go up when the economy is stable. It could talk of the legacy of slavery, it could talk of generations of casual dismissal of blacks to inferior schools, loathsome housing, and a passive ignorance among whites of the consequences of both.

It could talk of the terrible lives and the early deaths that the urban drug traffic represents. It could talk of the psychological connection between the black experience and the need to escape through drugs. There is not a police officer in the country who does not know that drugs are involved in the tremendous majority of the burglaries, killings, assaults, hold-ups, car thefts, bank robberies and forged checks that involve the acquisition of quick money. There are also very few police officers who do not know what an overwhelming, enormous profit comes from the drug traffic. If it is true, as has been conservatively estimated, that there are 250,000 heroin addicts in America (most authorities think this number is low), and if each addict requires something on the order of $50 a day (probably also a conservative figure), then we are talking about receipts of (again conservatively) something between $4 *and* $5 *billion each year* from this one drug alone in the United States. That money, with some slippage for independent entrepreneurs, flows mainly to organized crime. It provides an enormous pool of cash with which to bribe and otherwise compromise public officials in order that the traffic may continue.

This approach would be complicated, serious, and unquestionably unpopular. It is hard to believe that sponsors could be found for programs on which the authorities would deal with black criminals and then try to explain graphically, visually and with all the talent that Hollywood has available, why this is so. It would be difficult to present the fact that black criminals are as unrepresentative of their race as are white criminals—it is easiest to think simple thoughts, and easier for an audience to condemn a race than to examine the complicated problems of our society. The disciplines of history, sociology, anthropology, psychology, and a host of recent urban studies would have to be dramatized before the full impact of what we are doing in our cities could come clear. So it is not done.

The third way to deal with the problem is the way the networks are "dealing with it"—ignore the black once again, this time at the moment not of *his* greatest need for understanding, but of *ours*. Treat crime as essentially suburban, white collar, and middle class, overload prime-time police forces with black officers, and hope that no one will notice—more precisely, that no will want to notice.

Television's "niceness" in this respect is not confined to blacks. Organized crime is a favorite subject of television programming, usually in the context of a policeman who does not want to arrest "the small fry" because he hopes they will lead him to "Mister Big." It is well known that many members and particularly leaders of organized crime have Italian names (save for that statistically significant slice who are Jewish). But on those television shows that portray organized crime, nobody has an Italian name except the occasional policeman. Here again, the complicated historic and social circumstances that create a major problem in America are ignored in favor of a kind of "inoffensiveness" which is of course, in reality, a good deal more offensive than the truth, just as ignoring the role of the black in urban America is a more offensive form of racism than treating it honestly. Real treatment of organized crime would, of necessity, involve a depiction of its links to organized labor—particularly the Teamsters Union—as well as the complicity of segments of American business in the use of pension and welfare funds by the Mafia.

But these are things many Americans know, and when they see organized crime *capos* with names like Smith and Jones, or when they see big city police forces dealing intensively with white collar crime, viewers sense the disparity—and the alienation from institutions is heightened. No studies exist on the subject—but it is highly likely that exacerbated racial feelings on the part of enormous numbers of Americans are caused by the clear inability and unwillingness of television to face the facts in everyone's experience.

The racial crisis in America's cities is real and it is in large part a media crisis. Newspapers and magazines give us the facts of real crime—with pictures and accounts of blacks prominently featured. Television gives us a totally unreal, almost lily-white crime world, except for the police. But neither gives us the true facts, or the explanations that might lead us to peace.

5 SEX ROLES: CO-OPTED LIBERATION

History—and life—have been as much the result of the interaction of specific groups in the population as of the impact on everyone of outside influences. During the time of television—roughly the postwar years since 1950—American lives have been affected in a major way by the emergence of two new groups, blacks and women, as powerful and discrete social and political forces that have significantly changed American norms and American power relationships.

For a quarter century television has been at the center of our consciousness in these struggles, whether on the road from Montgomery to Selma or in a legislative hall where the Equal Rights Amendment is being debated. Change, almost by definition, has come with drama and speed in the Age of Television, once the decision has been made behind the camera that a particular change is on the national agenda.

In Washington journalist Sally Quinn's book about her short, unhappy life in television newscasting, *We're Going to Make You a Star*, she quotes novelist Gore Vidal: "There are two things one always does, my dear, when one has the chance—sex and television."

The two have gone together more and more—and not just as chic imperatives. Twenty years ago the television camera, even in the most "modern" situation comedies, never entered the bedroom. Nor did the characters talk about what went on there. Ten years ago, if the mother and father in *The Brady Bunch* were ever in bed, they were either reading on opposite sides, or there were enough blankets bunched up between them to make the shot "harmless" to the viewer.

Today, there is hardly a "family" program without some leering reference to sex. On the evening news, we have come from a tolerant smile by Walter Cronkite after a fierce women's liberation meeting at which childbearing is denounced—all the way to Howard K. Smith's endorsement of the ERA. In the entertainment sector, sex has replaced violence in the Family Hour time slot.

The original impetus behind Family Hour—at least as it was handed down from the Congress, to the FCC, to the networks, to the NAB, to the producers—was to reduce the amount of both violence *and* sex on television, specifically in those hours when children would be most likely to be watching. By the time Family Hour got to the television screen, after all the strategy sessions, the television audience, child and adult, has got more sex and less violence, rather than something else instead of both.

Thirty years ago, in an extraordinarily perceptive pamphlet, "Love and Death," Gerson Legman analyzed contemporary American fiction and concluded that violence, specifically physical violence by men against women (and only occasionally vice versa), was the dominant theme in our popular culture, to the almost complete exclusion of love—particularly physical love. Legman thought that the Puritan tradition had so enforced a standard of prudery on our literature as to create two kinds of fiction—the popular, in which violence was always a satisfactory substitute for adult love, and the classic "great" American novels, which treated of love of a person, to be sure, but almost always of one man for another.

This same theme (with scant credit to Legman, by the way, whose title was subsumed and mention of whom was confined to a footnote) was considerably expanded by Leslie Fiedler in *Love and Death in the American Novel,* published in 1960. The point was the same: there are no American novels worth mentioning that treat of love between mature men and women, and our popular culture is full of violence and devoid of sex.

Modern television has changed popular culture: it is immensely popular—admittedly with no claim to "greatness" in fiction or drama—and it is full of sex (adult love is still largely absent). The fictional figures with whom Americans identify or whose adventures, at least, they follow and discuss, are almost always involved in some "sexy" problem. Mary Tyler Moore's Mary Richards is on the pill and often fending off suitors who would like to spend the night. Rhoda is on the town, and her mother wonders whether to have an affair with her doctor; Phyllis wonders about an unsatisfactory relationship and discovers the man is gay; and the girls on *Charlie's Angels* don't seem ever to have anything else on their minds but sex, with or without their mysterious employer. Maude has an abortion, Archie Bunker's daughter thinks about having one, Maude's husband seems to be having an extra-marital affair and so, once, did Archie himself. The new maturity is not without a little kinkiness, too: Archie gives mouth-to-mouth resuscitation to a woman who turns out to be a female impersonator, and the continuing sub-plot of *M*A*S*H* seemed to involve a sado-masochistic relationship between a bumbling doctor and the chief nurse. A successful comic detective program, *Barney Miller,* often seems determined to come close to the Gay Media Task Force's quota of "one gay bank robber, one gay cop."

The Family Hour device—whether or not ultimately allowed to remain as a formal television requirement—sets aside some time in the evening relatively free of overt physical violence and fills that time with some "advanced" talk about sex. That may constitute an advance toward some kind of liberation. It must also be said, though, that the advertising that surrounds all this advanced talk is remarkably retrograde.

In between the commercials, the women come and go, talking of abortion, affairs, and homosexuality, but during the commercials nothing has changed. There the talk is of "ring around the collar," "shouting out" ugly greasy stains, and of which "bathroom tissue"—by test!—is softer and thus a better family buy. The women on television commercials have hardly changed from that clinging, insecure American woman of the forties, to whom Philip Wylie once said all advertising is directed with but a single message: "Madam, are you a good lay?"

The women's movement is by no means a monolithic grouping, either in political and social objectives or even in agreement on the interpretation of available data on women's roles in America. One thing, though, on which there is general agreement—not only within the movement but among its opponents and neutral observers—is that we form our notions of appropriate sex roles early in life, and that the image of those roles given to young boys and girls do more than anything else to determine the roles they will play in adulthood.

On the very day that the Equal Rights Amendment, in a highly publicized vote, was failing of passage in North Carolina (which was a major story on the evening news on all three networks), the results of a study among four-year-old children were announced to virtually no publicity at all. The study was a simple one: children were shown a short film, about a child's visit to a doctor's office to receive an apparently painless inoculation. In this film, however, traditional roles were reversed: the doctor was a woman and the nurse a man—otherwise, everything was familiar. The nurse greeted the child and prepared the injection, while reassuring the child that it would not hurt. Then the doctor entered, examined the hypodermic needle, and administered the "shot." After the nurse had rubbed the child's arm with alcohol on a cotton pad, the child skipped out of the office. But when the children were questioned about the short drama, and specifically, of course, about the identities of the man and woman, within a very few minutes *all* the children agreed that what they had seen was a child in a male doctor's office with a female nurse, Dr. Bob and Nurse Nancy.

Now it cannot be said, of course, that television is responsible for all this. Generations of rigid sex roles are difficult to reverse. Dick and Jane have taught more, earlier and quicker, to children, than have the best anthropology texts. Indeed, the earliest targets of the women's movement in the past decade were precisely those children's books that seemed, in the words of the movement's leaders, to "reinforce role stereotypes."

The book series that made Dick an active game-player, racing around the yard with Spot, while Jane watched Dick run or held her dolls or "helped" her cake-baking mother; showed a grown-up Dick's ambitions fulfilled as a doctor, a pilot, or a father coming home from work with his briefcase, while Jane fantasized herself as a nurse, a stewardess, or a bride—these were early subjects of women's protests. The books supposedly helped the child learn to read by showing printed words about a familiar situation—in spite of considerable evidence that nearly half those adorable cake-baking mothers spent their days on the job, working. These books reflected, rather than molded, the culture—or so the theory went.

Television has an impact beyond that of books, though, and even the theory that commercials just reflect how it is in life does not hold. Television can change those patterns of role perception, and it can change them in one generation. Children between the ages of five and twenty watch, on the average, twenty thousand hours of television—and what they see will greatly affect what they believe about life, particularly if what they see is as lifelike as the finest dramatic and technical talents of the age can make it.*

* With an increase in contemporary settings for television shows, instead of scenes from another time or an unfamiliar place, children's identification with the values on a program will increase. The depiction of violence, for instance, in what is clearly a fantasy, such as in a fairy tale or by characters in identifiable historic costumes, is much more of a curiosity and much less a signal of behavior to those with weak inhibiting systems, than is violence in a readily recognizable, everyday, contemporary context. We don't know how ineffective as behavior-models cartoons and fantasy shows are, though—and they would need to be zero-effective, perhaps, to leave a healthy impression in the face of the following figures:

—In June, 1975, the Media Action Research Center, a research organization funded by church groups and foundations, studied children's Saturday morning programming and reported that there was one act of violence "every three and a half minutes of actual program time on the commercial networks."

—One 1972 study of Saturday morning children's programming found that 30 per cent of the shows were "saturated" with violence, and that another 58 per cent contained one or more violent acts. An extraordinary 88 per cent of children's programs in 1972 contained violence—at exactly a time when the networks were claiming that great strides against violence in children's programming had been made.

—In 1973 an unpublished study found that on San Francisco television screens, children's cartoon programs contained an average of one violent deed per minute (and worse, almost 8 per cent of all violence was rewarded).

Syndicated columnist Jack Anderson quoted a spokesman for the National Association of Broadcasters as saying that the Media Action figures were "unimportant" because

Although we have seen that whatever progress has been made in terms of children's (and other viewers') perception of race as a result of saturation television viewing is somewhat ambiguous, this point of *changed* perception of roles is easily demonstrated with respect to race. Research has documented fairly conclusively that after repeated exposure to the racially integrated world of television, children in fact do become "color-blind." *

While the research does not focus on reasons for this trend—and countless parents can recite incidents in which a child will talk about and describe a favorite teacher or playmate, totally ignoring race as a descriptive factor—it would seem a good hypothesis that it is the integration on television of sports and commercials that accounts for it, since the same degree of awareness has as yet not reached actual programming. As we know, entertainment programs are less likely than in an earlier generation to show black performers in only menial or comic roles, but not *much* less likely, and the difference between the highly praised *Sanford and Son* and the much-condemned *Amos and Andy* is almost impossible to discern. But sports and commercials are more integrated racially on television than the rest of life is, one honestly and the other less so.

Sports programming on television is rather honest to the extent that it is simply a video presentation of a sports event that would happen—as most of the sports events would happen—whether or not the cameras were there to cover it. Black players constitute a substantial proportion of the total in football, basketball and baseball (hockey, for a variety of reasons, is something else again); therefore children who watch these events in their living rooms understand quickly the irrelevance of skin color to performance, and to acceptance by the team, the audience, and—by extension—the larger society.

When it comes to commercials, however, the influence on perception of race is easier to see, and, it must be said, less honest. When television advertisers became aware in the 1960s that there was a substantial untapped market of black people with money to spend for the products they sold, they had a problem to solve. Should they make "black" commercials for the "black" market, and "white ads" for everyone else, or should they integrate the same old commercials—for everyone? They chose the latter course, probably because it made very little sense financially to do anything else.

The result is an astonishing picture of our society. The America of

children can tell the difference between cartoon characters and real human beings. But the NAB spokesman did not question the statistics' validity and made no apology, nor did he urge members or advertisers to get rid of children's cartoon *commercials* as, by the same logic, clearly ineffective in inspiring imitation.

* See page 120 for the description of other studies with similar results.

television commercials makes it seem as if we have accomplished, in scarcely ten years, the reification of Martin Luther King's dream, "black and white together."

In this America, a Little League team will include two or three black players, even a girl or two, plainly a false picture. Gather a collection of youngsters at the beach for a late swim and an evening wiener roast and, wonder of wonders, a few of the teenage boys and girls in the spontaneous, happy group will be black, a scene unduplicated at any beach in America. If three housewives gather around the laundromat to compare starches and brighteners—one of them will be black. And when, in the country club locker room, four members emerge from behind their lockers to sing about their after-shave lotion, one member of the clean-shaven, grinning quartet will be black.

This is all contrary to the America of the 70s, which is in many ways as rigidly segregated—at voluntary, personal social activities, as opposed to public and commercial activities, where there has been great progress—as it was fifty years ago. That is fact, but it is not apparent to the young. The child sees the "reality" of life on the screen—there are the mommies talking about laundry, there are the daddies playing golf—and draws one logical conclusion: people come in all colors, and they are found everywhere in roughly the same proportions. It may be a dishonest presentation, done through the basest of financial motives, but that result is undeniably a healthy one.

It might be asked then: if the industry, out of pecuniary motives, can alter reality and produce a beneficial result where race is involved, then why not do so out of humanistic motives where the role of women is at stake? The question must become an insistent one, because it is clear, from an examination of the role of women (black or white) on television commercials, that we have never moved from Dick and Jane. In between commercials, Mary Tyler Moore may be producing a news program and Bea Arthur (Maude) be running for state office, but when the fadeout comes and it's time to sell things, the women are worried about ring around the collar, just as before.

There is agreement that this depiction of roles does harm to children from such a non-feminist source as the National Advertising Review Board. Commenting on a 1975 survey of women in commercials, panel member Robert L. Ficks, Vice-President for Advertising of the Ethan Allen Furniture Co., said that "sometimes in women-related advertising, [the] image is negative and deprecatory. Unfortunately, such images may be accepted as true-to-life by many men, women, and children, especially when they reinforce stereotypes of a time gone by." Ficks suggests that advertisers should ask themselves, "are the attitudes and behavior of the women in my ads suitable models for my own daughter to copy?" That is a strong departure for a man whose business responsibility is for the mass marketing of highly traditional furniture for the middle-class American home.

With precious few exceptions, what television commercials are saying about American women is: women are homemakers, are fashion plates, are sex objects. Women are naturally subservient, simple-minded, and concerned to the point of single-mindedness that their colors be more colorful and their whites whiter than anyone else's. In less than one per cent of their commercial appearances are women independent of their traditional chores. In one oven-cleaner advertisement, a woman is seen and heard telling us that with the new product, she is free from drudgery and can spend more time "on my own life." And her own life turns out to be—doing more things for her husband and her children.

These commercials do not appeal, of course, to the woman's potentialities, talents, or leisure-time play, as does most of the advertising directed to or employing men, but to fears, guilts, and insecurities. The discovery, identification, and exploitation of these guilts and insecurities has been refined to a high art indeed. There are commercials that show us that women are not very bright. A popular typewriter, for example, gave us a strong message that it could be used successfully by all secretaries—no matter how small their brains or how large their breasts. Women as professionals, or as self-dependent individuals in control of their own lives, are almost totally absent in television commercials; and when a professional woman is shown, she is likely to be a strikingly attractive news interviewer with a wristwatch for each personality—for the exciting job, the exciting cycle ride, or the romantic date. It is clear where the priorities are.

Furthermore, television commercials never hesitate to put men and women in their place—and the place for women is with their men and their children. "He touched me, and suddenly nothing is the same"; "My wife—she cares for herself, and I love her for it"; "If he's comfortable, I'm happy." There are even the "equal rights" ads, in which men and women seem to be doing the laundry together. "Better for him," says the wife, "and better for me"—meaning that this miracle suds gives him a clean shirt in which to work, and saves her time on wash day.

Perhaps the most graphic demonstration of the sex roles assigned by television is that almost all of the sick adults receiving attention are men, and almost all of those providing the care are women. And the same can be said by substituting "hungry" for "sick" and "food" for "care." It is never the helpful waiter or counterman in the diner who dishes out the mugs of coffee and runs a simple test to determine which paper towel lasts the longest, which headache remedy is the quickest, or how to spell "relief" from excess stomach acid (of course if the headache remedy is being recommended by someone playing the role of a professional, a pharmacist or doctor—then it's a man).

If women are put in their place by the commercials, so are men—and that place is the one of authority. According to a 1974 Screen Actors' Guild study, only 7 per cent of the off-camera voices on television commercials are women's, and of the on-camera speaking roles given to women, more than 60 per cent are in cosmetics commercials. The idea behind this allocation, no less in television newsrooms than along Madison Avenue, is that both male and female Americans are more responsive to and trust the male voice more than the female's.

The helplessness and inferiority of women is stressed almost every time a woman appears in a commercial. The dumb reiterated phrase is far more likely to come to us from a woman than a man. Thus: "What would you do if your son stole home and most of the dirt around it?" "I'd 'Shout' it out," laughs the unworried housewife. Mother in *The Brady Bunch,* rebuffed by one of her daughters in an offer of help ("Mom, I've got to speak to Dad; this is a *math* question") to appreciative canned audience chuckles, seems to be playing Everywoman.

Downey Fabric Softener had a commercial that defined the uncertainty and limits of women's experience in this prime-time world. The new bride offers her husband his laundry: "did I wash it right?" He nods approvingly, and her fulfillment is registered joyfully. "He noticed," she exclaims; "I'm a wife!" If this is the test of marriage, it is scant wonder that the divorce rate has climbed to nearly one marriage in two.

When women are not made to feel insecure about housework, it is their assumedly poor sex performance that is under attack. By removing unwanted hair (Nair), my dear, you can wear the newly fashionable short shorts. Eat Breast O'Chicken tuna and develop for yourself a new "lean machine," just like those leggy models up there on the screen. Milk has just the nutrients to make you stand straighter, feel more lively, and be more—well—sexy. Baggy pantyhose are a new menace—everybody can see, even your daughter. For the great and abiding American concern with breast size and appearance, the brassiere commercials are a broad field of fire. There is Jane Russell for "us full-figured gals," here is a cute medium-sized thing full of enthusiasm (she even starts to take her off her blouse, but then she—and, one imagines, the network continuity department—thinks better of it and goes to a voice-over filmed dummy) for the "cross my heart" firmness technique. And over there is a small-breasted young woman, arguing with her "Jewish" mother over what bra to wear. She finally gives in, wears the advertised brand, and returns radiant, late at night with her date. "Mom, meet Dr. _____."

"Put your money where your mouth is," one girlfriend urges another, discouraging sexy clothes as the way to get her man interested again, and insistently urging the right brand of toothpaste instead. It always works; at the fadeout the man is back, and it's clear the investment paid off. One toothpaste conducted a long commercial campaign in 1976, purporting to poll famous show-biz types. "How's your love life?" was the single-entendre question, and the answer was always some variant of, "Don't ask." It took the toothpaste with "sex appeal" to change the answers, and the scoreboard.

On television, women serve. They do it gaily, uncomplainingly, usually singing while they do, frequently in unison with their colleagues. They serve hamburgers, medicine, frozen concentrate for imitation orange juice, iced tea, and cake frosting. Men receive. They protect and defend. If they confide, it will almost always be to another man ("My broker is E.F. Hutton, and Hutton says . . ."), and when they buy a deodorant, it may well be (as in the case of Right Guard) so as not "to leave your family defenseless."

As the decade began, Whitney Adams of the National Organization for Women summed up the organization's view in testimony before the Federal Trade Commission. In effect, she laid upon television advertisers the responsibility for reinforcing old stereotypes and profiting from them, rather than taking any steps to achieve more realism in the medium:

> Women have been reared and trained to believe that the ultimate achievements and fulfillments of their lives are the attraction of males, success in getting a husband, satisfying completely all his needs, and placing the welfare of family and home above all, including themselves. To many women, the failure to attain these long-range goals reflects only on their own inadequacies.
>
> Advertisers are aware of this and actively seek out these vulnerabilities, attempting to play upon them to induce women to buy products. The ads are deceptive because they lead the viewer to believe that the use of the product will achieve the result of pleasing the opposite sex, leading to matrimony or maintaining a contented household.

Ms. Adams presented the result of research in Washington-area commercials: women's advertising was twenty-three times more likely to appeal to anxieties about personal appearance than that directed toward men.

As the decade goes on, little has changed. If anything, the image in the commercials is stronger and more sexually explicit. So in the "liberated" mid-seventies, there is now, in addition to the "sex appeal" toothpaste, a soap which lets a woman be "some body" and a specific bath oil for "the man you live with." "All my men wear English Leather [cologne]," says the provocative model in a famous prime-time vignette, "or they wear nothing at all." And for a rich (well, upper-income) fantasy life, there's always the handsome stranger from the sandwich bag company. The desired sexiness can even come from a career. Flight attendants on airlines who are female—in real life the holders of a wearying job combining the most tiring elements of waitress, barmaid, and stand-by rescue-team leader—have virtually become love affairs waiting to happen, thanks to the airlines' commercials. "I'm Cheryl, fly me," or "I'm going to fly you like you've never been flown before," could hardly be more explicit. And when the cute chorus swings into "at Continental Airlines, we really move our tail for you," is it any wonder that the occupational hazard assigned by real flight attendants to their work consists of fending off passes from aroused passengers, particularly when Cheryl has a "tempting meal served aloft" in one hand and "your favorite beverage" in the other? *

The degree to which all this might consistute "false and misleading" advertising, and thus come under the stern purview of the FTC, or even the FCC, has yet to be explored. From time to time, complaints have been filed with the FTC concerning the treatment on television of various groups, but these are generally turned away on the ground that the Commission's mandate relates only to "material fraud in connection with the sale of the product."

Some understanding of the dimension of the problem can be seen in analyzing the sharp criticism leveled by Joyce Snyder of the National Media Reform Task Force. Speaking to a conference on Women and Consumerism in Louisiana in 1974, Ms. Snyder took on the FTC on a few fronts.

> While the Federal Trade Commission represents itself as regulating unfair and false advertising in the public interest, it merely winks at advertising's consequences for women. Reviewing some of the decisions on deception handed down by FTC in the last few years, a double standard clearly emerges.
>
> The FTC ruled against Lysol for presenting this ad claim: "Lysol kills flu virus wherever you clean." The FTC declared this statement unfair, for viruses on environmental *surfaces* do not play a significant role in transmitting upper respiratory diseases and these germs are usually absorbed from the *air*. Yet when the Lysol commercial "We women are sniffers" burst on our home screens, the FTC obviously dismissed the fact that this falsely depicted women as obsessed with cleanliness.
>
> Advertising that has the tendency or capacity to mislead is unlawful. The law should be applicable to misleading portrayals of women. Ads

---

* This role is reflected in real life by the female flight attendants themselves, who are presumably not immune from the impact of thousands of commercials. "Good afternoon and welcome aboard," runs the customary greeting before takeoff. "Your flight today is under the command of Captain Smith, with Captain Jones as co-pilot" (and sometimes *Mr.* Brown as first officer). "In the front cabin to serve you are Nancy and Linda, and in the rear cabin Lucy, Marcy, and me—Patti." Rarely a last name, and surely never a Ms. Not even a Miss or a Mrs.

showing women sniffing and serving mislead women into a limited lifestyle and deceive men into thinking it both natural and proper to treat women as inferior beings.

In a landmark ruling the FTC majority opinion found that Wonder Bread was not an extraordinary growth-producing food, despite the ads showing a little squirt transformed into a towering specimen of health, and stated that the deception here was based "on the totality of the impression and representations which we believe are conveyed."

Shouldn't they likewise take notice of all the ads where the haggard housewife is made "presto chango" into a stunning Cinderella? Or ads for a product that promise an insecure young woman that with its use she will be ripe for the marriage market and be plucked for male consumption in due time? Or advertising that claims to save a marriage on the rocks by the clever use of a cake mix? If the totality of these product claims is false, they are illegal and should be curbed.

This statement is set forth at length because it is an important one, and contains the seeds of two or three important ideas, particularly in view of the activist tendencies at the FTC in the past few years, tendencies presumably heightened for the Carter years. The problem, if the Media Reform Task Force—and others who share its concern over the view of women on television advertising—is serious, lies in the law and in the state of public opinion.

As Ms. Snyder correctly pointed out, the FTC regulates "unfair and false advertising in the public interest." Unfortunately, that mandate is confined by law to "material fraud in connection with the sale of the product," and while that could be fairly easily demonstrated in the first Lysol case, it could not in the second, and complaints of this type are regularly dismissed. The problem lies with that language, "material fraud in connection with the sale of the product." When FTC jurisdiction was first established, and even when it was later refined, that seemed a reasonable ambit for its activities. After all, we were concerned that we not buy a product under false pretenses.

Hence, if Lysol says it will kill flu viruses "wherever you clean", and you clean on surfaces, and flu viruses aren't on surfaces, but in the air, then the ad is misleading and the FTC, quite properly, will order it off the air. But the standard says nothing about material fraud or slander in connection with the dramatic action in the advertisement, and so "we women are sniffers," with all its obnoxious social implications, goes untouched. After all, the reasoning runs, whether the ad said "We women are sniffers" or "We women are senior accountants and nuclear engineers" it would not constitute an extra claim for the value of Lysol. Under this narrow, and so far prevailing, view, since it isn't women who are being sold to the public, there is no fraud.

That is why, for example, the FTC took no action a few years ago when Spanish-surname groups were incensed over corn-chip advertising featuring the "Frito Bandito," a classic Mexican stereotype complete with sombrero, serape, and bandoliers. The Commission held again that there was no fraud in connection with the sale of the product, and bucked the matter over to the Federal Communications Commission—which also took no action.

But the publicity connected with the protest, and the militant and well-organized stance of the protesters, accomplished what the lawyers had been unable to: the ad was pulled off the air, if one may say so, pronto.

But the reaction to "Frito Bandito" is the key even to the second question raised about women in advertising. It is clear that the role of the woman in the ads for toothpaste ("gives your mouth sex appeal"), hair conditioner ("the closer he gets, the better you look"), or deodorant ("takes the danger out of being close") *is* "connected with the sale of the product;" indeed, it is the very essence of the sale of the product. When advertising says, ceaselessly, that this toothpaste or that soap will attract Mr. Right, it is skating very close to the edge of fraud. No case is in litigation on this point, and the defense would almost certainly be that this is nothing more than an example of the ancient art of "puffing," traditionally defended by the courts. Customers, the reasoning goes, know that this is an advertisement, and expect a little hyperbole. That defense might well succeed—and it would be almost sure to succeed against a broader claim, that this goes beyond mere puffing to an image of women in general that is damaging—not so much to women as to all of society.

A good case can be made—though not a good court case—that such "puffing" *is* damaging to society, and especially to children. Children seek role models everywhere, but they find them most often on television, and particularly in the commercials. After all, it isn't likely that the children who identified Dr. Bob and Nurse Nancy in the face of visual evidence to the contrary got those ideas from books: they don't read very many books.

Most likely, new legislation would be necessary, broadening the traditional boundaries of fraud. However, the speed with which "Frito Bandito" was yanked off the air indicates the strength of group protest regardless of legal strength. The difference, of course, is that Chicanos are somehow more visible than women, perhaps because they are a smaller and less-publicized group. In any event, if thousands (or hundreds of thousands) of women were to make it clear to the advertisers and the networks that the prevailing image of the group is as obnoxious to its members—at least the protesting ones, who would be seen as speaking for many more—as would a steady depiction of shiftless blacks, drunken Irishmen, or money-lending Jews, the results might be striking.

Certainly this technique has worked for others beyond those offended by the "Frito Bandito." Spokesmen for Italo-American groups have accomplished a result amazing to those concerned with law enforcement and organized crime; whenever the Mafia is depicted on television, its leaders all have names like Cartwright and Wickersham. The cigar manufacturers have largely succeeded in eliminating the stereotype of the big-shot criminal as the only cigar-smoker in the crowd. In fact, in a related development, they may have given some cause for concern to the cigarette makers—almost every smoker on a prime-time dramatic program is now identifiable, by that habit, as on the wrong side if not of the law, at least of good morals. In the television universe, smokers don't get promoted to the top jobs, they don't win the big cases, and nice girls don't marry them. It may be only a matter of time before the protests begin.

The 1974 survey conducted by the Screen Actors' Guild yielded some interesting facts. The Guild, concerned about the increasing re-use in prime time of programs that had already been played (prime-time "weekly" programs produce only twenty-four new shows a year, since each is re-used once, and other programs or special events usually pre-empt about four of a show's spots), got what it wanted in the responses. Most of the respondents said they didn't like the use of so many re-runs; they wanted, presumably, SAG members to have more work.

But there were other opinions logged. Of those questioned 67.4 per cent said they would like to see women appearing in positions of authority, and 63.4 per cent said they would like to see more women in leading roles on other than variety and talk shows. The Guild had also monitored programs and advertisements, and established that these were legitimate concerns—women were vastly outnumbered by men not only in roles in dramatic productions, but also in commercials. Off-camera male voices, for example, dominated the field of women's product commercials, and 71 per cent of all off-camera singing principals were men. Even on camera in commercials, the survey found, women are confined largely—70 per cent—to non-speaking roles. And suggesting that some deep sexist beliefs are operative here, the survey also found that discrimination against women on commercials as well as in dramatic programs increases with the age of the performer.

As for the opinion portion of the survey—a fact of considerable interest, in light of the dissatisfaction with the ways women were portrayed when they were portrayed at all, is that only 15 per cent of those responding were men. Of the respondents—85 per cent women—71 per cent said they felt the relationships and roles did not mirror women's lifestyles; 66.2 per cent felt that television portrayals did not encourage young girls or women to aspire to a useful role in society; 72.2 per cent thought sex was overused to sell products; 89.5 per cent said that television is generally fantasy rather than fact. And in spite of those whopping majorities, 52.3 per cent said that television commercials influenced their choice of products to buy. No wonder that an article on the survey appeared in *Variety* under the headline, "In TV, You've Come a Short Way, Baby."

If the majority of women aren't pleased with the way they see themselves on television, the problem would seem to be largely one of organization. Women are the major determinant in the American family as to which products are purchased—thus the line of organizational activity seems clear. Television marketing executives are probably surpassed in their lack of independence only by public school administrators, with the result that one complaint earns attention, 10 complaints rate the participation of a vice-president, 100 can produce a meeting to decide what to do, 1,000 can cause a change in agencies, and 10,000 will make heads roll. What would 10,000,000 protests accomplish? Those ugly rings, those spots on the crystal, even all that unwanted hair, might literally vanish overnight. One can imagine the question, "Madam, if your airwaves portrayed you and all women as simpering fools, what would you do?" And the answer, one would hope, "I'd shout it out!"

SOME PROGRESS FOR SOME HOMOSEXUALS

An example of the success of organized protest against the bastions of television can be found in the vastly changed image of male homosexuals on the screen. To be sure, a mincing lisping actor (but not actress) can still get laughs with the same portrayal of male homosexuality as could be found in vaudeville more than half a century ago. Thus, some of the many portrayals of gays on the comedy police program, *Barney Miller,* are of the old style, even while others—and the way in which the police discuss gays—are far more modern. Archie Bunker can talk of his club, "The Kings of Queens," and be asked, by a prospective member, "Is that that gay bar over on Queens Boulevard?" (And, typical of the latitude which Norman Lear has carved out for this program, the prospective member—a black man, asked to join the club only to meet the law's requirements—can announce that he plans to bring in his friends, his business colleagues, and his family, and then proclaim loudly, "You better change the name of the club to "The Kings *and* Queens—of Spades!"")

Under heavy pressure from organized gay activists, television has for the most part, though, been instrumental over the past decade in helping homosexuals "come out of the closet," individually and collectively. We can find dramas, explicit and sensitive, on the subject, as well as a generally dignified treatment elsewhere:

—A network special on Walt Whitman in 1976 dealt with a part of his life—his homosexuality—hardly even mentioned in high school and college courses.

—*Hot l Baltimore,* a situation comedy about life in a seedy, run-down, residential hotel, included among the "regulars" a quarreling homosexual male couple.

—On *M*A*S*H,* a regular character, Corporal Klinger, while not gay, constantly wears women's clothes (in a constant and unsuccessful attempt to get out of the Army as "crazy"), and the character is so skillfully written that the "drag" persona seems to emphasize his masculinity, at least in traditional terms. Klinger the transvestite performs his Army duties competently and at times bravely, and seemed, in 1975, to match the real-life performance of ex-Marine Oliver Sipple—a homosexual who was the hero who foiled the attempt to shoot President Ford in San Francisco.

—*Mary Hartman, Mary Hartman,* Norman Lear's meteorically successful sort-of soap opera, included in its cast of "ordinary people" two gay lovers, living together but posing as brothers.

—On a Family Hour program, Phyllis finds her date unresponsive, and she asks if she is to blame. Not at all, replies the young man, it's just that I'm gay. There follows a merry half hour in which Phyllis convinces him to come out of the closet at a reception given by his parents, who think they are announcing his engagement to Phyllis. His "coming out" consists of running up to each guest and announcing "I'm gay." Everyone, including the studio audience, laughs, much as if he were announcing that his wavy hair is really a wig. While there is no doubt that this is an enlightened treatment by the standards of the Gay Activists' Alliance, one wonders about the use of Family Hour to demonstrate—presumably to millions of children whose parents have not put the subject on the family agenda for the evening—the humorous and light-hearted consequences of homosexuality, or for that matter just what it is.

Acceptability on television of female homosexuality has not come so easily or, indeed, at all. In the almost entirely male world of television decision-making, female heterosexual aggressiveness is threatening enough without going one step beyond. The leading demonstration of lesbianism on the home screen, remains the NBC production of *Born Innocent,* including the horrifying scene in which a group of tough girls rape a teenager with a broom handle. The play drew angry protests, which have yet to die down, and at least one lawsuit from a parent who believes her daughter's rape, following the production, was prompted by what her assailants saw on the screen. Nevertheless, NBC ran the program a second time, although some affiliated stations declined to do so.

It is hard to assess the role of television in the new awareness of male homosexuality. To a large degree, it is a reflection of the changing view in society as a whole—or at any rate the changing view in that portion of society on both coasts to which television executives and creative people belong. Courts have ruled against the more flagrant examples of discrimination based on what is now called "sexual preference," and many major corporations have proclaimed on employment application forms that "sexual orientation will not be taken into account."

In the last few years, homosexuals repeatedly placed themselves at the center of news attention. A decorated, professional Air Force sergeant, for example, made his status public voluntarily in 1975 and challenged the armed forces—and, in effect, the nation—to justify the unwritten policy that a man cannot be gay and a good soldier at the same time. Sergeant Matlovich lost his case, as did others who followed his path, but not until he had had sympathetic treatment in cover stories of national news magazines, extensive television news coverage, and in-depth analyses of the case in magazines and newspapers throughout the country.

There is no doubt, however, that this discriminatory policy will be changed and forgotten by the end of the decade, if not sooner. One can see the change coming in the increasing acceptance of—if one may use the locution—straight gay characters on prime-time entertainment television; and more especially in the attitudes taken by television personalities on comedy and talk shows.

When Anita Bryant—herself a pure television personality, the commercial spokesperson for Florida orange juice—began what turned out to be a successful crusade against a local ordinance removing some barriers to gay public employment, she became not a heroine—as she would have, twenty years ago on network television—but the butt of jokes and hostility on the networks. Since talk-show hosts and comedians never express minority national political opinions or extreme social attitudes, their unanimity on the issue would seem to adumbrate a national consensus on the other side from Ms. Bryant. Twenty years ago, she could have parlayed her hard-line opposition attitude into a political career; in the 70s it has jeopardized her job and her public acceptance, for the time being—the former because of the loss, or at least the "controversiality," of the latter.

But if all this suggests that television's increasingly favorable treatment of the homosexual merely *simply* reflects continuing acceptance in the larger society, the suggestion masks the degree to which the two work together, and in which a favorable television image at least hastens general acceptability.

Before television, homosexuality was, in the view of the American

Psychiatric Association, a mental disorder; to the overwhelming majority of the public at large, it was a sin, if not a crime. In fact, until the Supreme Court ruled the statutes "void for vagueness," many states permitted the arrest of recognizable homosexuals on the ground that they had committed "the infamous crime against nature." One reason for the change—as opposed to any substantial change, as we have seen, in the portrayal of women—has been the militancy and precision of gay organizations. Most programs dealing with homosexuals are now "cleared" by groups such as the National Gay Task Force or Gay Media Action; these are increasingly sophisticated groups, who are permitted an increasingly significant input by network program executives and writers.

Gays claim to represent 10 per cent of the population (a figure much harder to verify than those dealing, for instance, with minority racial groups, or with women, or with those constituting other pressure points in society, such as the handicapped or members of particular religious communities), and their instructions to the networks are quite explicit. Whether in memoranda to writers or in testimony before the NAB Code Review Board, the gay position is stated simply and forcefully.

"You can't be a little bit gay any more than you can be a little bit black," one such statement began. "That telephone call your dentist got between bouts of drilling was from his lover . . . He wanted to know whether it was his turn to cook. Our lives are not a joke. And we're angry about being constantly equated with violence, depravity, or disease."

Gays want, as itemized in 1974 testimony by Ronald Gold of the National Gay Task Force, "an end to invisibility," no more fag and dyke jokes, no more leering put-downs or limp-wristed put-ons. Gays point out, quite accurately, that stereotypic impressions of them have lasted far longer on television than of, for example, blacks, Jews, or Catholics. (An exception to this assessment might be black stereotypes—*The Jeffersons, Good Times,* and, above all, *Sanford and Son,* deal in ancient stereotypes as gross as any purveyed by Aunt Jemima; the difference is they now have black approbation.)

The goal, in the words of one Gay Task Force spokesman, is to "have a gay policeman for every gay bank robber." That goal, however broadly stated, is not much different from the goal of blacks or other racial minorities, and it is met by the television establishment in much the same way. How, it is asked, can there be legitimate drama or art if every interested societal group, however justifiably, demands proportional representation? As for gays, this is a more insistent question, since no one is in a position to say what fair quotas would be. Gays, in this case, are in a position not unlike that of the major oil companies—only *they* have the information about their own reserves.

There remains the reality, though, that after the presentations

generation of Americans modeled itself after Clark Gable or Lana Turner, but there is no indication that very many of the Television Generation followed the sexual lead of—let us say—the young people on *Father Knows Best* or *Leave It to Beaver*.

From the movie stars of the 30s and 40s, we learned the appropriate sexual gambits, depending upon whether we felt more comfortable as the suave operator (Robert Taylor), the "aw shucks" country boy (Jimmy Stewart), the seductive siren (Lana Turner), or the schoolmarm-*cum*-girl next door (June Allyson). But the sex lives on television in the 50s and 60s of the juveniles and ingenues were so prim, so universally proper and sanitized, there was nothing to learn.

Measure, for example, the lives of the characters on two "nostalgia" programs of today—*Happy Days* and *Laverne and Shirley,* in theory re-creating the 1950s—with those of characters in the programs made in the 50s. Beaver's older brother, or the young folks in Ozzie and Harriet's family, or even in *My Little Margie,* were chaste and proper, and agonized over nothing more "sexy" than whether the kid could get the family car (for a "heavy date" at the most). But the Fonz and Laverne and Shirley are into sex in a big way—or at any rate they talk about it a lot.

Both programs, in fact, seem to tell us that the lesser breeds among us—the so-called "ethnics"—are fantastic sexual animals with small brains. Fonzarelli is all grease, leather jacket, and motorcycles, and spends his time—and most of the plots—showing his straight but brainy WASP pals how to make out with women—or, as he puts it, "broads" and "chicks." He speaks with a recognizable "dumb" accent and scorns any intellectual activities. The WASP girls cluster around and seem anxious for what can only be described as sexual humiliation—to the extent that television can provide it—as they submit to the Fonz's orders as to which of them go with him and when. He is, in short, television's equivalent of Lady Chatterley's gamekeeper.

Laverne and Shirley, on the other hand, are the objects of sexual advances by male ethnics, and almost as giddy and yielding as the girls on *Happy Days*. It is amazing that both programs are as popular as they are, and that both are described, with straight faces, by television critics as demonstrating the importance of a new consumer bloc—the "ethnics." Actually, the programs are highly elitist, and demonstrate a New York/Hollywood view of ethnics as condescending as it is invalid.

But the important thing is that in these characters, television has presented a sexually charged atmosphere. It is a concession, not evidence that television has brought about any of this new consciousness level. It is to other media that one must look for the sources of the change in sexual attitudes.

In addition to motion pictures—the kind you go out to see, not the ones made for television—books, magazines, and the classroom have certainly led the way. Words and descriptions once confined to smudged paperbacks sold furtively in the back of the cigar store or mailed in plain envelopes, now are also found in stylish, best-selling fiction and non-fiction. Illustrated sex manuals—of which *The Joy of Sex* is perhaps the best example—that could be found a generation ago, if at all, locked in a case at the Public Library, now sell by the millions, and have become a part of contemporary literature. Sex magazines—short of real pornography, whose future in the short run seems uncertain as a result of ambiguous Supreme Court decisions about "community moral standards"—have become a part of the mass culture. On the newsstands across the nation, *Playboy* has become tame and centrist, surpassed in explicit sexual content by a multitude of magazines whose quantity—and sales figures—may be limited only by the number of expressive single-syllable words and sexually explicit photographs.

Newspapers and general-circulation magazines have also far surpassed the "mass media" in sexual liberation. Once-prohibited words are now found in such publications as *Time* and *Newsweek,* and there seems little doubt that the squeamishness displayed by almost all newspapers in refusing to quote directly the scatological language of former Secretary of Agriculture Earl Butz in 1976 will not be repeated the next time.

In schools, most of the battles over "sex education" are over, almost all settled in favor of more explicit and "advanced" material and teaching techniques. The result is that, at least for children from junior high school upward, the fancy talk on prime-time television is quite understandable and reflects a world they largely comprehend. The problem arises with younger viewers (most of the situation comedies are on the air during Family Hour), who may not be ready for themes dealing with abortion, homosexuality, or vasectomies, and whose parents, in any event, have not had much say in whether or not their children will be exposed to these words and ideas on any particular evening.

William S. Rubens of NBC put the matter this way:

> Sexual matter is rarely presented in television, and is treated circumspectly when it is. In this sense, commercial television may be the last bastion of puritanical thinking left among the media.

Mr. Rubens is overstating the case: "circumspect" defines the treatment on *Maude,* for example, only if one is comparing it to *Midnight Cowboy* or *Deep Throat.* Even so, he is pretty close to the mark. When the President of the United States, addressing a crowd of civil servants and, beyond them, everyone watching the evening news on television—as Jimmy Carter did early in his administration—can urge his listeners to get married if they are "living in sin" (a state he had described earlier in

Playboy as "shacking up"), and if both he and the audience can then laugh easily at what he has said, then we have, indeed, passed through a sort of revolution. Television has been a part of it—sex now shares with violence a central place in American drama—but hardly a leader.

EMPLOYMENT OF WOMEN
IN BROADCASTING

Women have been mobilizing for increased opportunities in broadcasting, as have other groups traditionally discriminated against in employment. Largely in response to organized pressures, the position of women in television has been improving. In 1974, women were 24 per cent of the total work force at American commercial television stations, and the percentage had been increasing steadily for several years. The percentage of women in non-clerical positions also showed a steady increase. More than one examination of the industry was made, and the figures generally coincided.

Much of this improvement, though, is only on paper, as throughout the industry employers—whether stations, networks, or agencies— change job titles to make file clerks and secretaries into assistant production managers and associate producers. (In the motion picture credit hierarchy, "associate producer" usually denotes either a brother-in-law or a large investor; in television it probably means an ambitious and talented secretary who has already received all the pay raises the budget can stand.) Furthermore, hundreds of new "management" and "professional" jobs, all filled and to be filled by women, began to appear along with federal scrutiny of hiring practices.

Even the Public Broadcasting System, theoretically a special bastion of social enlightenment, could not escape the charge of sexism. A 1975 report of the Task Force on Women in Public Broadcasting concluded that PBS presented a distorted view of women in society, largely because women were so under-represented in "meaningful positions."

In 1975, the New York City Commission on Human Rights found that NBC had practiced discrimination against women in hiring— discrimination designed, among other things, "to place females overwhelmingly in clerical positions regardless of their qualifications, and to withhold from them the opportunity to move up afforded to men." This was accomplished, according to the Commission, by steering female job applicants into secretarial designations, and then by neither training nor considering secretaries for higher, non-clerical positions. NBC's response to this indictment was strong and detailed, pointing with pride to statistics that showed that since 1971, "the percentage of women in ex-ecutive and management positions at NBC in New York has nearly doubled, increasing from 6½ per cent to 12 per cent." In other words, like every other giant American corporation (including the other net-works), NBC discriminates against women in hiring.

But if television was neutral or inhibiting in the sexual revolution, if it is just another American industry when it comes to hiring practices, it can claim some leadership in the progress the women's movement has made in the past decade. NBC (and CBS and ABC as well) shows the progress it *has* made in hiring—reflected throughout the industry—because of enormous public pressure. And that pressure has come be-cause of a highly publicized movement, which could not have had nearly the success it has without television.

The feminist movement, after all, did not spring full-grown from the brows of Ti-Grace Atkinson and Germaine Greer. The ideas which ani-mate the movement have been in America at least since Abigail Adams admonished her husband, John, to "remember the ladies." They have passed through phases of emphasis from educational and vocational op-portunity, to moral equality, to suffrage. The movement never acquired a mass following except briefly, at and after the time of the Suffrage Amendment, after which it more or less went to earth for forty years. Today's movement is a frontal assault, which could not exist without the availability of mass media—that is, television. This is true, of course, only now that the issues raised by the movement have become precise and specific, and capable of a certain quantification on news pro-grams—Equal Rights Amendment, Social Security inequities, liberal-ized abortion.

In the early days of the modern movement, when the emphasis was on organization and philosophical principles ("equal rights," rather than the Equal Rights Amendment) television was probably inhibitory and ultimately hostile. In those days, militants talking about burning bras and refusing to have children were the staples offered to viewers, along with highly threatening figures on talk shows.

But when the movement began to grasp the importance of political participation, public opinion shifted toward, rather than away from, its objectives. Television news cannot accommodate a philosophical discus-sion of *anything,* much less anything that might make us think seriously about new ideas; but if a "women's caucus" can be created to serve as a voice for a definable group, then thirty or forty-five seconds will almost automatically be available, particularly if a·controversy is thereby precipitated.

Thus, bound by the Iron Law of television news—the Trivial Drives out the Serious—we have seen and heard very little serious debate about the ideas that animate the women's movement; but at the 1972

Democratic Convention, for example, hours of debate and learned analysis were devoted to the fate of six male delegates from South Carolina who were challenged by the Women's Caucus.

That South Carolina challenge was a splendid example of how television works, and especially with respect to "hot" and visible controversial matters such as those raised by the organized women at the Miami Beach convention. The rules of the Democratic Party called for fair representation of women in state delegations. The Women's Caucus decided that the South Carolina delegation, many of whose members had been appointed by party authorities, was out of line. No issue was raised of how the delegation's vote would be cast; only who would cast them. So half of the male at-large number was challenged.

The leading candidate for the nomination, Senator George McGovern, was supportive of the rules in question and, therefore, of the South Carolina challenge. But he had other concerns, mainly that after the South Carolina vote, there would be a challenge—wholly bogus, but in a posture to be heard and voted upon—to 152 of his delegates from California, and in the case of California it *would* affect the state's vote on the nomination.

Due to a complicated parliamentary situation and some equally complicated rulings of the chair, it became vital to the McGovern forces on the floor of the convention to see to it that the challenge by the women either won or lost by a substantial margin. A close vote—within five or six either way—would open up parliamentary inquiries that could endanger McGovern's majority on the key California vote later in the evening.

When it became clear that a close but losing vote on South Carolina was indeed a strong possibility, the McGovern floor leaders adopted the strategy of peeling votes away from the pro-challenge totals, so that the California vote forces might be unchallenged. The result, of course, was to defeat the South Carolina women's challenge by a larger margin than it would otherwise have suffered. And the result of *that* was anger in the women's ranks, who felt they had a guarantee from Senator McGovern that had been betrayed.

The real story of what had happened was far too complicated for television, which then settled for substantial interviews with telegenic representatives of the Women's Caucus—and to this day remnants of the bitterness engendered by that coverage remain. It was a classic case of television, with limited coverage possibilities, opting for the attractive, the controversial, or the colorful as representative of women in general.

The women's movement has no greater intellectual impetus today than in the early years of the century when Emma Goldman was writing, nor when Simone de Beauvoir's *The Second Sex* appeared in the early 1950s; why did it achieve no general acceptance—even among women—until nearly 1970? For that matter, why did it not become an important factor in our political life in 1775, when Thomas Paine wrote of women "robbed of freedom and will by the laws"?

The answer, of course, is that these advocates were creating linear statements, which were read, even if widely for printed literature, by a narrow minority of our people. Even into the Age of Television, the point was not grasped. Betty Friedan's *The Feminine Mystique*—certainly the seminal work of the modern feminist movement—first published in 1963, failed to recognize the power of television. Ms. Friedan saw television only as a potentially liberating educational force—she marveled that while only thousands of nineteenth century women were able to see or read Ibsen's *A Doll's House*, millions of American housewives watching the play on television could hear and see Nora slam that door.

But Ms. Friedan either did not notice, or did not think it important to notice, that there was but one Nora in a throng of Lucy's, and that both before and after the action of the Ibsen play, those millions of American housewives could and did see themselves as dolls again, shrieking with delight as DUZ did everything and puzzling over which twin had the Toni.

In fact *The Feminine Mystique* accepted, almost casually, not only the ubiquity of television, but an intrinsic aesthetic and emotional value as well. Ms. Friedan, in the course of demonstrating the emptiness of most women's lives, quoted a suburban professional woman who lamented that her neighbors had little time in which to find themselves as individuals. As a result, she said, they have no time for being "alone, or watching TV or reading a book." In 1963, even so prescient an observer as Ms. Friedan could not see that it was precisely that time "watching TV" that made those women accept themselves and stay in their place.

Other leading books of the early 60s made the same omission, ignoring the potential for television either to promote or inhibit progress, and the early communicators of the feminist message were either selected, or self-selected, without television at all in mind. The result was that television news particularly was able to present some highly unattractive stereotypes of "women's libbers," an image that to some extent still persists. By the late 60s, before the movement became media-conscious, Americans could and did perceive it as full of women compensating with stridency for their lack of physical attractiveness, frigid, hating children, perhaps lesbian, and favoring the widespread use of test tubes in lieu of more orthodox methods of procreation. Although the number of brassieres actually burned could be counted on the fingers (perhaps the thumb) of one hand (the number of draft-card burnings was much smaller, too, than the impression we had), *that* was the image that stuck, and the comedians and talk-show hosts had a field day.

But the shift, at the end of the decade, to leaders such as Gloria Steinem, and to issues like those subsumed within the Equal Rights Amendment—equal pay, equal access to credit, control of one's own finances—was aimed straight at television and other key media, such as the *New York Times*. Ms. Steinem, Billie Jean King, Representative Shirley Chisholm, Shirley MacLaine, and Representative Yvonne Brathwaite Burke—all talking about tangible and palpable injustices, and all obviously achievers in the "real" world—were a far cry from the early stridency of a militant, philosophical (and to many men, highly threatening) position.

Within a few years, the public—particularly female—perception had changed. A study of mass media and the feminist movement published in 1974 by the Russell Sage Foundation reports that:

> . . . of those respondents who had joined [the movement] after 1969 only about one-fourth had learned about the movement exclusively or primarily from other people. In contrast, about half were influenced by both personal contacts and the media, and most interestingly, about one-fourth decided to look into the movement entirely on the basis of what they had learned from the mass media. A number of NOW (National Organization of Women) chapters, including those in New York City and Los Angeles, noted a sudden influx of new members following the protests of August 26, 1970.

The study goes on to point out that the mass media—television, particularly—made the modern feminist movement possible because it spread its ideas and images so rapidly. In addition, by the very fact that it selected what it chose to disseminate, television shaped the story while telling it.

"Perhaps," concludes the Sage study,

> it would have taken a different form if the media had not emphasized dramatic but often unrepresentative events and figures and if potential members as well as opponents had not learned about the movement through the media's often sensational presentation.

True enough, but without television neither members or opponents would have learned about the movement at all in sufficient numbers to make any difference, and without the "often sensational presentation," television would not have bothered.

That is the central dilemma of television news: how to present the news within the essentially "entertainment" framework the medium demands—or at least seems, and is believed, to demand. It is a dilemma that the women's movement began to appreciate as it began to direct its attention to television, at the turn of the 60s into the 70s. In 1971, the National Women's Political Caucus was formed, created almost entirely to provide the "entertainment" without which the news becomes, in Hamlet's words if not his meaning, "weary, stale, flat and unprofitable."

It has accomplished its ends. All the networks maintain extensive news bureaus in Washington, and to justify this there is an enormous amount of news broadcast each day from the national capital. In fact, it can be argued that the existence for the past twenty-five years of national television news organizations, network news programs, and large Washington bureaus whose correspondents hold the most coveted assignments, has contributed substantially to the growth of federal power and its concentration in Washington. One way to reduce the power of the presidency would be to put the network Washington bureaus —personnel and salaries intact—in, let us say, Omaha. Then it would turn out that Nebraska was the center of the Free World and the Strategic Air Command the proper source of most news.

The National Woman's Political Caucus and its related organizations understood the Washington news scene, and as a result the publicity for the movement has become far more favorable, and far more reflective of the simpler, one-dimensional issues the Caucus has promoted and television prefers. The result is that dramatic changes in public opinion have occurred:

—A 1970 Harris poll found the public "favor[s] most of the efforts to strengthen and change women's status in society," but just barely—42 per cent were in favor, 41 per cent were not. A 1975 poll found that support increased to 63 per cent, and opposition dropped to 25 per cent.

—By 1975, the Gallup Poll found that 71 per cent of those polled felt the country would be as well or better governed with more women office-holders, and that 73 per cent would vote for a woman for President, up from 31 per cent since 1937, and up 7 per cent since 1971.

—Women themselves began to have a different image of themselves and their roles—a 1974 study by the Institute of Life Insurance found that young women want less and less to be housewives and more and more to have professional careers. "Career" seemed capable of a wide definition; FBI figures showed that the number of crimes committed by women in 1972 were 246 per cent of 1960 women's crimes; and that the number of women arrested in 1974 was 9 per cent greater than in the previous year, where the comparable figure for men showed an increase of only 2 per cent.

—In legal as well as illegal activity, women's role is rapidly changing. Over 40 per cent of the work force is now female; over 22 per cent of all American households are now headed by a woman; by 1970 the percentage of mothers who held paying jobs had risen to 42 per cent; and more than one-third of all women with preschool children are in the work force.

All of this is change, but not necessarily progress. The highly visible women's activities may be sustaining confidence and public opinion on specific issues, but there is a danger that publicity can be equated with forward movement. It is true that ERA would probably not be on the agenda were it not for the women's movement's use of television, but it is also true that the rather thin and often elitist campaign presented in its behalf has not succeeded as of this writing, and success is not likely soon.

It is true that Barbara Walters is a skilled and successful network newscaster—certainly the highest-paid—but women are still seriously underemployed in television news. And with few exceptions, women who are not physically attractive as well as capable of news broadcasts are totally unemployed in television.

At the level where the "women's issue" cuts the deepest, the Department of Labor reported in 1976 that the gap between the incomes of full-time male and female workers is *widening*. Women, says the Labor Department, continue to be chronically undertrained and underemployed, and undercompensated when they are employed. These are areas where it would seem that broad media access and virtually unlimited forty-five-second television interviews with female leaders or elected officials are simply not enough. Television news cannot sell some things, and the early abandonment of deep-seated psychological barriers appears to be one of them.

Until the beginning of this decade, almost no women were continuing stars of prime-time dramatic or situation comedy programs. By the middle of the decade, there were nine—13 per cent of the total. Programs that were male-oriented or had male leads comprised 63 per cent of prime-time programming, and general or family-oriented programs made up the rest. Since 1975, the number has stayed almost exactly the same.

Very few of these heroines have done much more than earn top billing—they're still playing the kinds of characters women did when the men ran the living-room-screen families, offices, and detective agencies. Some of them, like Charlie's Angels, are unabashedly sex objects and use that, almost exclusively, in their work—in this case as the agents of a sort of phantom satyr who, for reasons never clearly stated, is against crime. Some, like Phyllis and especially Rhoda, have jobs but spend all their visible time involved in their private and romantic lives. A Norman Lear situation comedy of the 1976-77 season, *All's Fair,* purported to star Bernadette Peters as a liberal Washington career woman, to play against the hero, a conservative Washington columnist. But the program was almost entirely about their love life, and her career—in this case photography—seemed about as relevant to her life as Elizabeth Ray's. Furthermore, the sexual stereotyping in behavior continues. Women get emotionally upset and cry, for example; men do not. Even the redoubtable Maude, on her first day on a new real estate job, broke down in tears and stormed out in what could only be called a snit. Even on *Police Woman,* where Angie Dickinson often shoots it out with the street criminals as unrealistically as any male officer, the plots frequently reveal sexually stereotypical thinking—the attractive Ms. Dickinson is frequently used as a decoy for suspected rapists and molesters.

In one typical episode of *Space 1999,* a successful program about a hopeful future, "our" space patrol members are tracking down a vicious but unseen creature. Just before they are about to confront the monster, the patrol leader (naturally, played by a man), turns to the female member of the team. "Helena," he says, "maybe you ought to wait here." Although she is as well armed as the others, she waits while they continue to stalk the hideous prey. Even in the future, the program tells us, men will be braver than women—who, in turn, will accept male protectiveness graciously.

In the Age of Television, anything is better than to be invisible, and feminist groups see great potential in these programs. *Ms* magazine, for example, praised a short-run series starring a black woman policeman, *Get Christie Love,* for "attempting to change the stereotype of the TV policewoman who is usually seen handling only juvenile or rape cases." But the program replaced only one stereotype with another, and added an emerging one—black female police officers are saucy and sexy. Except for that, Christie Love was just as false a figure as other police officers, and the program did nothing to narrow the gap between the living-room reality and the station-house reality.

And it should not be forgotten that even Mary Tyler Moore, whose news-producer role was perhaps the most career-oriented of all those played in prime time by women, was not exempt from the casual sexism of television. Of all the people in the newsroom, even the ones over whom she had nominal executive authority, she was the only one who continued to the final program to call the chief Mr. Grant. Even more revealing was that she called him Lou only once—during an episode in which, for a brief and quickly reconsidered moment, they "dated." Women on television, it appears, are equal only when sex is in (or, more properly, on) the air.

SOAP OPERAS

There is hardly an American who does not know what is meant when someone describes a real-life situation as "something right out of a soap opera."

The "soaps" on television are a national institution. Each week day, without fail, they are attended by over 20 million people, far more than attend many of our better recognized and catalogued institutions. Churches, for example, are virtually empty except for a few hours each week, and trade union meetings increasingly attract a diminishing share of the members.

As with all established institutions, soap opera teaches and demands certain values, foremost among which is loyalty. The prime sin, to a soap opera viewer, is to Miss an Episode, and as a result millions of lives are regulated by whether *Love of Life* appears before or after *As the World Turns*. On college campuses, some students select their courses on the basis of how they conflict with the soap opera schedule. In Congress, an unabashed cadre of members openly sits in the cloakroom watching their favorite soaps, with little regard for what may be happening on the House floor.

At least one Supreme Court justice is an avid viewer. Office workers arrange coffee breaks, truck drivers juggle schedules, and college professors scurry from classroom or library—all closet soap opera addicts (there are few casual viewers). Soap opera achieved an American success pinnacle on January 12, 1976, when it was the subject of a *Time* magazine cover. Employees of at least one federal agency pooled resources to purchase an "audio feed" from local television stations, enabling them to catch the daily episodes without breaking civil service regulations against television sets in offices. Soap operas are regularly watched by patients in mental hospitals, and physicians and psychiatrists use them for therapy. And there are at home those 20 million housewives, homemakers, and other domestic-chore-bound people who watch in between tasks.

The economic impact of soap opera deserves some note. Although rates are lower than in prime time, advertising time-buyer Walter Stabb estimates that over $450 million is spent annually to reach the viewers. The advertisers are almost exclusively manufacturers of housekeeping products (waxes, polishes, cleansers, and, of course, the products from which the genre takes its name) and cosmetics. And, as is no longer the case with prime-time programs, the sponsors take an active hand in story ideas, casting, and character development.

The networks' profit margin is enormous. The cost of one week's programs for one show is about $150,000, less than one-half the cost of a single prime-time hour. That weekly cost is almost completely recouped by one day's advertising revenues. Daytime programming, thus, becomes the most active profit center in any network's overall operations.

Such is the intensity of soap opera followers that more than a dozen fan magazines, with titles like *Daily TV Serials* and *Day Time Television* are published—these magazines have a weekly circulation in the millions. Plots are summarized, stars interviewed, and articles featured along the line of "On-Screen Weddings of the Year." Many of these magazines serve to keep people informed about the doings of their television companions when work, travel, or other real-life pressures force them to miss episodes. In addition, in some major television markets, local morning talk shows bring viewers up to date with weekly or biweekly summaries of the soap operas, and some newspapers provide running summaries and previews.

Soap opera is more than just regular, daily drama on the home screen. For one thing, it is radically different from prime-time drama in three specific ways. First, the time cycle is slowed down almost to that of life itself; in prime-time, nothing takes very long—arrangements are made and broken, people marry and separate, children are born and grow, diseases are contracted and cured, in the space of a few minutes. But in soap opera, if two people begin an illicit love affair, it may last for months, or even years. If a woman becomes pregnant, and does not decide to have an abortion, she will be pregnant for nine months of daily episodes. If a character becomes terminally ill, it will take months until death. Comedians have attempted to satrize soap opera in this "nothing happens" aspect, but it is almost impossible to satirize.* Not much does happen on each day's program as the story gradually develops—but this leisurely rhythm of the dramatic life on the screen is one of the appeals of soap opera; we are not required to absorb more events in a day than we would in life, and there is time to explore nuances, and consider implications.

Second, soap opera is the only place on television where, as part of an entertainment program, serious social questions are discussed and acted out. A typical soap opera plot will concern such themes as abortion, venereal disease, euthanasia, incest, drug addiction, suicide, marital infidelity, child abuse, impotence, and even political questions such as the Vietnam War.

The third major difference between soap opera and prime-time drama is that some issues on the soaps are never entirely or satisfactorily resolved. In prime time, no loose ends are ever left dangling: if it is a medical

---

* Bob and Ray once kept a soap opera satire going called "The Life and Loves of Linda Lovely, Girl Intern," in which on a typical episode someone would get into a car and close the door. "Tune in tomorrow," the announcer would say, "and we will hear Linda start the car." It was too much like the real thing.

161   •

show, the patient is cured and the emotional problems of his family are cured as well. If the program stars a lawyer, the client is freed and the guilty parties arrested or killed. If it is police drama, at the end of the hour the guilty are in custody or dead, and the baffling case is solved. But in soap opera, as in life, very little ends so tidily. Love affairs sort of dwindle into nothingness; ill patients may linger, or just remain afflicted with the disease; lawsuits, as in life, last for months or years, and sometimes are never satisfactorily settled. Operations are botched; some love is unrequited.

These differences are important. They help to make 20 million soap opera viewers into what *Time,* in its 1976 cover story, called "participants" and residents of a "separate nation." Psychologists, media critics, university professors, and others who have analyzed the world of soap opera (and of soap opera viewers), say that the lasting popularity of the programs stems from a general restlessness in our society, the breakdown of family life, and the increasing isolation of the individual, which has inevitably accompanied fast technological development. The Washington *Star,* early in 1976, asked of soap opera: "What's going on here? Have we become so compartmentalized, so sealed in isolated and insulated niches that many of us must have this vicarious injection of typical—and bizarre—experiences to compensate for a presumed barrenness in our own?"

The question, really, is whether that "presumed barrenness" is really there. Soap opera certifies all the awful things that happen, so that a mother who discovers that her thirteen year old is pregnant, or the teenage viewer who discovers that cops can be brutal, may be less stunned by this evidence of life. But the steady diet of unrelieved crises, the unchanging cycles of marriage, adultery, and divorce, infidelity, pregnancy, and abortion, eventually dull our senses. Ceaseless sensation eventually becomes no sensation at all, and the soap opera lives come to seem as barren—presumed or not—as our own.

6 READING, LEARNING, AND BEHAVIOR: ELECTRONIC CHILDHOOD

Each year, nearly every high school student in the U.S. who even thinks about going to college takes the Scholastic Aptitude Tests, called the SATs. There are two SATs, one to test so-called "verbal skills" and the other to test mathematical ability. The tests are designed to measure the mastery, or potential mastery, of these skills, as deemed necessary for successful college and university work; increasingly, a students' SAT score is perhaps the single most important determinant of whether or not he or she gets into the college of his choice.

SAT scores are non-competitive; they are not rated on a so-called "curve," but on how many questions a student answers correctly. The lowest possible score is two hundred, awarded for simply showing up and taking the exam; the highest possible score is eight hundred; and most top-flight American colleges and universities require a score—at least on the verbal exam—of somewhere between six hundred and six hundred and fifty.

The first SATs were given in the mid-50s, and until 1963—in keeping with a general trend in America—the average score rose steadily. But then, full-fledged members of the Television Generation—children born after World War Two—virtually all of whose educational and learning years have been accompanied by near-saturation viewing of television—began to take the tests. The first year in which a post-World War Two baby would be old enough as a high school senior to take the SATs was 1963.

What happened then has contributed to one of the most alarming patterns in recent American social history: the SAT scores began to drop, they have dropped steadily every year since 1963, and they are dropping still. Although this decline continued with painful predictability through the 1974-75 school year, it was virtually unnoticed by the general public. Then, with a flourish that warranted a front page story in the *New York Times,* the annual rate of decline in SAT scores more than doubled. The "sharp drop in scores," reported the *Times,* "represents an intensification of a twelve-year trend whose causes are one of the most puzzling and debated issues in American education today."

This debate—amazingly enough—has proceeded with virtually no attention to the effect on the scores (and consequently on the reading skills of high school students) of television, the one drastically different element in their lives since the decline began. Discussion in the academic community, and to some extent in the popular press, has been conducted almost as though television does not exist. Needless to say, neither the drop in scores nor television's contribution to that drop have been mentioned at all on television news programs; one might think that a steady decline in verbal and mathematical skills could have been the subject for a public-affairs documentary on some network in the years since the matter became of public interest, but such has not been the case—although any number of other public issues, from the disappearance of certain endangered animal species to the quality of drinking water, have been rather thoroughly analyzed.

The puzzling debate noted by the *New York Times* has so far offered four possible explanations for the decline in SAT scores: (1) errors in test content or grading procedures; (2) changes in the composition of the student body taking the tests; (3) weaknesses in the nation's educational system; and (4) external forces acting upon the students who have taken the tests since 1963.

In his 1975 address to the College Entrance Examination Board (which commissions the SAT), CEEB President Sydney P. Marland, Jr., former U.S. Commissioner of Education, seemed to eliminate all the possible explanations except the fourth. His staff has spent years, he reported, examining and modifying its procedures to see if errors in how the tests are "constructed, administered, evaluated, and scored" could be responsible for the decline. The conclusion, he said, was a firm negative.

Marland was equally blunt about the possibility that the decline might be caused by a change in the composition of the student body taking the tests. This is a critical area, because it is widely known that the expansion of community colleges and state universities' so-called "open admission" policies and "affirmative action" programs have made post-secondary education available to students who had been hitherto excluded, and many experts would gladly blame the decline in scores on the presence of more blacks taking the SATs. But Marland gave them no comfort. Acknowledging that open admission policies and the general democratization of higher education had lowered the academic abilities of the average college freshman, Marland nevertheless warned his colleagues not to be misled into parallel conclusions about the decline in SAT scores. He said:

> This explanation seems plausible until it is pointed out that the changes in the number of such [less capable] students are still small, relative to the total population tested, and that there has also been a concomitant reduction in the scores in the upper ranges—over six hundred—so in truth the depression of the average is a function of both more lower scores and fewer high ones.

In other words, students from "gifted" family backgrounds and schools were also doing less well with the SAT material, and the notion that an infusion of disadvantaged students had brought about the decline in scores, simply is not supported by the data.

Of the third possible explanation, weakness in the nation's educational system, Marland warned, "the SAT was not designed as a measure of school performance and should not be used that way. To single out schools as being responsible for the decline is unwarranted, unfair, and scientifically unfounded." Marland concluded that a variety of other forces, from "busing and its related stresses" (less than 7 per cent of all students, elementary and secondary, are bused for reasons of racial balance. Was Marland throwing a bone back to the anti-open-enrollment folks?) to "the phenomenal increase in television viewing," have been largely responsible for the drop in scores.

The reactions to Marland's speech—and for that matter, the major portion of the speech itself—are studies in scholarly coyness. The CEEB head, having eliminated all but one of the causes for the decline, then refused to draw specific conclusions, except to include television along with a variety of other possible causes, most of which were very weak sisters indeed. The inclusion of busing is a case in point; in 1963, and for many years thereafter, there was *no* inter-neighborhood busing to achieve racial balance or achieve anything else except getting children to school. Then Marland appointed a "blue ribbon" panel of educators, social scientists, and experts in statistical analysis, to determine the specific reasons for the decline.

At its first meeting, the panel announced it would "give primary emphasis to examining the SAT itself, and to the changing population of the students taking the test"—precisely those possible explanations already eliminated by Marland. All explanations of the decline would be "inventoried" they said,* for "future study by educational groups, government agencies, foundations, or independent researchers."

There is a substantial body of scientific data available, including interviews with teachers and other education professionals throughout the country, almost all of which indicate it is no coincidence that a major literacy crisis has emerged concurrently with the Age of Television. To be sure, all complex phenomena have complex causes; but there can be no question that television is both a fundamental and major factor in this continuing crisis.

Perhaps the most compelling proof of television's impact on reading and related intellectual abilities comes from events that seem independent of—and perhaps far more important than—the steady decline in SAT scores. When taken as a whole, these show that we are indeed in the midst of a literacy crisis:

—A 1976 study by the American College Testing Program (an Iowa City-based organization that administers the only tests similar in purpose to the SATs) concludes that "colleges and universities have adapted to declining admissions test scores by enrolling and retaining students with lower ACT test scores than previously." To that could be added that the same is true with respect to declining SAT scores.

—ACT issued the report because its own tests, first given in 1964-65, also show a continuous drop during the past twelve years.

—In March, 1975, the Department of Health, Education and Welfare released a special study showing that reading skills have been declining for about ten years.

—In 1973, the General Accounting Office analysis of multi-billion-dollar federal programs designed to close the gaps in reading abilities between children from poor families and children from middle class families, found the programs' achievements to be "debatable at best. Most of the students were not reading at levels sufficient for them to begin to close the gap . . ." Prominent educators praised the program, but were disturbed to discover that fully 60 per cent of the disadvantaged students fell further behind despite the best efforts of professional educators.

—Similar disappointments followed the twenty-five "innovative" educational programs sponsored by the Ford Foundation during the 1960s.

—In the early 1970s the Educational Commission of the States surveyed the reading habits of about 100,000 young people of all economic classes and levels of educational advantage. Their findings included the following:

(1) "Nearly half the thirteen year olds and more than one-quarter of

---

* "Inventoried" is not, of course, a blue-ribbon expression for a learned group to use, particularly a group brought together to study the decline of language.

the seventeen year olds (it was worth remarking that this latter group is one year away from voting) were unable to read a passage containing two conflicting statements and arrive at the conclusion that one of them had to be wrong." In contrast, only 33 per cent of the thirteen year olds and about 15 per cent of the seventeen year olds "had difficulty reading and then answering questions about a common TV schedule."

(2) At age nine, 20 per cent of the white children and 40 per cent of the black children still cannot "identify the dictionary as a book that tells what words mean."

(3) Of the nine year olds, about one-fifth cannot answer questions like "Complete the sentence with the words that make the most sense. The boy wanted (a) a new ball (b) under dinner (c) rode his bike (d) to the circus (e) stopped raining (f) I don't know."

—Since 1969, the National Assessment of Educational Progress has been evaluating the writing skills of Americans ages nine to thirty-five. In 1975 it reported, "There is no evidence here that the schools must 'go back to basics,' indeed, the basics seem well in hand . . . [However, there is] a movement away from established writing conventions towards those of the spoken word."

—School systems across the country are discovering that younger teachers of English—themselves members of the Television Generation—cannot read well or write well. Half of the recent applicants for English-teaching jobs in Montgomery County, Maryland, the nation's wealthiest and best-educated county, failed to pass a test in fundamental grammar, spelling, and punctuation. The public schools in Stamford, Connecticut, now require that all teachers take written and oral English tests; those who fail must attend special remedial courses. The problem is nationwide. Visitors to teachers' lounges across the country can frequently overhear conversations about fellow English teachers who begin work without the skills that they themselves are supposed to teach.

To what degree in this chain television is responsible for the decline in test scores is a question that cannot, of course, be answered definitively. It seems clear that whatever forces are at play are dominated, though, by television, if for no other reason than that the average high school graduate spends more waking time in front of the television set than in a classroom—or anywhere else.

VISUAL MEANS

There have been widespread changes in schooling techniques, which many critics blame for the decline in test scores; for the most part, these changes have been in the direction of teaching children based on *aural* as opposed to *written* techniques. In other words, teachers have frequently adapted their classroom techniques in order better to reach a student body trained since its earliest days to pick up messages and information from what is heard rather than from what is read. Dr. Robert McGee, a Texas educator, says that too many teachers and school administrators believe "that reading and written expression are outmoded, that logical thought is pretentious, and that one can acquire all of the data one really needs through visual means."

Why would educators come to believe that reading is ready to be replaced by visual techniques? For one reason—put bluntly—if you can't beat it, join it. An examination of the scholarly literature on the subject reveals that such notions have been introduced into the nation's schools during the past two decades as a response to the children, whose orientation is visual. Teachers' use of visual techniques has been, for the most part, limited and reluctant, a rear-guard action against a force far beyond their control.

Novelist Jerzy Kosinski taught elementary school for a few years and came away with some fascinating and frightening observations:

> Once, I invited students (from ten to fourteen years of age) to be interviewed singly. I said to each one, "I want to do an interview with you, to ask you some very private and even embarrassing questions, but I won't record our conversation or repeat to anyone what you tell me. To start with, do you masturbate?" And the kids, quite shocked, usually answered, "Well, you know, I don't know what you mean . . ." Then I asked, "Do you steal often? Have you stolen anything recently?" Again, the kids all hedged, "I don't know, uh . . ."—more mumbling. The girls were invariably more embarrassed than the boys.
>
> When I finished, I said, "Now, I'll tell you why I asked you all these questions. You see, I would like to film the interview and show it on television . . . Your parents, your friends, strangers, the whole country would see it . . ." All the students assured me they were willing "to try harder" to answer [the same questions] . . .
>
> Once the equipment was installed, I started the video camera and it was time to address my first "guest." "Now tell me," I asked . . . "do you masturbate? If you do, tell our audience how and when you do it." The boy, suddenly poised and blasé, leaned toward me. "Well, yes, occasionally I do. Of course, I'm not sure I can describe it. But I can try . . ." An inviting smile stolen from the *Mike Douglas Show* . . . After Tom described all, leaving nothing to the public's imagination, I changed the subject. I said, "Everybody will be interested in your experiences as a thief. Have you ever stolen anything?" Pensively, as if recalling a pleasant childhood incident, Tom said, "Every once in a while when I go to the Five and Ten, you know, I like to pick up something . . ."

Kosinski reports a similar response from about twenty-five other children. Each, he said, was willing "to be interviewed about the most incriminating subjects, ranging from less common sexual experiences to acts of violence, the very betrayal of one's family, friends, etc. Often I pretended to be embarrassed by what they said. But trained in the best talk show tradition, the guests were not put off by their host.

"Their manner was so familiar—the easy posture of the TV conversationalist, the sudden warmth and openness, the total frankness . . . looking directly into the camera with a straight face, mumbling a bit, pretending to reflect, but in fact covering up for a deeper verbal clumsiness. Suddenly, these youngsters seemed too old for their years; each one a blend of actor, author, professor . . ."

Kosinski left his teaching experience depressed and discouraged. He seems to feel that his teaching ability and the ability of all teachers, no matter how talented—may have been irreparably damaged by television. "How long can [we] compete with all the channels . . .? Go into any high school and see how limited students' perception of themselves is, how crippled their imagination, how unable they are to tell a story, to read or concentrate, or even to describe an event accurately a moment after it happens. See how easily they are bored, how quickly they take up the familiar 'reclining' position in the classroom, how short their attention span is."

Interviews with teachers across the country confirm Kosinski's assertions. Many teachers, even at the college level, report that classroom behavior has become remarkably similar to living room behavior while a television program is on. Thus, students will talk more to each other during a lecture (theater people report that Broadway audiences, in the legitimate theatre talk more now too, during the play), and some students will even get up during a class period and leave the room, perhaps to return later. This is, of course, the general pattern of behavior while watching television; the figure on the screen surely does not mind being interrupted by a conversation, the preparation and consumption of a snack, or even a trip to the bathroom.

Teachers who remember pre-television students talk emotionally about longer attention span, greater imagination, more fantasies and creativity, less passivity, and an infinitely greater tolerance for situations that are not immediately gratifying. The one-hour span of a typical television program, and the inevitable satisfactory resolution of all problems raised during that period, has contributed unquestionably to a decline in the willingness of a whole generation of Americans to postpone—however briefly—gratification.

Younger teachers, many themselves members of the Television Generation, have similar complaints, "I feel every day as if I'm competing with the characters on *Sesame Street*," sighs a third grade teacher.

"Whenever I start a project or a lesson I have the children's attention for about two minutes. Then, unless I'm really entertaining, or unless I've stayed up the night before to make up some sort of picture display, or unless I've arranged for some sort of film or slide show, I lose them. I can see them dropping out. I'm not interesting any more, and they're waiting for something new to come on."

Reports educator Dorothy H. Cohen:

> As teachers talk to each other, details begin to mount. They flit . . . They can't seem to stay with anything for very long. It's as though they have no patience with themselves . . . They seem to expect quick results . . . They give up too easily and put up a fight against trying.

Caroline Potamkin, a reading specialist who has taught both high school and elementary school, says that television has also created the "can-but-won't reading syndrome"—students who are competent, or even excellent, readers, but who refuse to read because it is not sufficiently interesting and takes too much time and effort. One typical example: a fifth grader was referred to her for special training by an exasperated teacher who could not get the child to read. Ms. Potamkin gave the student a fifth grade test and he read it easily, not just phonetically, but with comprehension. He handled a sixth grade test with similar ease. This child not only had no reading problem, but was able to read with comprehension above his grade level. He had what the jargon of the trade terms "superior reading skills." When asked if he enjoyed reading, the fifth grader replied "No, not really." When asked what he enjoyed doing with his spare time, he replied, also not unexpectedly, "I don't know—watch television sometimes." Ms. Potamkin informed the boy's teacher that "he was not performing because he didn't want to. He was uninterested, passive, and uninvolved. He was going to grow up to be a nonreader and another alienated personality." Our schools are turning out many more just like him, in her opinion, based on many similar experiences—intelligent children whose minds have been captured by television.

This is not the kind of "reading problem" that shows up "in the test scores," Ms. Potamkin notes. "This boy would come out well in any standardized test of basic skills. He would be one of those who helped to raise the statistical average of the school system." Reading skills, then, may be even lower than the test scores indicate.

Child psychiatrist Nicholas Long believes that one of the reasons children do not read is that they see so few adults reading—the adults they emulate watch television. "After seeing things done so quickly and easily on television all of the time," says Dr. Long, "then it's just unreasonable to think that a child will want to read a two-hundred- or three-hundred-page book." Dr. Long has served as a consultant to *National Geographic*, helping them produce a new magazine for children from eight through twelve. It is designed, he says, to beat its chief competitor—prime-time television.

Another reading expert, Dean Everett Jones of the English department at UCLA, reports that among the college freshmen he talks to, "book" has become synonomous with "textbook." Books have become something to read when one has to, he notes, not because one might want to. The impulse that once sent children to the public library, or the family bookshelf, now sends them to the television set.

Jones also cites, mournfully, the virtual absence from the life of young people of what he calls "trash literature." By this he means the standard teenagers' fare such as *The Rover Boys, The Hardy Boys* and *Nancy Drew,* but he also includes the dime novels, paperback mystery adventures and Western stories that were so common on the newsstands and hidden under the mattresses of teenagers in the years before World War Two. These books used to be standard equipment in any American home with growing children. Virtually heirlooms, they were passed on from child to child and from generation to generation. Even the collections of Doc Savage, Zane Grey, and Ellery Queen—as well as the paperback Westerns (which so delighted President Eisenhower)—were also treasures fit for collectors. But television has practically driven them all from the market.

Dean Jones argues convincingly that this body of literature, while never acknowledged to be of a high standard, was at least written in complete English sentences, and it gave adolescents a body of writing that was adequate, colorful, generally grammatical, capable of expanding the vocabulary—and it defined at least the meter and rhythm of written speech. Whether they knew it or not, American teenagers were becoming acquainted with books and literature.

For all of these books we now substitute television. While it cannot be said that *Cannon* or *Mannix* or *Petrocelli* was inferior in literary content to *The Riders of the Purple Sage,* it is true that one is linear and the others are not. One "taught" reading, and the others do not. Confronted with exams like the SAT, or for that matter with any work that requires reading and writing skills, the student whose idle time has been filled with trash television instead of trash literature is at an extraordinary disadvantage. The results are in. No amount of discussion of test methodology or of the changing constituency in SAT aspirants can obscure that point.

College and university professors cite problems similar to those pointed to by teachers at the lower levels. Nearly every college student in this country is a member of the Television Generation, and their professors report—with alarming consistency—that most cannot read and write at minimally acceptable levels. The students have large vocabularies and can speak well, but much of their conversation seems to be molded on television dialogue. Teachers and professors seem lonely and self-conscious in their complaint; some even appear to believe that the failure to overcome television's impact reflects their own professional failure; but most strongly believe that to the list of barriers between students and teachers, between the uneducated and the educated, has been added a new, ominous, and perhaps dominant force—television.

So acute is the problem that many colleges and universities now give academic credit for remedial reading courses.

The flood of illiteracy and non-literacy, many educators now feel, threatens to change the meaning of scholarship, from the Ivy League to the most isolated community college. Students who cannot or will not read cannot learn from Aristotle or Spinoza. Students with short attention spans cannot learn differential calculus or master basic engineering principles, and students who are impatient cannot solve—or even seriously consider—complex problems, or learn to make the reflective distinctions that are the mark of an educated mind. Popular wisdom once had it that illiteracy is limited to the disadvantaged groups in society; now it is evident in the children of the middle and upper classes, who have enjoyed from nursery school the advantages of the best suburban education.

At UCLA, entering freshmen must take an exam known as "Subject A." (The name of the exam comes to us trailing the mists of antiquity; at one time, to graduate from high school, students had to demonstrate a proficiency in Subject A, English; Subject B, Mathematics; Subject C, History.) The exam requires only that the student write a six-hundred-word essay on any of a variety of subjects. Those who fail it must take the Subject A English course. The theory behind the examination and the course (known, to be sure, as "Bonehead English") is that if the student cannot write a collection of simple English sentences, he will be unable to write cogent examinations at the ends of his courses, and so the Subject A course—a simple one, directed solely toward creating the ability to write a simple essay—is required before a student can get into serious academic trouble.

It should be understood that this examination is administered only to freshmen who have already passed the stringent entrance requirements. UCLA considers applications only from those who have attained a high B average in a California high school, and the standards for out-of-state students are even higher. From that pool, only certain students are admitted. It can be seen that those who take the Subject A examination are already high-scoring achievers.

But Dean Everett Jones, who administers the program at UCLA, notes sadly that over the past twenty years, while the standards applied by those who grade the exams have steadily declined, the number of those who fail the exam has steadily increased. He believes this to be caused by at least two changes in secondary schools. One is that, through the operation of a variation of Gresham's Law, "Everything drives out composition." More and more, he notes, California high school students are required to do less and less composition work, in part because they do it badly and in part because other "audio-visual" techniques are available. Second, the reading and grading of compositions takes up an extraordinary amount of teachers' time, particularly when the compositions are so badly written. So rather than teach or grade essays, high school instructors pass the students on the basis of other, non-linear, achievement.

At Yale, the English department has recently reinstituted a course in basic composition.

> [Too] many Yale students cannot handle English—cannot make a sentence or a paragraph, cannot organize a paper, cannot follow through—well enough to do college work,

explained English Professor A. Bartlett Giamitty in the *Yale Alumni News*. The list of schools that have, like Yale, reinstated or are preparing to initiate similar programs reads like a *Who's Who* in American higher education. Interviews with faculty members concerned with the problem always come around to one cause: television.

In the meantime these universities, like the secondary schools before them, are turning out graduates whose basic skills are much less than adequate. Graduate schools report that a shockingly high percentage of their applicants—including many graduates from the nation's best colleges—cannot read or write adequately. The most common failings are spelling, grammar, punctuation, and word usage. The Federal Civil Service Commission, state civil service commissions, and major corporations report similar problems with college graduates who apply for jobs. The students possess the requisite degrees, but the degrees don't seem to mean as much as they once did. They represent just as high—or perhaps higher—standards of intelligence, but they no longer guarantee that the student holding the degree can express himself in a literate way in his native language.

In addition to remedial courses and a new emphasis on fundamental skills, colleges and universities have back pedaled to absorb the wave of non-literacy. Many schools, particularly private institutions hard-pressed for dollars in light of the declining school age population, are accepting students with SAT and ACT scores that previously would have denied them consideration for admission. The higher-education establishment has also successfully pressured the nation's college textbook publishers to lower the basic reading level required to understand the books. Using "readability" formulas that measure students' capacity to comprehend long words and complex sentences, recently, publishers simplified their textbooks.

More evidence—much more evidence—can be cited; but a major systematic problem is clearly at hand. Some educators, politicians, and journalists have become overly anxious to receive and interpret good news from the reading front. When given a chance, they have been known to present test results with misleading optimism.

Thus, many New Yorkers rejoiced in 1975 when tests taken by the city's 580,000 public school students showed that the percentage of students reading above the national norm for their grade level had risen from 33.8 to 45.2 in only one year.* Public acclaim and gracious bows from school officials took place despite muted explanations that the rise occurred only after the officials had decided to administer a different test from the one used in previous years. Among other differences, the new test used a 1973 sample to define "grade level," while the older test had used a 1968 sample, and most if not all of the 1975 "increase" in reading ability simply reflected the sad fact that national reading norms had declined significantly between 1968 and 1973. A more realistic perspective on these 1975 results can be found in the public plea one year later for reading tutors in the city schools—to contain the flood of students with literacy problems.

Another doubtful glimmer of hope came in the National Assessment of Education Progress' 1971–1974 study of functional illiteracy. That study discovered that in 1974, only 17 per cent of the nation's seventeen year olds were functionally illiterate, a distinct improvement over the 37 per cent listed for 1971. Rejoicing newspaper headlines greeted the report, even though Assessment Director Roy H. Forbes emphasized that "this assessment is only of the very basic reading skills essential in everyday life—reading road signs, maps, advertisements, forms and reference works." Several of the exercises, in fact, merely required knowledge of the alphabetical organization of dictionaries and telephone books. Even on a test containing these undemanding reading skills, the best scores came in respone to questions that contained "drawings and pictures." It was the visual items, the strength of the televised generation, that accounted for most of the increase. "The trouble," reported the Washington *Post,* "lies deeper in the students' sense of language and, evidently, in the way they think . . . electronics makes it harder to persuade children that they need to know how to write coherently . . ." The *Post* went on to find "real hope for public education" in the very

---

* Of course, to be "normal," 50 per cent of a school system's students should be reading above the norm and 50 per cent below; so there was slight cause for celebrating that 45.2 per cent were above the norm.

fact that the Assessment exists; that is something like a political candidate who faces a landslide defeat and finds "real hope" in the fact that the Gallup Poll exists.

The last real furor over reading ability came in 1955 with the publication of Rudolf Flesch's best seller, *Why Johnny Can't Read*. Flesch's assertions prompted considerable charges and counter-charges about the nation's teaching methods. For several years, the teaching of reading in public schools was an emotional and political controversy of the highest order. Just as no political candidate can run for public office today without taking a strong position on crime, no candidate in the mid-fifties could campaign without explaining how he planned to get Johnny to read. Flesch precipitated a national educational crisis—but still a crisis which, in today's terms, was eminently manageable. After all, he only urged that classroom techniques place more emphasis on phonics, and less on the so-called "see and say" method then widely in use—a change easily within the grasp of all but the most heavily indoctrinated recent graduates of teacher's colleges.

The television-induced reading crisis will not be so easily solved. Its cause lies not in classroom teaching methods, or in the curricula of teachers' colleges. It lies in almost every American living room. Perhaps this is why no major politician has yet seized upon the issue, and perhaps it is why no provocative book like Flesch's has been offered—despite the vast array of current books critical of American life in every respect from how we eat to how we talk to our plants.

Television is too much with us, too much an irreplaceable part of our lives, too ingrained in our thinking, and too central to our verbal and cognitive patterns. It can no longer be addressed directly. Furthermore, it is now impossible to provide totally unimpeachable, scientific data because television has affected everyone, tester and test subject as well as skeptic. In 1952 or 1953 such tests would have been possible.

Whichever critic approaches the problem, he concludes with a plea for more and earlier attention to reading in the schools, and that leads inevitably to an analysis of the most publicized and most successful use of television techniques for the purpose of teaching and improving reading. *Sesame Street* has been hailed as the best hope for reversing the trend toward illiteracy in the young, and an extensive analysis of its success and problems is clearly in order.

SESAME STREET

Sesame Street, in the words of its founder, president, and guiding genius (the word is apt), Joan Ganz Cooney, "is the longest street in the world." An estimated 9 million children ages two to five watch it at least once a week, joined by several million older children and adults. There are slightly fewer than 12 million preschool children in the United States; more American children watch *Sesame Street* than attend nursery school. It is also watched in 20 per cent of the homes with no preschool children. Of all people of all ages who watch any program on public television, fully 50 per cent watch *Sesame Street* or its sister program, *The Electric Company*. Designed to reach children in second through fourth grades, *The Electric Company* has 7 million regular viewers.*

In the nation's ghettoes—*Sesame Street*'s prime target audience—its reach is nearly total. Surveys taken from the early 1970s found that from 78 to 94 per cent of the inner-city homes in New York City, Philadelphia, and Chicago are tuned in to *Sesame Street.*

Sesame Street has won for its producing company among other honors the Peabody Award, the Prix Jeunesse International, the Japan Prize, and countless Emmy's. In one form or another it reaches forty countries and territories—France has *Bonjour Sesame,* Germany has *Sesamstrasse,* Brazil has *Vila Sesame,* Mexico and other Spanish-speaking countries have *Plaza Sesame,* and Indonesia, Crete, Saudi Arabia, and Samoa have used the English-language version. Saudi Arabia will soon have its own Arabic-language version. Anthropologist Margaret Mead has called *Sesame Street* "the most important program that has been developed for children as a way of introducing them to some of the basic tools necessary for the attainment of literacy." John Matthews, education writer for the Washington *Star,* says that "there is no doubt that *Sesame Street* has had a greater impact on how and what preschool children learn and think than virtually any other teaching tool in this century . . ." The United States Office of Education has given producers of *Sesame Street* more money than it has given to any other single grant recipient—one "of the best things we've ever invested in," the Office of Education says.

The Children's Television Workshop (CTW), *Sesame Street*'s producing company, describes itself as "an applied research laboratory that creates experimental television programs which have specific educational or informational goals presented in interesting ways." Since its

---

* The subsequent discussion focuses upon *Sesame Street* as a case study of what can— and cannot—be done with television. *The Electric Company* is a strong entity in its own right. The major difference between the two programs is that *The Electric Company* is used by teachers in many of the nation's classrooms (and most schools are equipped with television sets). Policy makers of *The Electric Company* encourage this practice, and adapt the program's curriculum accordingly.

There are also a number of other education-oriented non-commercial programs, which involve much hard work and dedication. All are of the *Sesame Street* genre, although some specialize in the teaching of math skills or in reaching specific minority audiences.

founding in 1968, it has accumulated an extraordinary amount of power and influence, which it uses to provide—without exaggeration—the best that television has to offer. There is, however, a nagging problem: it is still television.

From the outset, CTW planners decided to model their program after patterns already embedded in the minds of the members of the Television Generation by the commercial networks and their advertising clients. "Why shouldn't the teaching be done with the sophisticated and entertaining techniques of commercial television, especially the commercials?" asked Ms. Cooney. The chief academic adviser, Harvard education specialist Gerald S. Lesser, explained that CTW decided to take advantage of commercial market research on what holds children's attention, "change of pace and style, catchy jingles and rhymes, broad comedic devices, and short, simple, straightforward presentations."

Thus, CTW programmers developed their now-famous format. The programs are non-sequential, with short segments of a few minutes each followed in rapid-fire order by totally unrelated segments. Slow-motion action and cartoons are mixed to enhance the "reality" and the impression of speed. Stop-action, zoom closeups, repetitions, instant replay, and frequent songs, further minimize the need for viewer concentration. "This show is really put together from a show business point of view with a spinal column of education to it," explains CTW producer Jon Stone.

Ms. Cooney calls *Sesame Street* a *"Laugh-In* for children," and producer David Connell says, "We stole everything from *Laugh-In.*" The references to *Laugh-In* are instructive. The show was a prime-time comedy hit in the late 1960s, and specialized in quick, punchy, sometimes daring joke sequences, which introduced the American people to such expressions as "Sock it to me," and "Verrrry interesting," as well as to the talent of Lily Tomlin. Its serious intent and impact were limited to occasional one-line jibes at the foibles of politicians, and one 1968 appearance by presidential candidate Richard Nixon. Nixon's bit—which consisted of appearing for a moment to ask, "Sock it to me?"—marked the high point of both *Laugh-In*'s involvement with politics and Nixon's career in comedy.*

If *Sesame Street,* as the best that television has to offer, is indeed a *Laugh-In* for children, then the Age of Television may be more limited in what it can offer young people—and limiting—than we ever realized.

---

* The current successor to *Laugh-In* is NBC's *Saturday Night;* on which President Gerald Ford, seeking to surpass the record of his predecessor, appeared twice one night (once to introduce the program and once to introduce his press secretary, who served as master of ceremonies), and then presumably watched as the program went on to make him appear a clumsy oaf. Included was a tasteless sketch in which a woman commentator questioned the value of television's concentration on what she called "the presidential erection."

For the first few years, academics and educators had little but praise for *Sesame Street*—after all, it towered over its competitors in children's programming, completely overshadowing the likes of *Road Runner* cartoons and reruns of *Hogan's Heroes* and *Gilligan's Island,* the major alternatives offered on television to capture what *Variety* calls the "tot market." In the early 1970s, as the tremendous reach of *Sesame Street* became apparent, criticism began to emerge. An article in a prominent scholarly journal argued that *Sesame Street*'s use of non-sequential short-action segments might be promoting—however unintentionally—some undesirable side effects, including a short attention span. A short attention span might lead quickly to boredom once the children reach school, and the need to read books, and might lead to an increased desire to watch more television in general. Other critics warned that *Sesame Street* "is a Madison Avenue sell of the alphabet" and that "the continuum of the life experience is everywhere destroyed."

Such warnings did not emerge from a vacuum. Rather, they reflected complaints that were being voiced by more and more teachers throughout the country. Children do learn a great deal from *Sesame Street,* the teachers were saying, but they also seem to be picking up the notion that everything worthy of their attention must be entertaining. Dr. Edward L. Palmer, Director of Research for CTW, dismisses this complaint on the grounds that he "hasn't seen any evidence" to support it.

Many teachers began to focus on the undeniable fact that learning from *Sesame Street* is by definition passive. Good educators believe that learning must be more than a spectator sport, and that if we have learned anything over the painful progress of teacher training since the early days of John Dewey, it is that the child must be involved in the learning process. Even the most conservative critics of modern primary education would not return to the days of a century ago when children sat quietly for hours while teachers lectured. But television—including *Sesame Street*—may have already accomplished that reversion.

It is one thing for a cartoon character to reveal with comic emphasis that 3 plus 2 equals 5, and quite another for the child to struggle with the concept himself—perhaps with Cuisinier rods—to reach the same solution. Many teachers use films, Jean Piaget wrote in 1969, because they mistakenly believe that "the mere fact of perceiving the objects and their transformations will be equivalent to direct action of the learner in the experience." This is a "grave error," Piaget explained, because "action is only instructive when it involves the spontaneous participation of the child himself, with all the tentative gropings and apparent waste of time such involvement implies."

The producers of *Sesame Street* are highly qualified professionals who are well aware that this participation problem exists. But they are bound by the need to attract children to sit down voluntarily in front of a television set—and that by definition creates passive viewers. Indeed, it is CTW's success in attracting and keeping an audience of children which makes the program a success—and CTW knows it. Thus *Sesame Street* not only does *not* encourage children to learn through some sort of individual struggle, but it is designed to give the child the impression that the program will not require any effort that could be even remotely unpleasant. The only concessions to the need for participation are cosmetic, such as the decision not to let the adult characters on the program adopt a child character, because child viewers would feel jealous and lose their sense of participation. One might well ask, "What sense?"

The problem of participation and its effect in later years is well put by psychiatrist William Glasser:

> Because I work extensively in elementary schools, I am often asked to suggest ways to cope with five-to-ten-year-old children who seem to have no sense of social responsibility. They cannot cooperate in the necessary give and take of the classroom. Often disrupting the class because they cannot settle down or listen . . . when asked to become actively involved in learning (to read, for example), they are passive. Used to receiving, they do not know how to put forth an effort.

As early as 1960, Bruno Bettelheim was worried about the inducement to passivity that television watching—even "instructive" television watching—inevitably produces. "My concern," he wrote, "is less with content and much more with what persistent watching does to a child's ability to relate to real people, to become self-activated, to think on the basis of his own life experience instead of in stereotypes out of shows . . ." Further, he said:

> The emotional isolation from others that starts in front of television may continue in school. Eventually it leads, if not to a permanent instability, then to a reluctance to becoming active in learning or in relation to other people. By adolescence, this inability to relate is apt to have ever more serious consequences because then the pressure of sexual emotions begins to unsettle a personality that has never learned to internalize or sublimate them, or to satisfy them through personal relations.

This encouragement to passivity was a major reason why the British Broadcasting Corporation refused to run *Sesame Street*. BBC spokesmen say they felt the program emphasizes a hard-sell technique, that *Sesame Street* prepares children for school but not for life, and worst of all, it encourages "passive box-watching."

John Holt, a teacher whose comments in a series of books and articles are perhaps more widely read than those of any other serious critic of

education today, complains that even the children on *Sesame Street* itself learn passively, as though they themselves were watching the program. Says Holt:

> Learning on *Sesame Street* means learning right answers and right an-
> swers come from grownups. We rarely see children figuring anything
> out . . . we rarely see children *doing* anything.

On *Sesame Street,* children are not permitted time to figure out whether
there may be more than one correct answer to a question, or even why a
particular answer is correct. Frequently the program does not even
allow itself enough time to provide an explanation. The result, many educators say, is that children may be learning to give correct answers in
response to specific, but irrelevant, cues. The child watching *Sesame
Street* knows these cues will be visible and entertaining, and that if he
does not use them to pursue the correct answer, he can sit back with
the calm confidence—always justified—that it will be forthcoming anyway, also in an entertaining way. The children are thus totally shielded
from the need to master deduction, a process that may be more important to education than the correct answers to *any* set of questions.

There is also the danger that children may adopt at an early age the
notion that there *is in fact* a correct answer to *every* question. The effect of this on children confronted at a later stage in life with questions
that have no correct answer is incalculable. It is easy enough to dramatize in a skilled and entertaining way the answer, for example, to a
simple and relatively unimportant question such as "What is the largest
city in the world?" But a more difficult question (admittedly perhaps no
more important, but one to which there are complex—and consequen-
tial—answers) is, "What is the best city in the world?" And to that there
is, of course, no "correct" answer; there are differing answers, which
might be "correct" in particular contexts for particular children as they
grow older. It is much more this latter type of question with which people have to deal for most of their lives.

Sesame Street also exacerbates the Television Generation's unique notions about problem solving. Nearly every television program tells
viewers that all problems can be presented, understood, and then completely and satisfactorily solved in a half-hour, or at the most, in an
hour. *Sesame Street* speeds up this process, providing solutions that are
"correct" within a matter of seconds or minutes. This speed is part of
the program's successful effort to keep children's interest, but it may
also convey a lesson that transcends the immediate educational purpose: the lesson may be that if any problem is worthy of one's attention,
it can be solved before it causes any emotional discomfort. "The mere
manipulation on the program of letters and numbers does not make a

program educational," runs a typical complaint in an educational journal. "It can be misleading if the mechanical counting and recitation of the alphabet is accepted as a major achievement without finding out if that behavior can be transferred to other problem-solving tasks."

Further criticism has come from the use on *Sesame Street* of "commercials." CTW is highly critical of *real* commercials. Ms. Cooney wrote, in a 1972 article in the *New York Times:*

> Direct costs aside, the indirect costs of a commercial program are incalculable but enormous. They range from our children's bad teeth to a warped value system and the possible psychic damage that is done to hundreds of thousands of our youngsters who are urged to buy and own what their parents cannot possibly afford to get them.

But CTW seems to believe that only the *content* of commercials can do damage to the Television Generation's psyche, health, and values—the producers of *Sesame Street* are happy to utilize the commercials' *form.* "This portion of *Sesame Street* has been brought to you by the letter 'M' and by the number '8'," a somber adult voice intones at the end of a particular *Sesame Street* segment. Children and adults alike are delighted when this happens. These fake commercials have an air of authenticity, and they help to make *Sesame Street* "real," to link it to the real world.

Unfortunately, the fake commercials do more than cause the adults in the audience to chuckle. They reinforce and legitimize—although one should never go so far as to blame them for—a world in which no news or entertainment is real or worthwhile unless it is "brought to you" by someone with something to sell. On *Sesame Street* the products are abstract numbers and letters, but later in the child's life they will be candy, toys, and games, and still later, automobiles and deodorants. The link between the Television Generation and the television commercial is deeply rooted and outlasts childhood. There are very few parents in America who have not heard their children happily singing television commercials—most likely for a soft drink or a hamburger chain. The children are obviously unaware that they are singing anything unusual, although their parents may be surprised. They shouldn't be.

The fake-commercial technique is also used on *Saturday Night,* the NBC late-night program that is a successor to *Laugh-In. Saturday Night's* popularity with older members of the Television Generation impressed even the most conservative industry skeptics within weeks after its introduction in 1975. One fake commercial on the program showed a loving couple, modeled after a then-current Geritol commercial in which husband and wife seem bound together after the age of thirty-five by the regular use of the patent medicine. This *Saturday Night* couple, however, is all male: "My wife—I think I'll keep him." Another shows a new foamy spray, which functions as both a dessert topping and a floor wax. One of the most insightful parodies of a television commercial on *Saturday Night* was a take-off on Gillette's new "miracle" Trac II razor. "Trac III," intoned the announcer at the end of a typical recital of its virtues, "because—you'll believe anything."

NBC reports that Gillette, Geritol, and manufacturers of other real-life products subject to these mimicking commercials, don't complain. In fact, they welcome the unsubtle criticism of their advertising. They are happy, NBC says, because they know that anything evoking their product's image or name in any viewer's mind is a solid plus. They know that for members of the Television Generation in particular, form and substance have merged to the advantage of steady, well disciplined consumer behavior. One *Saturday Night* commercial showed ex-radical Jerry Rubin, doing a typically frantic and hysterical, late-night sales pitch, promoting wallpaper with 1960s political graffiti. Many members of the Television Generation, gathered in their living rooms and bedrooms, thought this commercial was real and inquired where they could send checks and money orders.

The producers of *Sesame Street* seem to hope that somehow the same unthinking loyalty to form may attach itself to letters and numbers, but detach itself later when the letters and numbers assume the substance of unwanted or unaffordable commercial products. It seems unlikely, and the ultimate cost may be difficult to determine.

Another commercial aspect of CTW, this time purely imitative of commercial programs, with no suggestion of satire or fun, is the $25 million annual sale of wristwatches, paper cups, books, records, puzzles, comic books, and teaching machines that have the "official" endorsement from Cookie Monster, Big Bird, or other *Sesame Street* characters. It may be captious to complain, but one wonders whether the parents of the young *Sesame Street* viewers should be pressured into buying these items, particularly when the program is tax-subsidized and "non-commercial."

Valid as these criticisms are, there remain many compelling arguments in favor of *Sesame Street*. Most of them come down to the fact that the choice is not whether children will watch *Sesame Street* or read a book, or watch *Sesame Street* or play outdoors. The choice is whether children will watch *Sesame Street* or whether they will watch whatever alternative junk—violence- and commercial-filled—the other channels make available at the same time. Even those parents who carefully and diligently monitor, restrict, and guide their children's television viewing (and many parents are unable, by sheer economic force, to do so) know that a certain amount of time in front of the television set each day is inevitable. The choice then clearly is *Sesame Street* or something worse, and the inevitable preference, of course, is for the CTW program. "To

pass through childhood, when one's imagination, one's sense of the possibilities of the world is developing, and have it touched only or mostly
by a piece of boffo-funny mechanistic slap-trap such as *McHale's Navy*
seems a damned shame," writes Michael J. Arlen in *McCall's* magazine.
And, there is obviously no question but that *Sesame Street* is more than
a less objectionable alternative to that kind of programming; it does
make a contribution to the child's imagination and his "sense of the possibilities of the world."

Indeed, the arguments made against *Sesame Street* are those best
made against television itself—the passivity, the simplicity, the stifling
of imagination, the behavior modification, the shortened attention span,
the training to be an avid consumer, and the distortions that character-
ize all learning from television.

But given the severe restrictions imposed by the medium, CTW
seems to be doing extraordinarily well. Its programs have entered the
child's world and have taught some lessons that are socially and educa-
tionally useful. To be sure, some of *Sesame Street*'s sins, such as the use
of commercials and an over-reliance on fast action sequences, could be
avoided. These sins seem rather minor when compared with the alternatives, and may even have been necessary in order for *Sesame Street* to
do what television demands of nearly everything broadcast: attract a
large audience.

For an educational program to defy this demand means instant and
unnoticed death. For an educational program to yield to it, as the CTW
programs have done, is to accept, as a price for remaining on the air
with a useful and helpful message, the likelihood of imposing some
damaging effects upon young children. This is a deal the CTW planners, reluctantly it would appear, were willing to make. In doing so,
they struck what must ultimately be considered a good bargain. Probably no American broadcasting or educational institution has been more
self-critical or more closely examined from the outside than has CTW.
Yet one can examine the voluminous literature on it in vain to find constructive suggestions that do more than offer peripheral improvement—such as more frequent depiction of women as independent professionals.

At its best, television would begin to offer a variety of *Sesame Streets*,
each designed to teach a different age group, and each scheduled for
repeated daily showings so as to be readily available to all children. The
absence of such programming (the absence of even heading toward
such programming) is CTW's greatest failing. It is perfecting what is
very good (while largely ignoring its flaws), but not moving on to what
the people in CTW know should be its goal. Ms. Cooney and her colleagues had originally hoped to develop programs so popular that the
networks would be forced to respond with imitations. Their concept of a

children's television heaven consisted of age-specific programs that ran through late afternoons, early evenings, and Saturday mornings. Their optimism about the networks' response to *Sesame Street* and its sister programs was misplaced. Perhaps this was because of public television itself, which has rarely—even with Sesame Street—reached an audience that makes it even faintly competitive with commercial stations in the ratings. (In fact, the most watched public television programs in prime time, such as *The Forsyte Saga* or *Upstairs, Downstairs,* rarely achieved in the ratings, when compared to the poorest rated prime-time commercial programs, what the Weather Bureau would call "a trace.")

The CTW programs still stand out as testimony to the networks' indifference to significant positive children's programming. All three networks have improved their children's programming with a few more culturally or socially defensible shows, but these were introduced in response to parental and political pressure as much as to the competition from CTW. The networks, for the most part, still avoid weekday children's programming (although ABC in the 1975-76 season introduced some original children's *After School Specials,* which are very promising) because it is so unprofitable, and still maintain a Saturday morning bubblegum and sugar-puff wasteland because it brings in large profits. All network programs—even the crime shows in prime time—continue to have a broad appeal to the two to eleven age group, a target audience defined by advertisers as profitable.

Sesame Street has yet another problem, which may reflect the Age of Television more than anything else: if the test results are to be believed (and they seem reliable), the program is having only a marginally positive impact on basic reading and writing skills, while making a deep impression upon children's behavior. These results may be precisely opposite to those Ms. Cooney and her colleagues intended and still expect. Ernest Hemingway used to warn would-be writers not to "confuse movement with action," but it is a dictum largely ignored by television, and the ratings inevitably suggest to those responsible for television that they were wise to ignore it. Praise for CTW programs comes from parents who are impressed when their children can recite the alphabet at age three, or count to twenty before they go off to nursery school.

Gerald Lesser points out that *Sesame Street* gives us "our first real evidence, beyond scattered anecdotes from parents, of the remarkable rate at which young children can learn from television . . . On *Sesame Street,* when we used existing guidelines of 'normal' development we found that we constantly underestimated how much three, four, and five year olds could learn from *Sesame Street,* and did not even have the foresight to anticipate that our most responsive audience would be children even younger than three years of age." But such learning—however dramatic and impressive, particularly to parents previously concerned that their children had memorized only a McDonald's jingle and the desire to play Batman and Robin—may be the result only of an infatuation—temporary, and not followed up, or sometimes at odds with the child's maturation level, so that like the tricks a monkey learns but does not assimilate, the knowledge will quickly wear off.

The emphasis on learning the alphabet is not accidental, nor is it stressed by CTW for purely educational reasons. Dr. Edward L. Palmer, the remarkably candid research director for CTW, admits that one reason the alphabet is maintained so strongly in the *Sesame Street* curriculum is to impress parents with what their children have learned, thus convincing them of the value of *Sesame Street* and that their children should keep watching. Viewers of *Sesame Street* do indeed improve their performances on standardized tests that measure vocabulary, "mental age," and IQ; teachers also frequently praise the CTW programs because they prepare children better for school, in terms of vocabulary and ability to count. But other teachers argue that these gains dissolve quickly as the child undergoes normal maturation, during the first few years of school. Ms. Cooney dismisses this with, "You can't put them (*Sesame Street* viewers) on a diet of filet for two years, then a starvation diet afterwards, and expect filet."

Probably the most impressive and potentially powerful uses of *Sesame Street* are the individual experiments by mothers who expose their children of less than twelve months to *Sesame Street*. They find that these children, at age two, are responding to words, counting, and communicating in a quite extraordinary way.

While such progress among very young viewers is clearly significant, as of now it is impossible to tell whether it will be retained in later years or whether it is simply an earlier-than-usual revelation of precociousness and innate intelligence. Furthermore, this experimentation is limited almost by definition to the children of well educated, concerned parents—probably the children who need help the least.

Independent tests conducted for CTW, summarized below, have defined the impact of *Sesame Street* and *Electric Company* in these terms:

—Viewing CTW programs does not demonstrably change a child's attitude toward reading.

—Gains seem to have only one year's impact. A pre-schooler who watches one year of *Sesame Street* unquestionably learns from it, but he learns nothing new from watching a second year unless the program contains a change in curriculum. In other words, a child may learn six of twelve concepts in a given curriculum, but will probably learn no more if he watches the same curriculum the second year. Children quickly "peak" and level off while watching the programs. Similarly, viewing two years of *Electric Company* seems to have the same effect as viewing only one year.

—Three-year-old first-year viewers of *Sesame Street* gained more in general skills and intelligence measurements than did five-year-old first-year viewers.

—Second-year *Sesame Street* viewers made "significant gains" in learning "functions of body parts, naming geometric forms, role of community members, matching by form, naming letters, letter sounds, sight reading, recognizing numbers, counting, relational terms, classification (single criterion) and sorting." As the song says, "One of these things is not like the others."

—*Electric Company* has a positive impact on the reading abilities of children in the first through fourth grades. At the same time, watching *Electric Company* does not improve overall reading skills so much as it contributes to the prevention of reading difficulties.

—*Sesame Street* does not close the gap between the disadvantaged and the advantaged children, although disadvantaged frequent viewers gain more than do advantaged infrequent viewers. A corollary finding is that only frequent viewers, advantaged or disadvantaged, make "significant gains."

But a 1975 re-evaluation of this data, sponsored by the Russell Sage Foundation, reached significantly different conclusions.

The Sage study analyzed two groups of children watching *Sesame Street,* those encouraged to view" and those "not encouraged to view." The first group received considerable attention, all from researchers and others outside the children's family. The children were visited regularly by grown-ups. They were given materials related to the program and some—if they needed it—were even given television sets to watch *Sesame Street.* They were—and they knew it—clearly the products of an experiment. The second group merely watched the program, without any assistance, advice, special materials, or special knowledge.

The non-encouraged children, who watched heavily for up to a year, showed a slight increase of comprehension of symbolic representation (numbers and letters) and a slight increase in ability to recognize letters.

But the "encouraged" children showed more improvement along a whole range of number and letter skills. The Sage Foundation research attributes this, significantly, not to viewing the program, but to the personal meetings with the staff, and the feelings of worth and importance the attention conveyed. In other words, the encouragement to watch the program had a more significant effect upon the children than did watching it.

There was no significant evidence that the heavy viewing by either section had a meaningful impact on school progress. In fact, among those children who were not encouraged to watch, heavy viewers gained less in cognitive skills than did light viewers.

The Sage researchers also concluded—as previous research, including CTW's had indicated—that there was no evidence that the gap in ability between advantaged and disadvantaged children had been narrowed in any way. Their report concluded ominously that if the gap had been affected in any way, it had widened; as one significant review of the Sage material put it, "to the limited degree that *Sesame Street* has intellectual benefit, it benefits most the children who need it least."

Some of the Sage findings are supported by the insight of Harvard psychologist Burton L. White, one of the nation's leading experts on the development of children under the age of three. In a 1975 book, White tells parents that "exposure to programs like *Sesame Street* probably will, in a modest way, have an impact on the child's level of language development, but rest assured if he never sees a single television program he will still learn language through you in an absolutely magnificent manner."

One final footnote: The Sage conclusions have been hotly contested by CTW. Dr. Lesser, in a blistering reponse, says they are "full of false premises and misleading analyses . . . a mixture of accurate and inaccurate descriptions . . . [The] inexplicably negative conclusions and accommodations . . . should not be allowed to obfuscate the fact that the data do establish the effectiveness of the series." But however valid his specific complaints—and many are compelling—Lesser never really refuted the main conclusions of the Sage study.

Despite the controversy over how much or how little *Sesame Street* has helped to promote reading and other school-oriented learning, there is little diagreement, even from the program's sharpest critics, with the proposition that *Sesame Street* has a tremendous impact upon children's attitudes and behavior. This consensus has prompted CTW to pay attention to the non-learning aspects of its mission.

Perhaps responding to the limitations in the capacity to "teach" reading, CTW several years ago began plans to initiate change in *Sesame Street*'s goals, and hence in its methods. The pace of the program slowed down noticeably and the content—since the 1971-72 season—began to move away from the previous emphasis on reading, arithmetic, and related school skills, and more toward social training. CTW now openly tries to help children deal with their feelings, and to master concepts such as cooperation, friendship, justice and fair play. *Sesame Street* now includes discussions of emotion, some current and trendy political issues such as "ecology," and some advice on how to assess personal strengths and weaknesses. Special efforts have even been made to reach the mentally handicapped.

Throughout this shift, *Sesame Street*'s planners have remained acutely aware of the enormous power they exercise. "Until we discover more about the risks of the medium, we decided to be cautious about raising social and emotional issues," writes Dr. Lesser, chairman of

CTW's board of advisers. Lesser goes on to explain that the program has not yet even exploited its potential for showing children how to avoid physical dangers in their environment—ingesting a harmful medicine, or crossing the street unsafely—because children may not "connect the consequences with the activity" and may walk away from the television set believing only that crossing the street or invading the medicine cabinet for pills is a new kind of activity in which the adults who make television programs have told them to be interested.

There is a connection here—indeed a very direct one—with the finding that violence on television, for children and for weakly inhibited adults, is often not connected in their minds with the consequences of that violence. If ever there were a simple admission of television's enormous power over children it is in this observation of Lesser's.

The reluctance of CTW to try to show children even the simplest cause and effect relationships with respect to danger in their own environment is highly laudable. To the *Sesame Street* decision makers, the question obviously has been not whether to exercise their power, but *how*.

Sesame Street spokesmen maintain, with sound reason, that they are teaching (or at least consciously teaching) socially acceptable behavior such as "kindness, warmth, and even simple courtesy." But some staff members are concerned that they may be engaged in dangerous social engineering. Every behavior pattern, they point out, may have debatable or undesirable manifestations, depending on its social context. In this connection, *Sesame Street*'s greatest asset, its immediate and total availability to everyone with a television set, creates concomitant liabilities, because its social messages reach a widely disparate audience. "Cooperation" is a good example of the kind of virtue that may not be unmixed. Most adults would agree that cooperation is a socially useful—even a socially necessary—skill. It is good, they would say, to teach children that working together is necessary to solve a complex problem or complete a complex task. But the same sort of teamwork may be needed—and used—to deceive a teacher or organize a street gang. The socially beneficial value is not only in the cooperation or the working together *per se*, but in the ultimate end to which the cooperation is directed. CTW's planners are very much aware of these possible ambiguities, and it is one reason the change in direction of *Sesame Street* has proceeded with speed as deliberate as it has.)

In any event, *Sesame Street*'s success in social teaching is well documented. A child specialist at Washington State University, for example, monitored the behavior of children before, during, and after one week of watching *Sesame Street*, and discovered that it "increased the children's giving of positive reinforcement and punishment to and social contacts with other children and adults in the preschool"—and that this increase was limited to children who had shown low amounts of this behavior before watching the program. This suggests that watching *Sesame Street* may initiate an awareness of social skills in those who had not held them, but does not reinforce or strengthen the values already held.

"Of course, it is frightening to think of the influence of television," says CTW President Ms. Cooney, and that concern is not limited to those within CTW. Michael J. Arlen, of the *New Yorker,* warns that both *Sesame Street* and the *Electric Company* teach "within a context of propounding what are generally called white middle class values— perhaps one might even call them *higher* white middle class values." And a Boston *Globe* commentator in 1971 warned, not too facetiously, that "if the tube abrogates to itself the power to inculcate the Golden Rule, the Beatitudes, and the Civil Rights Act of 1964, it is also perfectly capable of trying to persuade that Aryans are superior or that the good citizen welcomes the opportunity to pay higher taxes . . ."

Closely related is the danger that *Sesame Street* and similar programs will teach children to accept, rather than question and challenge, the status quo. John Holt points out that the CTW asks itself, "How can we get children ready to learn what the schools are going to teach?" and not, "How can we help them learn what the schools may *never teach* them!"

MISTEROGERS NEIGHBORHOOD

Fred Rogers is an ordained Presbyterian minister who lives in Pittsburgh. He has his own television program, which reaches nearly 5 million people daily. *Newsweek* says that "his *rapport* with the three-to-eight set borders on the mystical," and former Senator John Pastore, famous for his crusty cross-examination of witnesses who appeared before his committee, once responded to a plea by Rogers for better children's television with no more than a soft "I feel goose bumps."

Rogers' program is called *Misterogers Neighborhood,* and he is unabashed about what he believes to be television's power over children. "Have you ever observed a baby at its mother's breast?" he asked a 1972 symposium at Yale. "Did you notice how carefully that baby watched its mother's face as it sucked and drank her milk? Do you ever notice a similar sight with people watching television? Older children eating popcorn and cakes, younger ones sucking their fingers! If this association is by any means a valid one, then television viewing must be considered as having its root at the very core of human development."

Rogers strongly agrees with those critics of *Sesame Street* who argue that all learning from television is passive. The difference between sucking at a human breast and television, he says, "is that a human mother can help the baby develop active modes of dealing with what he or she is seeing and feeling, while a television set invariably presents some kind of stimulation and lets viewers drink it in as they will." Along with his counterparts at the Children's Television Workshop, Rogers is one of the most potent draughts American children have available.

In sharp contrast to *Sesame Street, Misterogers Neighborhood* is a quiet, easygoing program, with none of the technical gymnastics, animation, and non-sequential action in which CTW takes so much pride. A normal episode opens with Rogers taking off his suit jacket and putting on a comfortable stay-at-home cardigan sweater, all the while softly singing a song of welcome, "It's a Lovely Day in the Neighborhood." Then follow thirty minutes in which he discusses, perhaps, friendship, or why people feel so many different emotions, or why there are so many different kinds of birds. His props are simple, including an on-camera walk over to a friend's backyard, or perhaps scenes from a large illustrated book. He used to jazz up his jacket change at the beginning by also flipping his shoes up and catching them, but he stopped when he learned that too many of his less-coordinated young viewers were hitting themselves in the head with their own shoes.

Rogers, with his unimposing features and gentle eyes, may be the perfect television personality—the children's Perry Como. He is gentle in manner and soft of speech, with a splendid combination of the "good teacher" you remember all your life and the favorite uncle to whom you ran when your parents acted unreasonably. Rogers communicates an unmistakable sense of integrity, kindness, and decency. You would buy a used car from Fred Rogers, you would trust him with secrets. He affects children the same way he did Senator Pastore. He is believable, thoughtful, and above all, interested. He looks right into the camera and calls each child "my friend." He is *there*. Children frequently talk to Misterogers while he appears on the screen; an excellent showman, he seems to know this, and times his dialogues to make it appear as though he is responding.

All in all, we should be thankful that Misterogers is on the right side. He deals with fears, fantasies, and everyday occurrences, such as how to ride a bus or how to respond to the tumult of the circus or even—classically—how to come in out of the rain. He sings songs with titles such as "When A Baby Comes to Your House," and "What Do You Do with the Mad That You Feel?" After the assassination of Robert F. Kennedy, he spent some time talking about death.

Rogers feels that he helps to fill a vacuum created by the impermanent, impersonal life situations that dominate America today. "Before we got so mobile in this country," he once told an interviewer, "there were always the grandparents or an uncle who could give a child undivided attention. I think that maybe I'm this adult who stops in."

The children who watch Misterogers, and their parents, do not need prodding to tell what he means in their lives. Doctors thank him for showing that the pain from shots is eminently bearable, dentists appreciate his showing that pain in the dental chair is neither inevitable nor permanent, and children's barbers appreciate his humanizing of haircuts. Even advocates of early sex education admire his explanations that boys are "fancier on the outside" than girls.

Such testimonials make Rogers the example most often cited when educators and child specialists argue that the power of television should neither be cursed nor ignored, but turned to pro-social purposes. Experiments have found that just a short thirty-second commercial "selling" pro-social behavior is sufficient to change children's play habits. Robert Keesham, better known as the ageless Captain Kangaroo of CBS, feels that the medium is the most potent home molder of children. The right children's programs, he says, could "change the face of the earth."

There is no doubt that this power exists. Just as children emulate and are affected by the violence they see on television, so, too, are they trained and guided by what might be considered the "pro-social" messages.

Dr. Eli Rubenstein, who supervised the work of the Surgeon General's committee on television violence, writes that

> a pro-social example shown on television can under some circumstances increase a child's willingness to engage in helping behavior. Furthermore, the research findings show that such television programming can feature action and adventure and still have a salutary rather than a negative social influence on the child viewer.

In this area of the assumption by television of a "pro-social" role, the following research findings exist:

—Children who watch adults on television make "moral" judgments, e.g., whether or not to cheat, emulate the judgments when faced with the decision on their own.

—Kindergarten children who watched only four episodes of *Misterogers Neighborhood* "learned and generalized several themes—helping a friend, trying to understand another's feelings, knowing that wishes do not make things happen, and valuing a person for inner qualities rather than appearances."

—Behavior models on television can quite clearly affect children's willingness to help and hurt other children over the short term. This is true of children as old as elementary age and even into adolescence.

—Cooperation, helping, sharing, understanding others' feelings, and positive forms of interaction increase when children see pro-social programs.

—Children who have viewed *Misterogers Neighborhood* "increased task persistence" and "became somewhat more likely to follow classroom rules with adult supervision."

—Imaginative play increases after children view programs that stress its importance.

—Children who watch special Saturday morning cartoons learned carefully predesigned messages well enough to repeat them back to an interviewer. The messages included how to handle the arrival of a new baby, what to do during the divorce of parents, the importance of traffic signs, pride in a father's occupation even though it is "menial," and the justification of pride in American Indians.

—Children can learn pro-social skills and messages from carefully designed programming and this learning affects positive social behavior, self-regulation and imagination.

The studies also find that pro-social effects are marked and noticeable even after one brief viewing, that behavior viewed on television can be generalized and applied to real-life situations that are somewhat dissimilar to those portrayed, and that the effects of viewing can be measured for months afterward.

Again, as in the case of behavior stimulated by television violence, these results vary widely according to age, adult supervision, and methodology.

So potent and volatile is television as a behavioral modifier that many researchers and broadcasters worry—as the producers of *Sesame Street* worry—about "boomerang effects." A child, shown a program about another child who is afraid of the dark, may become frightened of the dark himself even though the message at the end of the program is that the fear is unwarranted. Or, a child shown behavior he should not engage in, such as abusing a younger sibling, may emulate the behavior no matter how unattractively it is depicted. This is best demonstrated when, as in the case of most television violence, the antisocial behavior has no adverse consequences—as when the victim of a shooting or a beating emerges in the next scene little the worse for wear; or when the violence has even positive consequences, when it is seen, and intended to be seen, as an effective solution to an otherwise apparently insoluble problem.

On one program, Misterogers demonstrated that bathroom drains are too small to suck down a child—apparently a major fear of some children. Rogers even eased himself down on a toilet seat while singing a catchy song he had written, called "You Can Never Go Down the Drain." This undoubtedly reassured many children, but it also suggested a new fear to others.

This worry over initiating new fears has kept Rogers from dealing with divorce or with the possibility of the death of a person loved by the child. "I'd love to make special tapes for children who have had significant losses—a parent or grandparent who died—or for children whose parents are getting a divorce," he says, "but I really feel I want to know that the kids who are going to see those rather packed programs are children who are going through the experience." For other children, exposure to death or divorce could introduce fears and problems that—he feels—would otherwise appear only years in the future, if at all.

IN CONTEXT

The violence in so much of television programming is in sharp contrast, of course, to *Misterogers Neighborhood;* and the sincerity of concern for television's affects that Misterogers shows is not widely shared in the industry.

The networks, of course, reject such assertions, insisting instead that Family Hour, for instance, constitutes a sincere concern for the public's needs and that television violence has indeed declined. The CBS Office of Social Research maintains its own "violence count" and it shows that after one season of Family Hour, violent incidents declined by 24 per cent, with only 11 per cent of the incidents occuring during Family Hour. Psychologist George Gerbner, though, explains that their "decline" was built into the methodology—because CBS did not count what it calls "comic violence."* All three networks maintained a continued public relations assault on the Gerbner count because it failed to take into consideration the dramatic context in which action occurs. Yet, the type of context deemed desirable by the networks may be more harmful than the old shoot-'em-up type. The producer of a popular police drama notes:

> [A] particular scene may be leading up to a certain act of violence, and the scene can be just as scary and suspenseful without the actual violent act . . . we can use stop-action technique to freeze the frame and avoid a situation where the screen is covered with blood.

Psychologists and phychiatrists have known for years that a source of information is more compelling if it, as it were, forces the individual

---

* Gerbner's own count defined violence as "the overt expression of physical force against others, or the compelling of action against one's will on pain of being hurt or killed, or actually hurting or killing."

receiving the information to work along with the source. That is why it is difficult to do anything else while seriously listening to a dramatic program on the radio. Very few people can read, do serious homework, or balance the family checkbook while listening to more than music. But most people can, and do, perform these and other tasks while "watching" television. Adults skim the evening paper, children write compositions, and a surprisingly high number of television viewers engage in conversation while a dramatic program is in progress before their eyes.

This habit of talking while watching television seems to have spread during the past several years to other types of received "entertainment" as well. The decibel count in Broadway theaters (and Off-Broadway) is up, as it is in movies, during the performances. What has happened is that members of the television generation are treating everything as though it was television. After all, if Telly Savalas or Bob Newhart are not offended if one takes a telephone call, eats a sandwich, or discusses a scene with one's watching companion—all while the action is progressing before one's eyes—why would "live" actors object?

In fact, college teachers report the same phenomenon. During lectures, it is no longer uncommon for students not only to talk rather freely, but even to get up and walk out of the lecture class in a professor's midsentence—sometimes to return just as casually, sometimes not. Professors who once thought this "rude" now see it as merely an extension of television-watching habits into other aspects of the lives of young people. Not only is most information received over a screen, but the professors themselves are often likely to be televised, rather than "live." The audience reaction, increasingly, is the same whether the professor or his televised image is present.

For many viewers, television is part of the social background, something that is present while eating, walking in and out of the room, talking on the telephone, or discussing the day's events with one's spouse, children, or peers. Its demands are limited, largely because the viewer's imagination is left dormant. To read a play, or to listen to it performed on the radio, leaves little room for any other cognitive effort. The reader or listener simply has too many imaginative responsibilities. He must give all the characters faces and features; they must be tall or short, pretty or plain. He must provide clothes, mannerisms and modes of expression. He must invent personalities, based on the way each character listens, talks, or cries. He must be an architect and an interior decorator, constructing in his mind everything from entire cities to bedspreads and carpets. This can be hard work, but well worthwhile in the case of some dramatic material—because it is an irreplaceable learning and growing process. (It is interesting in this connection to ask adults of the pre-television generation about the appearance and mannerisms of the *radio* heroes and heroines with whom they grew up. One obtains a startling variation on such questions as the height of the Lone Ranger, the color of Jack Armstrong's hair, or the ages of Fibber McGee and Molly. The reason, of course, is that each listener imagined these characters as he or she wished. No such discussion, of course, is possible with respect to the famous characters on widely viewed television programs. Everyone knows the style of Mary Tyler Moore's hair, or the way Archie Bunker dresses.)

The power of imagination has been perhaps best demonstrated by a study of subjects possessing a natural interest in sex—male university students. A number of these students were divided into two groups with all extraneous factors such as age, intelligence and aggressiveness held constant. Each student was wired to a special theater seat with devices which measure vital life signs such as body temperature and heart beat rate. Each group then viewed a motion picture identical in every respect but one. The plot of the flim included a violent gang rape. In one version, the movie showed the rape in graphic and gruesome detail; in the other, the story faded in and out around the rape. One might expect that the group actually viewing a gang rape, complete with concrete physical acts, would have become more excited. Such, however, was not the case. By every measure, the group who only *imagined* the rape registered a higher *physiological* response. Clearly, each member of this group acted out in his own mind the most exciting, titillating rape fantasy possible. Each, in short, gave himself the best possible show, and each was imaginatively involved.

Writers and dramatists have known about this long before the social scientists confirmed it. It is surely no accident of dramaturgy that Shakespeare had Hamlet's father describe his murder to Hamlet; every member of the audience was forced to make that particular death, in his own mind, as sinister and demonic as possible. An episode of *Police Story* contained a more recent example. In the episode, two men drag an attractive, blonde, miniskirted waitress from a car off into the woods while their wives wait in pickup trucks. The camera (and thus the viewer) lingers on the waitress's look of horror as she realizes what is about to happen, and as she pleads with the other women for help. No violence occurs on the screen. The woman is firmly but without "violence" taken from the car and led off into the woods. Soft background music accompanies the camera as it shows one of the wives fingering a Bible. No noise, no violence. A few moments go by and the men return. One of them appears to be adjusting his trousers. He slides back into the pickup truck and hands his wife a crumpled waitress uniform, while telling her something to the effect that it's about time she went to work, too. Violence count: zero. Violence in the viewers' mind: enormous. One can only speculate on the thoughts that must have gone through the minds of hundreds of thousands of younger teenagers of both sexes who watched this program.

There are as many such examples as there are "violent" television shows. On an ABC "action" drama, *Starsky and Hutch*, in 1975, young hoods were depicted as about to execute a young drug pusher whom they believed to be a police informer. The pusher falls to his knees, begging and pleading for his life as his executioners' faces remain stoic and tough. He continues to cry as the camera slowly fades out. Commercials are shown. When the program resumes, it is the next morning and the police are examining the dead body of the victim. Violence count: again, zero.

The absence of "real" violence can often even make the scene, in a curious way, more attractive. Thus Judith Rossner, the author of a successful book (*Looking for Mr. Goodbar*), which ends in a horrifying (and inevitable) rape and murder scene, has observed that rape on television almost always seems rather attractive for all the participants, and that the victim seems frequently to invite her fate. Ms. Rossner is correct in this perception; most rape victims on television are extremely attractive physically, walk provocatively, and seem almost to glance invitingly at the camera (previously established to be shooting from the rapist's point of view) just before either the actual physical assault occurs on screen or—more frequently—just as the rapist, his face grimly set, stalks his victim as the scene ends. Here again, there is no explicit violence, but the level of titillation is extremely high and what is more, an unhealthy and false lesson is taught once again—that rape is probably often merely the inevitable consequence of *the woman's* seductive actions. Here, as we observed in Chapter 5, the violence is done to the entire social fabric.

Gerbner's compilations revealed that by the late 1960s the use of violence by "bad guys" was indeed declining. But the use of violence by "good guys," the very people the networks present as pro-social examples, was climbing steadily. Gerbner also reported in 1973 that television violence had come "closer to home"; that is, more and more of it happened in the present time (as opposed, for example, to the stylized Western past), in urban environments and domestic settings. This trend has continued until the present.

This finding is particularly disturbing. It has been demonstrated that violence in an abstract, highly fictional setting has less of an adverse effect upon children and adults than does violence to which they can readily relate—which lends, of course, some credence to the NAB's claim that (particularly older) children can tell the difference between real and cartoon characters. That very ability, though, contributed to greater aggressive behavior when the children saw that the violence was being done, not by "make believe" characters but "people" as real as their parents or even themselves. But it also meant that a quantitative decline in violence may be meaningless, in terms of its actual impact upon viewers, as the use of violence on television becomes less and less a tool of the villain to frustrate and frighten decent people and more and more the tool of the hero to be used in resolving a difficult problem.

THE OTHER PARENT

Programs like *Misterogers Neighborhood* remind us daily that in this Age of Television we have given up much traditional control over our children. Television enters their lives at an extraordinarily early age. Studies show, for example, that twelve-month-old toddlers keep their eyes on a television screen fully 12 per cent of the time they are in the room with it, and that by the age of thirty months an almost adultlike total fascination seems to have set in. The average child enters kindergarten having already spent more time in front of a television set than a college graduate has spent in his classrooms.

This makes television as important as an additional parent (in some cases, more so), and a powerful cue-giver. Stealthily, if not silently, it has entered into and upset some of our most important relationships. William V. Shannon writes in the *New York Times,*

> In the past twenty years, television has become a powerful intruder in the traditional processes by which parents and teachers impart values to children. It is a dangerous intruder because it portrays excessive violence, gives children a silly picture of adult life, encourages a deadly passivity, and creates a fantasy world in which entertainment is the highest value and every problem is readily solved.

So sure is Shannon that this "ruthless competitor" has stolen the minds of young Americans that he urges parents simply to turn it off. Not to do so, he says, means that parents must "recognize that in almost everything they do guiding their children they are rowing against the tide . . ." In this feeling, he is joined by Coleman McCarthy, a writer on intellectual matters for the Washington *Post,* who in a celebrated article a few years ago wrote that anyone who keeps a television set in the house with children "is guilty of child abuse." McCarthy threw television out of his house, and reports a peaceful aftermath.

Similar warnings come from the conservative end of the political spectrum. Semanticist S. I. Hayakawa, who achieved national fame in the 1960s for his tough policy toward campus demonstrators in California, parlayed that reputation into a seat in the United States Senate

(California is the ultimate television state, and its politicians become manipulative screen stars as quickly as its screen stars become manipulative politicians).

Hayakawa warns that the Television Generation has been "absorbing messages parents did not originate and often do not even know about." These messages, he says, teach by omission as much as by commission, and have, for example, usurped the roles of teachers and parents in guiding the political socialization of children. The result, he says, is that television has produced a generation that has not *lost* faith in democracy—but never had any:

> Militant young people, far from being "disillusioned" with democratic processes, are totally unacquainted with them, since they are rarely shown on television—the arduous day-to-day debates, fact-finding, and arguments by which social decisions are arrived at by every democratic body from town councils to the Congress of the United States, are never shown.

Hayakawa is telling only half the story. Television exerts such a powerful presence that even if it showed those processes, it would inevitably change them. Much has been made, for example, of the desirability of televising the Congress, and good-government organizations have long decried Congress' refusal to let the cameras onto the floors of the House and Senate. If the cameras were there, the workings of Congress would change, irrevocably. It is clear that those "arduous day-to-day debates" of Hayakawa's would be far less arduous, and take far less time, and involve far less of the necessary tedium, if they were televised. For one thing, Representatives and Senators would immediately become, perforce, journeyman actors (and many splendid legislators would be promptly retired from public life because of their inability to become even apprentice actors). The legislative process—discussions, manners, decision-making—even topics—would be subverted.

The example most often used of the democratic process at its best on television—the meetings of the House of Representatives Judiciary Committee considering the impeachment of Richard Nixon—is really not in point. That was an extraordinary proceeding, made all the more so by Chairman Peter Rodino's refusal to permit television to enter into the committee room until *after* he and counsel John Doar had literally stuffed the members with evidence, and seen to it that they absorbed it. The sight of more than thirty Representatives reading documents closely, asking endlessly technical questions and receiving equally obscure answers, would have been extraordinarily boring; and as that message began to get back to the committee members, the pace would have quickened, the evidence become simplified, and the entire process been distorted.

The same reasoning—and wise reasoning it is—has so far kept criminal (and for that matter, civil) trials off television. If every lawyer, juror, witness, and judge knew that the audience for his performance was unlimited, and that the camera might at this very moment be moving in for a close-up, there is no question that the conduct of American trials would change. What would be seen at home on the screen, then, would in no way be an accurate depiction of what happened in courtrooms before television.

But whether we are dealing with the millions of American children who watch *Misterogers Neighborhood* or *Sesame Street,* or with the millions more who watch *Starsky and Hutch* or the *Six Million Dollar Man,* nowhere is television's role more significant than in its increasing domination of children's socialization into our political and social process. This is the function of teaching children about "the system"— about the value of debate, checks and balances, individual rights, majority rule, dissent, fair play, and all the other complicated, contradictory, sophisticated, and yet uncompromisable principles that make a democracy work at the national and personal level. It once belonged to parents and teachers, and, in a child's later years, partly to newspapers, magazines, and radio. Now, in the Age of Television, parents and teachers must increasingly accommodate their own ideas and ideals to what is taught—by omission and by commission—on television.

More and more intelligent teachers, those most alert to the environment within which their students live and from which they take their cues, are using television rather than fighting it. As will be discussed later in this chapter, they are using materials derived from television news and from popular television entertainment programs and working them into classroom techniques and exercises. Many teachers developed these materials individually; others have joined non-profit organizations that regularly provide them with materials; and still others are fortunate enough to teach in school systems that have developed television-related instructional kits. But the general characteristics of all of these teachers is that they have observed that television is a power, and rather than fight it they are doing their best to use it.

Parents, though, are essentially on their own. Television has largely usurped their role, and there is truly very little they can do about it. Psychologist Kenneth Keniston, chairman of the Carnegie Council on Children, has concluded that "television has become a flickering blue parent occupying more of the waking hours of American children than any other single influence—including both parents and schools." Nearly one million school-age children do not attend school; another million children return from school daily to a house with no one home. For these two million, a television set is ready and waiting—and the statistics indicate that each of these two groups is increasing, rather than decreasing, in size. There can be no doubt who is raising the children while no parent is at home—skilled producers of television programs and commercials.

Parents who *are* at home must also deal with the presence of television. Child psychologist Bruno Bettelheim has pointed out that children are often engrossed in television at times when a parent may want to spend time with them, and the parents are often busy when the television schedule has "freed" children to share things with their parents. "I think we [parents] are resentful of television because it's given the children another measure of freedom from us," writes Bettelheim, "only we also depend upon that freedom." No studies precisely on the point exist, but surely there is no safer bet in this Age of Television than that modern American parents, when variables like family income are held constant, spent less time reading to their children, telling stories to their children, singing with their children, or sharing their own childhood with their children, than did parents of three previous generations.

Parents face a persistent dilemma. They can do what the networks—perhaps tongue-in-cheek—suggest they do: firmly turn off the television set whenever they don't want their children to watch. At first glance this seems, of course, the surest and safest way to reassert the traditional parental role, but it is not so easy as it seems. Strictly to forbid all television, even to ban it outright from the home, is to turn television into a tantalizing forbidden fruit to be sampled, perhaps, at a friend's house, or to be the subject of splendid fantasies. Common sense and even a cursory knowledge of child psychology tell us that this option carries significant dangers.

Many parents—one imagines, most parents—try to control how much television children will watch, and which programs. This may make television a constant source of tension in the home between parent and child, but it is unquestionably better than total abandonment at either extreme, that is to say, either abandonment of television or of the child to it.*

Even children's play, now given much less time than the television set, has been changed as well as diminished, over the past generation. Many children's games today are, quite understandably, based upon television models, whether it is cops and robbers (now more likely to be

---

* This middle course also provides parents with a carrot and stick with which to guide children: "If you don't eat your spinach, there will be no television." Surely there are not many American families in which some variant of that dialogue has not taken place within the past twenty-four hours. By using this technique, parents are, to be sure, sanctioning television as something *good,* to be denied in response to bad behavior. It is, then, no wonder that children become confused on a Saturday morning when a parent enters the television room, shuts off the set, and says, "Go outside and play." Most children will be grown with children of their own before they recognize—if ever—what those parents were trying to say.

S.W.A.T. and snipers) or the crew of the *Emergency* ambulance. Whatever game is played based upon television models is usually less imaginative and less active than was customarily the norm. The *New York
Times* reports that fifth and sixth graders from the public schools recently visited a Bicentennial exhibit on colonial life. "Why did people in
the olden days have so many musical instruments?" asked the teacher.
"Because they didn't have any television," was the children's response.
Those children know what has happened to their lives. Few of them
may think it is for the worse.

Television's usefulness as a babysitter is, for parents, addictive. It is
always available, it is free, and it keeps the children "out of trouble," so
that adults can do adult things without thinking about children, or talking to them. First Lady Betty Ford undoubtedly spoke for most American mothers of her generation when she wrote to Walt Disney Studios,
thanking them for sending her a button for the *New* Mickey Mouse
Club (a new version of a popular program from television's early years).
Mrs. Ford was effusive: "You have no idea how many hours I used to
spend with the children watching the *Mickey Mouse Club,*" she wrote,
"it was the greatest babysitter of all time. Just before dinner, when it is
quite hard to keep four young children happy."

One should not be too hard on Mrs. Ford. It is indeed difficult to keep
the children happy while cooking dinner; it is even more difficult to
remember, perhaps, what parents did to keep children happy before
there was television. There must have been something: games, chores,
music lessons, homework—something. But now, children are kept "out
of trouble," and part of the price to be paid is that they will come to the
dinner table singing in the cadences of candy and toothpaste commercials or, in this instance, humming "M-I-C-K-E-Y-M-O-U-S-E."

The pre-dinner hour provides just one more example of how the
sounds and rhythms of childhood are increasingly the sounds and
rhythms of television. The average child—let us say it again—watches
20,000 hours of television before he grows up. He carries away with him
a vision of the world defined by all the characteristics described in the
various chapters of this book. The images are short and simple, and the
pattern of life that is perceived is fragmented. Violence works, heroes
never fall, consumption is a desirable end in itself, and problems are
always solved neatly and within an hour. When Gary Trudeau's *Doones-
bury* characters gathered in their comic strip commune one Christmas
to sing carols, it came as no surprise that the Vietnamese baby they had
adopted was sitting in her highchair banging away with her spoon and
happily singing her own carol, courtesy of Burger King, "Hold the pick-
les, hold the lettuce, special orders don't upset us——"

A child's mind constantly seeks to be filled, and in finding this
nourishment from the television set he will rely less and less upon

parents and teachers. Whether we like it or not, television has been admitted as a full-fledged faculty member in the children's academy. Its addition to the curriculum is vigorous and carefully planned, and includes many subjects that parents and teachers might not have chosen. Television not only assumes a teaching function, but it determines the appropriate time for the lesson. How many family dinners are timed by the child's favorite program? How many bedtimes are set by network programming decisions?

Even more important, consider the routine programming decision made in 1975 by the producers of *All in the Family*. It was decided that on a given Monday night at 9 (8 PM Central and Mountain time) Archie Bunker's daughter would announce her pregnancy to her husband. It would appear that conception had occurred during the weekend when the daughter had left her "pills" at home—perhaps, her husband thought, deliberately. Her husband, at first pleased, then accused his wife of deliberately leaving the pills at home and of "seducing" him by wearing a bikini. The daughter charged, "You could have taken a cold shower," to which her husband replied, "I did take a cold shower." The topper for this sequence was then the daughter's line: "Yes, but you took it with me." In the next scene the daughter and her mother discuss the pregnancy and the possibility of an abortion.

How is a child to digest all that? As soon as the program entered millions of living rooms, millions of American parents had to face children's questions about abortion, conception, and, perhaps, the role of cold showers in this process. It is quite likely that many parents handled this well, and it is also quite likely that many did not. But the producers of *All in the Family* decided for both sets of parents when they would discuss these problems with their children.

It can be argued in response to this that any of the parents could have turned the set off or switched channels, but this is a somewhat spurious argument. Programs on other channels would have provoked other questions. Turning the set off would raise the kind of tantalization problems mentioned above and, in any event, is too much to ask of almost any parent in modern America. Indeed, such an act would be likely to incite enormous curiosity about the subject matter of the program:— you don't know before the picture and the sound have come into your home, after all, whether they are sounds and pictures you want to postpone explaining—and then it's too late. But the producers are not at fault either; they are, after all, only doing a job and in the case of *All in the Family,* doing it well. The point is that television is exercising an important child-rearing role, one that is not always recognized.

Television may well be, as Betty Ford has said, "the greatest babysitter of all time"—if it is, then only in the sense that it holds children's attention and keeps it from wandering. But who in his right mind would hire as a babysitter a skilled salesman, equipped with the most up-to-date research tools and with the virtually limitless financial resources that the nation's largest corporations can muster? Who in his right mind would choose as a babysitter, a person who tells endless stories—extremely skillfully and colorfully—that portray a highly unrealistic, and frequently dangerous, version of life? Television provides both kinds of "sitters," and no other. For the child—and even the parent—who tries to resist, the contest is unequal, even where the programs are so-called "good ones." And don't forget that commercials are even more skillfully presented than the shows—and the children are learning to be consumers while no consumer advocate is present. The children are being taught, and taught, and taught that ownership of products is the route to happiness—and they are at more of a disadvantage than the defendant on the crime program they are probably watching.

THE USES OF ADVERSITY*

Popular television programs are now being brought into classrooms across the nation to assist in teaching children to read. Prime Time Television, a non-profit organization operating in Chicago, has helped over 200,000 teachers coordinate classroom instruction using popular television programs. Prime Time Television provides teachers with kits containing related materials and questions for discussion. A popular police-crime program, for instance, may provide an opportunity to discuss some of the causes of crime, the use of violence, or even the importance of Constitutional protections. Other topics taught in this way include social values, news and how to interpret it, politics and general economics. Teachers using this material generally agree that they are reaching students in a way that would have been impossible without the involvement of the television programs.

Even more exciting is what's happening with an idea worked out by Philadelphia Superintendent of Schools Michael Marcase and his colleagues Bernard Solomon and Michael McAndrew. The educators edited the film *The Vanishing Shadow*, a 1934 movie matinee serial, interposed slow-motion and stop-action sequences, voice-overs, and superimposed words. A television station in Jacksonville, Florida, made it into a television series, then—and the episodes were broadcast nightly on a regular commercial channel for three weeks during the school year in

---

* "Sweet are the uses of adversity; which, like the toad, ugly and venomous, wears yet a precious jewel in his head." William Shakespeare, *As You Like It,* Act II, Scene 1.

Jacksonville. Students were instructed to take their scripts home and follow along, reading as they watched. The next day, the class discussed what happened in the episode the night before—and the next evening's script is ready in the classroom.

Dr. George Mason, of the English Department of the University of Georgia, surveyed the Jacksonville teachers involved after the first three-week program was broadcast. The teachers reported "real and significant" increases in the students' vocabulary and an enhanced student interest in reading. Moreover, shy children who had never previously volunteered in class now began to step forward. School attendance increased, discipline problems declined, and general reading scores improved. Some former D students became the best readers in class. *The Vanishing Shadow* series has been officially endorsed by a number of Boards of Education across the country, and has been cited by the National Education Association for its "learning implications which warrant national attention."

The Vanishing Shadow is not alone, although it seems to be the first to combine classroom discussion, reading, and home viewing of television in any systematic way. Another concept suggested and inspired by Drs. Marcase, McAndrew, and Solomon is the use of videotapes of programs like *Gilligan's Island,* (a marooned-on-an-island series, rather silly), *The Rookies* (an urban police program), and *Kung Fu* (a sort of Confucian Western, with police action overtones) in the classroom. If the classroom has a television monitor and videotape player, the students watch parts of the program; are instructed to read along with the script; to act out the episodes after viewing it, using the script for that purpose; or to use the script to produce their own version of a scene or the entire program, and then observe how the "real" actors dealt with the words on the printed page.

Even educators who consider this use of third-rate commercial programs to be at best "gimmicky" have been forced to admit that the technique helps significantly to improve reading scores. Public schools in Mount Vernon, New York, for example, used these programs for five months, and then tested twenty-eight students to determine the impact. Nearly 90 per cent showed marked improvement in reading skills and more than half of the students gained *two years or more* in reading levels in the five months that this "third-rate" television had entered the classroom. The program helped good readers as well as poor ones. One student's reading level rose four grades during the five months. In Philadelphia, where the program originated, reading levels of minority students were raised from low percentiles to the national norm.

Many teachers who have participated in the program used words like "fantastic" and "exhilarating" to describe the results. "Just about the most exciting thing I've run across as far as motivating students," says one; another comments, "You could get those kids to do just about any-thing you want them to do just by using television."

These teacher attitudes are perhaps best summed up by a fifth grade teacher who explained, "Kids identify with the television characters and want to be part of their world." Philadelphia Superintendent Marcase concedes that "people in Hollywood and on Madison Avenue know much more about reading and motivating kids than we do," and sees no danger—at least within the narrow focus of increasing reading interests and skills—in co-opting that special knowledge.

But if it is true that "kids identify with the television characters and want to be part of their world," then another problem has been stated. If, as appears to be the case, educators must *join* television (as opposed to fighting it or at least seeking ways to counteract it) then the Televi-sion Generation is indeed a permanent one in so far as reading, writing, and related intellectual abilities are concerned. Interspersed with teachers' praise for programs like *The Vanishing Shadow* are sad, rueful comments about decreased attention span, passivity, and other television-induced problems. As in the case of *Sesame Street,* even im-aginative uses of television programming for educational purposes do little to combat these negative side effects of television viewing, and may even be said to institutionalize and legitimatize them as a price worth paying in order to get children more interested in reading *any-thing*. This may be a high price, but it also may be unavoidable. Mem-bers of present and future television generations are going to watch an average of three hours of television in each twenty-four hour period, no matter what happens in the classroom, and unless the entire struc-ture of the broadcast industry is to be radically changed, those three hours are going to be filled with programs which approximate *Gilligan's Island* in quality. The question then will be not *how* much is watched or *what* is watched, but what *use* is made of it. The only real choices for the teachers and parents may be whether to use television to teach read-ing skills and how best to do this.

One must question how valuable, whatever its success in reading scores, programs like the *Vanishing Shadow* really are. The following di-alogue is a typical exchange taken from the scripts provided for the children to read:

GLORIA: "Stanley! Stanley! Stanley!"
VAN DORN: "Kill!"
STANLEY: "Look out, Gloria! That ray gun will kill you."
VAN DORN: "Keep back, Stanfield! I'll burn them to a crisp!"

The plot itself is not much: two inventors team up to perfect an invisible ray machine. They get it started early in the series and the hero straps it around his waist, turns it on, and vanishes. His partner, the slightly gloomy but good-hearted scientist, tries to ward off the bad guys with his death-ray gun, but often succeeds in killing only a few plants. Much is made of their attempts to rescue the hero's girlfriend.

The program is filled with violence. Threats, beatings, car crashes, fist fights, and potential destruction by death ray ("to a crisp") dominate plot developments. This violence is, in fact, emphasized and exaggerated by the captions added by the authors of the reading program. "You fight Stanley, I'll fight the girl," reads one. Others include, "I'd rather fight than switch," and the caption for a choking scene, "ring around the collar." This use of phrases from irritating commercials may be a good pedagogical way to reach students, but it is a sad admission by the teachers of linguistic bankruptcy.

Not surprisingly, there is a commercial advantage to be squeezed from even these educational programs. Children in the Washington, D.C., area, for example, were required to watch *The Vanishing Shadow* as a homework assignment. At the same time, they were exposed as a consequence to, among others, McDonald's, Cocoa Puffs, and Burger King.

But such objections often mask the most significant conclusion to come from these recent experiments—television *can* be used to get children interested in reading and to improve their reading skills. Any doubter has only to visit a classroom in Philadelphia and see children begging to stay after school in order to finish their reading lesson. There, children watch a scene from—let us say, *Gilligan's Island* or *Sanford and Son,* the set is turned off, and the teacher asks for volunteers to "read" the parts in the scene just played. The children clamor to play the leading roles, and invest them with considerable animation as they read the part from the script. Then the teacher, working from a comprehensive guide, begins to stray from the script, but the childrens' enthusiasm does not wane. They begin to talk—in the case of *Gilligan's Island,* for example—about the geography of an island and other elements of geography. Then they may go on to acting out the next scene before it is seen on the monitor screen, so that the children will get a double dose of reading the script while their enthusiasm remains high.

Still another application of this concept was launched when Superintendent Marcase negotiated an arrangement where the morning newspapers carried a script of the ABC special, *Eleanor and Franklin.* The ratings in Philadelphia exceeded that of other major cities for the broadcast—perhaps because 150,000 school children were given free copies of the newspaper and script. Since such a tremendous response was witnessed from the entire Delaware Valley, Philadelphia went even further by placing Shakespeare's *Midsummer's Night Dream* in the newspaper to correspond with a local TV production of the classic.

Again, the powerful attraction of television brought unprecedented numbers of children to read along with Shakespeare.

But what if some of Hollywood's finest talent—Norman Lear, for example—were to develop popular television programs with reading instruction in mind as the primary objective? This possible marriage between the best of Hollywood and the most imaginative, street-wise reading educators, if developed and marketed with the same intensity with which high ratings are sought, might possibly stem the tide of illiteracy.

Something new is clearly needed. Not only do reading scores continue to decline across the country, but there is substantial evidence that television has *permanently* shaped the reading habits of the Television Generation. It was with more than the usual Madison Avenue enthusiasm that advertisers promoted a 1964 edition of Marshall McLuhan's *Understanding Media* with the words "books will soon be obsolete." Consider the following conclusions of recent studies:

—Books that are dramatized on television, in whatever form, become widely read. Sales of *Helter Skelter,* for example, jumped by several hundred thousand during the days immediately after its dramatization on four hours of CBS prime time.

—A similar piece of luck hit Irwin Shaw's *Rich Man, Poor Man* after its successful run on ABC; new paperback editions were published and gobbled up in the hundreds of thousands, and other Shaw novels were rebound for the paperback racks, with the legend, "by the author of *Rich Man, Poor Man.*" NBC now is serializing, in its own words, "best-selling novels." But the network has its causality mixed up; whatever the original sales figures, the books *will be* best-sellers because NBC chooses to serialize them.

—Children living in middle class suburban homes from which all television has been removed for a period of time do *not* spend more time reading. Time devoted to all other leisure-time activities—ranging from listening to music to conversation—does increase.

—The amount of television watched by a child is unrelated to his performance in school, his interest in reading, or his intelligence quotient, once sufficient television watching has taken place and the availability and possibility of television watching has been established.

THE FUTURE

The average IQ is rising, recent studies strongly indicate. Children are getting smarter, a fact confirmed by many of the nation's teachers, even those who lament the decline in literacy. They observe that children possess more "facts," are more sophisticated, and have a higher capacity to absorb new, and even startling, truths.

IQ tests are adjusted every few years—questions in the exam are sometimes discarded as "outdated," other, "contemporary" questions are added, and the tests are "standardized"—the average IQ, the way the scale works, is an IQ of 100. The most recent standardization came in 1972 (the previous one had been in 1960). Educators examined representative samples based on the scores achieved by 20,000 children in each grade level who took the test. The results showed that a new notion of "average" had emerged; the average IQ for a four year old was 110 in 1972, based upon 1960 standard scores. At age five and one-half, the average IQ in 1972 was 111 (again, on the 1960 scale). Between the ages of roughly six and ten years, the average child lost one IQ point each year, dropping down to about 102. The average then rose again, reaching approximately 105 or 106 during adolescence.

John L. Debes, III, visual-learning coordinator for Eastman Kodak, says that from these numbers "one thing is certain: today's children under the age of five and one-half know more than their peers of twenty or more years ago." Recognized by the teaching profession as an expert on visual learning, Debes argues that television is responsible for the rise in average IQ. Never before in history have millions of people evidenced such a dramatic rise in intellectual capacity, he says, so it must be more than just a coincidence that this rise coincides precisely with the first exposure of an entire younger generation to a medium as pervasive as television.

Dr. Robert Thorndike, past president of the American Educational Research Association, also credits television with the increase. In his 1975 presidential address to the Association, Thorndike pointed out that for years numerous independent tests, based on different analytic procedures, have been providing solid evidence that the average intelligence of young children has been rising. IQs went up, Thorndike reported, because "the amount of verbal stimulation that the preschooler was getting was enormously more than that available to the typical preschool child in the 1930s [when the tests were originally written and standardized]." This stimulation, he explained, came mostly from television, as well as from better educated, more aware (also because of television) parents.

Does this mean that members of the Television Generation are and will be smarter when they reach adulthood? Or are television's effects transitory, most dramatic in preschool years and then disappearing with maturity? No one knows. Serious testing of the relationship between television and IQ did not begin until the late 1960s, and the oldest children of the Television Generation whose progress has been charted are still in their teens. Thorndike, however, has some very strong ideas about what is happening. He points out that the loss of IQ (slipping back to the earlier normal levels) begins at precisely the same time that children begin to attend school. He acknowledges that some critics may "point a finger of reproach at our schools by asking what they're doing wrong," but he asserts that the real culprit may be the entire educational system's refusal to come to grips with television:

> We should recognize that with television the world of the child has changed, and that the beneficial aspects are experienced primarily, perhaps even exclusively, in the preschool years.

Further evidence of this unique boon to children of preschool years comes from the Brookline Early Education Project (BEEP)—an educational experiment conducted in Brookline, Massachusetts, since 1972.

The project is based upon a ten-year study of young children's learning patterns conducted by Harvard psychologist Burton White and a team of colleagues. Their conclusion: what happens to a child during his first three years shapes his future capacities. "Of course, this doesn't mean you can't ruin a child after three," White told an interviewer, "but if he develops poorly during the first three years, he is not likely ever to catch up—he will simply fall further behind."

BEEP is an effort by White and the Brookline public schools to begin a child's education *before* the age of three. Specially trained BEEP teachers visit new parents soon after their baby's birth; the visits are repeated about once a month. The teachers work with parents on how best to understand their children and to shape future behavioral and intellectual patterns. Dr. Donald E. Pierson, the project director, explains the type of advice given by these teachers—"They never say, 'Read to your children,' for instance, though they might ask, 'Do you ever read to your child? Does he enjoy it?' " White claims that BEEP could be the basis for "a total re-evaluation of our educational priorities." "What we do now," he says, "flies in the face of reason. We spend nothing on a child's most important years, when the foundations of his educational capacity are being set. Then we spend more and more as he grows older, when he needs it less and less."

The BEEP teachers are attempting something that has previously been left exclusively to television. They are trying systematically to enter a child's life, to touch him, and to affect his development before he enters school. Until now, the only non-family institution trying to do this has been the broadcast industry. If the first three years are as important as the IQ scores and White's findings indicate, then the influence of television—and the need better to understand and direct that influence—takes on an added urgency.

Further evidence of television's impact comes from studies that examine whether the rise in preschoolers' IQ has been uniform in all items tested. Thorndike calls the results a "surprise." The change, it seems, has not been uniform: "non-verbal, pictorial, perceptual and memory" questions have become easier for preschoolers to answer. This is manifest only when the children are about four and a half years old.

"We should recognize," Thorndike explains, "that with television the world of the child has changed, and that the beneficial aspects of that change are experienced, primarily, perhaps even exclusively, in the preschool years."

Leonard Berman points out that the gap between teachers and the Television Generation is a result of this new visual stimulation received by the children before they enter school. "Theirs is a world of images rather than of sentences," he wrote in the *Humanities Journal*. "This generation came to school aware and armed with images. They came to school with images of action, creativity, of destruction. They came to school, and we gave, and continue to give them, what we understand best. We give them words."

Debes goes deeper into this visual component; he beleives that television is training children to use both sides of their brains, as opposed to a pre-television population which has used only one side. This different use of sides of the brain gets a bit tricky, but Debes explains it best by emphasizing the distinction between *verbal* language and *visual* language. In verbal language, each letter stands for a distinct sound. The letter "A," for example, represents a sound unlike all others, and the configuration A-P-P-L-E stands not for a sound alone but for a unique piece of fruit. In visual language, each symbol stands for a particular object, and the image of a real apple, or an image that represents a real apple, takes the place of the five letters.

Debes argues that pre-television generations have employed only one hemisphere of the brain to engage in language, all verbal, but that members of the Television Generation engage in verbal and visual language, using the brain's full capacity.

Psychiatrists and neurosurgeons agree that Debes is on to something. Most right-handed people, so the explanation goes, rely almost entirely on the left hemisphere of the brain for language, with the right hemisphere called upon only for commonly-used expressions, and what UCLA psychiatrist Warren F. Brown calls "a surprising vocabulary of swear words." (A roughly reversed relationship applies to left-handed people. Although their use of brain hemispheres appears to be more complicated.) Until recently, physicians considered the right sphere of right-handed persons "silent." They based this judgment on case studies that repeatedly show that a right-handed person who has a left-hemisphere stroke suffers an inability to read or write; the right hemisphere is unimpaired by the stroke, but apparently has nothing to do with language.

But, according to Dr. Brown, recent research shows that the "silent" hemisphere has "special abilities . . . which include the appreciation of spatial relationships and patterns, imagery, fantasy and dreams, music, and the recognition of facial expression and body language." Debes and others argue that the Television Generation is developing this "silent" hemisphere in ways not previously thought possible.

This thesis of Debes's does not go against any existing medical evidence, and it seems to be supported by a great deal of research that has already been conducted. Some of the best evidence comes from Japan, where many literate Japanese really master two languages. One is *Kanji,* derived from ancient Chinese classics and visual in construction. The other is *Katakana,* a verbal language in which words are constructed by letters much as in English. Medical evidence seems to show that a right-handed Japanese who has a left-hemisphere stroke retains the capacity to read and write in the visual language (*Kanji*), even though he loses his capacity for verbal language (*Katakana*). From this, Debes deduces that Television Generation children, like well-educated Japanese, are using both sides of their brain. This conclusion has yet to be proved, but recently published research indicates that one brain hemisphere is indeed uniquely developed in the use of verbal language.

Further evidence is found in the fact that reading disabilities in Japanese children are practically nonexistent; Japan does not even have teachers trained as "reading specialists." In the United States, on the other hand, experts say that anywhere from 20 to 40 per cent of all schoolchildren have some form of reading disability that requires special attention, and the correction of reading disabilities is a rapidly growing professional speciality for teachers. The reading disability problem in European countries, none of which have Japan's linguistic duality, is roughly similar in size to our own.

Medical science does tell us that the visual, television-stimulated capacity of the brain to learn is incredible. It is estimated that a full 10 per cent of the cerebral cortex—250 million sense receptors—are reserved for sight alone. The ears, in contrast, command only 50,000 sense receptors. Some scientists engaged in neurological research speculate that the thickness of the tissue layer covering the two brain lobes is increasing due to the demands made by television.

Marshall McLuhan once quoted J. Robert Oppenheimer as saying "there are children playing in the streets who could solve some of my top problems in physics, because they have modes of sensory perception that I lost long ago." Oppenheimer correctly perceived that television-trained children were developing a new kind of literacy, but he was probably wrong in believing that he himself had ever harnessed the senses of sight and sound to the degree that today's children have done.

Some recent experiments published in *Scientific American* indicate that sight actually dominates the sense of touch—exactly the opposite of what philosophers and scientists have believed for centuries. The experiments found, for example, that when a person views his own hand in a position distorted by a prism, he soon begins to believe it is where his eyes—and not his hand—tell him it is.

In another experiment, subjects felt a square block of plastic while at the same time viewing it (but not their hands) through a prism that made the block look rectangular. *In every instance,* they believed that the block was rectangular, even though their fingers provided direct sensory evidence that the opposite was true. "[Vision was] so dominant," write the authors, "that most subjects said the square actually *felt* the way it *looked.* If subjects closed their eyes while grasping the object, they often thought they felt it changing its shape from a rectangle to a square."*

If these studies are really pointing in the right direction, then television may be tapping an immense reservoir of brain power. Fully to use and channel this new power may require revolutionary changes in the nation's educational techniques. Debes feels very strongly that schools, because they force children to use exclusively verbal as opposed to visual language, are responsible for the drop in IQs that occurs once children reach the age of six; like Thorndike, he argues that schools should support and build upon, rather than resist, the change. As a consequence of this resistance, he says, "visual experiences to sustain the rise in IQ are not offered."

As partial proof, Debes cites a research project among minority-group preschoolers in Buffalo, New York. The project revealed that children from poor, black families, who watched more television than did their white, wealthier counterparts, scored higher in tests measuring visual language. But once the children began to attend school, where language competence is all verbal, the gap opened up between the two groups once again.

A study of children ages seven through twelve, with above-average intelligence and with reading difficulties, reveals that all share—if one can penetrate the jargon—"superior three-dimensional spatial visualization and analytical skills." This raises the possibility that a great many children deemed unintelligent and poor readers may really be quite bright, with capacities we stifle rather than recognize and encourage. Some ex-

---

* Shakespeare also noted this dominance of the eye over the mind. "The error of our eye directs our mind . . . Minds sway'd by eyes are full of turpitude." *Troilus and Cressida,* Act V, Scene II. This is not much different from the analysis of the Matthean Gospel given us during the 1976 presidential campaign, through the courtesy of *Playboy* magazine, by President Jimmy Carter. There really is nothing new.

perts estimate that anywhere from one-third to one-half of today's schoolchildren possess this visualization capability.

Debes asks:

> If so large a portion of the population is inclined to the visual, and if that portion of the population is exposed to television from infancy until they finish school, how can we expect such youngsters to prefer anything except a sequential visual language with which to learn or to communicate?

Child psychologists Barbara R. Fowles and Gilbert Voyat perhaps sum up the dilemma and the suggested direction of change most completely, writing in the *Urban Review:*

> When we ask that [Television Generation] child to use print, we ask him to derive from a single source the message normally carried in several partially redundant channels. This is difficult enough. But we complicate the task even more when we present both the print and the richer, more directly representational information and, in effect, require a child to ignore the latter in order to master the intended instructional goals.

Television has unquestionably put us on a steady decline from earlier and higher plateaus of literacy; there are strong hints that television may also offer us the tools with which to reach newer highlands.

7 CREATING CONSUMERS: THE BOTTOM LINE

Television is an enormously profitable industry. It has been said that while it is possible, with deliberately bad judgment and a staff top-heavy with incompetents, to lose money in one year of operation of a radio station, it is impossible under any circumstances to do so with a television license. That is why, for example, of the many newspaper corporations across the country that also own television stations, no more than a very few (the Washington *Post* may be the only one), if required by a divestiture order, would sell the television property rather than the newspaper.

What is more, television is recession-proof. Just as the motion picture industry thrived and prospered during the Great Depression, because it provided cheap, almost-constant diversion for the idle, so did television know no slump in revenues when the recession of 1974-75 came along. It is the cheapest mass entertainment, and any decline in the affairs of advertisers, and a consequent reduction of commercial minutes, was more than made up by an increase in viewers, higher advertising rates, and new customers waiting to advertise in whatever time periods had become open.

The profit figures are impressive. Overall television industry profits rose from $3.8 billion in 1974 to $4.1 billion in 1975. All three networks showed substantial increases, and despite the ratings battle, none of them had reason to complain. According to the Federal Communications Commission, the three networks had pre-tax income of $454 million in 1976, up 44.5 per cent from 1975. ABC's pre-tax income was $150 million on revenues of over $1 billion; CBS had a $215 million pre-tax-income on revenues of over $1.4 billion; and NBC had pre-tax income of $115 million on $955 million in revenues. These figures are for television broadcasting alone.

It is not only the networks that prosper. Dr. Johnson once was asked by the widow of a brewer friend of his who had recently died, if he would help as the auctioneer when the brewery was sold by the estate. He agreed, and announced to the assembled bidders that what they saw was not just a "parcel of boilers and vats, but the potentiality of growing rich beyond the dreams of avarice." He might have been describing the towers, transmitters, wires, and studios of a modern television station. With the license, it is a property more valuable than any brewery.

There are 974 television stations in the United States (excluding the UHF band, where one finds most public stations, and others with weak signals and whose channels, in any event, are difficult to dial on many sets and impossible on many more). Of these commercial VHF stations, 600 are affiliated with one or another network (198 CBS, 212 NBC, and 190 ABC), and the remaining 359 are independent—a few of these independents are non-commercial. The networks own, outright, 15 stations—5 apiece. Any single owner is limited to 5 stations. Each network owns one station in the three largest markets, New York, Chicago, and Los Angeles, and one in each of two others.

These owned and operated stations—called "O&Os" in the business—are tremendous profit centers for the networks, since not only are they powerful entertainment outlets in huge markets but their existence makes all kinds of profitable accounting maneuvers possible. Since no law as yet requires a separate public accounting for wholly owned divisions within a conglomerate—which each of the networks surely is—it is impossible to know just how profitable the O&Os really are.

The "independents" are what the name suggests; they may produce their own programming—but few do—or purchase programs from any source. However, if a network affiliate exists in the same market, it will have first call on network products. Occasionally, a local affiliate will refuse, for whatever reason, to carry a particular network program, in which case it may be available—on a one-shot basis—to an independent.

The affiliates make more money than the independents, for the most part, because they have first call on the most highly rated prime-time programs—those emanating from the affiliated network. The affiliation is for a period of years, and the agreement generally provides that the affiliate will, during the hours the network is programming, take the programs and play them at the suggested hours. The money from the national advertisers is split between network and affiliate—thus the affiliate gets sizable advertising revenues during network time, for no effort beyond that of turning on the network switch.

In addition, the affiliate has some "reserved" spots each hour, usually around the station breaks, for local advertising, from which it keeps all the money. And, of course, on its own programming—almost always local news, sports events, and an occasional Sunday morning public affairs program (usually called *Focus* or *Spotlight* or, if the station is fulfilling its "community service" obligation, the program title will probably use the word "rap" or "soul")—the local station, independent or affiliate, will sell the time and harvest the proceeds.

The key to network success can thus be seen to be both the number of affiliates (at least in the larger markets) and the continued good feeling of the affiliates toward the network. Thus, for example, all three network news departments are convinced of the desirability of an additional one-half hour of national network news each evening. They have so far not proceeded to execute this idea, however, because of almost solid opposition from the affiliates, who see the revenue from one-half hour of local news programming disappearing if the network takes the time. The affiliate would have to split revenues with the network if that half hour were network news.

In addition, news is a source of irritation between the network and the affiliates. It causes "controversy" and sometimes—as during the Watergate coverage—it brings to the local screen facts the local owner would rather suppress or at least not see. CBS denies it resolutely, but it was—and is—widely believed in the business that protests from pro-Nixon affiliated station owners finally forced the network to move correspondent Dan Rather from his White House beat after President Nixon's departure. His sin, in their eyes, was in reporting—not wisely, but too well.

Network programming can be generated within the network itself, although this is now almost entirely confined to news and public affairs, at least in prime time. Other programs, the purely entertainment segment of the schedule, are bought by the networks for a fee from "independent" producers. These producers are either the major film companies, such as Universal, Warner, or Paramount, or they are themselves "independents"—such as Norman Lear, Quinn Martin, or Grant Tinker—whose record of successful series has enabled them to take permanent studio facilities (sometimes leased from a "major") and, in effect, run their own production houses.

These producers are paid directly by the network for use of their product, under complicated production/distribution agreements in which production financing is advanced by a bank or other financial institution, with the product as security. The network then pays an agreed sum per episode—approximately $300,000 for a one-hour drama. This will, most of the time, be somewhat less than the total cost of production, but that figure includes generous—at times staggering—sums for the principals as "salary" or production fees.

This leaves the really enormous profits in television production to be made in syndication—the name given to the transactions in which programs that have finished, or are about to finish, their prime-time run, are sold for mass reruns to stations around the country. Some of these may be network affiliates, indeed sometimes the very affiliates that ran the original programs. The producers of the programs earn huge sums from the rerun syndication, and if a program is on the air for five years, it is said to be a prime syndication candidate.

Twenty-four new episodes of each weekly program are produced each sesson and sold to the network, if it exercises its options and the program is successful enough to stay on the air through the entire period. Each episode is rerun once during the season, and provision is made for at least four pre-emptions, when a program's time is taken for another program, either a one-shot special or perhaps a news or sports event.

In the end, it all comes down to ratings—that is to say, the number (and kind) of people assumed to be watching a particular program. If a network thinks a program will be popular, or even if it thinks it will help other programs be popular, it will buy it and put it on the air. If it does not draw a large enough audience, the options will be canceled and the producer will be left with a few episodes and no syndication market.

The ratings are believed, and they govern the whole industry. If even a tiny rise in a program's ratings is seen, it's cause for celebration by the television people connected with that show. If there's a drop in the ratings, they are desolate. Ratings, after all, determine how much that show's advertising-time slots will sell for; they are where the money is, and that is the bottom line. Since the number of measured families—the ones selected to participate in a ratings survey—is very small, the viewing habits of just a few can make the difference—for a star, a writer, a producer, or a network executive—between just an ordinary, and maybe shaky, job in a glamorous industry, or "the potentiality of growing rich beyond the dreams of avarice." Since ratings are the great throbbing engine of television—all television: entertainment, news, soap opera, documentaries, specials, children's shows—it is a subject worthy of some study.

RATINGS

Although they often deny it publicly, or when quoted by name, network executives admit privately that they are in the business of selling (or, actually, renting) an audience.

The size and demographic characteristics of this audience are the principal, and sometimes the only, criteria upon which programs are selected. High ratings mean that a large number of viewers—measured both in absolute numbers and in the size among the general viewers of the most desired demographic group—are watching a program. The most desirable prime-time group, by current thinking, is women, ages eighteen to forty-nine. Sponsors are willing to pay huge amounts of money for commercial time during programs viewed by high numbers of this desirable group.

Happy Days, the nation's number-one prime-time program (as of May, 1977), has approximately 52 million regular viewers, 22 million of whom are in the eighteen to forty-nine age group. ABC charges $60,000 to show this audience a thirty-second commercial. *Spencer's Pilots,* one of the 1976-1977 season's lowest-rated programs, was watched by 15 million people, 6.5 million of them viewers in the 18-49 age group. CBS accordingly charged only $31,000 for thirty seconds of access to the *Spencer's Pilots* audience.

Audience demographics became important in the early 1970s when Paul Klein, then in NBC's audience research department, sold the networks and the advertisers on the notion that quality of an audience is equally important as, and perhaps more important than, the absolute size of an audience. Ratings should measure more than numbers, he said. They should measure *quality* of an audience, its interest in the product to be advertised, and its capacity to buy when once it's convinced.

Klein's suggestion promised increased profits to both networks and advertisers. By changing the definition of "high" ratings, and offering the prospect of a wide variety of shows with "high" ratings, it appealed to the network people who set the price for commercials; and by focusing in more narrowly on a specifically appropriate group of consumers, it offered advertisers "more bang for the buck." Thus, the Klein notion became the norm almost immediately after its inception.

More surprising, however, was the selection of one of the target groups, women ages eighteen to forty-nine, as *the* best audience for prime-time television. This decision, which has done as much as— perhaps more than—any other to shape contemporary television, reportedly resulted from market research that dertermined that they, not men, are the principal consumers of the types of products most widely advertised on television. Men may have nasal congestion or hemorrhoids, the reasoning went, but chances are they also have women in their lives who buy them something to provide relief. Furthermore, many of the industries most dependent upon television advertising—cosmetics, household goods, and soaps—are trying to reach women anyway; the few all-male products like shaving cream can be sold on specialized programs with high male demographics, such as sports events. The research also demonstrated that, even in the purchase of supposedly male "big-ticket" items such as cars, women dominate the decision-making.

While the decision to go with women *seems* to make sense; no one in the broadcast industry seems to know how the precise age designation was derived. Why not seventeen to forty-six, for instance, or twenty-one to fifty-three? Ratings have become such a precise process that even such a seemingly small shift in the target audience could make a difference in programming.

The genesis of this grouping seems to be somewhere in the mysterious Nielsen bureaucracy, where it was decided that the eighteen to forty-nine age bracket provided a logical vehicle, for reasons that are kept dark, for rating data. Accepting this as a given, the broadcast industry seems to have just blindly followed along.

From time to time network executives and local station managers try to maintain the myth that factors other than profit maximization go into programming decisions. In the early 1970s, when they spoke to civic groups, students, or congressional inquirers, they invariably claimed that artistic creativity, corporate responsibility, and technological exigencies were often the most important considerations. Often, they claim or accept credit for guarding the First Amendment. But the greatest energies are reserved for the dollars, not the corporate image. Every year, CBS, NBC, and ABC battled over which network would emerge with the highest overall ratings and ability to charge higher rates of commercial time. (Like professional athletes, networks are paid according to their previous year's performance). During the height of the 1970-71 battle, Les Brown of the *New York Times* interviewed the presidents of all three networks and found "all of them denying the importance of a ratings competition." Brown concluded that the open crassness of the competition "embarrassed the network presidents. It was a little like street fighting, and they wanted to represent themselves as being above that."

But by 1975, a subtle shift seemed to have taken place. Buoyed perhaps by confidence in the public's indifference, the networks openly admitted that ratings and profits are what it's all about. "Commercial television programming is designed to attract audiences to the advertisers' messages which surround the programming," wrote ABC programming Vice President Bob Shanks. "Inherent creative aesthetic values are important, but always secondary."

Ratings determine what gets on the air—and they do more. They define television's view of society. The people who control television believe that if a program receives high ratings, it must be what the public wants, and if it is what the public wants, it is what the public should get. (The March Hare again: "You might just as well say that 'I like what I get' is the same thing as 'I get what I like'!")

One manifestation of this mentality dictates that television programs come in clusters. At least two or three such clusters are always identifiable, whether they be Westerns, doctors, lawyers, police, single-parent comedies, *Amos 'n Andy*-type social commentaries, or happy family life during hard times. In recent years, emulation has also taken the form of procreation. Thus, *All in the Family* begat *The Jeffersons* and *Maude,* which begat *Good Times.* In another line, the *Mary Tyler Moore Show* begat *Rhoda* and *Phyllis,* and became a grandparent when *Rhoda* begat *The Nancy Walker Show.* "Examine those ingredients which have been recurrently successful and reshape them without shame," ABC's Shanks advises anyone trying to sell a new program idea to the networks.

According to Les Brown, television's *weltanschauung* also generates fear. Like many major league athletes just before game time, the individuals who determine what gets on the air are guided, not just by the desire for victory, but by the desire, very important to most of us, to avoid embarrassment.* A top network official, interviewed by Brown, analyzed the decision process:

> We don't pick the shows we think will have the best chance of becoming popular. To be honest, we're attracted to those that seem to have the least chance of failing.

Writing in the *New York Times Magazine,* journalist Jeff Greenfield offers another reason for the fear: "The business is so good that it literally cannot afford to be different." Les Brown points out that at least one network president annually, with painful predictability, "makes the clarion call for originality and promises to lead a new wave of creativity in the medium. It never materializes. Never, because it cannot." It cannot, because network profits have risen so high that only a foolish businessman would risk such a good thing.

This let's-play-it-safe attitude breeds a particularly pernicious perception of the viewing audience. An apocryphal story, reportedly told by a top CBS official, sums it all up:

> You know about the African tribe who saw their first movie? It was *King Kong,* and after it was over there were big cheers. The next week they were shown a movie again, and they tore down the tent and the screen and trashed the projector—because it wasn't *King Kong.* I think the people want to see that same thing week in and week out.

---

* Indeed, at the end of each television season a few top network executives are fired for outright failure or insufficient success, just like the managers of professional sports teams. Perhaps this phenomenon is endemic to professions whose performances come under close and regular public scrutiny. In any event, many of those fired are later rehired, sometimes with a promotion, at another network or film studio. This is also true of major league managers.

Moreover, the tighter things get among the networks, the *less* difference there will be between programs. Competition in a capitalistic system is supposed to make for diversity, but in television broadcasting—where there is effectively a monopoly—it makes for sameness. When ABC made its 1975-1976 move for the number-one spot, an anonymous CBS executive told the Washington *Star,* "Frankly, the tighter things get among the three networks, the less innovation you're likely to see on the screen, the more the inclination to go for the tried and true."

Such beliefs prompted CBS in mid-season a few years ago to replace *Joe and Sons,* the failed story of an Italian-American widower with two sons, with *Popi,* the story of a Puerto Rican widower with two sons, which then failed.

The individuals who make these decisions, are, for the most part, well educated, well read, well bred, and well meaning men who love their children and their country—but they are also people who have risen to the top of a highly competitive industry that still believes that the ability to get a reservation at the latest restaurant is worth as much as good character, in fact may even *be* good character. Les Brown, who has probably spent more time with these people than has any other outsider, described the most successful contemporary programmer, ABC's Fred Silverman, as a man with "an extraordinary perception about the television audience that was uncomplicated by conscience, taste, idealism, or a personal life." On first meeting Silverman, who originally made his name bringing *Bomba, the Jungle Boy* and similar movies to the children of Chicago, Brown wrote, "It was hard to believe that a grown person had such a passionate involvement in a program that was meant only to exploit the young."

The value of his contributions may be measured by what happened to the market value of ABC on the New York Stock Exchange when news arrived that Silverman had jumped ship from CBS. It rose somewhere between $69 and $85 million. When Silverman joined ABC, he commanded an annual salary of $250,000 plus stock options and incalculable fringe benefits, and since then he has lived up to his price and his promise. In less than a year, ABC moved from third place among three networks to number one, where it has remained.

The Age of Television's Fred Silvermans feel they live in a one-minute-to-midnight world in which Important Decisions must be made with Up-to-the-Minute Information. They watch the ratings with religious intensity, often making decisions with what Mark Twain termed the calm confidence of a Christian holding four aces.

Programs are created, introduced to millions of Americans, changed, nursed along to success, and destroyed on the basis of clearly defined rules and procedures. For example, "program flow" dictates that there must be a well planned sequence of programs so that the early evening audience will be carried along on the same network until bedtime. Thus, an early evening family-oriented program will be followed by a slightly more serious medical show, rather than a violent police program, on the theory that the demographics of the audiences for the latter two shows are radically different from each other. In another version of program flow, a popular show may be scheduled at 8 PM, followed by a weak program at 8:30, and at 9 another popular show whose appeal is to the same type of viewers as the first. The idea is that the audience will stay with the weak show, giving it high ratings, because they will not take the trouble to switch over to another station for the middle half hour.

Another rule, "counter-programming," resembles a schoolyard argument among three children—in this instance the three networks—each trying to have the last word. CBS may announce that a new comedy program, in which it has invested significant amounts of money and prestige, is scheduled for Thursday night at 9. NBC may then schedule one of its strongest comedy programs, presumably drawing from the same audience, at the same time. ABC may then schedule a strong violence-filled detective program opposite these two, since the entire non-comedy preferring audience is up for grabs. CBS then re-schedules its new comedy program, setting off a whole new round of counter-programming.

Sometimes programming decisions make so little sense that it is almost impossible to avoid the conclusion that a program has been condemned to death before its birth, probably to enable network planners to claim that different-from-the-mold programs can never succeed. This is what seemed to be happening in the fall of 1975, for example, when NBC scheduled into Family Hour a comedy about the pseudo-sexual exploits of a not-so-young divorcee trying to make it on her own professionally, while surrounded by opportunities for sexual intimacy with her former husband and a variety of other men. The program's scripts were—as it were—emasculated to fit into Family Hour restrictions, and then the show itself—*Faye*—was canceled just three weeks after its premiere. NBC decision-makers defended their actions by pointing to the new techniques that made ratings available on a daily basis, and telling the *New York Times* that "fast input makes fast output." But the truth is that the condemned program touched many topics still taboo on network television. Its demise permitted network executives to proclaim that programs that are too true to life invariably fail.

The system used to compile ratings seems as silly as it is powerful.

The A. C. Nielsen Company of Chicago, Illinois, has little black boxes attached to television sets in about 1,170 homes scattered across the country—that is, it samples seventeen-one-thousandths of one per cent of all the homes with sets. The black box, called an audiometer, activated when the set is on, makes a taped record of the time and station. The "Nielsen families" mail this tape back to the company's headquarters every two weeks, for which they receive, according to the *New York Times,* about $2 a month.

The identity of Nielsen families is one of the nation's best-kept secrets. Rumor has it that the producer of a Judy Garland special in the 50s did discover some names and somehow managed to stack the ratings in his favor. Dick Adler of the *Los Angeles Times* actually located and interviewed a Nielsen subject, whom he nicknamed "Deep Eyes". "Deep Eyes" knew exactly what he was doing. He purposefully left the television on to help keep his favorite network programs, and he gleefully manipulated the ratings of local programs, which responded most dramatically to his machinations. His set was on for about 50 hours each week, whether or not he was watching. But Deep Eyes' best revelation was how Nielsen selected him. It seems that he moved into a house already equipped with an audiometer. So much for the scientific basis of Nielsen's national sample.

While they do issue detailed and sophisticated explanations of their statistical techniques, the Nielsen people also keep secret the answers to such questions as exactly how they select their so-called "typical" families, how often the families are changed, and on what basis such changes are made. A few tidbits are known—for instance, until late in 1976, Nielsen families did not include a representative number of poor families.* According to Michael Wheeler's 1975 book *Lies, Damn Lies and Statistics,* people remain in the Nielsen sample for as long as five years. Furthermore, the Nielsen Company admits that for an average day's viewing, the number of available tapes is about 150 fewer than the total number of homes equipped with audiometers. Why these tapes fail to materialize is not clear, nor is the question of whether these no-shows are a valid cross-section of what was already a small national cross-section.

Amazingly small. Wheeler points out that only "twelve households make a Nielsen rating point," and that only eight constitute a share point."** Since many shows live or die on the basis of a single rating

---

* Until the fall of 1976, Nielsen selected its families only from homes with listed phone numbers. This introduced obvious biases—many poor people have no listed phone.

Nielsen apparently figures there are 2.2 viewers per household in the sample—if that is so, it shows a fairly strong distortion of the sample. Clearly they aren't very big on families—children, that is to say—in the Nielsen families.

Also excluded were a significant number of college students.

**"Rating points" measure the number of households watching a program at a given time; "share points" measure the percentage of all sets in use at a given time watching a particular program.

point, twelve of Deep Eyes' colleagues together exercise an extraordinary amount of influence on the country.

Another mystery is the size of specific sub-categories within the Nielsen sample. For example, if Nielsen tells the television industry that a certain program attracts 46.7 per cent of the men under 25, upon how many such men is the company basing this assertion? 10? 156? 213?

Perhaps the greatest weakness of the rating system is that the entire Nielsen sample consists of consenters, people who agreed to have a little black box in their homes in exchange for money. This already makes them, by definition, atypical. Furthermore, no matter how conscientious a family may try to be, it must always be aware that the box is *there*, and whether they know it or not, this has to affect their behavior.

The findings of various competitive companies, some using audiometers and diaries, and others using alternative measures like telephone calls after a program's conclusion to test reaction, are also used by the networks and advertising agencies. Generally, their findings fall in line with Nielsen's, although major discrepancies invariably set off strident debates. Huge amounts of money are at stake—a drop in just one rating point for one show can cost the networks millions of dollars, and a rise of one point can cost advertisers an equal amount. These debates are not conducted on a basis of trying to find the facts, but on the interest of each party in arguing for the findings most supportive of its economic interests. In politics, it is said that anyone of influence who is against you is a boss, and if he is on your side he is an enlightened leader. Similarly, a rating system that puts your program high is accurate, and one that says otherwise is based upon a biased sample.

For example, in late 1975, Nielsen announced that the average daily time each American household spent watching television had dropped from the previous year's 6:07 hours to 6:02 hours. This was the first reported drop in the history of television broadcasting, and set off howls of protest from broadcasters, who knew that advertisers buy audiences by size. They blamed the supposed decline on Nielsen's techniques and on unusually warm Fall weather, which kept many Americans outdoors instead of in front of their television sets (where, presumably, they belonged). Arbitron, a rating company that specializes in measuring local markets, then announced that viewing in the thirty-three markets it examines had gone up, not down, a finding hailed by the trade press. The two companies use different techniques for gathering and analyzing,* and neither would release enough information about its operations to make a valid comparison possible. The issue drifted off into the nothingness of broadcast industry committees, with talk that maybe some-

---

* Arbitron selects families in each market by random telephone calls, and then sends out a diary which the families are asked to mail back. Arbitron visits black families each night to obtain the information.

thing should be done to make the rating system more accountable.

Like the first witness to arrive at an accident scene, the networks are now hypnotized by "overnights," a relatively new Nielsen service that gives, by 10 AM, the Los Angeles and New York City ratings (available because in these cities Nielsen homes are hooked into a central computer). "Go into any office around 10 AM and every executive in sight will be asking, 'Are the overnights up yet?' 'How'd we do in the overnights?!" writes ABC executive Shanks "It is an idiotic and masochistic ritual and I participate in it every day."

How can a powerful and pervasive national institution like television be dominated by something as mysterious and covert as Nielsen ratings? No one seems to know. The dominant attitude at the networks is that the ratings are to be taken for granted, and complained about only when they're not going your way. Most top executives seem to believe that the ratings, if they are inaccurate or unfair, are consistently inaccurate and unfair for everybody. One might think that the FCC or Congress might step in to see that the public is also taken into consideration. But the FCC, as usual on any matter in the economic interests to the broadcast industry, has played the role of the watchdog who sleeps by the fireplace. The last congressional hearings on ratings were conducted in the early 1960s, and they failed even to stir up a public reaction.

Reflection on the ratings system yields the conclusion that in a way, the system works to the maximum benefit of advertisers. They simply have to pass on the word through their advertising agencies, or, more likely, agree with the agency's insight, that they want a certain type of audience, and then they can sit back and let the system serve up programs designed to deliver that audience. Under this system, the prime skill upon which network executives are selected and promoted is their ability to sense beforehand what programs or stars will achieve the highest Nielsen ratings with the right demographic characteristics. Thus, if Silverman does indeed have a unique skill, it is to select programs that will please the women eighteen to forty-nine—not all of them, even by representation, probably; only the few hundred who live in Nielsen households. This skill, and not much else, is what defines success for the people who control television.

Advertising people are happy to sit back and say that under our system of free choice, they would not dream of even trying to disrupt the great American public's mystic relationship with its favorite television programs. They abdicate all responsibility for program content, saying, in the words of Michael Moore of Benton and Bowles, "We just pick and choose among the alternatives they offer to us. We really have little to say about what programs go on the air."

This leaves network executives free to make the really important decisions, like whether to schedule *Police Woman* at 9 PM on Thursday or 10 PM on Fridays, and whether to introduce two new doctor shows and only one new widow show, or to introduce two new widow shows and only one new doctor show.

Frequently fancying themselves to be sort of institutional Harry Trumans, reassuring a troubled nation about where the buck stops, network executives are quick to assert their independence from advertisers. ABC's Shanks writes, of advertising people, "The most conscientious ones read all the available scripts and outlines for appeal (and client biases) and go watch the production or meet stars or creators in California. Some do not sleep as they sincerely ponder how to make shows better or more creative. But all of this is really just so much making love with your clothes on. The truth is, if these people do not like the programs . . . nothing much would be different."

It is fascinating to ponder what Shanks is saying life is like for those, like himself, who actually do make programming decisions. Unfortunately, outsiders have never penetrated these meetings. A few journalists have, however, interviewed the participants and pieced the story together. Jeff Greenfield did this for room 610 at 30 Rockefeller Plaza, where NBC put together its 1975-76 season. The process took three weeks, Greenfield reports, and involved about a half dozen decision-makers, "all white, all male, all but one between forty-five and forty-nine years old, all living and working in either the New York or Los Angeles areas, all earning between $40,000 . . . and $250,000 . . . [and all] acting as surrogates for the audience." Their thinking, with a few unthinking concessions to program content, was ratings.

According to a then-NBC programming chief, "Rumor had it that CBS would move *The Waltons* to Sunday at 8, and shift *Cher* to Thursday at 8." When both these CBS shows held to their original days, NBC found itself with a potential disaster, with a *Waltons* imitation, *The Family Holvak,* directly opposite the CBS original, and with a mystery— *Ellery Queen,* which would attract the same younger, urban audience— opposite *Cher.* Instead of *Ellery*'s carrying its demographically desirable audience into the *Sunday Mystery Movie,* it risked failure in the competition with *Cher.* So NBC slipped *The Family Holvak* into the Sunday 8 PM slot, hoping to draw strength from its 7 PM show, *The Wonderful World of Disney.* It put *Ellery Queen* into Thursdays at 9, opposite ABC's *The Streets of San Francisco* and the CBS movies.

CBS's move of *All in the Family* and *Maude* to Monday at new times, coupled with ABC's *Monday Night Football,* meant that NBC could do nothing but move its one-hour dramas out of that Monday slot and sacrifice it with a movie night. That left *The Invisible Man* to compete with *Rhoda* and *Phyllis* on CBS, and *Barbary Coast,* a contemporary Western, on ABC. It was NBC's hope that *Invisible Man* would attract the teenagers and male action-oriented viewers turned off by the "women's comedies."

Greenfield reports that the network officials used six-inch folders, one for each prospective new program, and containing, among other things, test results from the "Magoo House," a phenomenon which future archeologists would do well to discover and analyze. The Magoo House is a small theater in Los Angeles and contains seats for two hundred volunteers from the public-at-large. Each seat is equipped with dials that can be turned from 0 to 16 and each volunteer is asked to turn the dial in reaction to what he is seeing at the time. Results are recorded on seismograph-like charts; 100 is the best rating and 70 is considered a good solid overall score. However, the whys and wherefores of various peaks and valleys are analyzed with the care of a bomb squad opening an unknown package. These presumably provide the network with invaluable insights into what sort of plots, character development, and action the American people want.

The Magoo House gets its name from a twenty-year-old animated cartoon, which is the first thing each test audience is shown in order to establish a norm for that particular audience. On any given evening, an audience may have what is termed a "low Magoo" or a "high Magoo." If the people off the streets enjoy Mr. Magoo, then network officials reason that any program they give a similar score is a program they liked. This in itself says a lot about why we see what we see on television, and the individual who selected Mr. Magoo to play this role certainly must have been one of the most influential men in modern America. It is fascinating to think how our society and our culture might have evolved differently had he chosen *Hamlet,* let us say, or *The Grapes of Wrath.*

Time correspondent Roland Flamini happened to be one of the members of the general public supposedly selected at random to visit the Magoo theater. "I say I am a taxidermist with a degree from Botswana University and I lie about my age," Flamini reports. "Out of the corner of my eye I see that the man in front of me, who has already volunteered to me that he works in a bank, has described himself as a doctor. So much for the demographic mix." Flamini discussed the Magoo reliance with most of Hollywood's most influential producers and screenwriters, and found them concerned that such testing "has become too powerful . . . no longer a tool, but a mechanical final authority." They also claimed that some of their colleagues create with Magoo in mind. They know there are certain rules to live by: "The appearance of a child or a dog in a sitcom will invariably send the needle up. Character development brings it down. In dramatic plots, violence and car chases produce the Magoos . . ."

Explained one writer, "If the private eye has to explain anything, he'd better be doing something interesting at the time, like walking a tightrope over Niagara Falls or screwing his female client." A serious question is raised by the increasing dependence of book publishers and theatrical producers—presentation of the work on television is more and more often spelling the difference between success and failure of a book or play. In the future, will only those that lend themselves to television advertising and promotion—in substance, style, and economics—be offered to the public? Will only the "mass" and the potentially "popular" culture drive out the serious, the specialized, or the difficult? The novel has already been affected. Leading agents now say that the television rights to fiction have become as or more valuable than even the motion picture rights. There is not only, then, the promotional and advertising potential to be considered, but the question of whether a book or a play can be "successfully" adapted for the television screen—and that factor will have an effect on future creators of those works. It is one thing to contemplate the impact on our culture of the opinions of a handful of dramatic or literary critics, when the potential audience affected by their favor or disfavor may number in the thousands. It is quite another to realize that the chiefs of three television networks can set in motion forces that can create a mass culture without reference, or even much of a bow, to the mass culture and the other culture that existed before.

Despite this comfortable arrangement, advertisers sometimes move into the open, and display their muscle.

In the fall of 1975 CBS planned to air *The Guns of Autumn,* an hour-long documentary about hunting in America. Long before the program was even broadcast, thousands of people wrote to CBS stating that they had already seen the program, found it unfair and offensive, and planned to boycott all of its sponsors. Under this same sort of pressure, which had been organized by the National Rifle Association and local gun clubs, all the program's sponsors, except for Dart Drug, which had purchased two thirty-second spots, cancelled their ads.

CBS went ahead and broadcast the program with only the two commercials. "It is curious that these people [the gun group] think they can keep us off the air or from doing journalist programs by putting heat on advertisers and forcing them to withdraw," CBS Senior Vice President Bill Leonard told reporters. "They don't know how this thing works."

Leonard could not—alas—have been more incorrect. They—and the advertisers—know exactly how The Age of Television works. The people who pay the bills ultimately call the shots (in this case, rifle shots). Advertisers were treating *The Guns of Autumn* exactly the same way they treat every program: basing their payment of money to the network on an assessment of how the audience would respond to commercials. It makes little difference if the audience is turned off by poor plotting on a situation comedy or by the content of a news documentary. The result is exactly the same. Even though they failed to kill *The Guns of Autumn* (and indeed, stirred up a great deal of popular interest in it), the sponsors, by responding so docilely to the gun lobby, effectively forced CBS to air a follow-through *mea culpa* program entitled *Echoes of the Guns of Autumn.* The incident left little doubt that CBS would think twice before trying to broadcast a program, whether it be generated by the entertainment or the news department, that might offend any vocal big interest group. It is too possible that advertisers would desert and not return. Furthermore, for all of Leonard's commendable courage about independence, those who read between the lines learned that CBS lost absolutely no money on the controversy. The networks' salesmen simply placed the cancelled ads on other CBS programs in time slots that might not otherwise have been sold. Indeed, the network's strong stand against sponsor pressure gave it invaluable publicity among those who admire that kind of independence.

The incident is far from isolated, and stands out only in that the pressure is rarely so open and menacing. In the late 1950s, Allstate Insurance Company forced a change in a Rod Serling drama in which a sheriff, who permitted the lynching of a black, committed suicide out of remorse. In the Allstate version which was aired, the sheriff simply died at the hands of a younger man with a faster draw. In 1970, NBC wanted to broadcast *Migrant,* the story of migrant workers in Florida, who are employed primarily by Coca-Cola. Les Brown reports that "efforts to suppress *Migrant,* or at least to dilute it, began about a month before the telecast." These efforts failed, as did a request from the Florida Fruit and Vegetable Association for equal time. But several months later, Brown says, Coca-Cola moved all of its business over to CBS and ABC.

Most attempts at censorship are more subtle, but are censorship nonetheless. Cereal companies request that programs they buy heavily into do not have characters who eat bacon and eggs for breakfast. In Abby Mann's *Judgment at Nuremberg,* the American Gas Association succeeded in having all references to extermination by gas omitted; and the American Florists Association has successfully kept bereaved characters in television serials from saying that contributions to a charitable organization should be made in lieu of flowers. Such a notion, if it gained popularity among even a small percentage of prime-time television viewers, could wreak havoc upon the florist industry.

Another, even less widely known means of advertisers' control, is program barter syndication. This system takes many forms, but basically large syndicating companies will buy the syndication rights to a previously popular program that is past its prime—or even a new "special"—and then give the program to local stations.

The syndicating company takes, in return—still no cash has changed hands between the syndicating company and the local station—a certain number of commercial spots during the programs, which it will then sell to advertisers, many of whom it has already signed up.

From a profit point of view, this makes sense for all those involved, but for the viewing pubic it means once again that programming decisions are made in corporate board rooms and in Madison Avenue advertising agency suites.

ADVERTISING AND VIOLENCE

A dramatic statement was made in late 1975 by Arch O. Knowlton, the Media Services Director for General Foods.

Not many Americans know Mr. Knowlton, but he is quite influential. Knowlton supervises perhaps the third or fourth largest advertising budget in the nation. He is authorized to spend, on behalf of General Foods, approximately $35 million dollars annually for prime-time television commercials alone.

So the broadcasting industry at least listened on November 19, 1975, when Knowlton addressed the annual conference of the American Advertising Council. His remarks are quoted at length here, not only because of their serious treatment of an important topic, but because they come from a man who rose to the top of a business in which such things are rarely discussed—and even more rarely discussed out loud and in public:

> I can become violent about the subject of violence on television. It's time to stop the dialogue about whether broadcasting violence into people's homes has a negative impact on society or not. Violence may be a reality of life, but that doesn't give anybody the right to overload everyone else with violent programs. Let's be on the safe side and speculate that it can't do anybody any good. The tempo of the times we live in today is more explosive than ever before, which is what makes this issue more important than ever before. We know that violent crimes depicted on television are very often experienced in real life in the next several days. We also know that crimes seem to come in bunches like the recent series of attempts of President Ford's life . . . Damn it, I think that if there is any chance, and clearly that chance does exist, then let's do something about it now.
> Who knows, the life you save may be your own.*

* An earlier and equally eloquent statement came in a little-noticed letter to *Advertising Age* from W. C. Bartlett of the W. C. Bartlett Advertising Agency, Wallingford, Pa. "In the last analysis," Bartlett wrote, "it is the hand that signs the check that cradles the gun."

And with that surprising and clear sentiment on the record, Knowlton then announced that General Foods would no longer buy any commercial spots in or adjacent to violent television programs.

The industry response was extremely muted. Leo Singer, president of the much smaller Miracle White Corporation (annual television advertising budget, about $2 million), had made a similar announcement in 1973 in testimony before Senator Pastore's committee. The press had given the testimony considerable prominence, and Singer received nearly one hundred thousand letters of praise. But Singer's had been a lonely voice within the advertising industry in 1973; he was dismissed as a headline seeker. His was not the kind of statement other corporate presidents expected from one of their number, and industry spokesmen were quick to point out that Miracle White did almost all of its advertising during daytime soap operas and would lose very little exposure by its high-minded determination to avoid violent settings for its commercials.

Hearing of Knowlton's speech, Singer immediately sent a congratulatory letter. "[T]he campaign has been a long, lonely uphill fight," he wrote, "and I'm delighted that a man of your stature at long last is joining the fray." But if Singer thought that his new alliance with Knowlton would bring real results, he was mistaken.

Dennis C. Beaumont, Director of Marketing Services for a food company with $11 million to spend annually on television commercials, hailed Knowlton's comments as a "courageous, overdue move." But Beaumont hastened to point out that his company bought television commercials according to a "scatter plan" (a method of purchasing commercial time in which, for a given sum of money, the network will literally scatter the commercials through its schedule, without concentrating on any time segment or type of programming), and thus the company could not boycott violent programs. In fact, three telephone calls could change the "buy" and accomplish such a boycott.

Spokesmen for a few other companies joined in with similar words of praise, but felt compelled to explain to Knowlton (who understood very well) the facts of commercial advertising life as defined by "scatter" buying. "We don't even know what shows we buy time on until we sit at home and see the commercials along with everybody else," was the general response. The response added up to claims from other representatives in the industry that much as they would like to join Knowlton's crusade, it was economically impossible "to be pure," and besides, any systematic boycott of television violence would be likely to bring an antitrust suit either from the government or from the television networks, alleging a conspiracy in restraint of trade.

In fact, the reliance upon "scatter plan" buying as an excuse was a sham. Scatter-plan buying in fact increases, rather than decreases, the sponsor's flexibility. As opposed to previous systems under which a sponsor typically purchased an entire program to sponsor (i.e., *General Electric Theatre,* or *Philco Playhouse*) or segments of certain programs on a regular basis ("This portion of *The Untouchables* is brought to you by . . ."), scatter-plan buying frees sponsors to pick and choose their time and programs at will.

Under a scatter plan, sponsors buy a large number of commercials spread out over as long a time period as they desire, thus minimizing the risk to them should any specific show or group of shows fail to draw its anticipated rating. The advertising agency—and if it wishes, the advertiser—knows exactly in what programs time is being purchased.

CBS reports, for example, that one major advertiser—whose name the network asks to be kept off the record—will not permit any of its commercials to appear on a program produced by Norman Lear (*All in the Family, Maude, Sanford and Son, The Jeffersons, One Day at a Time, Good Times, Mary Hartman, Mary Hartman*). These programs, says the company, have too much sex and too many "liberal" ideas.* The company's request, of course, is honored; after all, it pays the bills. The same cooperation would surely be extended to any sponsor who wished to boycott violence.

The defense that to move from sponsorship on violent programs would risk an anti-trust action is even more absurd and the risk even more remote. Detergent manufacturers long ago decided to concentrate on daytime soap opera (hence the name); and is it actionable evidence of a common conspiracy that razors, after-shave lotions, and athlete's foot remedies are sold during "breaks in the action" at televised sports events?

But most companies advertising on television apparently don't even take the trouble to find out how much violence they are supporting. A class in developmental sociology at the University of Washington monitored network programs and sponsors on three Seattle stations for the week of February 22, 1974. They found that McDonalds led the list in commercials appearing on violent programs; the manufacturers of Rice-a-Roni, the owners of Shakey's pizza parlors, and the manufacturers of other child-and-teenager-oriented goods were not far behind. When class members called the corporate headquarters to ask for comments, they discovered that most of the corporations seemed totally and genuinely unaware of the situation. Some of the corporations using violent programs for their commercials offered excuses, such as "buying decisions are made months in advance of programming and [it] is not always possible to know the specific content of programs appearing in that particular time slot." Others attacked the survey, charging that vio-

---

* It would be interesting to know if the advertiser relented in the case of Lear's 1976-1977 program, *All's Fair,* in which the hero was a conservative Washington columnist.

lence counts are unfair, or that parents who objected to the violence could simply turn off the sets. All admitted that they bought commercial time according to audience demographic studies, and that they paid little attention to program content.

"We knock ourselves out to maintain a family image," explained the director of public relations for McDonalds. Like the other sponsors, he may have realized that the tabulations, if given sufficient publicity, might blur the meaning of McDonald's famous advertising slogan, "We do it all for you."

Whether or not McDonalds, Rice-a-Roni, and the others will be able to continue the successful combination of enjoying a family image and reaping the rewards of high demographics in the placement of commercial time on violent programs remains to be seen. An *Advertising Age* editorial has warned that "the public makes no fine distinctions. It looks to the advertiser for signs of his concern and restraint. Unless that sign is forthcoming, the public will work its will—in the market place or through regulatory restrictions." Walter Staab, one of the nation's leading independent time buyers, has told his clients that "the deplorable dumping of corporate responsibility for programs because of 'scatter plan' buying simply won't wash in 1976."

At the same time, an *ad hoc* series of citizens groups opposed to violence on television began to make itself known. From Joplin, Missouri, an evangelical group delivered what it claimed to be more than 500,000 letters of protest to all three network presidents. The District Attorney in San Diego County (who prosecuted the young axe murderer who killed his family after watching the Lizzie Borden program) began to urge that civic groups initiate organized protests. Help America Reduce Televiolence began mass mailings out of South Bend, Indiana, urging concerned citizens to write to the networks and sponsors. Morality in Media, church-supported and centered in New York City, organized chapters across the nation so effectively that even its high school essay contests (typical question: "Do you feel that the many television programs featuring sex and violence have a harmful effect on family life?") received good local press coverage. The activist Action for Children's Television maintained a steady barrage of sophisticated studies and effective congressional testimony.

Five sponsors withdrew their support for weekend horror movies on television when threatened with a boycott by the Los Angeles-based National Association for Better Broadcasting.

The 1976 convention of the American Medical Association adopted a resolution that called on AMA members to boycott the products of advertisers who bought time on programs that included violence. And public opinion polls showed that a significant segment of the American people thinks that something should be done about television violence.

In early 1977, one of the largest, and potentially most powerful, groups entered the battle against continued television violence. The National Congress of Parents and Teachers (PTA), after holding a series of public hearings on television violence, adopted an "Action Plan for Television." If the PTA sticks to its guns and can mobilize even a substantial fraction of its national membership, its Action Plan poses the greatest threat yet to continued excessive violence on the home screen.

The organization has formally joined in a petition to the FCC seeking a change in Commission rules so as to allow local stations more time to view a proposed network offering and then decide if it wishes to present the episode in its local community. The proposal is full of peril for the networks, which have relied on the complaisance of their local affiliates and the short time available to view episodes to guarantee that what the network puts on the line from New York will be performed at nearly 200 affiliated local stations. It is that "guarantee" that keeps the rates up for national advertisers.

But if local stations are going to have to take the local heat for violent programming, instead of being able to pass off protests to the network ("we didn't have time to check it"), then there will be many more refusals by local stations to take the network product. The refusal of four or five stations to carry *Death Wish*, for example, is manageable—a steady refusal of twenty or thirty on any given night could change the structure of television advertising; that is to say, of television.

The PTA has gone even further, and is prepared, it would seem, to strike at the "soft underbelly" of television—the advertiser. The organization has supplied the names and addresses of prime-time advertisers on violent programs to its membership. Each of the 33,000 local PTAs have copies of such lists; in addition to PTA's 6 million members, others may obtain them.

The organization, in effect, gave the advertisers—and through the advertisers, the executives of the industry, until the start of the 1977-78 season to—in the words of Ann P. Kahn, the national secretary of the PTA—"clean up their act." As this is written, it is still too early to make firm predictions, but the action of the PTA is the most promising yet in the field of citizen action to control violence on television.

Such indications notwithstanding, much of the trade press downgraded remarks such as Knowlton's. A *Broadcasting* editorial explained, for example, that "This [Knowlton's] is a perfectly rational suggestion. The only trouble, in our opinion, is that it won't work." And *Advertising Age,* which seemed to lack a corporate memory about its earlier editorial stance, joined the dominant propaganda line by saying that "deploring violence in TV entertainment is fashionable in the advertising community as elsewhere now, but how many sponsors do you suppose rushed to get in line for openings in the new *Starsky and Hutch* series once the favorable early ratings came out?" *Starsky and Hutch* was not only a highly rated program from the start of the 1975-76 television season, but also, by any count, one of the most violent.

In fact, it could be said that the broadcasting and advertising industry, after a decent interval of faint praise, decided to let Knowlton twist slowly in the wind. One executive even gave Knowlton an extra push, using as a tool an attack on the Nixon Administration and on exposed corporate corruption. "The high government officials who have been most vocal in their criticism of television," he said, "have been convicted of lying, bribery, stealing, robbery and worse . . . We must restore the faith of the American people in the moral integrity and ethical conduct of its leadership and eliminate contempt for law as the national pastime. Until that has been accomplished, *I would refrain from joining the chorus of abuse being directed at the television industry."* *

The generally philosophical and moral tone of Knowlton's address was not entirely consistent. At one point, toward the end of his remarks, he sounded a positively dollars-and-cents note that did not go unnoticed by his colleagues in the business. "[O]n a hard-nosed business basis it's entirely possible," said Knowlton, "that a commercial *will work harder* in a program that reflects positive social interaction as opposed to one dealing with blood and guts."

Arnold Grisman of J. Walter Thompson, the world's largest advertising agency, agreed. Describing post-Family Hour programming as a "ghetto of blood," Grisman called for a "cooling-off period" before a "sensory overload" deprived all commercials of their impact. "As media heat up more and more," Grisman declared, "they may indeed create an environment that is hostile to advertising, either by reducing the power to attract attention, or by building associations that distort the intended response." Grisman was soon joined by the Thompson agency's president, Don Johnston. Citing a special study of two hundred adult viewers, Johnston warned the American Advertising Federation that 10 per cent of consumers might consider boycotting sponsors of violent programs. "[H]ere is a programming environment that can actually turn off sales . . . I cannot imagine any advertiser who would risk negative sales of these proportions," Johnston said.

This was the kind of warning that the business world can understand. As we have seen, "proof" that violence in television programming can lead to aggressive, anti-social, and even criminal behavior in viewers was generally discounted by television executives and advertisers on a variety of grounds. But the mere suggestion that there might be "proof" that a violent environment surrounding a given commercial might

---

* It is a nice notion; by this logic, any group attacked by Nixon has a license—for a few years at least—to misbehave.

cause a decrease in sales prompted by the commercial quickly caught their attention.

Rumors that such a study had been conducted circulated up and down Madison Avenue early in 1976. Les Brown of the *Times* reported that such a study was under way, but that the findings were not complete. The strong suggestion in industry circles was that the early statistical evidence from the study would back Knowlton's and Grisman's allegations. Arthur Taylor of CBS said he was familiar with the study and the agency (which he declined to identify), and strongly implied that he anticipated similar findings. On the other hand, the Advertising Research Foundation announced that it knew about nearly every marketing survey ever done in the United States, and that no such study existed. (When pressed about all of the reports that there was evidence that violence hurts advertising, a Foundation spokesman replied, "Yes, never put a ketchup commercial on a Western.")

Apparent evidence that some studies had been undertaken, however, came in the regular newsletter to clients published in the winter of 1976 by Ogilvy and Mather, one of the nation's largest advertising agencies. The newsletter said that the preferences of women in the eighteen to forty-nine age group were turning more to general drama, situation comedy, and variety, and away from violence. Since this age group is the prime target audience of most national television advertisers, the trend could have a major impact. Feeling confident of its prediction, Ogilvy and Mather chastised the networks for acceding to the Family Hour proposal: "Normal competitive pressure would have forced many action-adventure shows off the air . . . Broadcasters gave up some freedom unnecessarily."

In late 1974, one of the nation's most respected jurists, David L. Bazelon, of the Court of Appeals for the District of Columbia, told broadcasters "abuse of the immense power of television for the private profit of a few" threatened the continuance of television free from closer government control. "The programming executives and their advertiser clients must stop their single-minded purpose to achieve higher ratings, more advertising, and greater profits, and stop to consider what greater purposes television should serve," he warned.

Judge Bazelon's warnings are particularly poignant when considered in conjunction with an observation made by Les Brown. Brown's *Television: the Business Behind the Box* describes in great detail the rivalry in 1970 between NBC programming chief Paul Klein and Michael Dann, his CBS counterpart. Within the same week, each resigned, although each was still at the peak of his power. "Each professed to have reached a point in his life when he desired to make a meaningful contribution to society," Brown wrote. "The reader may make what he will of the fact that two men with great influence over the program matter of the most pervasive and powerful communication forces in all history were giving up the office from a desire to do something *important*."

INSTITUTIONAL ADVERTISING

Some mention should be made of non-commercial advertising on television—the so-called "institutional" messages. Sometimes, regular commercial advertisers will shift to an "institutional" framework for a cycle of television messages—such as when one oil company or another will urge on us the virtues of horizontal and vertical monopoly ("the pieces all fit together"), give us the benefit of imaginative and shielded accounting techniques to say that there is only a minute profit on each gallon of gas, or show us that oil company shareholders are all little old retired schoolteachers ("Who owns America's oil companies? You do!" is the message, to which an appropriate reply might be: "Then why don't we get a seat on the board?").

Other institutional advertising is used to sell the status quo through the National Advertising Council, the country's largest ($500 million annually) single advertiser. The Council is a "voluntary" association of advertising agencies, and takes on a number of "public service" campaigns each year, roughly one-third of which are commercials in support of some government program. These range from the Peace Corps to, for example, President Ford's ill-starred WIN program, a proposal to "whip inflation now" by cleaning your plate and planting a vegetable garden.

But the Advertising Council does more. It proposes to end industrial pollution by cracking down on litterbugs, points to "loss of desire to work" and other evils of marijuana use, and encourages greater worker productivity as a cure, presumably, for unemployment and inflation. The anti-crime message of the Advertising Council is a simple one: don't leave your keys in the car. It has also come out against bad vision, mental retardation, and physical handicaps. Advocates of anything "controversial" are routinely denied access. Examples of things the Advertising Council considers "controversial" include Planned Parenthood and saving certain commercially hunted species (such as whales) from extinction.

Television stations have become conditioned to carrying the spots and messages of the Advertising Council; it consists, after all, of representatives of the very customers stations and networks deal with all the time. A petition currently before the FCC as this is written, presented by the Media Action Council, a public interest law firm in Washington, would go far—if granted—to break up the Council's virtual monopoly on public service time. It would limit to one-third the proportion of public-service commercials that could be sponsored by one organization, would require one-fourth of all public service announcements to be originated locally, and would require stations to make production facilities available.

If these rules were adopted, or if even anything approaching them were adopted, it would end the virtual stranglehold the industry—through the Advertising Council—has over its "public service" messages. The reason is that stations must carry a certain number of such spots, in order to fulfill the requirements imposed as a condition of the license.

CREATION OF DEMAND

It is simply not true that television commercials tell viewers who want a certain thing—toothpaste, a new car, to smell better—where they can find the *best* of that thing, although this is the most frequent claim made by spokesmen for the industry when the time comes—as it does with increasing frequency—to defend the excessive use of commercials.

What is true is that television commercials create demand that did not exist before. People are stimulated to buy and seek products in response to needs they had never before acknowledged—because the sense of "need" is newly created, under the strong influence of the ad writers, ad artists, social scientists, market researchers and product manufacturers—all brought together in the "mass media," television. Unfortunately, the evidence seems strongly to suggest that this is particularly true in the case of non-prescription drugs, where the target market includes millions of children.

Senator Gaylord Nelson of Wisconsin, whose hearings over the past several years have convinced him of the dangers in some widely advertised non-prescription drugs, thinks television commercials may be socializing children to look to pills as the answer to a variety of personal problems. An article of Nelson's in *Family Health* magazine, told of a mother who wrote him, upset because commercials for sleeping pills affected her children:

> My six-year-old daughter and eight-year-old son have on several occasions got out of bed and told me they couldn't get to sleep and nagged me for pills. Neither my husband nor I take prescription or

over-the-counter sleeping pills, and my children have admitted to me
that the idea that they should take the pills comes from television commercials.

Senator Nelson juxtaposed this letter with one he had received from a
physician at a methadone center that treated hundreds of heroin addicts
daily:

> TV advertisers are teaching our children to use drugs. It seems to me
> that any child or emotionally immature adult subjected to the daily and
> incessant barrage of messages offering "fast, fast, fast" or "instant"
> relief from every care of life by simply swallowing pills would be
> tempted to try them—and, finding they do not live up to the glowing
> promises, would then resort to stronger ones . . . That many arrive at
> heroin is not surprising. *I know of no drug except heroin or morphine
> which will produce the dramatic relief from all worldly cares TV viv-
> idly pictures.* (Emphasis added.)

The senator writes that on the basis of such letters, and six years of
investigation by the Senate subcommittee he chairs, he is convinced
that millions of children and adults have turned to pill-popping in response to television commercials. It is primarily members of the Television Generation, he says, who grew up singing the commercial jingles
for drug products, and who have turned into what some physicians call
"electronic hypochondriacs."

There is also mounting evidence that for many individuals this consumption of pills translates into serious drug abuse. In 1975, an article
in the *Annals of the American Academy of Political and Social Science*
presented an overview of research into "Drugs and the Mass Media." It
presented evidence that both the *act* of watching television—

> the kinship of the LSD and other drug experiences with television is
> glaringly obvious. Both depend on "turning on" and passively waiting
> for something beautiful to happen.

and the *content* of what is viewed—

> there is ample a priori evidence from these studies that advertising
> messages encourage one to swallow, chew, or otherwise ingest sub-
> stances not only for medical symptoms, but also for psychological well
> being

can contribute to a push toward the drug culture.

The networks, and their allies in the over-the-counter drug industry, bound together by a strong cash nexus, dispute these claims, of course. But as with the overwhelming evidence linking televised violence with real-life violence, they answer the wrong questions, by preference. Still, there has been a statement, after years of research, in which NBC concedes that television advertising does lead to the use of over-the-counter drugs.

The statement—the conclusion of a study—could hardly have been otherwise, once one considers where it was presented. J. Ronald Milavsky, director of social research for NBC, presented this finding at the 1975 annual meeting of the Proprietary Drug Association. His audience was the top brass of the pharmaceutical companies that manufacture over-the-counter drugs—and pay to advertise them on television.

The study NBC did was extensive—and really involved dragging a large, quite red herring across the trail. It is appropriate to ask whether non-prescription-drugs advertising leads directly to the abuse of illegal drugs (the study asked, and got a negative answer). But the study did not ask whether the success of that advertising does not promote, with bad consequences, a widespread attitude of "take a pill if you have a problem and be like everyone else" in the population—promote it particularly to the younger members.

NBC and other industry defenders love to ask, and answer, another question that was in their lengthy study—the study did not show that the use of over-the-counter drugs leads to the use of illegal drugs. Surely poverty, helplessness, and a sense of alienation are causes of drug abuse and, for that matter, heavy television watching. But even that common-sense conclusion is difficult to "prove" scientifically; let alone "proving" with laboratory certitude that there exists a two-step causal chain leading from drug commercials to the heavy use of non-prescription drugs to the use of illegal drugs.

The more provable question—the answer to which is provided by the network every day as its salesmen solicit drug advertising—is whether television commercials make us take more pills than we think we need? To that question, the drug companies themselves provide an answer when they spend over $300 million a year for the commercial time; they are not in the business of *limiting* the use of their products.

Another partial answer, alas, comes from the reports of children who poison themselves on overdoses of drugs they see advertised on television. Vitamins have been sold over television virtually as candy, and other children's pills have been hawked as "making you grow up big and strong." Figures from the Department of Health, Education and Welfare's National Clearinghouse for Poison Control Centers show 5,146 cases of vitamin overdose poisoning in 1973, with children's aspirin ranked a close second with 4,275 cases in the same year. Those are only the cases reported to the Poison Control Centers; many are not.

Robert Choate looks at the problem from a statistical point of view. A public interest activist in the field of children's television commercials, Choate estimates that the average child sees over one thousand drug commercials annually. Basing his further calculations on 1975 broadcast industry statistics, Choate estimated that there were over 6.2 *billion* instances each year in which a child sees an advertisement for drugs on television.

Pharmaceutical companies who make and market *prescription* drugs have a different interpretation of the data. "Bombarding the young mind with the pill-for-every-ill philosophy is reaping its grim harvest as these children grow into adolescence and begin seeking their kicks in their own drug world," the American Pharmaceutical Association told the National Commission on Marijuana and Drug Abuse in 1972.

"Advertising and promotion of non-prescription drug products," said the APA, " 'pre-sell' the patient, not only on what product to purchase, but also on what is ailing him."

Other testimony is not difficult to find:

—In 1973, the New York Temporary Commission to Evaluate the Drug Laws reported: "Although there is no proof that such [drug] advertising actually encourages the misuse of drugs, there is a great deal of evidence that unnecessary use of drugs and chemicals (with resultant profits to their manufacturers) is the goal of such advertising." That was about as revolutionary a finding as would be one that the aim of the merchants, since the time of Adam Smith, was to buy cheap and sell dear—but the Commission was not through. It cited as an example an hour-long television documentary on "emotional stress" that contained "two commercials for Excedrin, one for Excedrin PM, one for Congesprin, three for antiperspirants, one for a hair spray, and one for a cough syrup."

—A compendium of articles on "Television and Human Behavior," issued by the RAND Corporation in 1975, lists more than twenty studies showing a positive correlation between heavy viewing of television commercials and children's use of over-the-counter drugs.

—Dr. Anthony Kales of Penn State University School of Medicine told a Senate committee in 1975 that drug advertisements on television "encourage the widespread use of drugs for what usually are responses to the normal frustrations of life."

—And Alistair Cooke, an observer of American life, has complained that "the thing that bothers me most about commercials is the medical brainwashing that the family gets on television. It seems to me that it easily outweighs any lessons in chemistry or biology that the child picks up in school . . . The body of our knowledge about medicine is fed to us from a very early age by commercials—and it's idiotic medicine. Mostly, its either harmful or useless."

The stakes in drug advertising are high. Over $300 million each year is spent on television advertising of over-the-counter drugs. The Federal Trade Commission has reported that the drug industry spends 14 per cent of its *gross dollar volume* on advertising—90 per cent of that is on television. Figures for comparable industries include: tobacco, 6 per cent; candy, 9 per cent; and food, 3 per cent. Of the drug total, $20 million in television advertising is aimed explicitly at children. To put these statistics in more understandable proportion, one commercial on television out of every six advertises a drug or a chemical.

A 1975 article by two professors at the Wharton School at the University of Pennsylvania demonstrates that advertisers now have the tools to determine not only what we want before we know it, but to make us want what we want before we know we want it. This significant experiment established that people in surprising numbers and percentages can be made to feel strong preferences for some beers and strong dislikes for others, even though all the beer is identical.

These researchers first spent more than two years perfecting tests and questionnaires to separate what they termed four distinct types of "personality spaces," each a measure of such characteristics as sociability, confidence, and a sense of self-worth. Then they examined and categorized (by personality type) 250 beer *aficionados*—without their knowledge. The beer drinkers believed they were engaged in market research—indicating a preference for commercials—for four prospective new brands of beer for Anheuser-Busch. The names selected were "Bix," "Zim," "Waz," and "Biv," names the researchers had determined to be value- and connotation-free.

Unknown to the beer drinkers who were the subject of the test, each of the brands was exactly the same, having been drawn from the same brew in the same vat. The drinkers then watched story-boards (drawings) of the proposed "commercials," each designed to reach one of the four personality types. For example, one series of drawings showed a working man arriving home from a presumably hectic day and sitting down with his—let us say—"Bix," as the cares and sounds of the day slowly faded away. This was designed to reach those who feel pressured by the world, who drink beer as a reward, and whose idea of peace is solitude.

After watching all the story-boards, the subjects were permitted to drink all they wanted of the four "different" brands, while at the same time discussing the merits and demerits of each brew with their fellow drinkers. The results were most significant. All of the drinkers said they could tell a difference among the various brands, a significant number selected one particular brand as their favorite, and many said that one brand or another was "not fit for human consumption."

Most important of all, the advance personality typings served as a reliable prediction of what both the likes and dislikes of the subjects would be.

The research experiment then called for in-depth interviews with 1,200 beer drinkers in six American cities, which yielded the finding that as a result of advertising campaigns then in use—dealing now with real and different beer brands—"each beer was perceived as having an appeal to particular personality clusters," that "those who drink each brand of beer do in fact fall into these perceived clusters," and that "the personalities associated with each brand not surprisingly correspond to those of the people usually shown in the brand's commercials."

In other words, people select and defend a brand of beer not for the taste, or even for the package, but because the perceived personality of people in the various commercials most resembles the personality they imagine for themselves.

The scholars concluded—not intentionally—on an ominous note. Their findings, they wrote,

> show how much can be done with even a little understanding of the consumer . . . The personality theory described herein obviously applies to other products which have psycho-dynamic effects; that is, modify the personality of the user . . . The potentialities of the theory have only begun to be explored.

resultant apathy. This began to change in the early 1960s and by now, these same professors are saying that an increasing number of Americans have declined to register or failed to vote, not as a characteristic of social class and not from apathy, but as a conscious statement of alienation and distrust.

This lowering of expectations, this loss of trust and confidence in our public officials and in our great political and private institutions, and the surge in political alienation bespeak a crisis—in our politics, in our daily lives, and in our national spirit.

This crisis may be ascribed, obviously, to many causes. The war in Vietnam, during which for the first time Americans became aware that Presidents not only lie but lie intentionally, and that the official establishment promotes and justifies the deception, was perhaps the leading cause. Another, of course, was all the official deceit, corruption, subversion and criminality loosely known as Watergate. Another was the long series of revelations of crimes committed by such once-trusted institutions as the FBI, the CIA, and major corporations.

Another of the basic, fundamental causes of this decline was television. Television has had a powerful effect, and a complex one.

It was television, after all, that defined and sustained each of these other causes—Vietnam, Watergate, criminal FBI-CIA-corporate actions—and that determined its place on the public agenda. We have had wars before—even unpopular ones—but never have the about-to-die, the dying, and the dead been displayed regularly in our homes; and our leaders have lied to us about war before, but this time we saw them talking on the same screen where we saw film from the war. Presidents have lied to us before about official corruption, but not when the corruption was discussed and displayed to millions of us—for hours a day, week after week, month after month, in painstaking detail. Never before have Americans had the opportunity daily to look directly into the eyes of a President who is wilfully deceiving them.

Americans tend to trust television—faith in television increased though our faith in institutions declined. The Louis Harris organization has been surveying Americans' trust in a list of kinds of institutions since 1966. The answers are profoundly disturbing. Confidence in physicians, organized labor, the military, religion, big business, and the courts, is fading—just as is confidence in our government.

It is television that may well have changed our attitudes toward how the political process is supposed to work. For example, research at Syracuse University has turned up a relationship between the amount of television viewing and voting: the more television a person watches, the less likely he is to vote. While causality here is obviously complicated, the professors go on to suggest that people who rely heavily on television for information are likely to believe that events are moving too fast to be affected by an individual citizen.

Commenting on this same phenomenon, the *New Yorker* wonders worriedly whether the American people have "lost the capacity for believing in the reality of events in their own lives." Citing the nation's response to New York City's financial crisis in 1975, the magazine points to "the drawing up of sides, the stereotype of New York as sinful villain or virtuous hero," with indifference to the real economic consequences for the nation." People's reactions, the magazine noted, were more those of "an audience at a play than of citizens watching the approach of a catastrophe."

News programs on television, in their efforts to entertain, change the news they show. The brevity of each news story means we, the audience, have no time to react very deeply to what we're shown, to feel involved—to experience much of an empathetic connection with even, say, a now-homeless victim of a fire, or to feel affected by, for instance, a government decision to shift a budget priority from housing construction to highway construction. The style of news on television also changes the events themselves*—in addition to changing our view or them—as was discussed earlier, in Chapter 3.

Beyond the narrow field of news—which is only a small part of television programming—years of saturation television have contributed substantially to our increasing institutional mistrust, and an increasing drop in expectation and self-esteem.

We will examine in this chapter the depiction on television of some major American institutions—medicine, law, police work, and the gen-

---

* In the first half of 1976, the evening news almost always included one or more of both parties' candidates for the presidential nomination, participating in what is now scornfully called a "media event." They were unlikely to be speaking straight to the viewing audience, as they might have in a newsreel of the forties or a television program of the fifties; instead, they would probably be discussing inflation with the amazed patrons of a supermarket. "Amazed" because one is usually not borne down on by a horde of cameramen, electricians, sound men, reporters, cables, cameras, lights, candidates, and aides, while patrolling the aisles of the supermarket in search of bargains. If one of the candidates for President is also a real President (as happens some of the time), then he will be engaged in a "media event" as well, but it will be a *presidential* media event. Perhaps the outstanding media event in the brief history of presidential use of television was Mr. Nixon's trip to China in 1972, a journey whose accomplishments could have been achieved diplomatically and without the visual trappings, but that would not then have furnished brilliant color film for his 1972 election campaign. For that matter, the *Mayaguez* incident became a spectacular Ford media event. The President was shown on television in meetings, sober, concerned, disciplined, and then laughing and congratulating his chief aides as the event ended "successfully." Left for the viewers to dig out of printed news accounts were all the complex subtleties of the *Mayaguez* case, including the facts that the *Mayaguez* had been warned of hostile action in those seas, and that more Americans were killed than were rescued. Mr. Ford's prestige was vastly buoyed by the *Mayaguez* media event; and American prestige may ultimately have suffered.

eral administration of justice—to see if the "reality" of television has not established a bench mark that the "reality" of reality cannot hope to reach.

MEDICINE

When the nation's top health officials and prominent members of the bar speak of "the Marcus Welby syndrome" as a major cause of the malpractice crisis, which has gripped and in places threatened to paralyze American medicine, this syndrome is worth examining. The television doctor—and he has been available for consultation in two or three places on the dial almost every day·of the week for years—is a skilled diagnostician; he is never wrong, and is always supremely confident. In the space of one hour, or at least that portion of the hour that fits between the commercials, he will diagnose a patient, effect a complete cure, and in the process straighten out the patient's emotional life. There will be some interaction between the doctor and other members of the hospital staff. Both the doctor and the hospital will seem to have no other patients in their care. There will be no discussion of insurance or payment of a fee. At the end, the doctor and the audience will be looking forward with confidence to next week's miraculous cure, previewed in short, dramatic takes.

Real doctors have a mixed reaction to these medical shows. They know that their patients are more knowledgeable than ever before, but at the same time the patients make unreasonable demands. Frequently, they insist on the same treatment a patient on television has received; and they expect, as a matter of course, a quick, painless, and total cure. Is it any wonder that real patients confronted with real doctors, who for the most part are overworked and increasingly uncertain about diagnosis and diagnostic tests, come to feel that they are the victims, if not of malpractice then at least of something less than the treatment to which they are entitled?

In real life, a doctor can seldom diagnose with absolute certainty—or with speed. Doctors order only those tests that a patient (or his insurance carrier) can afford. Often, a doctor has difficulty getting hospital space—and a real-life patient will have trouble paying for it. Being sick means feeling sick, usually, and for quite a while. Being sick is not always temporary, either—some illnesses and body malfunctions can be only partly cured or relieved, and some kill. On many counts, going to a doctor in real life does not measure up to what is seen on the screen in the living room every night.

THE LAWYERS

Lawyers are seen on television in two roles, neither of which is likely to enhance or even stabilize the standing of the profession. One role follows the tradition of Perry Mason, in which an attorney—like his medical counterpart—will devote himself entirely to one client at a time, and right a terrible wrong in the process, usually via some climactic confrontation in the courtroom. His client is almost always accused of crime but the attorney does not discuss a fee with him. He does, however, discuss the case with his partners and associates, sending them around the country looking for crucial pieces of evidence and key witnesses. It appears that entire law firms are devoted to one particular (innocent) client at a time, and that there is no other type of client or representation.

The other kind of lawyer appears on the police programs. This attorney represents criminals (not defendants in criminal matters, but criminals), and often participates in and counsels their illegal schemes and conspiracies. He can be identified early in the program because he smokes, is exceptionally well dressed, probably has a moustache, and is surrounded by beautiful women, none of whom is his wife.

Neither characterization of the profession is likely to create much confidence in the bar. Instead, each in its way tends to confirm an exaggerated view, against which the reality will inevitably suffer.

As for the police, they devote the time and energy of an entire precinct—if not an entire citywide force—to the solution of any crime that comes their way, at least as they are protrayed in prime time. They are always successful, often with the cooperation of a "private eye," and always within the same one-hour time segment. Real police are not so successful. They are, by and large, overworked, harrassed, and underpaid, and live a delicate balance between boredom and fear. Furthermore, on television *all* crimes are solved; and capture by the police means the criminal has been brought to justice. Either the bad guy is killed—most televised violence is done by officials of the state in the name of justice—or the bad guy is captured.

Television screenwriter Howard Rodman makes a telling point in this connection. All post-arrest administration of justice, he points out, is "telescoped" into a few seconds of action in which the police arrest the alleged criminal (often after shooting him), frisk him, and "book" him. That is the end of it, so far as the viewer is concerned. Law enforcement officers know, though, that is not the end, but barely the beginning. All of the difficulties and time-consuming aspects of post-arrest procedure are ignored on television. Arraignment, bail, plea bargaining, pleading, preparation for trial, pretrial testimony, motions, jury selection, the trial itself, the verdict, the probation reports, the sentence, appellate motions and dispositions, and perhaps the final serving of the sentence—all these are ignored and subsumed in the visual moment of arrest. This "telescoping," in Rodman's word, must cause serious problems if one believes at all that the message of television is carried into life. First of all, no post-arrest procedures are shown at all, and since the police and the "good guys" generally are pleased with the results ("he won't be harming any more people for a while, ma'am"), the assumption is that the arrested criminal is behind bars to stay. This ignores, of course, the possibility that post-arrest procedures do not work well, that a jury may fail to reach a verdict or that it may acquit, or that probation or a minimum sentence may result from a guilty verdict.

Second—and most important—this telescoping of post-arrest procedures focuses attention on the crime, the chase and the arrest, and no attention of any kind on the administration of justice. Thus, no attempt is made on television either to acquaint us with the enormous difficulties that system imposes, or with the enormous social values those difficulties are intended to guarantee. A survey of typical detective and police television programs by two University of Massachusetts professors in 1975 turned up enough illegal procedures by police (entering without a warrant, illegally seizing evidence, failing to warn defendants of their rights, etc.) to suggest that most of those prime-time "cases" would be thrown out on constitutional grounds, either before trial, at trial, or on appeal. Furthermore, it is entirely possible that the enormous frustration now apparent among Americans over the "failure" of the criminal justice system may be traceable to the assumption that all post-arrest procedures are successfully and swiftly completed following the televised arrest at the end of the program, and if they aren't, as is the case in non-television life, then—because of television—Americans think they ought to be.

In fact—in real life—the great majority of people convicted of crimes (not just arrested) do not serve sentences, and the overwhelming majority of people who commit crimes are not arrested. The reasons are complicated—some are good and some bad—but not so complicated that the average citizen cannot understand them.

Some depiction of the difficulties and the reasons might lessen this sense of frustration. But it is difficult, given the present state of the art, to imagine a prime-time police drama in which the case is not solved, or in which the wrong man is arrested, or in which the "right" man is arrested but is granted his freedom on a solid constitutional ground, which is presented as legitimate, justifiable, and important.

There are other problems in network television's reliance on action alone to solve a crime and dispose of the criminal. For one thing, most viewers watch not only police and private eye programs but "lawyer programs" as well. In the police and private eye programs the ultimate suspect is at least "guilty"; after all, we saw him commit the crime before our very eyes. But the following or preceding hour might have given us a lawyer program—on these programs, the accused are always innocent. The messages of television are thus not only simplistic but in conflict. People who are accused of crimes on television are either obviously guilty—in which cases they are counselled by shysters who are themselves in complicity in the crime, and the policemen will be frustrated for a time but otherwise quite perfect citizens; or else the accused are being railroaded by brutal and corrupt law officers and can be (and are) saved only by dedicated lawyers. Neither version is borne out in more than a handful of cases in real life, of course. Real-life situations, with people accused, cops, lawyers, and judges—almost always ambivalent situations—create extra tension and frustration in those whose views have been shaped by television.

Finally, there is a further serious point. From time to time, a policeman in a program in which the police are the heroes will speak disparagingly of the lawyer for the accused. It is not uncommon to hear Kojak or one of his colleagues in prime time say something like, "His lawyer will be down in ten minutes to get him out on some technicality." When that happens, it is never explained to the audience that the "technicality" is invariably a writ of habeus corpus or another Constitutional guarantee; further, that "technicality" is seen as just a sneaky ploy: often it is invoked by a lawyer we have previously had reason to identify with criminal activity. The heroic lawyers never acquit their clients on a "technicality," but always because of perjured testimony or freshly discovered evidence or witnesses. Thus, the Bill of Rights comes out disparaged or at best unnoticed all the time.

POLICE AND LAW ENFORCEMENT

Jeffrey Shufelt was a twenty-six-year-old Vietnam veteran. In 1975, he owned his own home in Hyattsville, Maryland; his wife was pregnant with their first child. One Sunday morning, without warning, Shufelt began to shoot from his living room into his neighbors' houses and into the street. Although he called police to say that he meant to kill as many people, including police officers, as possible, Shufelt seemed to be deliberately missing with all of his shots; he had learned in Vietnam to shoot accurately when he wanted to. Heavily armed police soon surrounded the house and, after a very brief and tentative effort at negotiations shot and killed Shufelt as he dashed across his front porch.

The incident had an aura of unreality about it. Shufelt had no history of mental illness, and his relatives and friends reported that he had never expressed any special animosity toward the police or his neighbors. Witnesses said that his shootings seemed more of a "cry for attention" than an attempt at murder. They also said that the dash across the porch in full view of the assembled army of police had all the marks of a suicide.

Having overheard the police radio calls, Washington *Post* reporter Elizabeth Becker telephoned Shufelt during the shoot-out. "I watch too much television," Shufelt said. The next day, his widow explained to Ms. Becker that he probably had said this when he realized that, unlike a television character, he was not going to be helped by the police. She agreed to the *Post* interview in part because of her hope that "it never happens again to anyone." It became clear during the interview what "it" was.

> [W]hen he said he saw too much television, he meant he watched *S.W.A.T, The Rookies, Emergency, Adam 12*. He did not want them to kill him. He wanted them to get him and take him and help him, but they didn't. I know from him . . . we watched them . . . they always saved the person . . .
> He loved the cops, yes . . . and that's why he called the police, because he knew, or he hoped, or he believed they could do something and help him because he needed help . . .
> [I]n those shows those policemen [are] really helpers. In TV shows they aren't really the way they are.

(During the shoot-out, Shufelt called his sixteen-year-old brother-in-law, David. It's not known what they talked about, but David says that "When he called it sounded like a World War Two movie going on." Every character in the tragic drama seemed to see himself in a film role.)

The police seemed to be re-enacting a television program, but with a different third act than Shufelt had imagined. It is clear that he saw himself as the guest star of an episode in which the police, recognizing the neurotic or psychotic mentality of the Vietnam veteran, call in psychiatric assistance and "talk him down" so that a few seconds before the final commercial he throws his weapon out and emerges with his hands over his head, crying that he never really intended to hurt anybody and to receive psychiatric treatment. In the Shufelt episode the police were following a more customary television tactic, shoot to kill. Thus, rather than wait until Shufelt became bored, or tired, or ran out of ammunition, and rather than call in a psychiatrist, a member of his family, or tear gas, the police moved in quickly for the kill. By ignoring solutions other than the use of force, the police were acting in one of the highest television traditions. They arrived on the scene, deployed the members of their tactical team, talked for a brief period and then killed the "bad guy"in plenty of time for commercials and previews of the next episode.

Jeffrey Shufelt had a lot to choose from in deriving his attitudes toward police because broadcasting executives seem to believe that it is impossible to entertain Americans without police drama. Thus, there is every type of policeman imaginable on television. Some are apparently slow-witted, but really keen-eyed and remorseless Italian-American detectives; others are fast-moving, wise-cracking, relentless Greek-American detectives. There are women police officers, bitter "rogue cops," and even a robot policeman. A homosexual purse snatcher on the popular ABC police program, *Barney Miller,* explained to his uniformed captors recently that he, too, wanted a career in law enforcement. "What's wrong with a gay cop?" he asked. "There's plenty of gay robbers." Sure enough, a few weeks later on the same program a gay police detective made his appearance.

One characteristic shared by the full variety of policemen on television programs is that they always get their man, and almost always by force. (Even the gay officer on *Barney Miller* successfully entrapped a gay mugger in the course of a stake-out at—naturally enough—a gay bar.)

This love affair with the police has characterized American television programming from its earliest days. A 1954 study of prime-time programs found 20 per cent of the characters to be law-breakers, each of course requiring the requisite number of police to discover and capture him. A similar study conducted one decade later determined that a full third of all 1964 prime-time characters were law-enforcement officers. The 1970s have recruited even more police officers to the television precinct house.

These members of the Prime-Time Police Department provide most of us with our notions of who policemen are and what they do—just as they provided Jeffrey Shufelt. With a few exceptions, Americans deal with real police officers only when they receive a traffic ticket or need directions in a strange town. Those Americans who maintain close or regular contacts with the police—usually unwillingly—for the most part belong to discrete subcultures: they are almost always poor, or black, or Spanish-speaking, or belong to a criminal sub-group clustered around gambling and drug traffic.

Some impressions of police come to the great majority, to be sure, from television, radio, newspaper and magazine news accounts. But when do police make news? Police make the newspapers or the six o'clock local television news when they go on strike or when some of them are caught taking bribes or accused of excessive brutality. The death of a police officer on duty is always newsworthy, and the funeral of a police officer is highly visual; television invariably covers it. Editors rarely ignore the visit of a distraught mayor to a new police widow. Police unable to solve a particularly heinous crime or series of crimes are occasionally portrayed through a spokesman, who anticipates an arrest "within twenty-four hours." Otherwise, however, they are not newsworthy. Policeman performing the grinding, boring, often dangerous daily work they are assigned are rarely, if ever, reported.

Futhermore, police entertainment programs are often consciously planned and designed to reflect and enlarge upon what we see on the news. One Hollywood writer says, "What are stories on the news are ideas and events on *Kojak* . . . the contemporary problems that greet us as soon as we click on the *Today Show,* by Sunday, *Kojak* has harnessed . . . into a story . . ." The alacrity with which television producers got on the air with rogue FBI and particularly CIA agents is a good example of this. While the U.S. Senate was still investigating the role of multinational corporations in manipulating foreign and domestic policies, Lieutenant Stone of the *Streets of San Francisco* was solving a series of crimes in which the agents of a large corporation were terrorizing—and in one case, murdering—the small property owners in a city block it wished to purchase for a new factory. At the end of the program, Stone explained to his partner that this was "a multinational corporation," which meant that it had no home base and strongly implied that therefore it had no morals. After a few commercials that same night, a program called *Harry-O* gave us a multinational corporation whose agents ingeniously killed a petroleum engineer during a flight on the corporation's private plane, because he had knowledge of important petroleum deposits the corporation preferred to keep closely held. The news provides pegs for the development of television programs, but that is a long way from saying that television programs reflect reality.

Every evening, somewhere between 40 million and 60 million Americans watch the Prime-Time Police Department in action during what are presented to us as routine workdays. They see a world of shootings, car chases, and crime syndicates totally unlike that which really exists. The cumulative effect is enormous. According to the best available broadcast industry statistics, nearly 10 million children between the ages of two and eleven are still watching television at 10 PM. Assuming that each sees or has seen one hour of police programs each day (a low estimate), this means that the average eleven-year-old American child has already spent more than one thousand hours in television precinct houses and police cars. By the time he reaches adulthood this figure, of course, will be multiplied many times.

What is the practical impact of this flood of unreality? Former New York City Deputy Police Commissioner Robert Daley warns that these "actors impersonating the way other actors have always impersonated policeman" may be "fabricating a police myth via television that will last for decades to come." "Our police departments are in need of help," Daley says, but so long as our police ideas and opinions are formed principally by television cop shows, "very little intelligent help can be forthcoming."

Does Daley attach too much importance to television? The hard scientific evidence is scarce. Although public funds have been allocated for studies of such things as the correlation between the size of a woman's breasts and her success as a hitchhiker, apparently no one has seriously and extensively examined how the public gets its ideas about the police. All we have are a few scholarly studies examining narrow apects of children's attitudes. Among the general conclusions reached by these studies are: the more a child "likes" the police the more likely he is to believe that the portrayal of police on television is realistic; most children subscribe to the same homogenous view of the police no matter what their real-life experiences and contacts with the police have been. According to these fragmentary studies, children also seem to believe that certain police shows are "true" because an adult voice has told them that the episode is based upon real events in a real department.

Probably the most thorough examination of children's ideas about police concluded that television ranked third, behind parents and friends, as a source of opinion about police work. But this study failed to ask the necessary next question—where the parents and friends learned about the police. It seems clear that the answer might well have been from television.

IN REAL LIFE

On a less scientific basis there is considerable evidence indicating that television has shaped the way in which we think about the police. The International Conference of Police Associations has cited at least one television program—*Police Story*—as "giving the public greater understanding and insight into professional police work." A *New York Post* editorial warned about "frequent cases in which hold-up victims, emulating television, carry guns and try to draw them and out-shoot robbers—and are quickly dead themselves."

The FBI and the Washington, DC, Metropolitan Police opened a fake fencing ring in 1976 and recovered over $2.4 million in stolen property from burglars who brought them the goods. "You guys are just like on television," ran a typical comment from one of their "customers" as he was being booked and taken away.

A Florida woman whose husband was murdered by his business partner carefully broke the news to her children, only to discover that they had suspected both the crime and the perpetrator almost from the moment of their father's disappearance. "It never occurred to me that such things can happen," she said later, "but my kids watch things like that every night and evidently thought such murders are a normal part of life."

When the apartment of the star of *Rhoda* and her husband was burglarized one night on CBS, for example, the police appeared. Rhoda began to ask them to perform certain investigatory tasks that police on television customarily perform, and the policemen then told Rhoda that they were not from *Kojak* or *Adam 12* or *Police Story* or any of the other police programs, all of which they listed. Rhoda's feelings are apparently duplicated around the country; a 1976 survey of detective work in major cities in America,* indicates that almost half of the things detectives do in the course of an investigation are done for "public relations" reasons. In other words, most of the fingerprinting, showing the victim mug shots, line-ups, and other details of detective work that American television audiences expect, are done by real police only because the television audiences—which presumably includes the victim of the real crime they are investigating—have come to expect it.

This is a truly astonishing finding, and it is unfortunate that television did not devote some time to the study, perhaps in a public affairs documentary if not on the evening news.

Police detectives all across America are drawing chalk lines around the body on the floor, taking endless photographs at the scene of the crime, dusting for fingerprints, showing pictures of suspects to the victim, and perhaps conducting line-ups from which the victim is to choose one, all because over the past two decades Americans have seen police do this on television and will not be content unless police do it in real life. It is entirely possible, although the Rand study does not go this far, that some of the tax money spent on law enforcement in the United States could be saved if the facts about the differences between real police work and television police work were the subject of a mass educational program. But, of course, the only way these facts could be presented to sufficient numbers of the American people, with sufficient intensity to have an impact, would be on television. Given the present economic structure of the industry, it is inconceivable that television

---

* The Rand report is explicit in other ways; it includes the discouraging conclusion that practically no crime will be solved unless by reliable eye-witness testimony. If the victim or a bystander knew or saw the criminal, the police will almost certainly get their man; without such testimony or first-hand knowledge, they almost certainly will not, unless the goods stolen are of such enormous value that separate insurance-oriented ransom demands are made.

would devote itself to telling the American people that not only is what they see in the evening about police activity false and misleading, but belief in it actually causes the loss of perhaps millions of dollars in tax revenue.

But it would be an interesting program. Real policemen, when confronted directly with the question, are unanimous about the lack of realism in television police work. In all of the interviews conducted for this book with uniformed and plain clothes officers across the country, not one failed to smile in derision when asked about the procedures and techniques used by television police departments.

Real policemen agree with Daley's assessment of the shows as "an incredible collection of prime-time half-truths, illusions, stupidities, and outright lies." Further interviews with police officers reveal not only derision but a great deal of frustration and anger at how they are portrayed. Many worry about what impressions their wives and children get from television non-truths and half-truths about their work; a young son or daughter must be continually reassured that Daddy does not get shot at every day and does not really conduct himself the way the policemen do in the living room. A wife needs to understand that the risks involved in her husband's profession, while very real, need not force her to live in constant fear of widowhood. Police wives on television frequently insist that their husbands quit the force "before it is too late"; real police wives sometimes do the same thing—without really knowing where they got the idea. A recent survey, for example, discovered that an average American policeman pulls his gun no more than three times in his entire career. And the commander of the Los Angeles S.W.A.T. team, the prototype not only for proliferating S.W.A.T. teams around the country, but also the super-violent team on television, points out with some pride that since 1968 when the unit was formed, his men have prepared their weapons for use only three times (including the shoot-out with the Symbionese Liberation Army).

Real police agree that television police programs are truthful only in their technical details. The removable blinking light that can be placed on the top of unmarked cars, the guns, belts, uniforms, and station houses depicted on television are indeed found in most city departments.* The most important discrepancies are not found in the sets, but

---

* Daley points out, however, that almost all the officers and cars shown on television are unrealistically new and clean. Police cars take a beating just like taxis and look it. From the real-life unattractiveness of police station houses he draws a larger lesson: "Police offices are manned almost exclusively by men, they are not used to impress anybody, no outsiders sees what they look like except suspects, who are usually too scared to notice. Such offices are often badly cleaned; this is partly because the people who man them don't complain and partly because they are in use so much of the day. There are no rugs on the floors and there are no books on the walls. This is a small point perhaps but it might help the viewing public to realize how shabby crime is . . ."

in the scripts, in the almost complete distortion by television of what a police officer actually does. On television, the typical officer spends a significant segment of his normal work day chasing (or being chased) by criminals. Sometime between breakfast and lunch he will be shot at, hit on the head, or otherwise threatened or menaced. Invariably, before the day is over, he will be in a deadly car chase. About 25 per cent of the criminals and suspects on television suffer bodily harm at the hands of police—and that's not counting bodily harm from shooting, and stomach-turning car chases. The television policeman's routine activities include pumping a few prostitutes (perhaps forcibly) for information; or exchanging jive talk with super-slick, exotically dressed and coiffed pimps; or perhaps some gunplay behind the thick pillars of a parking garage.

Theo Kojak, in one hour a week (less commercials) as a lieutenant for the New York City Police Department, decodes complex criminal schemes, outwits and outthinks at least one group of thugs, comforts the victims of crime while explaining life in "realistic"—that is, cynical—terms, all the while sucking on a lollipop which he extracts from the pocket of an immaculately tailored $300 suit, the supply of which (the lollipops and the suits) seems inexhaustible. He may have a moment of sentimentality. His life consists, thus, of nothing but exciting and glamorized events, and if he loses at anything, the setback is temporary. "If it would work that way," said an eleven-year veteran of the Dallas police force, "we'd all go out and buy lollipops."

Police work is tedious and slow; a real policeman's main enemies are boredom, psychological strain, emotional problems, and fear. The police suicide rate ranks second only to physicians in America.

On television, the victim of a crime is as falsely portrayed as the policeman. The victim is not the focus of the entertainment—the victim is seen sympathetically for a moment, but soon the camera abandons a victim, and gets on with the adventure. In real life, being the victim is very different—and it is a further shock for a crime victim to discover that the television police work is a lie. Victims of crime, particularly violent crimes in large cities, almost always have real horror stories to tell. A young woman who was raped recently in Washington, D.C., identified her assailant and swore out a complaint. He was found, booked, and then released on bail, as the Constitution and the Bail Reform Act required. A few weeks later, before any action was taken about trying him in a court of law, he returned to her home, this time accompanied by others. They gang-raped the woman and left. Police officers responded to her frantic second call, but were able to do no more than write down the details and prepare to find him once again. "When do you think you can catch him so this won't happen again?" the victim asked, reasoning perhaps that since the rapist had already been booked once, the police knew where he was and where he lived. "We don't know. It's a big city, and it could be weeks or months," was the unfortunately accurate reply. With a sense of panic, she asked what she could do in the interim, since she lacked money simply to pack up and move or leave town. Among the well-meaning suggestions she received from the police were to buy a gun, see if she had any friends in the Mafia, or, to move out and live elsewhere. None of the rapists ever were caught. Months later, the woman still lived in fear.

Her story is not unusual. As the *New York Times* reports, a recent study of crime in the Bronx discovered that "almost half of the victims . . . hid in their apartments for weeks after the crime. Many—deeply fearing another crime or intimidation to prevent them from reporting the crime or testifying about it—wanted to move, but did not have the resources to do so."

On television, these things would not happen. Two factors mitigate against it. First of all, it is not the purpose of commercial television to create anxieties or doubts or ambiguities or ambivalent attitudes about one's life during the entertainment portion of the program, lest these feelings be carried over into the commercial portion and lessen its impact. Second, repeated demonstrations of how crime really is in the United States would surely evoke such a wave of protest from official America, beginning with the Justice Department and working on down to local police departments, as to prove intolerable for the management of television—which depends upon peace and quiet at the ideological level for its continued operation. To the extent that realism might create questions about the nature of the station operation, it is sedulously avoided.

Perhaps the most potent difference between television police and real police—and the one that may contribute the most to the rising feelings of irritation and failure with respect to law enforcement—is that the television police never fail to solve a case or capture a criminal. In real life most cases—in some areas all cases—are never solved. The recent studies sponsored by the federal Law Enforcement Assistance Administration show, in fact, that in real life most of the time no one even *tries* to solve a crime.

One study was conducted over a two-year period and examined detective activities in 181 separate jurisdictions (because of its excellent record-keeping system, the police department of Kansas City, Missouri, provided much of the data). "Less than half of the reported felonies could be said to be worked on by an investigator," says the report, "and the great majority of cases that are actively investigated receive less than one day's attention." Most investigations receive "no more than supervisorial attention."

How are cases solved at all? Not by detective work, says the report: "It is not appropriate to view the role of investigators [that is, detectives] as that of solving crimes." The single most important determinant of whether or not a case will be solved is the information the victim supplies to the immediate responding patrol officer. If information that uniquely identifies the perpetrator is not provided at the time of the crime, then by and large the criminal will not ever be identified. Top priority thus goes to cases "in which the investigators' steps are obvious from the facts related to the incident report." In other words, the easiest-to-solve crimes get the most attention—because there is some hope of solving them.

On television, crimes are solved. The police, after examining clues (broken matchsticks, heel prints, hair under the fingernails, and, of course fingerprints) and after discerning the motivation of the gangster's plot, apprehend him. Sometimes they must surround a deserted warehouse (or parking garage), sometimes they arrest him while he's quietly eating breakfast at his girlfriend's apartment.

All the crime statistics bear out the unliklihood of a solution of a crime, and if the statistics are questionable it is on the high side because they deal, of course, only with *reported* crimes. (The most susceptible to error of perception are the FBI figures; the FBI has a much higher percentage of convictions in the cases it undertakes, because a tradition begun under J. Edgar Hoover insisted upon reporting every recovered stolen car as a solved case.)

But even so, in 1975, only 21 per cent of all the crimes reported nationally resulted in an arrest, and an arrest, of course, hardly means conviction and almost never means incarceration. In Montgomery County, Maryland, for example, 95 per cent of all people *convicted* of crimes are given probationary sentences; while Montgomery is an "enlightened" county—penologically speaking—those figures are not too far from the national average. If one extrapolates from that the number of arrests which do not lead to conviction, and the number of suspects who are not arrested, and the vast majority of crimes for which there is hardly even a suspect, the magnitude of one's dissatisfaction with real life as opposed to the orderly regulation of crime on television becomes apparent.

In most of our large cities there is a conviction in less than 5 per cent of reported serious crimes. Nationally, about four-fifths of all murders result in some arrest, but only one out of every five murders, or 20 per cent, ends in a conviction. Only one-fifth of all reported burglaries result in even an arrest, one-fourth of which (five per cent) end in conviction—that is, 5 per cent of the reported burglaries ends in a conviction. The arrest and conviction rate for murders is very high, compared to other crimes; it is because murder is the most easily solved of crimes, since the majority of murderers are involved with their victims—they are either family members, or in a business or social relationship—and are thus easier to trace.

Solving cases is what television police do; and on television, policemen are detectives. Very few of our police in real life are detectives—they're patrolmen.* It may not even be the job of the police to solve crimes, says James Q. Wilson, a respected Harvard criminologist:

> The average citizen thinks of the police as an organization primarily concerned with preventing crime and catching criminals. When crime increases or when criminals go uncaught, the conventional public response is to demand more or better policeman. When the crime rate goes down or a particularly heinous crime is solved, the police often get—or at least try to take—the credit.
>
> For some time, persons who run or study police departments have recognized this public conception is misleading. The majority of calls received by most police are for services that have little to do with crime but a great deal to do with medical emergencies, family quarrels, auto accidents, barking dogs, minor traffic violations, and so on. And those calls that do involve serious crimes such as burglaries, robberies, and auto theft, typically occur after the event has taken place and the trail is cold; the officer who responds can often do little more than fill out a report that will contain few if any leads for further investigations. The police themselves wish it were otherwise—most patrolmen would prefer to stop a crime in progress or catch a major felon—but only infrequently do they have the chance."

The way in which television has shaped the development by police of their own institutions can be demonstrated clearly in the case of S.W.A.T. In 1974, in May, members of the Los Angeles Police Department Special Weapons and Tactics unit engaged in a prolonged shoot-out with the Symbionese Liberation Army. Local television cameras arrived shortly after the firing began, and broadcast hours of the confrontation live, culminating with fiery death. The coverage was sensational—and magnified in the national news by the mistaken belief that Patricia Hearst was inside the besieged building, and among the dead S.L.A. members.

In the following television season, in an ABC program *S.W.A.T.*, three snipers set out to kill six policemen as revenge for their father's death. "We're at war," announced the television S.W.A.T. chief. Later, he tells

---

*The same holds true for the self-image of many private investigators. One real private eye says, "Often when I meet a girl and she asks me what I do and I tell her that I'm a private investigator, there'll be a sparkle in her eyes and she'll say 'Oh, you mean like Mannix?'

"Sure I enjoy it, but then when I'm asked for details of some of my most exciting cases, I feel almost ashamed to admit that I've never been beaten up by mobsters urging me to 'get off the case,' that I have never used a gun . . ."

a rookie member of the team, who has just killed his first sniper, "Welcome to the club." The television S.W.A.T. members travel about town in a "war wagon," and have a rather glamorous time, including lots of good fellowship in between heroic exploits. "When you get in trouble," says ABC's promotional advertising for S.W.A.T., "you call the police. When the police get in trouble, they call S.W.A.T." S.W.A.T. enjoyed considerable success in the ratings and in the toy market, where S.W.A.T. action figures found their way into hundreds of thousands of American homes. But it enjoyed another, and more significant distinction.

Around the country, new S.W.A.T. forces began to proliferate in communities that no more needed them than they did a fleet of submarines. The New York Times discovered that by 1975 there were more than 500 S.W.A.T. units in local jurisdictions around the country, and the Times reported that the S.W.A.T. television program had "introduced a paramilitary mentality inside some departments and that some local agencies are pouring money and manpower into units where there is little rational likelihood that they will ever be used." Since, on the authority of S.W.A.T. Unit, the "grandfather" of S.W.A.T., the unit has drawn its guns only three times in eight years, and that in Los Angeles—the Times conclusion seems correct that the force is hardly needed to put down crime in rather peaceful, juvenile-plagued suburbs.

The Times survey contains some interesting examples. Providence, Rhode Island, for example, has no S.W.A.T. force, but 36 of the 176 officers in one of its suburban communities were members of such a team. In Belmont, California, a placid enough suburb of San Francisco with a population of 20,000, a new S.W.A.T. force equipped itself with knives strapped across the chest and with Israeli-made sub-machine guns. The Times quoted one police expert's reaction to all of this: "It reminds me of the 1930s when some smart salesman went around the country selling submachine guns to every police department on the theory that they were all going to have a shoot-out with John Dillinger some day." Moreover, the television S.W.A.T., with it's "we got to shoot it out" mentality, has given most Americans the wrong idea about just what a S.W.A.T. force is and can be. The San Diego, California, police chief, commenting sourly on the image the television S.W.A.T. team gives to police departments around the country, said "that's just a bunch of guys sitting around in black baseball caps waiting for the phone to ring to tell them who to go out and snuff."

A good special weapons and tactics officer in real life rarely has to shoot. The chief training officer for the FBI's equivalent of a S.W.A.T. team describes a good operation as follows: "First step, clear the area, second step, wait . . ." The FBI devotes more time to training members of its special teams in abnormal psychology than in weaponry.

One police chief, who turned down the S.W.A.T. idea, told a *New York Times* reporter, "some of these men have lost perspective on their role in society and are playing mental games with firearms."

THE LAW

There exists in America today a tremendous, almost all-pervasive dissatisfaction with our system of criminal justice. Some Americans argue that it is too lenient, others argue that it is oppressive or at the very least capricious, but almost all agree that it does not work as it should—that too few criminals are captured, that the system of incarcerating convicted criminals is bizarre, and that incarcaration itself produces little more than hardier criminals capable of resisting the more ordinary strains of the social order.

Few things enrage Americans today more than to read or observe—as they may on any given day—that a convicted criminal is still on the street, or worse, that he appears to have committed another and perhaps similar crime during his time out of jail. This has led to calls for quick and sometimes mandatory sentencing, without an understanding of the enormous extra effort and money required to make the criminal justice system work swiftly and efficiently.

In England, for example, it is not uncommon for a lawbreaker to be arrested one month, tried and convicted the following month, and begin serving his sentence—with all appeals exhausted—the month after that. Admittedly, the British system is simpler because the country is simpler, and a single national system of administration of justice prevails. But it is a model many Americans would like to reach, without understanding the enormous change in our system and the enormous expenditures that would be required. It has led to some rather dangerous proposals.

The New York *Post*'s James Wechsler pointed out recently that this disillusionment with the system of law enforcement is so deep that a serious book on crime, published in 1976, suggested that "the preservation of society and social order finally may require that we subordinate charity and sometimes even justice to punish most severely what most endangers society and the social order, even when there is little guilt or none."

"In an earlier American era," Wechsler writes, "such pronouncements would be regarded as beyond the legitimate boundaries of rational democratic dialogue. But they are no more."

Television does not necessarily *create* this dissatisfaction. To a large degree, these beliefs are based on reality. Criminals do walk the streets after conviction on loosely-based probation. The Constitutional guarantees of bail do provide for freedom pending trial for people who have been accused of crime. And the statistics on recidivism show that these criminals are often likely to commit another crime.

But television does magnify and exacerbate the problems, by confirming the belief that our legal system is not working correctly unless all "criminals" are either killed or permanently removed from society once they are arrested.

There is no doubt that most Americans, whatever their sensitivities or instincts with respect to questions of civil liberties, would like to see crimes solved by simply locking up the criminal. After all, we know from what we think is overwhelming evidence that most crimes are committed by repeaters (actually, while the proportion is significant, it is not that large). So it makes sense to keep violent people in jail, particularly once the trouble has been taken to find and capture them and relate them, however tentatively, to a crime that has been committed. In pandering to this desire, however, the people who run television for the most part do so as a part of seeking the same goal which dominates almost all of their decisions—the maximization of profit. Most television viewers do not want reminders that crime is complicated and that its slow-moving measures such as, for example, work-furloughs, can have an appreciable impact on recidivism rates. So in order not to concern the viewer too greatly, television's solution to crime, as is its solution to almost every other social problem raised in prime time, must be swift and clear-cut.

The largest audience can be delivered to the advertiser not by a challenge to patience and understanding, but by escapism and the opportunity to see collective prejudices and fantasies fulfilled. Television needs (in order to deliver that audience) the visible and the easily explicable, and neither quality characterizes the real causes and possible cures where our present deficiencies in the administration of justice are concerned.

The demands for a large and basically quiescent audience also extend into television *news* coverage of law enforcement and the administration of justice. Home furlough programs—to take the same example—make news only when one of the temporarily released prisoners uses his new freedom to commit a new crime. Yet the Bureau of Prisons reports that for three typical months in 1974 it granted 6,153 such furloughs with an escape rate of only .52 per cent. The District of Columbia granted 38,000 furloughs in the fiscal year 1974, and only 87 escaped. These are impressive statistics, made all the more compelling by the fact that large numbers of prisoners have, in the process, been given a chance to visit their families, further their education, attend religious services, work at a regular job, and—to be sure—relieve sexual pressures. But none of these constitutes action, so these activities are neither news nor—assuredly—entertainment.

The same unfortunate treatment is also accorded the question of parole. In real life, the parole privilege is a mixed blessing, depending on how it is used by law enforcement officials. But parolees make news only if they commit new crimes. On entertainment programs, parolees are almost inevitably abused. One type of television parolee laughs at the law while planning his next heist. Other fictional parolees, who try to go straight, always seem to have a job at the local car wash, a loving family, a modest suburban home, and a front lawn they are mowing when a former associate comes by to pressure them to join in "just one more job." If he refuses in Act I, he is beaten or killed. If he accedes to the blandishments of his fellow parolee, he will probably be captured and led back to jail (again with no trial). The only honorable course, it would seem, and the one the majority of prime-time parolees follow, is reluctantly to join the new criminal conspiracy, repudiate it later, and then be killed while saving a policeman's life. Television has no time for explanations to inform or comment about the pressures and distortions with which parolees are required to deal, and since television has no time to deal with this problem, neither do its viewers.

But of all the errors of omission apparent in television's treatment of the administration of justice, none is more significant in its contribution to the gap between expectation and reality than its portrayal of a criminal justice system that exists without plea-bargaining.

Whether plea-bargaining should go on or not is a question very few people involved in the process care to discuss, or have time to discuss. In fact, it is that lack of time which makes it so crucial. Whatever the encrustations that have covered the American system of justice, they now make it physically impossible—or so the prosecutors believe—to dispose of more than a fraction of the criminal matters which come to the authorities in a routine way. That is to say, if every arrestee were to insist on his rights, and be tried by a jury for the crime with which he is charged, the delay in the court system would be so great that it would break down entirely within a few months. The delays are already extraordinary; trials are delayed for months and appeals for years. If it were not for the fact that the great majority of cases end in plea-bargaining—that is, in a plea of "guilty" to an offense lesser than the charged one, as a result of a bargain struck between prosecution and defense—then trials would take years, and appeals decades.

In the nation as a whole, about *90 per cent* of all criminal indictments and informations are resolved by plea-bargaining. Plea-bargaining has become the heart of our criminal justice system. The alternatives may be more judges, more automatic sentences, bigger and more jails, different laws, different punishments—but short of a solution, or several solutions, plea-bargaining will continue to turn our courts into a tread-mill in which there is no exit for the judge, the prosecutor, the defender, the accused, and although he is unaware of his status, the ordinary citizen. Awareness comes with involvement, and it is a rude shock to find oneself in court and a witness to the other-wordly processes.

None of this comes through on television, and the shock of seeing the consequences in real life is all the greater because we have not imagined it existed. Indeed, as we have seen, we are led to believe—hour after hour, night after night—that quite a contrary clean and "just" system exists, one in which people whom we have seen commit crimes are brought to justice swiftly, surely, and, presumably, fairly.

THE VANISHING CONSTITUTION

Another misleading lesson taught by television police/lawyer programs is that "technicalities—read 'Constitutional guarantees'—need not and should not get in the way of effective law enforcement." Both the NAB and FCC guidelines, for example, bar the depiction of astrology or numerology as "commonly accepted appraisals of life." They also require that no crimes go unpunished, but nothing is said about crimes committed by policemen during the course of their official duties, and the rules and regulations are totally silent with regard to unconstitutional action by the police. A spokesman for the American Civil Liberties Union, normally more zealous than any others in this area, admits that the ACLU has paid no attention at all to television police programs "since the early days of *Dragnet.*"

But two University of Massachusetts professors monitored eight popular prime-time police shows in 1975 to see how well the Constitution fared, and came away disappointed. Kojak kicked down the doors without a search warrant and Lt. Stone of *Streets of San Francisco* illegally stole evidence from a suspect's apartment. Other "routine" police activities including coercion of witnesses to obtain information, failure to inform suspects of their Constitutional rights, bribery, locking up suspects, and planting illegal drugs.

"The message was pretty clear," Professors Ethan Katsh and Stephen Arons reported, "the right to privacy, the integrity of the individual and the right to due process of law do not seem to be observed by successful police whose activities always subdue evil.

"Almost every episode of every television police show contains one or more violations of either the Fourth, Fifth, or Sixth Amendments . . . in the months of painfully packed police dramas, hardly an hour's viewing passed without an illegal search, a confession obtained by coercion, or the failure to provide counsel."

The two professors fear what these programs may be doing to public attitudes:

> When comparing our perceptions with those of non-lawyer friends, we discovered that police shows seem to reduce the ordinary citizen's awareness of Constitutional rights and responsibilities. Many people, engrossed in the drama of rapid-fire action or preoccupied with violence, fail even to notice blatant police-state tactics.

Arons and Katsh video-taped examples of illegal police activity and showed the tape to classes of pre-law students. Most of the students—all members of The Television Generation—did not understand why the video-tape was worthy of note; even with clues from the professors, few of the students could specify what Constitutional rights had been compromised.

Writing a few years after their initial studies, Arons and Katsh reached a new conclusion. After examining recent Supreme Court decisions, they warned that, "The Court has been legalizing outrageous police conduct, enacting into law principles much like those projected in the TV crime shows." How could this be possible? They suggest:

> What started off as merely fictional entertainment has now begun to have the political effect of "softening up" public opinion.

This phenomenon has important public policy implications. Americans have often been notoriously unsupportive of specific civil libertarian guarantees, especially when asked in the abstract to extend those guarantees to unpopular groups or the advocates of extremely unpopular positions. In a celebrated case in the 1950s, for example, the great majority of those questioned by pollsters thought that freedom of speech should not be extended to "Communists" and every so often during the 60s and 70s an enterprising public opinion specialist would roam the supermarkets and by-ways of the nation, trying to collect signatures in support of the language of the Bill of Rights, and would be turned down by substantial numbers who called it "subversive."

Television unquestionably has added to and heightened such feelings, especially when local police are widely reported as claiming they have been "handcuffed by the Supreme Court." Conversations with police around the country reveal that to a considerable extent, such claims are made as an excuse for failure—made so they can measure up to the invincible image the public has come to believe. If a criminal is not caught—it is easier to blame the failure on some "technicality" imposed by the Supreme Court, or to suggest that the police are forced by over-zealous civil-liberties-minded judges to operate with one hand tied behind their backs.

A good example is the famous *Miranda* decision, which required police to tell a suspect before any questioning that he has the right to remain silent, that if he talked anything he said might be used in court against him, that he had a right to an attorney, and that if he lacked the funds to hire an attorney, one would be appointed to represent him. The purpose is, of course, straightforward: to keep the police from extracting a confession by force or the threat of force. Almost every safeguard written into the Constitution, either explicitly by the founding fathers or implicitly by judges and legislatures over the past two hundred years, can be said to be in response to the famous dictum of a British police officer in India, quoted by the great authority on the law of evidence, John Wigmore: "It's easier to throw red pepper in some poor beggar's eyes than to go out in the hot sun looking for evidence." Miranda was just one more attempt by the Warren court to keep the police out in the hot sun and away from the pepper jar.

Very few Americans were aware, and very few more have become aware since, of the basis for the *Miranda* warning. With the exception of brief mentions on television news programs, the only exposure is through the prime-time police program. And what do we see? We see television policemen, for the most part, mumble as if by rote a few words, usually being read from a card, to suspects who snap back, "I know, I know my rights," and perhaps we then see dapper criminal types with diamond pinky rings and flashy cars bragging that they have a right to a free lawyer. To television policemen and criminals alike, the warning seems to be just a momentary pause in the day's occupation, a sop to some do-good outside force perhaps, but never an integral part of the unfolding system. At best, it seems to demean and distract the police while they seemingly should be busier with more important things.

Miranda is completely irrelevant to most criminal police work—the majority of arrests occur when a policeman himself, or else a complaining witness, catches someone in the act. With an eyewitness, a confession isn't needed. It is only detectives—a fraction of the police—who work on crimes to which there isn't a witness.

Even for them, all the available studies seem to show that *Miranda* has not in any way hampered police work. Five editors of the *Yale Law Journal* examined *Miranda's* impact on police in New Haven, Connecticut, and concluded that "not much has changed . . . the *Miranda* rules, when followed, seem to affect interrogations only slightly. The police continue to question suspects and succeed despite the new constraints." In 1975, defense attorneys around the country were asked about *Miranda,* and a typical response was that "most defendants will make statements to the police, the district attorney and, on occasion, even a judge *after* being advised of their rights." Indeed, for twenty years before the Supreme Court *Miranda* ruling, the FBI routinely required that *Miranda*-type warnings be given by its agents making arrests (with the exception of the guarantee of free legal counsel, a requirement the Supreme Court imposed only a few years before *Miranda*). J. Edgar Hoover required these warnings not through any zeal for civil liberties, to be sure, but because he knew that stronger cases could be built and appeals more successfully fought against individuals who had been warned of their rights.

But all of this is in harsh contrast to what is shown on the television screen, and should make us wonder anew how much Kojak and his colleagues have contributed to the public's distain for constitutionally guaranteed rights of the accused.

These criticisms, however, are largely applicable to the "good cop/bad lawyer" type of program on television. On the other hand, as has been noted, there is the "good lawyer/bad cop" program and here a different concept of civil liberties—equally at odds with reality—is presented. Mark Twain once said that he'd like to "close the jury box against idiots, blacklegs, and people who do not read newspapers." He was expressing the increasingly popular view that to keep from a jury peers of the defendant who have neither heard about the case nor formed an opinion is almost to guarantee the presence of nin-compoops and those who have no sense of civic responsibility. Had Twain lived in the middle third of the twentieth century, he might very well have added "people who watch too much Perry Mason."

Howard Schwartz a New York lawyer who worked for the Legal Aid Society in New York City's South Bronx, recalls the case of the jury that surprised him by acquitting his client. Later that day, he bumped into one of the jurors and asked what had happened. "It was the right to have a warning, about never saying anything without an attorney," the juror replied. "The prosecutors never read him his rights. We didn't like that." Schwartz then explained that the suspect had been caught in the act with eyewitness testimony available, and that the police had never even considered using any of the defendant's statements as evidence—hence, no warning was necessary. It did not seem to matter to the jurors, who had picked up a totally different interpretation of *Miranda,* unquestionably from television dramas.

Jason Kogan, an assistant U.S. Attorney in the District of Columbia, tells a similar story:

> It was a case involving possession of a pistol. There were several eye-witnesses to the defendant's possessing the weapon. These witnesses testified at the trial that the defendant possessed the weapon; the de-

fendant denied that he possessed the weapon. Afterwards, several of
the jurors told the prosecutor that the reason they didn't convict was
because the government didn't introduce any fingerprints. The prosecutor said, well, we thought it wasn't necessary because we had eye-
witnesses, but the juror said "well, we see it on television that there are
fingerprints on items and since you did not have fingerprints on this
weapon, we could not be sure beyond a reasonable doubt that he was
the person who had the weapon."

"What has happened in this country," writes Robert Daley, "is that
juries tend to believe so-called scientific evidence, and more and more
they tend to disregard all other evidence. Too often, if the prosecution
can't show that prints were found on the murder weapon, the jury will
refuse to believe that the accused could have possibly have used it to
commit the crime. Television viewers are potential jurors and errors
such as this have been perpetuated for so long that in the minds of most
of us they have turned into prejudice."

Lawyers also talk about the "Perry Mason syndrome." Mason has
been practicing on television now for nearly twenty years—in reruns for
the last several years—and has never lost a case. He almost always
brings a witness to tears or hysteria while successfully exposing the real
culprit in open court (his most popular contemporary imitator was Petrocelli, who always closed his cases with a vivid and correct recounting
of how the crime was committed, a courtroom equivalent of the older
fictional detective's "you're probably all wondering why I've asked you
here."). Many American lawyers fear that Mason's pervasive style has
taught too many Americans that it is the responsibility of defense attorneys to prove who is guilty. In truth, of course, the defense need prove
nothing, let alone provoke a confession from the real guilty party. The
burden of proof rests with the prosecution, but television directs our
thought processes in other directions.

"It usually comes up during *voir dire* (the oral questioning of prospective jurors)," explains Jackie Sands of the New York Legal Aid Society.
"We ask if the prospective juror knows how Perry Mason always wins,
and the answer is yes. Then we ask if he understands that it is the job
of the District Attorney to prove who's guilty. Then we go on to *Petrocelli*
and the other current shows to make sure that the juror realizes that
the real trial won't go that way—or at least that he can suspend his
belief." This is an interesting statement, suggesting that defense attorneys will count it a success, not if the juror indicates that he understands the American system of jurisprudence in its most rudimentary
form as it applies to him, but will settle for an understanding on the part
of the juror that "real" trials—that is to say, those on television—are
somehow different and that the "drama" being enacted in the courtroom
is, at least for today, being played under different rules.

Charles R. Garry, who has successfully defended a number of politically unpopular defendants, including San Francisco Bay area Black Panthers, warns, in a manual published by the National Lawyers' Guild, that the prospective juror must also accept the fact that the defendant "doesn't have to take the affirmative in bringing out the person who did the crime, if, in fact, the crime was committed." The Perry Mason syndrome also makes itself felt when the jury has to reach a solution. "Most jurors, in part because of television entertainment, wait for a defense lawyer to come up miraculously with the missing bit of evidence," writes New York City trial lawyer Martin Garbus. "They penalize the defendant if his lawyer is not overpoweringly bright. No surprise witness, no last-minute legal argument that successfully explains every bit of evidence and twists every fact to the defendant's favor—no acquittal."

An apocryphal story which seems to have become a law school tradition with student members of the Television Generation, tells the tale of the defense attorney at a murder trial, who completed his summation to the jury as follows:

> "I have something important to tell you now. I have employed a private detective—a very good private detective—to find the person who committed this crime. The private detective is going to bring that person here and walk through that door in just a few minutes."
> The defense attorney then sat down and waited in silence. After about two minutes had passed, he stood up and told the jury, "I just noticed that every one of you is glancing toward the door. You expected to see something. What does that tell you about whether you're convinced that my client is guilty beyond a reasonable doubt?"

This story does not reveal what the jury then decided; for the Television Generation process is almost always far more important than result. They know what has gone into their own development and they know that this same force undoubtedly helped shape the jurors.

Not all of the complaints about the law firm of Mason and Petrocelli and its associate members come from defense attorneys who feel they are harmed by the fact that on these shows the prosecutor always puts the wrong person on trial. The fear of misrepresentation is shared by many prosecutors. On almost every television program with a trial, so the prosecutors' argument goes, the state has not only brought to trial an innocent person, but a person whose innocence would have been clear to the District Attorney's office if only someone there cared about justice. Boston attorney Joseph Oteri, a member of the American Bar Association's Committee on Television, argues that *Perry Mason* and similar shows have done much to lessen the juror's bias that a defendant must be guilty if he has been brought to trial; but many district attorneys still cling to the traditional view, that television is pretty much devoted to the proposition that defendants are innocent. Walter H. Louis, a deputy district attorney in Los Angeles, wrote in *TV Guide* in 1974 that "the American public has been getting a tube-fed legal education about lawyers and law enforcement." Louis was particularly angry that in the shows on which he concentrated, *Perry Mason, The Defenders, The Bold Ones,* and *Owen Marshall,* people have learned that, in cases that do come to trial, (a) the defendant invariably stands unjustly accused by (b) the prosecutor, who is a rude obstructionist, a form of necessary evil. Louis called this a "body of distortion and misinformation" amounting to "a brain-washing, not an education," and called for television programs that would dramatize and, presumably, promote, the prosecutor as a central figure in the attempt to achieve justice.

Prosecutor Martha K. Kwitney thinks that television may have even gone too far in stressing the possibilities that defendants might be innocent. "Jurors have been conditioned," she writes, "to adopt a skeptical attitude towards the state's case. They are waiting for the prosecutor to call Kojak to the witness stand, and instead the prosecutor puts on the boy next door." Daley writes of a murder trial in which he witnessed the prosecutor subject "the defendant to one of the most scathing personal attacks that any man has ever had to endure. I watched the jury. It seemed to me that I had seen this scene before, and indeed I had, dozens of times on television. On television the murderer always cracks eventually and says something like 'I can't take it any more.' He suddenly breaks down blubbering and admits his guilt.

"But this defendant did not break down, he did not admit his guilt. He did not blubber. It seemed to me I could see the jury conclude before my eyes: ergo, he cannot be guilty—and indeed the trial ended in a hung jury . . . Later, I lay in bed in the dark and brooded about the trial I had attended. If television programs such as this one had never existed, would the jury have found the defendant guilty even though he did not crack? . . .

"What is the idiocy of programs such as this doing to our country?"

Still, this bias—if it is one—in favor of railroaded defendants is two-edged. The mistakes made by television prosecutors nearly always come from ineptitude or laziness—they rarely frame a suspect or ramrod an indictment past an indifferent grand jury and a guilty verdict past an indifferent or biased jury, as frequently happens in real life. And if a neighbor is lying or a jilted girlfriend is perjuring herself on television, conscience strikes long before an innocent person goes to jail. On television, the system always ultimately works, no matter how poorly served it may be by particular individuals.

"Television seems also to have had an effect on how *witnesses* conduct themselves. Due to the style of courtroom drama on the screen, the least significant witness now comes to court expecting to be tricked, ridiculed, and harassed by inquisitorial gimmicks," writes Washington defense attorney Edward Bennett Williams. According to Williams, "The number of argumentative witnesses has increased. As a result, trials slow down with unnecessary evasion. Double and triple meanings are heard when a lawyer, in the most prosaic style, is simply trying to establish a sequence of events that can then be corroborated by a second witness."

Somewhat the same effect is seen on defendants, many of whom come to court expecting their attorney to act as attorneys do on television. They want their lawyers to leap to their feet with objections, skillfully to manipulate and destroy prosecution witnesses, to produce all witnesses necessary to establish innocence (or better yet, the guilt of someone else), and most of all to be constantly acting—both verbally and physically—at all stages of all court proceedings. Sometimes, this can work to a defendant's detriment. Legal Aid lawyers report, for example, that sometimes it is best to remain silent during arraignment, allowing the testifying police officers and the young inexperienced deputy district attorney a chance to dig their own graves by admitting that certain evidence has been obtained illegally. Frequent objections, although highly desirable to a television-saturated defendant, may only serve, say the defense lawyers, to make prosecutors more alert and effective and less likely to make damaging admissions.

But whether used by a demogogue or simply as a central feature of the American myth, most of us, no matter what our cynicism, believe and have always believed, that the right to judgment by one's peers is an irreplacable element in our society. Whether on the frontier or in the drawing room, the judgment by a jury, the arguments, the logic, the evidence, even where the proceeding is as hasty and one-sided as it has often been—is still a central feature of our experience. So long as Americans think of themselves as a democratic, free people, they will continue to believe in the courtroom as the place where facts are determined, where all men are equal, and where appropriate judgments are rendered. Trials have always been—real ones as well as fictional ones—important in our literature and mass entertainment, and the courtroom has been the most popular stage upon which we enjoy acting or watching others act out our central social dilemmas and emotions.

Perhaps the most important impact of television has been that on the Bar. Edward Bennett Williams has lectured on college campuses and at law schools for more than fifteen years, and comes away with a somewhat disheartened view of the Television Generation: "I sense a disbelief in the students . . . [They] seem to have accepted the point that television dramatists have not consciously tried to make but have made almost subliminally: students have come to understand that criminal cases are decided by rhetoric; that the outcome depends on malevolent tricks; that the lawyer is always the key factor in winning or losing. The student has a definite impression that deception may be more important than the difficult and grubby discipline of the law. They would like to avoid the digging that turns the law student into a competent attorney.

"Television's dramatists, while observing the technical details, leave an impression that the scholarship of law is a bore—unnecessary to successful practice."

"The actual trial is often a dull, plodding affair to watch," says Williams. "It has to be. The rules of evidence generally reduce showmanship to farce." But television's courtroom is pyrotechnic and there is never time to show the actuality of carefully developed facts.

There is no question that today's lawyers, particularly those forming a part of the Television Generation, find themselves acting out what they have seen on television. George Gerbner, whose violence index is only one avenue to his acceptance as a television authority, tells the story of "a defense attorney who once leaped to his feet, objecting, 'Your honor, the prosecutor is badgering the witness!' The judge replied that he, too, had seen that objection raised on a recent television program but unfortunately it was not a legitimate objection listed in the state's code of civil procedures. "Anecdotes and examples should not trivialize the real point, that even the most sophisticated can find many important components of their knowledge of the real world derived wholly or in part from fictional representation," writes Gerbner.

One prominent Washington attorney, with a successful high-pressure practice, adamantly insisted in an interview that television had in no way entered his professional life. It had not prompted his specialization in trial work; it had not changed his style; it had not helped to shape his expectations; and it had never affected his thinking. "I can tell you with absolute certainty," he said, "that I have seen *Perry Mason* and similar shows and I have always recognized that they are fictional and have nothing at all to do with what goes on in a real courtroom." He was convincing until asked what thoughts go through his mind during the seconds while he is rising to address the jury. His answer: "I think to myself, this is *not Perry Mason,* and I am *not* going to get melodramatic."

Perry Mason himself, actor Raymond Burr, once told an audience of the National Association of Municipal Judges, "Without our laymen's understanding and acceptance, the laws which you apply and the courts in which you preside cannot continue to exist."

What are we learning from all this? One measure is the fan mail received by the actors who play television's "good guy" lawyers. It isn't the type of fan mail movie stars receive, nor is it the fan mail received by the stars of television variety or talk shows. It is from people with real legal problems asking for real legal advice. Somehow, Americans come to believe in the reality of those programs even though they must know they are fiction. Barry Newman, who played television lawyer-hero Petrocelli, comments modestly, "most of it [my fan mail] just comes from people looking for free legal advice."

The legal profession is badly served on television, although its leaders rarely complain. In prime time, there are basically only two kinds of lawyers, super-heroes and super-villans. But only a small proportion of the legal profession is involved in trial work, and even the lawyers who litigate often devote only a portion of their time to that activity. Most lawyers' time is spent with paper, and in extensive meetings, discussions, negotiations, and research. In Great Britain, this difference is recognized with the distinction between solicitors and barristers; only the latter do court work and do not have clients in the traditional sense. They are assigned trial matters by solicitors. American law schools and bar associations have traditionally resisted this distinction, clinging to the increasingly implausible notion that every law school graduate who makes his way past a state bar examination is equally qualified to handle all parts of the practice, including litigation. In 1973, Chief Justice Warren Burger, in one of his many observations about the American judicial system, estimated that about half of all American lawyers involved in "serious litigation" are unqualified. Burger did not release any scientific or even unscientific data to support the figure, but any serious lawyer who has spent any time in a courtroom—and for that matter most clients whose lawyers have spent time in a courtroom—are prepared to accept the figure as, if anything, conservative.

This lack of experience and often of competence in the American courtroom is made even more serious by the expectations raised by television. It is doubtful if Chief Justice Burger's 50 per cent of trial lawyers who are able, can measure up to the high standards set by prime-time law firms; it is certain that the other 50 per cent contribute to the decline in confidence which the legal profession has experienced over the last 25 years.

The people who produce the lawyer programs claim, with considerable justification, that not all of the blame for the disparity between the law as it appears on television and the law as we know it exists in real life, lies with the broadcast industry. Advertisers would not take long to discover if Americans wanted true legal realism, and after all it is they who determine—in a real sense—the content of network programs. But the clear distinctions between right and wrong, the certain verdict, success and failure, that are presently displayed, seem to satisfy a need of the television world.

Some of the people who introduced these programs admit that they are consciously creating new realities to replace those which occur in

CONCLUSION

As an attempt to assess the ways in which television has affected American life in the past quarter-century—the Age of Television—this book could have treated many other subjects. Nearly every aspect of American life is now shaped, in one way or another, by television. There are studies that demonstrate the degree to which voting behavior is influenced by the uses candidates make of the medium. Family relationships are changed by the members' perceptions of their roles as depicted by characters on the screen. Simpler questions—how to act after scoring a touchdown, for example—find answers on television.

The truth is that television programs sell more than cars, hair sprays, and life insurance. They sell a view of the world and that view, as Dr. George Gerbner has said, helps change our image of ourselves. As an example, he says if the television world contains more victims than perpetrators of violence, that will create a society in which most people view themselves as potential victims and respond to life more fearfully.

Television programs increasingly—at an alarming rate of increase—now provide the background, rhythms, and assumptions by which Americans live. In doing so, they enter our lives in ways so deep as often to be unrecognizeable, and often impossible to escape. The policeman pulling up to the scene of an accident or a crime, the lawyer preparing to address the jury or examine a witness, the doctor talking to a patient or scrubbing up for surgery—each cannot help but register images of what the scenes are like on television. He knows, in short, full well what his feelings and actions "should" be. Even if he does not consciously make this calculation ("Now, ladies and gentlemen, this is not a *Perry Mason* program . . ."), then he does so subconsciously. From the television image—and the difference between it and reality—comes much of his attitude and behavior.

In recognizing this, it is important also to recognize that television is—most emphatically—here to stay. There can be no successful latter-day Luddites, throwing out or burning their television sets to remove the temptation (although some church groups have conducted provocative mass television set smashings). On the contrary, most Americans now regard television as a basic necessity of life. Hotel and motel rooms are far more likely to have inadequate plumbing or lighting facilities, or no fire escape, than they are to lack a functioning television set. The law has come to recognize that status; in New York State, for example, a television set is included, along with pots and pans, essential tools, and prosthetic devices, among those necessities of life beyond the reach of creditors.

Along with admitting that television is here and will remain here, Americans must face just how important television is in our individual and national life. This book has attempted to point to that importance. We believe that the impact of television can be seen, not in complicated McLuhanesque analyses, but by simply looking at the world about us—a world filled with television, touching and informing our lives and our ideas, influencing the things we eat, the way we raise our children, and the songs we sing.

We should note as well that television is now accepted in artistic and intellectual circles where once it was scorned. Jean Paul Sartre announced plans on his seventieth birthday to write less and to direct a series of television programs. And the Librarian of Congress, social critic and historian Daniel Boorstin, whose books regularly note the influence of television, recently told an audience at the dedication of a new humanities center that "the crisis of our time, the next great crisis of human consciousness, has come with television."

We offer in these pages no set of solutions, no final chapter called, "Agenda for Reform." We have attempted to draw attention to the impact of television, and to do so within the context of accepting it as the most powerful external factor in American life. Television is here—in our bedrooms, our streets, our factories and offices, and in our children's classrooms. If we wanted to, we could not make it go away.

Furthermore, nothing in our research or in our interviews suggests that commercial television programming in the United States will change significantly in the foreseeable future. So long as the industry is based upon engaging an audience and delivering it to an advertiser, present tendencies—in one form or another—will prevail. This is not necessarily the worst thing or even a bad thing; if the alternative is government television, we have seen enough of political developments in 15 years to note the dangers of central control of communications. Charles de Gaulle often said—correctly, as it turned out—that whoever controlled television in France would control the country. We need not test that theory in the United States.

We are not left, however, with impotent acceptance of the status quo. There are many things that can be done within the framework of commercial television, and there are many fine and dedicated people and groups committed to those changes. These pragmatic options range from community cable systems—including so-called "pay" television—to seeking a more meaningful stance from the Federal Communications Commission.

A more muscular FCC could, without any change in the law, give new meaning to the "public interest" requirement for renewal of station licenses, and require—let us say—a reduction in violence by half, an increase in news, and free segments of time for political candidates. Television, in short, can be made more responsive to the public's needs, but television itself can never be made less powerful. That distinction is vital, no matter how obvious it may seem, once stated. The Age of Television, in other words, will pass through new and perhaps dramatically different phases, but these will mark only shifts in *what* television does to society, not in *how much* it does.

Andrew Fletcher of Saltoun, a Scottish patriot and philosopher, wrote in 1704: "If a man were permitted to make all the ballads, he need not care who should make the laws of a nation." In this nation, in this Age, it is television that makes the ballads.

BIBLIOGRAPHY

BOOKS

Aaker, David A., and Day, George S., *Consumerism: Search for the Consumer Interest.* New York: The Free Press, 1971.

ABC/Montreal *Star*/The *New York Times, How to Watch the Olympic Games, Summer, 1976.* New York: Quadrangle, 1975.

Altschuler, Richard, and Regush, Nicholas M., *Open Reality.* New York: G. P. Putnam's Sons, 1974.

American Bar Association, Special Committee on Youth Education for Citizenship, *Law-Related Education in America: Guidelines for the Future.* St. Paul, Minnesota: West Publishing Company, 1975.

Arlen, Michael J., *The Livingroom War.* New York: Viking Press, 1969.

Aronson, James, *The Cold War and the Press.* New York: The Bobbs-Merrill Company, 1970.

Bagdikian, Ben, *The Information Machine.* New York: Harper and Row, 1971.

Baker, R. K., and Ball, S. J., eds., *Violence and the Media, A Staff Report to the National Commission on the Causes and Prevention of Violence.* Washington, D.C.: Government Printing Office, 1975.

Balk, Alfred, and Boylan, James, eds., *Our Troubled Press: Ten Years of the Columbia Journalism Review.* Boston: Little Brown and Company, 1971.

Barrett, Martin, ed., *Moments of Truth? The Fifth Alfred I. Dupont-Columbia University Survey of Broadcast Journalism.* New York: Thomas Y. Crowell, 1975.

Barthes, Roland, *Writing Degree Zero and Elements of Semiology.* Boston: Beacon Press, 1953.

Bell, Daniel, *The Cultural Contradictions of Capitalism.* New York: Basic Books, 1976.

Berger, Arthur Asa, *The TV-Guided American.* New York: Walker and Company, 1976.

Bettelheim, Bruno, *Love Is Not Enough.* New York: Collier Books, 1950.
————————, The Informed Heart. New York: Avon, 1960.

• BIBLIOGRAPHY

Bliss, Edward, Jr., and Patterson, John M., *Writing News for Broadcast*. New York: Columbia University Press, 1971.

Bluem, A. William, *Religious Television Programs*. New York: Hastings House, 1969.

Bock, Richard, and English, Abigail, *Got Me on the Run: A Study of Runaways*. Boston: Beacon Press, 1973.

Bogart, Leo, *Strategies in Advertising*. New York: Harcourt, Brace and World, 1967.

——————————, *The Age of Television*. New York: Frederick Ungar, 1972.

Boorstin, Daniel J., *Democracy and Its Discontents*. New York: Random House, 1971.

——————————, *The Decline of Radicalism: Reflections on America Today*. New York: Vintage Books, 1970.

——————————, *The Image*. Middlesex: Penguin, 1961.

Bouton, Jim, *I'm Glad You Didn't Take It Personally*. New York: Dell, 1971.

Bower, Robert T., *Television and the Public*. New York: Holt, Rinehart and Winston, 1973.

Brecher, Ruth and Edward, eds., *An Analysis of Human Sexual Response*. New York: New American Library, 1966.

Breitman, George, *Malcolm X Speaks: Selected Speeches and Statements*. New York: Grove Press, 1965.

Broder, David S., *The Party's Over: The Failure of Politics in America*. New York: Harper and Row, 1971.

Brown, Les, *Television: The Business Behind the Box*. New York: Harcourt, Brace, Jovanovich, 1971.

Brownmiller, Susan, *Against Our Will*. New York: Bantom, 1976.

Bugliosi, Vincent, and Gentry, Gene, *Helter Skelter*. New York: Bantam, 1975.

Bunce, Richard, *Television in the Corporate Interest*. New York: Praeger, 1976.

Burdick, Eugene, et al., *The Eighth Art*. New York: Holt, Rinehart and Winston, 1962.

Bush, Chilton R., ed., *News Research for Better Newspapers*. New York: American Newspaper Publishers Association Foundation, 1969.

Campbell, Angus; Converse, Philip E.; Miller, Warren E.; Stokes, Donald Z., *The American Voter*. New York: John Wiley and Sons, 1964.

Cantril, Albert H., and Roll, Charles W., Jr., *Hopes and Fears of the American People*. New York: Universe Books, 1971.

Carden, Maren Lockwood, *The New Feminist Movement*. New York: Russell Sage Foundation, 1974.

Casty, Alan, *Mass Media and Mass Man*. New York: Holt, Rinehart and Winston, 1968.

Cater, Douglass, et al., *Television As a Social Force: New Approaches to TV Criticism*. New York: Praeger, 1975.

——————————, and Strickland, Stephan, *TV Violence and the Child: The Evolution and Fate of the Surgeon General's Report*. New York: Russell Sage Foundation, 1975.

Chester, Edward W., *Radio, Television and American Politics*. New York: Sheed and Ward, 1969.

Chester, Lewis; Hodgson, Godfrey; Page, Bruce, *An American Melodrama: The*

Presidential Campaign of 1968. New York: The Viking Press, 1969.

Christopher, Elias, *Fleecing the Lambs.* Greenwich,; Connecticut: Fawcett, 1971.

Cirino, Robert, *Power to Persuade: Mass Media and the News.* New York: Bantam, 1967.

Clark, Ramsey, *Crime in America.* New York: Pocket Books, 1974.

Cleaver, Eldridge, *Soul On Ice.* New York: McGraw-Hill Book Company, 1968.

Cline, Victor, ed., *Where Do You Draw the Line? An Exploration into Media Violence, Pornography and Censorship.* Provo, Utah: Brigham Young University Press, 1974.

Clouser, John William, *The Most Wanted Man in America.* New York: Stein and Day, 1975.

Cohen, Bernard, and Chaiken, Jan M., *Police Background Characteristics and Performance.* Lexington, Massachusetts: D. C. Heath, 1973.

Cohen, Dorothy H., *The Learning Child.* New York: Vintage Books, 1972.

Cohen, Richard M., and Witcover, Jules, *A Heartbeat Away: The Investigation and Resignation of Vice President Spiro T. Agnew.* New York: The Viking Press, 1974.

Cohn, Nik, *King Death.* New York: Harcourt, Brace, Jovanovich, 1975.

Columbia Broadcasting System (CBS) News Special Report, *Vietnam Perspective.* New York: Pocket Books, 1965.

Comstock, G.A., *Television Violence: Where the Surgeon General's Study Leads.* Santa Monica, California: The Rand Corporation, .1972.

Cook, Thomas D.; Appleton, Hilary; Conner, Ross F.; Shaffer, Ann; Tamkin, Gary; Weber, Stephen J.; *Sesame Street Revisited.* New York: Russell Sage Foundation, 1975.

Cosell, Howard, *Like It Is.* New York: Pocket Books, 1974.

Cottle, Thomas J., *Black Children, White Dreams.* Boston: Houghton Mifflin, 1974.

Crouse, Timothy, *The Boys on the Bus.* New York: Random House, 1972.

Dechant, Emerald, *Diagnosis and Remediation of Reading Disability.* West Nyack, New York: Parker Publishing Company, 1968.

Decter, Midge, *The New Chastity and Other Arguments Against Women's Liberation.* New York: Coward, McCann and Geohegan, 1972.

DeMott, Benjamin, *Hells and Benefits.* New York: Basic Books, 1958.

Department of Communication, The American University, *The Press Covers Government: The Nixon Years from 1969 to Watergate.* Washington, D.C.: Department of Communication, The American University, 1973.

Doctor X, *Intern.* Greenwich, Connecticut: Fawcett. Crest, 1965.

Domhoff, G. William, *Who Rules America?* Englewood Cliffs, New Jersey: Prentice-Hall, 1967.

Dorsen, Norman, *Frontiers of Civil Liberties.* New York: Random House, 1968.

Efron, Edith, *The News Twisters.* Los Angeles: Nash Publishing, 1971.

Ehrlich, Paul R. and Ann H., *The End of Affluence.* New York, Ballantine Books, 1974.

Ellison, Harlan, *The Glass Tent: Essays of Opinion on the Subject of Television.* New York: Pyramid, 1969.

Ellison, Ralph, *Invisible Man.* New York: The New American Library, 1952.

• BIBLIOGRAPHY

Ellman, Mary, *Thinking About Women.* New York: Harcourt, Brace, Jovano-vich, 1968.

Ellul, Jacques, *Propaganda: The Formation of Men's Attitudes.* New York: Vintage Books, 1965.

——————————, *The Political Illusion.* New York: Vintage Books, 1967.

Epstein, Edward Jay, *Between Fact and Fiction: The Problem of Journalism.* New York: Vintage Books, 1975.

Erikson, Erik H., *Childhood and Society.* New York: W. W. Norton and Company, 1950.

Evans, Rowland, Jr., and Novak, Robert D., *Nixon in the White House.* New York: Random House, 1971.

Fairlie, Henry, *The Spoiled Child of the Western World: The Miscarriage of the American Idea in Our Time.* Garden City, New York: Doubleday and Company, 1976.

Fall, Bernard B., *The Two Viet-Nams.* New York: Frederick A. Praeger, 1963.

Fang, Irving E., *Television News.* New York: Hastings House, 1972.

Fiedler, Leslie A., *Love and Death in the American Novel.* New York: Criterion Books, 1960.

Flesch, Rudolf, *Why Johnny Can't Read.* New York: Harper and Row, 1955.

Friedan, Betty, *The Feminine Mystique.* New York: Dell Books, 1963.

Friendly, Alfred, and Goldfarb, Ronald L., *Crime and Publicity.* New York: The Twentieth Century Fund, 1967.

Friendly, Fred W., *The Good Guys, The Bad Guys and the First Amendment.* New York: Random House, 1975.

Galbraith, John Kenneth, *The New Industrial State.* New York: New American Library, 1967.

——————————, *Economics and the Public Purpose.* Boston: Houghton Mifflin Company, 1973.

Gardner, George E., *The Emerging Personality: Infancy Through Adolescence.* New York: Delacorte Press, 1970.

Gattegno, Caleb, *Towards a Visual Culture.* New York: Avon, 1969.

Gilmour, Robert Scott, *Political Alienation in Contemporary America.* New York: St. Martin's Press, 1975.

Glasser, William, *The Identity Society.* New York: Harper and Row, 1972.

Golden, Harry, *Mr. Kennedy and the Negroes.* Greenwich, Connecticut: Fawcett, 1964.

Goldman, Eric F., *The Crucial Decade and After: America, 1945–1960.* New York: Random House, 1960.

Gornick, Vivian, and Moran, Barbara K., eds., *Women in Sexist Society: Studies in Powerlessness.* New York: New American Library, 1971.

Goulart, Ron, *An American Family.* New York: Warner Paperback Library, 1973.

Greer, Germaine, *The Female Eunuch.* New York: Bantam, 1970.

Greenberg, B.S., and Dervin, B., *Use of the Mass Media by the Urban Poor.* New York: Praeger, 1970.

Greenfield, Jeff, *No Peace, No Place.* Garden City, New York: Doubleday and Company, 1973.

Grey, David L., *The Supreme Court and the News Media*. Evanston: Northwestern University Press, 1968.

Grollman, Earl A., ed., *Explaining Death to Children*. Boston: Beacon Press, 1967.

Groombridge, *Television and the People*. Middlesex, England: Penguin Books, 1972.

Gross, Martin L., *The Doctors*. New York: Random House, 1966.

Guimary, Donald L., *Citizens' Groups and Broadcasting*. New York: Praeger, 1975.

Hall, Calvin S., *A Primer of Freudian Psychology*. New York: New American Library, 1954.

Hargreaves, Robert, *Superpower: A Portrait of America in the 70s*. New York: St. Martin's Press, 1973.

Harris, Thomas A., *I'm OK—You're O.K.* New York: Avon, 1967.

Harris, Louis, *The Anguish of Change*. New York: W. W. Norton and Company, 1973.

Hartmann, Paul, and Husband, Charles, *Racism and the Mass Media*. Totowa, New Jersey: Rowman and Littlefield, 1974.

Hayes, Harold, *Smiling Through the Apocalypse*. New York: McCall Publishing Company, 1969.

Henry, Jules, *Culture Against Man*. New York: Random House, 1963.

Herschensohn, Bruce, *The Gods of Antenna*. New Rochelle, New York: Arlington House, 1976.

Hersey, John, *The President*. New York: Alfred A. Knopf, 1975.

Heilbroner, Robert L., *Business Civilization in Decline*. New York: W. W. Norton and Company, 1976.

———————————, *An Inquiry Into the Human Prospect*. New York: W. W. Norton and Company, 1974.

Herndon, James, *The Way It Spozed To Be*. New York: Bantam Books, 1968.

Hersh, Seymour H., *My Lai 4*. New York: Random House, 1970.

Hilliard, Robert C., and Field, Hyman H., *Television and the Teacher: A Handbook for Classroom Use*. New York: Hastings House, 1976.

Hofstadter, Richard, and Wallace, Michael, *American Violence: A Documentary History*. New York: Random House, 1970.

Holt, John, *The Under-Achieving School*. New York: Dell Publishing, 1969.

———————————, *What Do I Do Monday?* New York: Dell Publishing Company, 1970.

———————————, *How Children Learn*. New York: Dell Publishing Company, 1972.

———————————, *How Children Learn*. New York: Dell Publishing Company, 1964.

Hunter, Beatrice Trum, *Consumer Beware!* New York: Bantam Books, 1971.

Hunt, Morton, *Sexual Behavior in the 1970s*. Chicago: Playboy Press, 1974.

Huxley, Aldous, *Brave New World Revisited*. New York: Bantam Books, 1958.

Johnson, Nicholas, *How to Talk Back to Your Television Set*. New York: Bantam Books, 1970.

Kahn, Frank J., ed., *Documents of American Broadcasting.* New York: Appleton-Century Crofts, 1968.

Kaye, Evelyn, *The Family Guide to Children's Television.* New York: Random House, 1974.

Kearns, Doris, *Lyndon Johnson and the American Dream.* New York: Harper and Row, 1976.

Kendrick, Alexander, *Prime Time: The Life of Edward R. Murrow.* Boston: Little, Brown and Company, 1969.

Kennedy, Robert F., *Thirteen Days: A Memoir of the Cuban Missile Crisis.* New York: W. W. Norton and Company, 1969.

Kesey, Ken, *One Flew Over the Cuckoo's Nest.* New York: New American Library, 1962.

Kimball, Penn, *Bobby Kennedy and the New Politics.* Englewood Cliffs, New Jersey: Prentice-Hall, 1968.

Knightley, Phillip, *The First Casualty: From the Crimea to Vietnam: The War Correspondent as Hero, Propagandist, and Myth Maker.* New York: Harcourt, Brace, Jovanovich, 1975.

Kohl, Herbert, *36 Children.* New York: New American Library, 1967.

Kosinski, Jerzy, *Being There.* New York: Bantam Books, 1972.

Kraditur, Aileen S., *Up From the Pedestal.* Chicago: Quadrangle Books, 1968.

Krickus, Richard, *Pursuing the American Dream: White Ethnics and the New Populism.* Garden City, New York: Doubleday, 1976.

LaGuardia, Robert, *The Wonderful World of TV Soap Operas.* New York: Ballantine Books, 1974.

Lang, K., and Lang, G. E., *Voting and Non-Voting.* Waltham, Massachusetts: Blaisdell, 1968.

Lesser, Gerald S., *Children and Television: Lessons from Sesame Street.* New York: Random House, 1974.

Liebert, Robert M.; Neale, John M.; Davidson, Emily S., *The Early Window: Effects of Television on Children and Youth.* New York: Pergamon Press, 1973.

Lindstrom, Miriam, *Children's Art.* University of California Press, 1967.

Lopate, Phillip, *Being with Children.* Garden City, New York: Doubleday and Company, 1975.

Lubell, Samuel, *White and Black: Test of a Nation.* New York: Harper and Row, 1964.

Lystad, Mary H., *A Child's World As Seen Through His Stories and Drawings.* Rockville, Maryland: National Institute of Mental Health, 1974.

Maddox, Brenda, *Beyond Babel: New Directions in Communication.* Boston: Beacon Press, 1972.

Magruder, Jeb Stuart, *An American Life: One Man's Road to Watergate.* New York: Atheneum, 1974.

Mailer, Norman, *The Idol and the Octopus.* New York: Dell, 1968.

——————————, *The Armies of the Night.* New York: New American Library, 1968.

——————————, *Advertisements for Myself.* New York: New American Library, 1959.

Manchester, William, *The Death of a President.* New York: Harper and Row, 1967.

Marcuse, Herbert, *One Dimensional Man.* Boston: Beacon Press, 1964.

Marsh, Robert, *Agnew: The Unexamined Man.* New York: M. Evans and Company, 1971.

Marsh, Spencer, *God, Man and Archie Bunker.* New York: Harper and Row, 1975.

Mayer, Martin, *Today and Tomorrow in America.* New York: Harper and Row, 1975.

——————————, *About Television.* New York: Harper and Row, 1972.

Maynard, Joyce, *Looking Back: A Chronicle of Growing Up in the Sixties.* Garden City, New York: Doubleday and Company, 1973.

McCary, James Leslie, *Human Sexuality.* New York: Van Nostrand Reinhold, 1973.

McGinnis, Joe, *The Selling of the President, 1968.* New York: Trident Press, 1969.

McLuhan, Marshall, *Understanding Media: The Extensions of Man.* New York: The New American Library, 1964.

McNeal, James U., *Dimensions of Consumer Behavior.* New York: Appleton-Century Crofts, 1964.

McQuail, Dennis, ed., *Sociology of Mass Communication.* Middlesex, England, 1972.

Mead, Margaret, *Culture and Commitment: A Study of the Generation Gap.* Garden City, New York: Natural History Press/Doubleday, 1970.

Melody, William, *Children's TV: The Economics of Exploitation.* New Haven: Yale University Press, 1973.

Metz, Robert, *CBS: Reflections in a Bloodshot Eye.* Chicago: Playboy Press, 1975.

Milgram, Stanley, *Obedience to Authority.* New York: Harper and Row, 1975.

Minor, Dale, *The Information War.* New York: Hawthorn Books, 1970.

Minow, Newton; Martin, John Barlow; Mitchell, Lee M., *Presidential Television.* New York: Basic Books, 1973.

Mintz, Morton, and Cohen, Jerry S., *America, Inc.: Who Owns and Operates the United States.* New York: Dell Publishing Company, 1971.

Morgan, Robin, ed., *Sisterhood Is Powerful: An Anthology of Writing From the Women's Liberation Movement.* New York: Vintage Books, 1970.

Morris, Norman S., *Television's Child.* Boston: Little, Brown and Company, 1971.

Mosken, Robert J., ed., *The Case for Advertising.* New York: American Association of Advertising Agencies, 1973.

Murdock, Graham, and Phelps, Guy, *Mass Media and the Secondary School.* London: The Macmillan Company, 1973.

Napolitan, Joseph, *The Election Game and How to Win It.* Garden City, New York: Doubleday and Company, 1972.

National Advisory Commission on Civil Disorders, *Report of the National Advisory Commission on Civil Disorders.* New York: Bantam Books, 1968.

National Commission on the Causes and Prevention of Violence, *Mass Media and Violence: A Report to the National Commission on the Causes and Prevention of Violence.* Washington, D.C.: Government Printing Office, 1969.

National Commission on Marijuana and Drug Abuse, *The Technical Papers of the Second Report of the National Commission on Marijuana and Drug Abuse.* Washington, D.C.: U. S. Government Printing Office, March, 1973.

Newcomb, Horace, *TV: The Most Popular Art Form.* Garden City, New York: Doubleday, 1974.

Newman, Edwin, *Strictly Speaking.* New York: Bobbs-Merrill, 1974.

Noble, Grant, *Children in Front of the Small Screen.* London: Constable, 1975.

Noll, Roger G.; Reck, Merton J.; McGowan, John J., *Economic Aspects of Television Regulation.* Washington, D.C.: The Brookings Institution, 1972.

Oberdorfer, Don, *Tet!* New York: Doubleday, 1971.

O'Brien, Larry, *No Final Victories.* Garden City: Doubleday and Company, 1974.

O'Connor, Len, *Clout: Mayor Daley and His City.* New York: Avon, 1975.

O'Neill, William, *Coming Apart.* Chicago: Quadrangle Books, 1971.

Packard, Vance, *The Hidden Persuaders.* New York: Pocket Books, 1957.

——————————, *The Sexual Wilderness: The Contemporary Upheaval in Male-Female Relationships.* New York: Pocket Books, 1968.

Pember, Don R., *Mass Media In America.* Chicago: Science Research Associates, 1974.

Percy, Walker, *The Moviegoer.* New York: Farrar, Straus and Giroux, 1960.

Plumb, J. H., *The Death of the Past.* Boston: Houghton Mifflin and Company, 1970.

Podgorecki, Adam, et al., *Knowledge and Opinion About Law.* Briston, England: The Barleyman Press, 1973.

Polsky, Richard M., *Getting to Sesame Street: The Origins of The Children's Television Workshop.* New York: Praeger, 1974.

Pollak, Richard, ed., *Stop the Presses, I Want to Get Off!* New York: Random House, 1971.

Polykoff, Shirley, *Does She or Doesn't She? How She Did It.* Garden City, New York: Doubleday and Company, 1975.

Postman, Neil, and Weingartner, Charles, *Teaching as a Subversive Activity.* New York: Dell Publishing Company, 1969.

Priestley, J. B., *Man and Time.* New York: Dell Publishing Company, 1964.

Quinlan, Sterling Red, *The Hundred Million Dollar Lunch.* Chicago: J. Philip O'Hara, Inc., 1974.

Quinn, Sally, *We're Going To Make You a Star.* New York: Simon and Schuster, 1975.

Reich, Charles A., *The Greening of America.* New York: Random House, 1970.

Reich, Wilhelm, *The Sexual Revolution.* New York: Pocket Books, 1962.

Research and Policy Committee, Committee for Economic Development, Broadcasting and Cable Television, *Policies for Diversity and Change.* New York: Committee for Economic Development, 1975.

Rivers, William L., and Schramm, Wilbur, *Responsibility in Mass Communication.* New York: Harper and Row, 1969.

Roman, Kenneth, and Mass, Jane, *How to Advertise.* New York: St. Martin's Press, 1976.

Rosenbloom, David Lee, *The Election Men: Professional Campaign Managers and American Democracy.* New York: Quadrangle Books, 1973.

Rovere, Richard H., *Senator Joe McCarthy*. New York: The World Publishing Company, 1959.

—————————, *Waist Deep in the Big Muddy*. Boston: Little, Brown and Company, 1967.

Safire, William, *Before the Fall*. Garden City, New York: Doubleday, 1975.

Sandman, Peter M.; Rubin, David M.; Sachsman, David B., *Media: An Introductory Analysis of American Mass Communications*. Englewood Cliffs, New Jersey: Prentice-Hall, 1972.

Sarson, Evelyn, ed., *Action for Children's Television: The First National Symposium on the Effect on Children of Television Programming and Advertising*. New York: Avon, 1971.

Schell, Jonathan, *The Time of Illusion*. New York: Alfred A. Knopf, 1976.

Schlesinger, Arthur M., Jr., *The Crisis of Confidence*. New York: Bantam Books, 1969.

Schramm, Wilbur, and Roberts, Donald F., eds., *The Processes and Effects of Mass Communication*. Urbana: The University of Illinois Press, 1972.

Schramm, Wilbur; Lyle, J.; Parker, E. B., *Television in the Lives of Our Children*. Stanford, California: Stanford University Press, 1961.

Schiller, Herbert I., *The Mind Managers*. Boston: Beacon Press, 1973.

Schrank, Jeffrey, *Deception Detection: An Educator's Guide to the Art of Insight*. Boston: Beacon Press, 1975.

Schultz, William J., and Mazze, Edward M., eds., *Marketing in Action*. Belmont, California: Wadsworth Publishing Company, 1963.

Schwartz, Tony, *The Responsive Chord*. Garden City, New York: Doubleday, 1972.

Seedman, Albert A., and Hellman, Peter, *Chief!* New York: Avon, 1971.

Seiden, Martin H., *Who Controls the Mass Media?* New York: Basic Books, 1974.

Shanks, Bob, *The Cool Fire: How to Make It in Television*. New York: W. W. Norton and Company, 1976.

Silberman, Charles E., *Crisis in the Classroom: The Remakings of American Education*. New York: Vintage Books, 1970.

Singer, B. D.; Osborn, R. W.; Gershwender, J. A., *Black Rioters: Sociological Factors in the Detroit Riots of 1967*. Lexington, Massachusetts: D. C. Heath, 1970.

Singer, Jerome L., *The Inner World of Daydreaming*. New York: Harper and Row, 1975.

Skinner, B. F., *Beyond Freedom and Dignity*. New York: Vintage, 1971.

Skolnick, Jerome K., *The Politics of Protest*. New York: Ballantine, 1969.

Small, William J., *To Kill a Messenger*. New York: Hastings House, 1970.

—————————, *Political Power and the Press*. New York: W. W. Norton, 1972.

Stavins, Ralph L., *Television Today: The End of Communication and the Death of Community*. Washington, D.C.: Communication Service Corporation, 1969.

Stein, M. L., *Shaping the News*. New York: Pocket Books, 1974.

Stein, Robert, *Media Power*. Boston: Houghton Mifflin, 1972.

Steinberg, Charles S., *The Creation of Consent: Public Relations in Practice.* New York: Hastings House, 1975.

Steincrohn, Peter, *Questions and Answers About Nerves, Tension and Fatigue.* New York: Hawthorn Books, 1973.

Steiner, G. A., *The People Look at Television.* New York: Knopf, 1963.

Sussman, Barry, *The Great Cover-Up: Nixon and the Scandal of Watergate.* New York: New American Library, 1974.

Toffler, Alvin, *Future Shock.* New York: Random House, 1970.

Tolley, H., Jr., *Children and War: Political Socialization to International Conflict.* New York: Teachers College Press, Columbia University, 1973.

Toynbee, Arnold, *Surviving the Future.* New York: Oxford University Press, 1971.

Tuchman, Gaye, *The TV Establishment: Programming for Power and Profit.* Englewood Cliffs, New Jersey: Prentice-Hall, 1974.

Turner, William W., *Hoover's FBI: The Men and the Myth.* Los Angeles: Sherbourne Press, 1970.

Ungar, Sanford J., *FBI.* Boston: Little, Brown and Company, 1975.

Voelker, Francis H. and Ludmila A., *Mass Media: Forces in Our Society.* New York: Harcourt, Brace, Jovanovich, 1972.

Wakefield, Dan, *Supernation at Peace and War.* New York: Bantam, 1968.

————————, *All Her Children: The Real Story of America's Favorite Soap Opera.* Garden City, New York: Doubleday and Company, 1976.

Walker, Tom, *Fort Apache.* New York: Thomas Y. Crowell Company, 1976.

Watters, Pat, and Gillers, Stephen, eds., *Investigating the FBI.* New York: Ballantine, 1973.

Watts, William, and Free, Lloyd A., eds., *State of the Nation.* Washington, D.C.: Potomac Associates, 1974.

Wells, Alan, ed., *Mass Media and Society.* Palo Alto, California: National Press Books, 1972.

Wertham, Frederick S. *Seduction of the Innocent.* New York: Rinehart, 1954.

Westmoreland, William, *A Soldier Reports.* New York: Doubleday, 1976.

Wheeler, Michael, *Lies, Damned Lies and Statistics.* New York: Liveright, 1976.

White, Burton L., *The First Three Years of Life.* Englewood Cliffs: Prentice-Hall, 1975.

White, Theodore H., *The Making of the President, 1960.* New York: The New American Library, 1965.

————————, *The Making of the President, 1964.*

————————, *The Making of the President, 1968.*

————————, *The Making of the President, 1972.*

————————, *Breach of Faith: The Fall of Richard Nixon.* New York: Atheneum, 1975.

White, William S., *The Professional: Lyndon B. Johnson.* Boston: Houghton Mifflin Company, 1964.

Wilkes, Paul, *Trying Out the Dream: A Year in the Life of An American Family.* New York: J. B. Lippincott, 1975.

Williams, Raymond, *Television: Technology and Cultural Form.* New York: Schocken Books, 1974.

Winick, Charles, *The New People: Desexualization in American Life.* Pegasus,
New York: Western Publishing, 1968.
Witcover, Jules, *The Resurrection of Richard Nixon.* New York: G. P. Putnam's
Sons, 1970.
Wilson, Jerry, and Fuqua, Paul Q., *The Police and the Media.* Boston: Little,
Brown and Company, 1975.
Woodward, Bob, and Bernstein, Carl, *The Final Days.* New York: Simon and
Schuster, 1976.

NEWSPAPERS

We relied upon literally dozens of newspapers from around the country to get a
feel for the impact of television. The following newspapers were particularly important in coverage of events specifically related to the television industry:

> *Christian Science Monitor*
> *New York Times*
> *Variety*
> *Wall Street Journal*
> Washington *Star*
> Washington *Post*

NEWSLETTERS, MONOGRAPHS, RESEARCH REPORTS AND PRESS RELEASES

All of the following organizations issue material directly related to television. We
reviewed most of what they made available between 1970 and 1976.

> A. C. Nielsen Company
> Action for Children's Television
> Alliance of Media Women: Ms. on Scene
> Alternative Educational Foundation
> American Association of Advertising Agencies
> American Bar Association, Legal Advisory Committee on Fair Trial and
>   Free Press
> American Bar Foundation
> American Broadcasting Company
> American Civil Liberties Union
> American Enterprise Institute Center for Health Research
> American Newspaper Publishers Association
> Arbitron
> Aspen Institute for Humanistic Studies
> Cable Television Information Center
> Carnegie Council on Children
> Carnegie Foundation

BIBLIOGRAPHY

Children's Television Workshop
Citizens Communication Center
Columbia Broadcasting System
Congressional Black Caucus
Corporation for Public Broadcasting
Council on Children, Media and Merchandising
Educational Development Laboratories
Educational Testing Service
Federal Communications Bar Association
Ford Foundation
Institute of Life Insurance
Institute of Politics, John F. Kennedy School of Government, Harvard
    University
International Communication Association
International Reading Association
International Visual Education Service
KNOW
Market Foundation
Marketing Science Institute
Media Industry Newsletter
Morality in Media
National Academy of Television Arts and Sciences
National Assessment of Educational Progress
National Association for Better Broadcasting
National Association of Broadcasters
National Association of Educational Broadcasters
National Black Media Coalition
National Broadcasting Company
National Citizens' Committee for Broadcasting
National Gay Task Force
National Organization for Women
Office of Communication, United Church of Christ
Rand Corporation
Society for Research in Child Development
Society for Visual Education
Television Information Office
Twentieth Century Fund
United States Catholic Conference
Woman's Action Alliance
Writers Guild of America, East

GOVERNMENT PUBLICATIONS AND REPORTS

Many government publications and reports were assimilated into our conclusions. Publications from the following were particularly helpful:

Department of Commerce, Census Bureau
Department of Health, Education and Welfare, Reports Studies and
  Analysis
Department of Health, Education and Welfare, Report of the Secre-
  tary's Commission on Medical Malpractice
Department of Health, Education and Welfare, Public Health Service,
  Health Resources Administration
Federal Communications Commission
Federal Trade Commission
Food and Drug Administration
National Commission on the Causes and Prevention of Violence
National Commission on Marijuana and Drug Abuse
National Institutes of Mental Health
New York State Legislature
Surgeon General's Advisory Committee on Television and Social Be-
  havior
U.S. Congress, House Commerce Committee, Subcommittee on Com-
  munications
U.S. Congress, Senate Committee on Commerce, Subcommittee on
  Communications
White House Office on Telecommunications Policy

JOURNALS AND MAGAZINES

We used literally thousands of articles and stories published in the following
journals and magazines. Not all of these addressed television directly. Many
were about American life and thought, and we extrapolated from them.

Access
Administration and Society
Advertising Age
American Academy of Pediatrics
American Behavioral Scientist
American Film Institute Magazine
American Journal of Orthopsychiatry
American Journal of Psychiatry
American Sociological Review
Annals of the American Academy of Political and Social Science
Archives of General Psychiatry
Atlantic
Audio-Visual Communications
Black Enterprise
British Journal of Psychology
Center Magazine
CHAI
Childhood Education

BIBLIOGRAPHY

Columbia Journalism Review
Commentary
Crawdaddy
Developmental Psychology
Ebony
Educational Broadcasting Review
Educational Technology
Family Health
Freedomways
Harper's
Harvard Business Review
Harvard Educational Review
Human Relations
Industrial Management Review
Journal of Advertising Research
Journal of the American Medical Association
Journal of Broadcasting
Journal of Communication
Journal of Dental Research
Journal of Experimental Social Psychology
Journal of Marketing Research
Journal of Marriage and the Family
Journal of Personality and Social Psychology
Journal of School Health
Journal of Social Sciences
Journalism Quarterly
Language Arts
Madison Avenue
McCall's
Media Decisions
Medical World News
MORE
MS.
New England Journal of Medicine
New Republic
New Times
New York
New Yorker
Newsweek
Nutrition Education
Pediatrics
Perceptual and Motor Skills
Phi Delta Kappan
Playboy
Progressive
Psychapharmacology Bulletin
Psychology
Public Opinion Quarterly

Public Telecommunications Review
Redbook
Saturday Review
Science News
Scientific American
Signature
Sloane Management Review
Social Problems
Society
TV Guide
Television Quarterly
The Australian and New Zealand Journal of Sociology
The Educational Forum
The Nation
The National Education Association Journal
The National Elementary Principal
The New York Times Sunday Magazine
Time
Toy and Hobby World
U.S. News and World Report
Washington Monthly
Washingtonian
Women: A Journal of Liberation

PUBLIC OPINION POLLS

The following organizations regularly publish polls which we found very helpful. Sometimes these polls measured television and its impact, but in general they provide an invaluable barometer of what the American people want and what they believe.

Cambridge Survey Research
The Gallup Organization
Louis Harris and Associates
The Roper Organization
Yankelovich, Skelley and White, Inc.

UNPUBLISHED MANUSCRIPTS

Numerous unpublished masters' theses and doctoral dissertations on television, as listed in Masters Abstracts and Dissertation Abstracts, have been used—particularly for background data.

INDEX